A History of the Holocaust

A History of the Holocaust

From Ideology to Annihilation

Third Edition

Rita Steinhardt Botwinick

Florida State University

PEARSON

Prentice
Hall

Upper Saddle River, New Jersey 07458

Library of Congress Cataloging-in-Publication Data

Botwinick, Rita S.
   A history of the Holocaust: from ideology to annihilation / Rita Steindhardt
Botwinick—3rd ed.
   p. cm.
   Includes bibliographical references and index.
   ISBN 0-13-177319-4
   1. Holocaust, Jewish (1939-1945) I. Title
D804.3.B68 2003
940.53818—dc21   2003054835

Editor-in-Chief: Charlyce Jones-Owen
Senior Acquisitions Editor: Charles Cavaliere
Managing Editor (Production): Joanne Riker
Production Editor: Julio Espin and Virginia M. Livsey
Manufacturing Buyer: Tricia Kenny
Art Director: Jayne Conte
Cover Design: Bruce Kenselaar
Cover Concept: Rita Botwinick
Composition: This book was set in 10/12 Times by Integra Software Services Pvt. Ltd
Printer/Binder: Courier Stoughton
Cover Printer: Phoenix Color Corporation.

Credits and acknowledgments borrowed from other sources and reproduced, with permission,
in this textbook appear on appropriate page within text.

Pearson Education LTD.   Pearson Education Australia PTY, Limited
Pearson Education, Singapore, Pte. Ltd.   Pearson Education North Asia Ltd
Pearson Education, Canada, Ltd   Pearson Educación de Mexico, S.A. de C.V.
Pearson Education–Japan   Pearson Education Malaysia, Pte. Ltd

10 9 8 7 6 5 4
ISBN 0-13-177319-4

For my husband
the man for all my seasons

and

in loving memory of Mikey, Evelyn, and Mark
who left us much too soon.

Contents

Chapter 8   From Ideology to Isolation   157

Chapter 9   From Isolation to Annihilation   181

Chapter 10   Resistance and Rescue   210

Epilogue   233

Preface

This text is the product of four decades of teaching the history of the Holocaust. It is intended to meet the need for a single volume on the topic and intended for use by the average university student. Although most high schools require some instruction on the fate of the Jews during the Nazi era, most can only devote a few hours to the subject. As a result, students are left with some superficial notions on the causes and implications of the Holocaust. This book seeks to explain the sequence of events that ended with mass graves and mounds of human ashes. Questions that arose in class discussions provided insight to specific insufficiencies or difficulties experienced by the students and whenever possible, relevant material was incorporated into the course material.

Why a new edition? The purpose of a revision is to update a text so that it may reflect new research, new approaches, new ideas. The publisher aids in this process by providing the author with the views and criticism of several professors who are experts in the field. These are thoughtfully considered in composing a new edition. Also, the author has the opportunity to make improvements in style, correct errors which inevitably occur, and update the bibliography. Most importantly, a revision offers the opportunity to include new considerations on the needs of students who use this text.

The second edition *A History of the Holocaust* included a summary on the fate of the Jewish survivors. Students were invariably concerned about their lives immediately after liberation from the camps. This, the third edition, considers another issue which is raised in nearly every class: Can it happen again? The ensuing discussion soon turns to instances of man's inhumanity to man which have occurred since the end of the Second World War. Whether called tribal warfare, ethnic cleansing, or political restructuring, the suffering of innocent victims is equally tragic. The picture which emerges is pessimistic at best, despairing at worst. But the ability to learn from the past is not a totally bleak picture; the current history of Germany allows us to hope that change is possible.

The new material in this edition deals with the present-day relationship between Jews and Germans. Some readers might object that this inclusion is extraneous to a history of the Shoah, the death of the six million Jews. That is true, nevertheless it has been included. Our young people need to see evidence that the human capacity for shame and regret can result in an effort to fulfill the biblical command to be our brother's keeper. Why are we teaching about the Holocaust? Whatever other aims any one of us may have, the Holocaust is a warning: these are the consequences of . . . A glimpse at contemporary Germany does not imply willingness to forgive, surely not to forget, but it speaks to the ability of people to learn. And that is very much to the point. Finally, a word on two words. First, a commonly used description of the murder of six million Jews during the twelve years of Nazi control of Germany is "extermination". This, the author believes, carries the unfortunate connotation of killing vermin and unwanted pests and should not be used to describe the mass murder of innocent men, women, and children. Second, not everyone agrees that 'Holocaust' adequately designates the events that culminated in the gas chambers. "Holocaust" is a word derived from Greek and is usually translated as "wholly burn" or "devoured by fire." When spelled with a capital H, it has become accepted as the Jewish genocide. In recent years the word Shoah has grown in usage. Shoah is a Hebrew word interpreted as calamity/devastation/ ruin. In this text both terms are used.

This book is not a history of all Nazi atrocities, but rather confines itself to the devastation of Jewish life in most of Europe. There were some five million non-Jewish civilian victims of Hitler. Their stories await a comprehensive history of their own. Unhappily, it is not possible to do justice to their sacrifices within these pages.

Finally, it is hoped that this book will provide the incentive to seek more knowledge, deeper insights. The amount of available material is enormous. Let this be the springboard to greater scholarship on a topic which continues to be critical to understanding ourselves and our world.

Dear Student

You have elected to study the history of the Holocaust. The subject matter you will investigate will make some extraordinary demands of you. You may encounter difficulties in dealing with the facts. The events, even when related in the sparest of terms, will pull you into a world of such savagery, that you may doubt their veracity. But facts cannot be altered to ease our offended sensibilities. This text deals with material which has been exhaustively researched and confirmed by responsible scholars.

You may find that the intellectual mastery of the material is less exacting and less distressing than its emotional impact. The murder of six million, men, women and children within four years will arouse your compassion and your abhorrence. You will become angry, sometimes depressed, and occasionally, much too rarely, experience a moment of elation. The students who have preceded you most often used "disturbing" as the word which best described their reaction to this study.

It is hoped that your research will take you beyond this text into areas of specific interest to you. Wherever your work takes you, questions will arise that this book is not able to explain. We know that the German state committed mass murder on an unprecedented scale, but, you will wonder, how was it possible for thousands of ordinary men to become killers? We cannot absolve the German people who saw their Jewish neighbors disappear and did nothing. We cannot accept the passivity of the Allies whose inaction gave encouragement to the Nazis. Nor can we gain any comfort from the response of the Christian churches when we inquire: Where was the spirit of Christ when you stood by as the innocent perished? And perhaps most disquieting of all is the search for the power and the mercy of God during the Holocaust. Is it enough to say that his ways are mysterious and beyond human comprehension? Perhaps the fields of psychology or philosophy can help you in your search for answers.

Despite the fact that the Germans never denied their guilt and have preserved tons of evidence to keep researchers busy for decades, you will meet people who insist that the Shoah is a vastly exaggerated Jewish ploy. No, I am not referring to certain Middle Eastern politicians, but to people you might meet at work or social gatherings. How should you respond to Holocaust deniers? It is my experience that such individuals are not amenable to a rational account of the facts. You can try, but it is unlikely that your efforts will succeed in changing a mind so firmly closed. Be prepared to walk away from a useless disputation.

As the history of the Holocaust is rigorous work for the students, so it is for the instructor. But the rewards are commensurate with the effort. Some of you will be among those who in the future will refuse to be bystanders when suffering is inflicted upon innocent victims, who will speak up and act up in their defense. If you are planning to enter the teaching profession, your influence might be like the ripple that grows ever larger on the surface of the water. Can any work be more important?

Best wishes,
R.S.B.

Introduction

Man is a slow learner. Why else do we need to teach the same lessons over and over? The search for peace and justice has been central since the beginning of human life on earth. How often have we been deceived, deceived ourselves? At the start of the twentieth century the western world basked in its certainty that soon human misery would be conquered. But, what began with such optimism, ended with bitterness and cynicism. Woodrow Wilson believed that the battlefields in France would make war obsolete; the liberators of the Nazi death camps thought that revulsion for the piles of bones, both dead and live, would stop future genocides; the United Nations was expected to fix the flaws of the League of Nations and fulfill its grand promise. No, we have not done well. Our world is still beset by hunger, anxiety, ignorance, terrorism, and deadly hatred.

While our marvelous technological advances astound the world, we have neglected to use our skills to rid the globe of greed and fanaticism, nihilism and ignorance. Technology has not joined with morality in the pursuit of human happiness; science appears intent to merely serve itself. In fact, contemporary weapons enable the traffickers of hate to commit ever greater crimes. Genocide bears some new labels for the same old malevolence: we must kill for the sake of racial purity, to achieve tribal domination, to avenge past wrongs, to promote political and economic advancement, to carry out the teachings of the faith, to create a state of our own. Acts of terrorism no longer occur amid primitive people in far away places. Our own lives have been altered by the Eleventh of September; the scars in the American psyche are permanent, our sense of security has been shattered.

What weapons do we have to counter the forces which would destroy our civilization? Only a few; vigilance, preparedness, anger, new arms, better intelligence. Such means, however, do not address the roots of the hatred that we see in all those angry faces. Only a change of minds and hearts can do that. And so we must rely on education to achieve what force cannot. We must do better to convince people to heed the wisdom of the ancient admonition: "to do justly and love mercy." How many generations will it take? Who can say? But we have no alternative, no other choice, no better defense. We must teach, by word and by example.

Among Holocaust scholars there are those who believe that the utilization of the Shoah as a tool to educate demeans its victims. This writer respects this opinion but does not share it. Holocaust History, so well documented, so near to contemporary times, is an excellent instrument to humanize, to sensitize, to universalize our responsibility toward each other. No other event can sound a better warning: Great evil happened because good people did nothing. "Never again" must become the watchword for all decent men and women. Education remains our best defense against genocide. Only knowledge can demand change. The very idea that mass murder can be made acceptable must be crushed no matter how persuasive the rationale. The role of the uninvolved bystander must be dishonored. " I did not do anything," "I minded my own business" must become unacceptable. To achieve such profound changes will require patience and commitment, especially when again and again events dash our hopes. Although progress may be imperceptibly slow, we have no choice but to continue. The recent indictments by international tribunals of mass murderers who carried out policies of genocide may give us some hope.

The Holocaust is more than a Jewish tragedy. It is a human disaster of unprecedented proportion in the modern world. It represents a watershed that diverted the flow of Western humanism into uncharted channels of killing innocents by lawful decree. Modern technology and organizational skills enabled relatively few men who managed factories of death to destroy millions of lives, not in combat, not in the heat of battle, but in deliberate, cold-blooded carnage. The causes of the Shoah are beyond reason; they bring a Danteesque quality to the tragedy. The ancient Greek concepts of the perfectability of man and his institutions were undermined and shattered. The Judeo-Christian principle of the inherent value of human life was discarded. The view that laws exist to protect citizens and their possessions was turned inside out.

The terrible waste of life and property during World War I started the questioning of man as a rational being. The Holocaust was the culmination of the process because it swept away so many cherished notions. The optimism of the nineteenth century and the promise that man's future would be based on rationalism and progress, was overthrown by the Nazi *Weltanschauung*. Even the concept of enlightened self-interest was subverted when the Nazis enacted policies that would eventually bring about Germany's self-destruction. A case in point: They murdered millions of Jews who might have been utilized as a much-needed work force of skilled laborers.

The Holocaust raised profound questions for religious communities. The oft-repeated article of faith that His ways are mysterious and unknowable rings hollow in the presence of Auschwitz. It is not within the scope of this book to examine the theological dilemma of faith in the presence of death camps, but it is proper to consider the actions of religious institutions. Churches that were obligated to bring the teachings of Christ into the lives of their members failed to meet the Nazis' challenge. Even after the disclosure of the death camps, the major denominations carried on their "business as usual." Few ministers and priests anywhere in the Christian world preached sermons on the Holocaust. The most common response to the question, "Am I my brother's keeper?" was silence.

The Holocaust stands as a catastrophe exemplifying both uniqueness and universality. The annals of history are replete with massacres and even genocide, yet the Holocaust is singular in its utter senselessness. When governments have waged war against their own citizens, they did so in order to achieve some desired political or economic end. The destruction of the Jews, however, was itself the sought-after end. The factories of death did not promote national religious unity or enrich the state or advance its borders. This genocide did nothing to promote public security or enhance the economy. Instead, the Holocaust deprived Germany of hands and minds desperately needed in the conduct of the war. The justification offered by the Nazis, that the elimination of Jews from Germany would result in the desirable Aryan racial purity for the master race, is utterly without scientific foundation. As a matter of fact, the vast majority of the victims never lived in Germany. We cannot know how many of the killers actually believed the myth of German Aryan superiority, but we do know that every German school child was taught the *Voelkerwanderung,* the centuries-long trek of tribes such as Goths, Vandals, and Huns across the center of Europe. The preservation of ethnic purity on the crossroads of such vast population movements is clearly illusory.

The scale of Holocaust killings within a brief four years is another unique aspect of the Holocaust. Concentration camp commanders reported with pride to their superiors that they fulfilled or exceeded their death quotas. The chilling cruelty and efficiency of the mass murders have been characterized as a return to savagery. But that is inaccurate. The man in the SS uniform who wanted to impress Himmler with his effectiveness was not a savage; he was an official of an established, legal authority. He did not run amok with a knife between his teeth; he sat in his office and issued orders. He may or may not have felt any emotion concerning his task. Certainly he did not view himself as a criminal. The murders committed within his sight and hearing were carried out by complex procedures involving many government agencies, with the cooperation of important representatives from German industry and technology, and with the acquiescence of a considerable number of Germans.

The number of civilians murdered by the Nazis—6 million Jews and 5 million Gentiles—staggers the imagination. The human mind cannot envision so many corpses. The unlimited power of a twentieth-century dictatorship was unleashed to expedite the killings. The scope of the operation required a total commitment to the task. Considerable organizational and scientific skill was required to keep the flow of victims coming into the killing centers. Disposing of so many thousands of bodies every day was a task that caused some camp commanders moments of despair. Medical and legal professionals became tools with perverted ethical obligations.

From the Nazi point of view, the business of mass murder was successfully carried out. With a little more time, continental Europe would have been completely

Judenrein (cleansed of Jews). When Allied armies closed in on Berlin, when the great cities of the Reich lay in rubble and the German people endured the suffering of total defeat, Hitler consoled himself that at least he had won his war against the Jews. That is the gist of his last will and testament.

Great historical events are generally subject to divergent points of view. Few issues are clear-cut; differences of interpretation are elucidated, defended, and attacked. But one cannot be pro- or anti-Holocaust. There is no justification, no defense, no rejoinder. There is only sorrow and guilt. Except for a small lunatic fringe that refuses to deal with facts, the world acknowledges that the Holocaust happened and that it stands as a landmark of man's faculty for evil. The amount of evidence is staggering. This would be true even if only German sources were available to historians. The intent and execution of the "final solution of the Jewish question" simply cannot be disputed. German governments since the fall of the Third Reich have acknowledged the culpability of their predecessors and have attempted to indemnify Holocaust survivors.

Although there can be no question concerning the reality of the Holocaust, a number of specific issues have given rise to conflicting points of view. Several such questions are treated in this text. The author offers no conclusions, but it is hoped that differing assessments will stimulate discussion and research. Among the controversial topics are the following:

1. Was the Holocaust the inevitable final step of centuries of antiSemitism, a pogrom of unprecedented magnitude, or was Hitler's persecution a distinctly different assault?

2. The Intentionalists and the Functionalists debate whether the destruction of the Jews had been Hitler's plan from the inception of his ideology or whether the death camps evolved from events originally not foreseen by the Nazis.

3. Did the victims go to their deaths like the proverbial sheep to the slaughter or was there significant Jewish resistance to the implementation of the Final Solution?

4. Under the Nazi regime, was Germany a goose-stepping, Hitler-heiling monolith of obedience or was support for the dictatorship less widespread than generally believed?

5. What were the reasons for Hitler's assault against the Jews? Was he motivated by desire for their alleged wealth? Fear of their supposed power? Or were the reasons for his hatred psychological rather than political or economic in nature?

6. What and when did the world learn of the Holocaust? What actions resulted from such knowledge? Could earlier intervention have lessened the magnitude of the disaster?

7. How should the operation of the *Judenraete* (councils of Jewish elders in the ghettos) be evaluated? Did their work as administrators of the day-by-day administration of the ghettos help or hinder the SS in the commission of their assignments?

8. How was it possible for some individuals, usually designated as the Righteous Gentiles, to remain true to their ethical standards? Though small in numbers, their courage and integrity testify that even in the midst of evil, there was goodness. What inner forces compelled them to risk their own lives to save others?

9. Can we, should we, forgive the men and women who perpetrated the genocide? What of those who stood by and did nothing? Are they guilty?

10. If we accept the premise that ordinary men committed extraordinary evil and extraordinary people risked their lives to fight them, then who are you? Who am I?

11. The final section of this edition examines the question of the relationship between Jews and Germans today. No doubt the policies of reunited Germany will arouse cynicism for some and hope for other readers. Perhaps a dose of both emotions is a healthy reaction.

This book is a history text. It is a narrative that delineates what happened, where, how, and when, to whom, and by whom. Holocaust study is humbling; the moral and philosophical questions remain unanswered. The Holocaust reminds us that civilization is but a thin veneer, that political apathy is very dangerous, that prejudice is a cancer that can infect and destroy an entire national body, that persuasive powers, particularly personal charisma, are no substitute for character, that there are no quick fixes for serious problems, that to stand aloof when others are oppressed is to participate in that injustice, and that each of us has to bear a responsibility for the protection of the powerless everywhere.

CHAPTER 1

The Nature and Roots of Prejudice

Most of us can recall a situation were we felt the sting of prejudice. Perhaps the job interview had gone well until you revealed something of your family background, or of your political affiliation, or your religious beliefs. Suddenly the opportunity for employment vanished. Do you recall a promising social encounter that never developed because the potential friend harbored some longstanding bias against your ethnicity? Was it not painful to be pre-judged by someone who did not know you? Had you decided to confront the hurtful individual, the reaction may have been denial, or something like, "That's how my folks feel and so do I."

You may believe that such a minor incident has no relationship to the events of the Holocaust. But you would be wrong. Just think back on a time when *you* were the person who demeaned another because of your bias. Did you find that moment of superiority pleasant? Now imagine that your government applauds, even rewards such behavior. In addition, the authorities that you have been taught to respect, tell you over and over that all your problems are caused by "them." No failure is yours, "they" are responsible. Could you resist the pressure to believe such soothing lies? The best answer to that question is, "I don't know."

The Shoah was the poisoned fruit of centuries of prejudice. It was possible because hatred for Jews was translated from thought to words to murderous actions. An estimated two-thirds of the Jews living in Europe were killed during the Nazi regime in Germany. The exact number of victims will never be known, but, among others, the renowned scholar Martin Gilbert, in his *Macmillan Atlas of the Holocaust* (Macmillan, 1982, p. 244), estimated that Polish Jewry suffered losses of 3 million, the Soviet Union 1 million, and the Balkan countries and Austria account for well over $1\frac{1}{2}$ million deaths. When Germany, the Benelux nations, France, and the Baltic

States are added, the total of over 6 million is reached. These figures are not deaths resulting from military action but represent mass murder carried out at the direction of a legally constituted German government. Hitler had achieved power lawfully, and his party platform clearly expressed hatred for the Jewish people. Of course, neither Germans nor Jews envisioned where this state-fostered ill will would lead. No sane person could have predicted that an entire people could be condemned to be unworthy of life itself.

SOME DYNAMICS OF PREJUDICE

Prejudice may be defined as a stereotyped negative attitude toward a person or group, an attitude that is unrelated to any factual information. Sociologists and psychologists agree that it is a learned reaction, not an instinct. Most often it is acquired at such a young age that the adult cannot recall its onset. Dislike, even hatred, of a particular group generally predates school age. Thus, prejudice is instilled before the child is capable of independent reasoning. The capacity to make critical judgments usually begins at age eight. Young children accept without question the values and mores of those in authority, usually mothers and fathers. It is not necessary for parents to verbalize their own intolerance; children will absorb their sentiments indirectly. Obviously, parental praise for conforming to acceptable attitudes or punishment for opposing them will reinforce prejudice, but the tone of voice or the dismissing gesture of the hand all have a language that children understand.

The bias accepted during early childhood is difficult to change even in the face of contrary information. We tend to cling to our early constructs even when they are harmful to ourselves and to others. To deny what mother taught me seems disloyal. It is not true that prejudices result from a disagreeable or frightening personal experience although such an experience may confirm an existing negative disposition. If all unpleasant encounters were to create prejudice, surely each one of us would be ill disposed toward everyone else.

PERSONALITY AND PREJUDICE

The environment is not the only determining factor in the formation of a prejudiced person. Individual personality differences play an important role in the willingness to accept or reject the social inheritance of one's culture. It is quite possible for siblings reared in the same environment to exhibit widely differing attitudes.

What factors or influences shape personality? The question is simple, the answers are controversial. Researchers are placing ever-greater emphasis on genetic predisposition. A growing number of characteristics, formerly ascribed to environmental factors, may well be of genetic origin. To the student interested in the causes of prejudice, the development of authoritarian personalities is particularly important because these appear to be particularly disposed toward biased behavior. They exhibit a strong need to conform to conventional values; their thinking is marked by inflexibility, and they are often preoccupied with concerns regarding status. Authoritarian personalities tend to be obedient to a fault and admire those who appear strong and powerful. One can note the connection between the men who committed acts of unspeakable brutality during the Holocaust and their claim that they were only carrying out orders. Blind obedience and the authoritarian personality seem threads from the same fabric. Clearly, such individuals rank the need for law and order as a prime priority. The theory has been advanced that such personalities harbor frustration, anger, and jealousy against the powerful. These emotions may become evident by acts of brutality against the powerless. These feelings, long hidden, pent up since childhood, may be released through violent behavior toward others who "had it coming." Ethnic minorities have always served as a convenient target for concealed antagonism. When prejudice is elevated to patriotism, to doing one's duty for the Fatherland, than excesses of behavior are possible, even probable.

Bigots look for the company of other bigots. They are followers rather than leaders and seek the approval of their peers. Fellow bigots, expressing similar views, will legitimize prejudices; in fact, when intolerance takes on the aura of communal acceptance, it provides comfort and cohesion to the group. Thus, it is possible to speak of institutionalized prejudice, that is, hostility by consensus. "Everybody hates. . . ." The bond of hatred is as strong as the bond of love. As we will see in later chapters, the organizations that executed the Nazi orders to commit mass murders were bonded into entities of common objectives and common guilt.

Prejudiced people avoid facing the irrationality of their intolerance by stereotyping. Their victims are invested with deficiencies that have little or no relationship to reality. For example, if their bias is directed against Jews, the single characteristic often used to taint all Jews may be their supposed avarice. Any positive traits of the Jews are ignored or denied. Charitable Jews are merely the "exception to the rule." Statistics proving that Jews contribute more money to the needy than other groups are seen as erroneous or falsified. Other collective victims of such stereotypes are the nondrinking Irishman, the law-abiding Italian, the intelligent Pole, and the enterprising African American; the list could go on and on.

Prejudice is not a static phenomenon, it has high and low tides that are pushed and pulled by economic condition. One is tempted to compare its fluctuations with those of the stock market. When the economy is strong and expectations high, minorities experience little bias. But as economic hardships return, so do prejudice and its kin, finding a scapegoat for whatever is wrong. Authoritarian personalities find it almost impossible to accept any blame for their own failures or reverses. They alleviate their disappointments, no matter what the cause, by placing the guilt on someone else. The greater the frustration, the more intense the culpability of the hated group. During periods of severe economic suffering, plunder and bloodshed may result, particularly when fomented by irresponsible leaders. Pogroms, that is government sponsored or tolerated riots against Jews, were suffered by generations of Russian Jews. They illustrate how mob action can result in arson, plunder and murder. Criminal acts seem acceptable when committed by a crowd. Even after the excitement of terrorizing defenseless victims has worn off, there is no sense of guilt, only justification. The outrages committed by the Ku Klux Klan after the Civil War are a familiar example of criminality by consent. Far from viewing themselves as arsonists and murderers, Klan members wrapped themselves in the flag of Southern patriotism. The suffering of the Jews nearly always had an economic component. As we will note in more detail, the Crusaders looted, the kings of medieval Europe demanded payments for protection, Ferdinand and Isabella expelled the Jews whose property was left behind, and the Nazis deprived them of all assets.

Prejudice wears many masks. Religious intolerance and its consequences are of such importance, they will be discussed in the following chapter. Most familiar to Americans is the scourge of racism. Until the second half of this century, the myth of Negro inferiority was given official sanction. The struggle to right this wrong has been long and painful and continues to the present day. Racism was also a basis for the dark chapter of American relations with Native Americans. A policy of their destruction and subjugation was endorsed, even implemented, by our government. As a consequence, the native tribes were decimated and their culture destroyed. These assaults were cloaked in patriotism, in the obligation to Christianize the heathens, in the right of greater might. As always, racism also had economic components. In the case of the Amerinds it was hunger for their land; in the context of slavery, free or cheap labor made cotton king.

THE COSTS

Social scientists have studied the reactions of both the victim and the victimizers of negative stereotyping. Both pay a dear price. The oppressor does not remain untainted by his power. In order to hate blindly, it is necessary to become blind. The act of prejudging another person on the basis of misinformation demands the suspension of independent thought and much of an individual's freedom of action. Bigots must stifle the impulses of compassion for those who suffer at their hands. In order to affirm and reaffirm the illusion of their superiority, they must play elaborate games of self-deception. They will search anywhere for distorted religious and ethnic confirmation to rationalize or sanctify their bias. That still, small voice that whispers to them in the quiet hours must be silenced. The greater the injustice of their conduct, the greater the amount of psychic energy required to maintain the facade of their superiority.

The victims of prejudice are, of course, deeply affected. They may lose more than personal freedom; they may lose their sense of wholeness, the self-respect that is so vital to human well-being. Whether actually or seemingly powerless, they may accept society's rejection as justified. The resulting self-depreciation will exacerbate their doubts. A sense of worthlessness, coupled with hopelessness, will weaken any efforts to bring about change. The need to fit in, to be identified with the majority, seems an almost universal human trait.

This herd instinct, especially strong during teenage years, exerts a lifelong influence. When the dominant element in society excludes a minority, individuals often react by questioning, even denying, the values of their own culture. For example, lightness of skin may be valued higher than darkness; aquiline noses are straightened and names changed to echo those of the majority; Jews convert to Christianity for non-religious reasons; traditions are abandoned as ill-suited to the main currents in society. In the process, pride in one's heritage, so essential in a well-adjusted personality, is traded for the plastic image of conformity.

Oppressed people respond in a variety of ways to their situation. They may withdraw from contact with the majority. Why chance the possibility of pain and rejection? So they stay within their own circle and create islands of self-contained neighborhoods. Communication with the world outside is restricted to business dealings; children are protected as long as possible from realizing the hostility they will encounter outside their protected home environment. Residents of the community insulate and culturally separate themselves from the larger society. Often, they resent and reject any proposal leading toward acculturation, speak their own dialect, or exaggerate their differences by wearing unconventional clothing or by having unusual hairstyles. Although these reactions are understandable, they obviously widen the gulf between cultures.

It requires no imagination to recognize that a common response to prejudice is prejudice. Hate begets hate and misunderstandings deepen. Generalized accusations are thrown into the air that further poison the atmosphere. "All white people are racist," "All Christians believe that Jews killed their Lord," "All men want to dominate women," "All Arabs are double-dealing," and so on. Stereotyping and scapegoating are handed down from one generation to the next like valued gifts.

SURVIVAL UNDER SLAVERY

The responses to slavery in the United States and to the degradation of the Jews in Europe during both the Middle Ages and the early modern era present a case for interesting comparison and contrast. Both groups, Jews and slaves, were denied the opportunity to enter the mainstream of society. Both were exploited and denied legal, social, political, or economic equality. Both experienced physical insecurity and psychological debasement. Both were regarded as separate but not equal. Both developed techniques of survival that involved creating a dual personality—one for the world within and another for the world outside.

The slave showed his master a protective and deceptive face of obedience. Bitter experience had taught him/her the futility of expressing either rage or despondency. So the overseer saw humility, the bowed head, and shuffling feet. Beneath the surface were dreams, sometimes actual plans of revenge, conspiracy, and revolt. One mode of expressing defiance was to deny the master the fruits of his labor by working as little and as slowly as possible.

Thus was born the myth of ineptitude and sloth; the portrait of the lazy, stupid Negro. Some slaves resisted their masters by means of sabotage, escape to free territories, and even self-mutilation. When hopelessness became overwhelming, suicide became the final epithet that expressed the anguish of captivity.

Slaves were not permitted into the schoolroom and thus were denied the consolation of education. Christianity and its promise of heavenly redemption provided solace for many of the oppressed. Prayer and song fused into expressions of hope and liberation in the next world. Perhaps the most devastating characteristic of American slavery was its denial of the right to establish and maintain a stable family. Children did not belong to their mothers, they belonged to their masters. The role of the father was minimal, and the owner, not the father, was responsible for providing the young with the necessities for survival. The heritage of the single-parent household, headed by the mother, is a familiar phenomenon. In this respect, the Jewish experience stands in sharp contrast to the ordeal of African Americans.

ORIGINS OF ANTISEMITISM

AntiSemitism, hostility toward the Jewish people, is a modern word for an ancient malignancy. One could begin to trace its history at various points. When the rebellious ancient Hebrews exhausted the patience of their Roman masters, they lost their national home in 70 c.e., and were scattered throughout the Mediterranean lands. Thus began the Diaspora, the dispersion. Unlike other nationalities who lost their homelands, they remained faithful to their monotheism, their language, and their heritage. Their history honors the martyrs who died, even at their own hands, rather than break the commandments of their God. And a jealous God He was who refused to become part of any pagan pantheon. The moral demands of that nameless, invisible, all-powerful, all-knowing God were onerous indeed. He commanded His people to adhere to ethical standards no other god required. Sacrifices and festivals in His honor did not suffice; this deity invaded the daily life, the very thoughts of His worshippers. Jewish rituals, such as circumcision and food taboos, although burdensome and isolating, did not diminish the zealous attachment of the Jews for their God and His law.

While many other ancient civilizations disappeared, the Jews maintained their religion and their culture without nationhood. Not until 1948, when the state of Israel was reestablished, did they regain their homeland. For nearly 2,000 years they lived in other people's lands, sometimes tolerated, more often as unwelcome outsiders.

After the fall of the Roman Empire, Arab peoples dominated the Middle East. The establishment of Islam by Muhammad in 622, was followed by great conquests as his followers swept across the Arabian Peninsula, fusing warring tribes into a religious nation. The wave of victories encompassed the eastern regions previously part of the now-disintegrated Roman Empire. In view of the present Arab-Israeli conflict, it is noteworthy to recall that Islam did not force the subjugated peoples into conversion. The Jews of the Middle East prospered under their Islamic masters. In fact, when the Moslems advanced into Iberia in the eighth century, large numbers of Jews settled in Spain. The Golden Age of Jewish culture was celebrated during the

Moslem domination of Spain. Jewish achievements in the areas of literature, science, philosophy, and religion remain monuments to an age of greatness realized by the virtue of the bygone spirit of Islamic tolerance.

CHRISTIANITY AND THE JEWS

The emergence of Christianity as the primary faith of the West marks the most important cultural revolution of the West. For the Jews, it was a disaster. As U.S. citizens, we accept the fact that it is possible for people of different faiths to live side by side in harmony. This concept, however, is a recent and wonderful New World innovation. The European record reveals an appalling history of mankind's inhumanity to the men and women who pray in different houses of worship. In the name of the Prince of Peace, religious persecutions among differing branches of Christianity and wars of atrocious cruelty lasted for hundreds of years. All major Christian denominations, however, were united on one issue: their animosity toward Jews.

For nearly 2,000 years, Jews were kept outside the Christian world. They were outcasts because they denied that Jesus was the messianic son of God. The accusation that Jews had killed their God was reiterated by generations of theologians, and the crucifixion drama was reenacted at Easter pageants throughout Europe. Jewish devotion to the faith of their ancestors was construed as both a challenge and an insult to Christianity. The conversion of the Jews was, and to some degree remains, an abiding missionary objective. It is impossible, as mentioned earlier, to separate purely religious from the economic antiSemitism as practiced during ancient and medieval times and in the era beginning with the nineteenth century, a racial component has been added. The latter will be discussed in connection with the rise of Hitler. At present we are concerned with the religious origins because these have the deepest roots and have sustained the entire poison tree of prejudice.

At first glance it might appear that the development of Christianity has no place in a Holocaust text. Many years of classroom experience convinced me that a discussion of the irrationality of the early hatred for the Jews is a prerequisite to understanding the susceptibility of Germans (and others) to the stigma of guilt placed on the Jews.

The historic Jesus, as opposed to Jesus the object of religious veneration, is shrouded in mystery. He wrote nothing at all. Later descriptions of his life were more concerned with his message than with his biography. We know that he was born in the year 7 B.C.E. during the reign of King Herod. The meager material available acknowledges the fact that Jesus was born a Jew and that he was baptized in a public ceremony by an Essene preacher named John.

The Dead Sea Scrolls, found in a cave near the Dead Sea in 1947, gave researchers a more detailed picture of the life and times of John and Jesus. The Essenes were one of several Jewish sects that arose in response to the challenges of Greco-Roman civilization and the degradation of Jewish existence. Its members lived ascetic, pious lives in communities isolated from the world. John exhorted all who would listen that the coming of the Messiah was imminent. God's promise of a heavenly kingdom on earth, which had been prophesied earlier by Isaiah, would soon be fulfilled. In preparation for that day, all sinners must repent. The contrite and penitent congregation then took part in a ritual of washing away past transgressions in the river Jordan. Among those thus baptized was Jesus.

Jesus began his work as a teacher when he was thirty. The best summary of his ministry is contained in his Sermon on the Mount: God's blessing has nothing to do with earthly wealth and power; the meek, the children, the peacemakers, those who live in purity and act justly, will receive mercy from the heavenly father. He stressed God's love and spoke of the power of faith. His teachings urged men and women to obey the law and to share their worldly goods. The empty rituals that had replaced the core of Jewish ethics were an abomination to Jesus, who preached that spiritual, not material values secured eternal life. He lived during a contentious time in Jewish history, when zealots, moderates, and conservative factions bickered endlessly with each other and with their Roman overlords. According to Jesus, the promise of salvation, that is, life after death, was open to all who lived righteously. His insistence that neither social standing nor worldly success won any merit before the throne of God offended both Jews and Romans.

Jesus' ministry probably lasted only one year, three at most. The influence he exerted in that brief time leaves us in awe. Because Jesus referred to himself as the Son of Man, as the Son of God, and as King, it is impossible to reconstruct how he viewed his role. The fact that he urged his followers to observe certain practices, now called sacraments, might imply that perhaps Jesus wanted more than to merely reform the Jewish faith. However, the institution of Christianity was not his work. The church was founded by his disciples after his death.

Jesus lived and died a Jew. In his own words, he had not come to destroy the law, but to fulfill it. He acknowledged that he was indeed the long-awaited Messiah and journeyed to the capital of Jerusalem to make a public pronouncement. There he denounced the leaders of the community for their hypocrisy and their materialism. The crowds following him probably grew in size and anger. The priests, who were responsible to the Romans for keeping the peace, feared that a rebellion was in the making. In that event, the Roman legions would descend upon the population and, as had happened before, kill thousands of Jews.

LEGACY OF THE CRUCIFIXION

The crucifixion of Jesus plays an important role in the history of antiSemitism. Few events have caused as much controversy and misrepresentation. It is generally accepted that Jesus was arrested on the night of the Last Supper, the Seder meal he shared with his closest disciples. It is also believed that Judas of Kerioth betrayed him and that the Sanhedrin, the Jewish court, indicted him and turned him over to the Romans for punishment. Accounts of the trial recount that, when questioned, Jesus replied that yes, he was the Messiah. This assertion confirmed the threat he allegedly posed to the tranquillity of the city. Because the Sanhedrin had no jurisdiction over capital offenses, such as blasphemy and messianic claims, the prisoner was turned over to the Roman procurator, Pontius Pilate. The biblical account of Pilate's reluctance to condemn Jesus was written almost a century later and may or may not be correct. We do know that the Romans used crucifixion routinely for political offenders.

The Romans governed dozens of diverse people and had much experience in dealing with revolts. There was no reason to assume that the death of this obscure carpenter would have any lasting effect. The priests, who had encountered numerous messianic claimants, surely could not imagine that this particular crucifixion would change the world after Jesus' death. After all, these so-called Christians (translated "followers of the messiah") were a mere splinter group in the total body of Judaism. The early Christians were Jews, observant of the law but differing from the majority in their conviction that Jesus was indeed the Messiah. The teachers of this small sect, led by the apostle Peter, lived according to the principles of brotherly love and shared their possessions. The only rituals they observed that were not part of established Judaism were baptism and the Lord's Supper. The most revolutionary doctrine concerned their certainty that Jesus had ascended to heaven after three days in his tomb and that he would return once again to earth to establish his kingdom.

THE NEW FAITH ESTABLISHED

The beginning of the amazing transformation of Christianity from a gentle brotherhood to a triumphant, worldwide church was largely the work of a Roman citizen named Saul of Tarsus, known as Paul in the New Testament. An observant Jew until his maturity, he experienced a vision that changed his life. He became, in fact, the founder of the church by detaching the Christian sect from the parent Jewish faith. Paul made the far-reaching decision that the Gentiles, that is, the pagan world, should be converted to the faith of Jesus. The church would be *catholica,* or universal. No longer was Jesus the king of the Jews, but the king of the entire spiritual cosmos. Paul's missionary zeal took him through much of the Roman world, and his success was extraordinary. In the process of that expansion, the simple faith of Jesus was elaborated and given doctrinal foundations.

According to Paul, the carpenter from Nazareth was not an ordinary human being, nor was he merely a great prophet. He was God's own beloved son. Paul ordained that circumcision was no longer required of converts. Dietary restrictions were removed. The concept of the Messiah of the Old Testament was thus revised. In the Jewish tradition, the redeemer would bring into existence an earthly realm of peace and plenty; the Pauline view elaborated on the heavenly kingdom that would reward the just, and clearly the distance between Jews and Christians widened. It became impossible for converts to be both Jews and Christians at the same time. The final rupture in the thread connecting the old and the new faiths took place when Paul, toward the end of his life, broke with Judaism completely. From the foundations he had constructed, other fathers of the church would erect a mighty edifice.

THE MEDIEVAL CHURCH AND THE JEWS

In the centuries following the crucifixion of Jesus, the Christian church spread across the Roman Empire and beyond. It evolved from a small band of persecuted martyrs to a privileged position. When Roman authority collapsed in the fifth century, the Christian church prevented the complete breakdown of civilization. As the influential Roman bishops assumed leadership on questions of orthodoxy, the papacy developed. Ultimately, Popes assumed preeminence in all religious, legal, economic, and organizational affairs of the church.

In an age that forgot how to read and write, where Roman law nearly disappeared, the Christian church filled the void. The human need for beauty was realized by the building of magnificent cathedrals, which often became focal points for the revival of towns. Monks, nuns, and priests provided hospitals, schools, and charity. The power of excommunication brought sinners to conformity, be they emperors or beggars. Not until the sixteenth century, when monarchies challenged the economic and political power of the church, was it possible to rival its authority.

The church was often challenged by heresies, doctrines that were declared unsound and unacceptable by the orthodox hierarchy. The bloody chapters of religious persecutions within the faith need not be examined here. It is sufficient to be aware of the absolute determination of the church to root out doctrinal opposition. Disobedience to a specific article of faith was (and is) a grievous sin. Tolerance, as we interpret that concept today, was not viewed as benign, not even acceptable, because diversity in religious thought was seen as destructive. Serious questions of faith were debated and usually settled by councils within the church. When it was not possible to reconcile the differing views and practices of eastern and western believers, the church split. The western Roman and eastern Orthodox churches have been officially separated since 1054.

Medieval Christianity granted neither indulgence nor sufferance to Jews. During the Age of Faith, the nearly 1,000 years between the fifth and fifteenth centuries, the church controlled life on earth and beyond the grave. Political, economic, and social activity was judged by Christian standards. Religion had hardened into the absolute conviction that Christianity, as interpreted by its hierarchy, was the truth—the only truth. No compromise was possible. Jews, who insisted on clinging to the error of their ways, were condemned to live in degradation. Their very misery was then exploited as a sign of God's punishment for their rejection of Christ. Isolation, economic ruin, false accusations, extortion, expulsion, and murder were methods employed in the attempt to eradicate the faith that once had been practiced by Jesus. From the time of the Crusades, which began at the close of the eleventh century, until the Age of Enlightenment in the 1700s, hatred for Jews was a common denominator within the diversity of European culture. Although the waves of persecution varied in time and place, the threat of disaster was ever present.

The Crusades were a watershed in Jewish history. The cry "God wills it" commanded the faithful, from kings to commoners, to join the war against the non-believers. With the exception of the Iberian Peninsula, the agitation swept across Western Europe. For nearly 200 years, wave upon wave of warriors for Christ trekked to the Holy Land. The original motivation was soon adulterated by the expectation of material benefits: wealth, land, trade, and freedom from serfdom. Self-appointed and officially designated churchmen crisscrossed central Europe and agitated for recruits. The appeal was hard to resist: a great adventure and the promise of worldly and otherworldly benefits.

But why wait to fight the enemy of Christ in faraway Jerusalem when there were infidels close at hand? Mobs razed Jewish houses of worship, schools, businesses, and homes. As the rioters fed on each other's violence, the destruction of material goods escalated into rape, plunder, and murder. The rabble that made up the Peoples' Crusade pillaged its way across Europe and attacked Jewish communities wherever they were found. Even church leaders were unable to restore order. The events in the German city of Worms are a case in point. About 800 Jews had been granted refuge in the Episcopal palace of Worms. Jews who had remained in their homes were butchered, stripped of their clothing, and left naked in the streets. Many corpses were mutilated. The bishop protested but was unable to exercise his authority. The rioters then attacked the palace. In two days they overcame its defenders and proceeded to murder nearly all the Jews they could find. Many had committed suicide before the killers could reach them; a handful were spared because they consented to be baptized. The cities of Speyer, Mainz, and Cologne fell victim to similar mania.

PERSECUTIONS CONTINUE

Long after the Crusades had disintegrated into movements fueled by avarice and the Moslems had retaken the Crusader enclaves, the hatred for the Jews persisted. The term "accursed race" became interchangeable with Jew. From the eleventh to the eighteenth centuries, Jewish history in Christian lands was one of affliction interspersed with periods of violence. The kings of France, England, and later Spain, as well as various German and Italian princes, ordered their expulsion. Always, they left as paupers. Sometimes they were permitted to return upon payment of a tax or duty. Some German rulers contrived a new indignity—their Jews were designated as chattel or possessions of the monarch, who had the right to sell their services and their future taxes. Conversion granted release from the bitterness of Jewish life. It was offered again and again, a simple ceremony that would gain acceptance and greater security. Against all reasonable persuasion, few Jews left their faith. The stronger the push toward the baptismal font, the greater the unwillingness of the Jews to accept Christianity.

What made the Jews so despicable to Christian eyes? One cannot understand anti-Judaism without its religious components. Jewish theology differs from Christianity in several major concepts. Foremost among these is the denial of Christ as the messiah and redeemer. But beyond the repudiation of the Godhood of

Christ, Jews reject other critical articles of Christian faith. They do not accept such doctrines as original sin or predestination, they reject the necessity for sacraments, they do not hold that priests act as intermediaries between man and God, and they dispute the Christian visions of heaven, purgatory, and hell. The stubbornness of the Jews who refused to acknowledge that Jesus had fulfilled God's promise was incomprehensible to the medieval world.

The notion that the Jews were in league with the devil took hold in the medieval mind. The attribution of supernatural powers made it possible to blame the Jews for all sorts of natural and unnatural events. Thus the Jews became scapegoats who surpassed even devils and witches in their culpability for disaster and misfortune. Added to Jewish guilt as Christ killers, even the most bizarre charges were believed. Among the most notorious accusations were the following:

Jews were infidels (nonbelievers).

Jews required Christian blood to prepare their Passover Matzos. A mysterious death or disappearance of a Gentile child served as "proof" of ritual murder.

Jews desecrated the host (wafer used during mass) by piercing it with sharp instruments, in that way reenacting the killing of Jesus.

Jews, as Satan's allies and assistants, caused droughts, storms, floods, and other natural disasters.

Jews poisoned wells.

Jews caused the Black Death, which annihilated one-fourth to one-third of the population of Europe.

God hated the Jews, as was evident by their miserable state.

The certainty that Jews were an abomination in the eyes of man and God was translated into decrees designed to prevent contact between the Christian majority and the infectious Jewish minority. Church councils, popes, and temporal rulers enacted laws designed to disconnect Jews from Gentiles. Within their own communities, the Jews could do as they pleased, but commerce with the world beyond was severely restricted. In most European communities the opportunities for Jews to make a decent living were few. This is a representative list:

Jews were prohibited from joining guilds, thus making it impossible for them to engage in nearly all business and manufacturing activities.

Jews could not practice medicine or law.

Jews could not own land.

Jews could not hold public office.

Jews could not leave their homes during Easter week.

Jews were forced to wear distinctive badges or hats in public to alert any unsuspecting Christians.

Jews could not intermarry with Christians.

The most restrictive laws concerned the separation of housing, giving rise to the ghetto. By forcing Jews to live in their own crowded and miserable quarters, their isolation was assured. Whether walled in or barricaded by fences, they lost contact with events outside their narrow world. Only a few were granted exceptions—these were usually Jews who achieved prominence in import-export trade, in banking, or as special "court Jews" in service of a ruler. Their unique circumstances did not diminish the general poverty of the ghetto dwellers.

Despised and segregated, degraded and fearful, the once-proud people of the Bible reacted to their plight both negatively and positively. It must be remembered that until the modern era, separation between church and state did not exist. Christian rulers, even when they disputed the right of the papacy to interfere in their public administration, were unlikely to offend the church authorities and become defenders of Jews.

EARLY GHETTOS

Within the confines of their ghettos, the Jews created a life significantly different from that of Christian neighborhoods. In the ghetto, religious observance was not a matter of weekly prayer but was ingrained into the fabric of daily activity. In churches it was common for women to outnumber men at services; in synagogues men made up the majority of worshippers. The most highly esteemed member of the community was not the wealthiest man but the scholar, the rabbi. His congregation took great pride in his reputation and his Talmudic learning. Teachers and students pored over the holy texts and subjected each word to discussion as well as contention. The mysticism of kabbalah found supporters who ardently pursued the search for secret meaning within the holy books. Kabbahlists were not granted a magical shortcut to understand God; this study was open only to the most learned members of the community. The hardships of ghetto life, particularly its poverty and insecurity, inspired the impulse to follow false messiahs who promised that the time of deliverance was at hand.

With the passage of centuries, the isolation of ghetto dwellers from the world beyond grew wider. Many Jews forgot how to play, how to enjoy the beauty of nature, and how to take pleasure from physical activity. Children were taught to avoid confrontations, especially with non-Jews. Most of the Jews whose ancestors had migrated eastward from German lands maintained a version of the German language. They spoke and wrote Yiddish and thus furthered the distance between themselves and life outside the ghetto wall. Any inroads from the world outside were strenuously resisted. A child who married a Christian was mourned as dead; his or her name was erased from membership in the community. Tradition hardened into stifling regimentation, which dictated even such matters as clothing and the shape of beards. The desire for individuality or privacy had no place in the crowded houses of the Jewish ghetto.

Lest ghetto life be perceived as unremittingly dreary, it must be noted that it also produced some positive responses. Jewish life was marked by a deep sense of community, a bond forged by shared suffering and shared values. The synagogue was more than a house of prayer, it was the focus of life. Religious, communal, and personal activity overlapped. In a world of illiteracy, most male Jews could read and write. The family was the source and center of joy and pride. The Sabbath meal, the celebration of the festivals, and the milestones in the lives of the children were occasions of collective joy. Sweet songs were sung by mothers to their babies, hospitality was gladly extended to visitors, and charity toward the poor was a public as well as an individual duty.

It is estimated that toward the close of the Middle Ages there were 3 million Jews in the world. Nearly all lived in designated quarters in villages, towns, and major cities such as Rome, Frankfurt, and Prague. This Jewish apartheid was supported and fostered by the church which feared that exposure to Judaism might be harmful to Christian beliefs. In light of the fact that Jews do not proselytize, the basis for this fear is hard to fathom.

The greatest challenge for ghetto dwellers was earning a livelihood. In many regions of Europe, the economic restrictions were so severe that one marvels that Jews survived at all. Closed off from farming and many crafts, they were forced into such occupations as rag picking, peddling, money-lending, and innkeeping. Wherever such prohibitions were relaxed, Jews turned their skills to tailoring, shoemaking, distilling beer and whiskey and gold- and silver-smithing. Of course, within the ghettos Jews provided for the needs of fellow Jews. As was common throughout Europe, skilled craftsmen passed their expertise from father to son. Because of the ban against Jewish landowning, ghettos depended on Christian peasants for much of their food supply although chickens, even a cow might roam the ghetto's unpaved roads.

While the scholar stood at the top of the Jewish hierarchy, in the Christian world the social order was fixed by birth. With the exception of the clergy, a person was born to be a serf, a free peasant or artisan, or a noble. Serfs made up the great majority; they were bound to the land, neither free nor slaves, burdened with long established duties and few rights. Their labor provided the food and feed that maintained the rest of medieval society. In towns, the small middle class was organized into highly restrictive associations of craftsmen and traders. They imported or manufactured the necessities and luxuries the upper class required. But Jews, physically isolated and socially scorned, did not fit into the established categories. There was no room for outsiders in the rigid class system of the day. Often, kings or lords accepted them as personal dependents or wards. Of course, for a price. They had the right to grant them residence or expel them, treat them with moderation or hostility, grant them justice or deny it. Sovereigns had no wish to administer ghettos, their major interest was tax collection. It was simpler to allow the Jews to govern themselves. Thus it was that in an era that knew little of representative government, the Jews maintained a form of democracy. Within their walls, they were autonomous; they elected their own leaders, established schools, held trials, made laws when biblical laws were not applicable, and administered the welfare system. But no decree could eliminate the squalor, the lack of water, the overcrowding which were the common miseries of ghetto life. To the Gentiles, this was an alien and evil world although the vast majority of Christians never saw a Jew. If they did, his strange appearance was likely to confirm the dehumanizing prejudices that had been instilled so early and so thoroughly.

While their pariah status was justified as God's will, the Jews as a people were permitted to survive. The church did not advocate their physical destruction. According to the New Testament, the Second Coming of Christ will be preceded by the conversion of the Jews and their in-gathering in the Holy Land. General acceptance of that doctrine hung as a double-edged sword over the ghettos; the Jews must live in wretchedness so that baptism would have the greatest possible appeal.

THE REFORMATION

The era of Middle Ages seems stagnant, but actually slow and uneven change was taking place. The Renaissance, that surge of renewed intellectual activity, was fueled by the spirit of inquiry. Many concepts accepted without question for centuries were opened to examination and interrogation. An obvious sphere for conflict and confrontation was the conduct of the church. The uses and abuses of its temporal and spiritual power had long disturbed men of courage and vision. For centuries, their pleas and warnings went unheeded. The church labeled them heretics, excommunicated them, and condemned them to die at the stake. Not until Martin Luther did a reformer succeed in defying the Catholic Church. In the process, he, and the men who followed his path of leaving the mother church, destroyed the unity of Western Christendom. The legacy of that revolt is pertinent to our commentary on Jewish life.

Luther came from within the church. He was an Augustinian monk and professor of theology at the University of Wittenberg. His personal crisis of conscience led him to protest the church's solicitation of money, known as indulgences. He opposed the practice because it led people to believe that donations could serve as a substitute for true penance and could thus shorten or ease the suffering of the soul in purgatory. His first act of protest was modest enough, ninety-five theses detailing his objections to indulgences. The complaint was written in Latin, hardly a cry of revolt to incite the masses. He nailed the text on the church door at Wittenberg in 1517 and hoped it might lead to a theological debate. His aim was simply to stop the sale of indulgences because they made false promises to sinners. But economic and political abuses of the church had readied great numbers of the faithful to confront a wide range of religious abuses. Common folk and princes, the Elector of Saxony prominent among the latter, united in a spiritual opposition that had economic and political components as well. Rulers begrudged the great wealth flowing from their countries to Rome. A developing national consciousness resented papal interference in political issues. As pressure mounted for and against Luther, the rift between his doctrines and the established tradition widened. A man of great personal courage, Luther stood by his convictions. Unlike some of his predecessors who died at the stake, his excommunication was not the prologue to a fiery death. Instead, his supporters multiplied. The split grew into a chasm that could not be bridged.

The establishment of the Lutheran churches in northern Germany was followed by other religious revolts. Once the principle was fixed that individuals, not the dictates of the popes, may interpret the Bible, a bewildering number of sects evolved. The meaning of every phrase, every word of the holy texts was weighed and measured. Differences in interpretations became the basis for the founding of many denominations, each claiming to be in sole possession of the truth.

In his relationship with Jews there are two Luthers. The early idealist believed that the long-sought conversion of the Jews was imminent. The Renaissance, with its cosmopolitan humanistic views, had ushered in a period of relief from the most severe oppression for some Jews. Protestant scholars, particularly the Calvinists, studied the Gospels with renewed vigor, often leaning upon the Jewish erudition of the Old Testament. Nonetheless, the pressure to convert the Jews intensified. Luther understood the Jewish origins of Christianity and had rebuked the Catholic hierarchy for its shameful treatment of the Jews. His pamphlet, *Jesus Was Born a Jew,* issued seven times in a single year, reminded Germans of the debt the Christian world owed to the Hebrew people. He fully expected that his anti-papal position and his admonition that Jews be treated with kindness would result in massive conversions. When it became clear that the Jews refused to give up their faith even for his revised edition of Christianity, Luther became violently anti-Jewish. Some of his tirades are comparable to Nazi propaganda. His later pamphlet, *Concerning the Jews and their Lies,* repeated the worst stereotyped vilifications. He urged civil authorities to raze the synagogues, confiscate Jewish property, and drive that obstinate people from the land. Unhappily, it is the second message that took hold.

THE ERA OF ENLIGHTENMENT

The winds of change blew gingerly indeed over the Jewish communities during the late eighteenth century. Here and there doors had been cracked open and provided the opportunity to prosper. Poland had provided a haven, as did Holland and England under Oliver Cromwell. Although Jews were not treated on a basis of equality with Christians, they were granted greater legal and economic protection. Generally, their improved status was the result of the growing rationalism of the educated classes coupled with the new materialism. Monarchs encouraged the pursuit of wealth by the middle class whose taxes promised to increase royal power. Jews could be helpful in the accumulation of riches because they were skilled in business, trade, and banking. No longer could the church persuade the faithful to shun possessions of this world in order to ensure a place in the next. The "just price" imposed by guilds, which had set limits on profits, was losing its hold. As the world of commerce and production expanded, it was possible for Jews to meet a growing economic need.

Social restrictions that had been in place for centuries also eased in many parts of Europe. Here and there voices were raised to declare the maltreatment of the Jews as a shameful injustice. Among these was the influential German dramatist Gotthold Ephraim Lessing. His play *Nathan der Weise* was an eloquent appeal for fraternity and tolerance. The Prussian counselor Christian Wilhelm von Dohm wrote extensively in support of political, economic, and educational equality. Several of the French philosophers, notably Montesquieu and Mirabeau, vehemently decried the inhumanity of the archaic Christian posture concerning the Jews. Austria's Emperor Joseph II, son of the anti-Jewish Maria Theresa, issued an Edict of Toleration in 1782. However, not all the philosophers of the Enlightenment shared an enlightened attitude toward the Jews. Voltaire's diatribes were echoed in the aversion for Jews held by his sometime friend, Prussian King Fredrick the Great.

The masses, as always, found the attacks on their cherished prejudices intolerable. The light of reason hardly penetrated below the level of the salons frequented by the intellectuals. Even so, the forces impelling a reshaping of society could not be held back forever. The middle class became aware of its importance and power and demanded its rightful place and society organized by hereditary privilege was no longer accepted as immutable. In the great upheaval of the French Revolution, the vestiges of feudalism were eradicated, absolute monarchy was shattered, and outdated class distinctions were demolished. The storm sweeping away so many inequities of the past in the long run also benefited the Jews.

THE FRENCH REVOLUTION

The changes wrought by the French Revolution stirred the entire continent. Despite the excesses of the Reign of Terror and the short-lived Republic, the principle of Égalité took root—not social equality, but equality before the law. For the first time in modern Western European history, the privilege of citizenship was granted regardless of religion. After a protracted debate, the legislative assembly voted in favor of Jewish citizenship, and Jews became Frenchmen in 1791. In the wars that followed the execution of Louis XVI, victorious French troops exported the ideals of the Declaration of the Rights of Man far beyond France. Holland was the second nation to tear down the restrictions under which large numbers of their comparatively prosperous Jews lived.

The phenomenal career of Napoleon Bonaparte extended the French influence across the German states. In his personal attitude toward the Jews, Napoleon vacillated between his desire to integrate them into French life and his acceptance of the well-worn allegation that Jews were incapable of patriotism. In the end, expediency motivated him to extend citizenship to Jews who might help to advance his grand designs. In total, his influence was salutary for the Jews. He went so far as to summon an assembly of Jewish notables in order to assure them of his willingness to lift them from their distress in return for their loyalty. Wherever French guns boomed during the Napoleonic Wars, ghetto walls fell; wherever members of Napoleon's family assumed the thrones vacated by fleeing rulers, Jews emerged from centuries of humiliation. There were instances of popular participation in the spirit of enlightenment. In the city of Bonn, for example, the Christian citizenry broke down the ghetto walls and jubilantly linked arms with the Jews. Sadly, after Waterloo many of the liberties were rescinded by the restored, so-called legitimate monarchies.

THE AGE OF REACTION

When Napoleon was exiled, so were many of the changes he had forced upon Europe. The victors met at Vienna in 1814 and tried to undo the novel concept that people are citizens, not subjects. The Age of Reaction attempted, and temporarily succeeded, in reversing the advances toward a more liberal society. Many of the old restrictions were reestablished by kings who assumed that whatever they did, they were executing God's will on earth. Reactionary autocrats supported one another as they muzzled every vestige of freedom of expression. Between 1815 and 1848, liberal ideas were anathema and Prince Metternich's firemen were quick to extinguish the flames of freedom wherever they might flare up. For most of the Jews, the Age of Reaction was a return to the medieval darkness of isolation and confinement in ghettos. From the Balkans across the German lands to the Spanish shores, the light of reason was extinguished in the narrow *Judenstrassen* ("Jew streets") of Europe.

But bayonets could not hold back the impetus for change. Fear of change by the conservatives was justified; political ferment was in the air. Inequalities accepted for hundreds of years were no longer borne in silence. The French Revolution had spread the message that the present need not define the future. The revolutionary spirit, long simmering beneath the surface, broke through. The German and Italian people, denied an independent national existence by the powerful Austrian hegemony, exploded into revolutions. Wherever suppression had become intolerable, from Spain to Poland, revolts shook the old order. Nationalistic enthusiasm combined with hopes for liberal constitutional governments. Patriotism was translated into rebellion in 1830 and, on an even wider scale, in 1848. Only England was spared. British governments, through evolutionary legislation, had permitted power to shift from the aristocracy to the middle class. By the middle of the century, the full rights of citizenship were inherent privileges of all Englishmen, regardless of their denominational affiliation.

INDUSTRIALIZATION

The mid-nineteenth century uprisings on the Continent met with partial success. Even repressive rulers, such as the Prussian king and Austrian emperor, could not completely return to the old order. Another revolution, one that transformed our lives beyond the pale of imagination, meshed gears with the cultural and political changes of the age. The economic upheavals of the Industrial Revolution changed not only the methods of manufacturing and influenced what people did but what people thought. A growing middle class was no longer satisfied with its second class status. Its power was derived from work and wealth, not nobility of birth, power that produced social and economic changes that gave entree to some Jews.

Fledgling capitalist systems needed men of ability in the boardrooms and the factory. The religion of either the financial director or the operator of a new machine was irrelevant. The Jews were willing and able to promote the industrial development of the nation, therefore they deserved political equality. Had not certain privileged

Jews, such as the House of Rothschild, proven that they possessed great business acumen? Their admirers wove a new myth (based on the exception rather than the rule), namely that Jews were born with the ability to make money. The age of the machine, of the investor, of improved quantity and quality of goods opened the door of opportunity to a wide range of underprivileged classes. Among these were the Jews, who streamed into the main currents of whatever nation they called home. Political emancipation followed the economic breakthrough. By 1870 the nations of Western Europe had liberated their Jewish population and given them citizenship. In return, Jewish gratitude was often expressed by ardent patriotism and by their contributions to the welfare of whatever nation they so proudly called their homeland.

TWENTIETH CENTURY

As the nineteenth century closed, Western and Central European Jews were found among factory owners and workers, teachers and shopkeepers, artists and inventors. Some grew rich, others achieved middle class status, while many struggled to escape their hand-to-mouth existence. Politically, their affiliations ran the gamut from the radical left to the moderate center to the conservative right. When public schools admitted Jewish children, the youngsters quickly adopted the vernacular, dressed and behaved according to the dominant cultures, and imitated the conduct of their contemporaries. The process of assimilation was underway. Complete acculturation, however, was never achieved. Only if Jews gave up their faith could they hope to "belong," and even then, converts found that many social obstacles were still in place.
　　The late nineteenth and early twentieth century were years of scientific discoveries that changed man's view of the world. Both Christians and Jews found their biblical articles of faith questioned. Darwin's theories, the new geology, chemistry, historical research, and psychology stimulated inquiry into every arena of faith and knowledge. Judaism was no exception. Were the ancient rites set immutably by the Patriarchs or was theirs a living, ever-evolving, religion? Would new forms, updated rituals, and modern interpretations of the holy books destroy Judaism, or would such action assure its survival? The ferment over reform or tradition was further agitated by the conflict over the degree to which Jews should keep pace with the world around them. Could one be a loyal Frenchman and devout Jew at the same time? The world of business operated on a Christian calendar. Work on the Sabbath or not? Eat in homes where non-kosher food was served or refuse and give the impression of standing aloof from your neighbors? Place your children in public schools or not? Would intermarriage result from such affinity? The practical and ethical implications were many. By the middle of the nineteenth century the split between the traditionalists and the liberals hardened into an open breach. The reformists created their own congregations as Reform Synagogues were established. The founder of this movement, Abraham Geiger, was convinced that Judaism must rejuvenate itself in order to better serve man and God. As the second millennium arrived, some of the divisions became permanent features of Jewish life.

The Renaissance and the Reformation, the emergence of the middle class, and the Industrial Age were movements whose influence stopped along the east German boundary. In Poland and Russia, the development of a modern economic system was delayed, perhaps by a hundred years. We have not yet dealt with the problems of Jewish survival in the Slavic states during the modern era, even though the greatest numbers of Jews lived there. The population of these nations suffered immense losses during the Holocaust. As a result, an entire culture disappeared. Hitler destroyed a unique civilization, a topic that will be discussed more fully in the next chapter.

It would seem that anti-Jewish prejudice in Central and Western Europe should have ended when it became clear that industrialism had no religion and that progress required the energies and abilities of all. The medieval preoccupation with the welfare of the soul after death had given way to goals of an earthly heaven of justice and plenty.

Increasingly, Jews entered the political and economic fabric of Western society. However, opposition to this integration did not disappear completely; there was always a segment of the population that resisted equality for the Jews. Repudiation to an open society came from some religious and some reactionary members of both the educated and the unlettered. However, their denunciations found few echoes, and the wrenching Dreyfus trial in France was viewed by many as the final gasp of a briefly revived antiSemitism. Alfred Dreyfus was a Jewish captain in the French army who was accused of selling military secrets to the Germans. His conviction was based on false evidence and he was sentenced to spend the rest of his life on the penal colony of Devil's Island. Much was made of the supposed fact that a Jew could not be a true Frenchman. Even when documentation proved that someone else had committed the treason, the military maintained Dreyfus' guilt in order to preserve the public's faith in the integrity of the army. All France watched with shame and chagrin as the press, particularly the famed writer Emile Zola, pursued the cause of justice and reversed the conviction. The victory of fairness to a Jew was viewed by liberals everywhere as symbolic of the modern attitude of decency toward all. The continued antiSemitism in Russia and Poland was seen as a symptom of the cultural backwardness of the benighted Slavic states. For Western Europe, assimilation seemed the key to an ancient enigma.

THE NEW ANTISEMITISM

Appearances, however, were deceiving. The roots of prejudice were still intact beneath the surface. Different circumstances demanded different modes of venting familiar hatred. The new face of the old aversion was less crude, less obvious, yet was as emotionally charged as the old religious bias. Modern antiSemitism (the term was introduced in Germany by Wilhelm Marr in 1873) emanated from two related sources: nationalism and racism. The advocates of the former claimed that Jews are forever aliens who cannot share the national ethos; the advocates of the latter asserted that innate racial differences prevented Jews from assimilating with the superior cultures of the host countries. Although several aspects of twentieth century discrimination were new, the historic religious bias fed this new strain of an old virus.

The forces of nationalism, stirred by Napoleon, had moved from rhetoric to action. The unifications of Germany and Italy and the expulsion of the Turks from nearly all European lands had been inspired by the passion for independence and self determination. Pride in one's national heritage swelled everywhere, and in many regions a competitive destructive chauvinism developed. In Germany, sentimentality merged with patriotism to create a mystical concept of Germanness. To be German, truly German, was not a mere matter of citizenship, it was based on an indefinable sense of common roots. Germanic blood and the German soil created an ethos that could not be acquired. Only an ancient shared heritage could infuse that *Voelkisch* spirit. German romantic writers spoke of a *Volksgeist,* a spirit that is particular to the blood and soil and the German people. The past, particularly the ancient past, was extolled as a time of spiritual perfection. Clearly, Jews could only pretend to be German. Their creativity and contributions in science, philosophy, literature, art, and music notwithstanding, they were forever alien.

Thus, German nationalism was burdened with a romantic, quixotic aspect from the outset. Johann Gottlieb Fichte was its founder. In 1807, he proclaimed the German spirit to be the spirit for human excellence. His aim was the unification of the many small German states into a single nation. The fact that Fichte argued against Jewish emancipation gave ammunition to several generations of antiSemitic politicians. The composer Richard Wagner wrote with a poisoned pen when he tirelessly and obsessively denounced the Jews. His revulsion seemed to stem from a conviction that German culture was "Judaized," that is, corrupted by Jews. His operas gloried in the Teutonic past, particularly its paganism. The notion that the German essence, sometimes described as its innermost or *Voelkisch* nature, went beyond the commonalty of language and heritage was reinforced by other German nationalists. Friedrich Ludwig Jahn (1778–1852) favored the natural, simple German peasant over the educated civilized man who was disconnected from the soil. Georg Wilhelm Friedrich Hegel, founder of the philosophy of dialectics, taught at the University of Berlin during the first quarter of the nineteenth century. He glorified the state and asserted that heroes function outside the norm of history even as they trample on ordinary mortals. A similar note was struck by Heinrich Treitschke who persuaded innumerable Germans that unquestioning homage to the state was the ultimate expression of love and duty. Friedrich Nietzsche, whose works were later shamelessly misrepresented by the Nazis, formulated theories concerning superhuman individuals who stood high above slavish parliaments and democratic disputations.

ANTI-JEWISH RACISM

German nationalists, whose writings appear rather muddled and self-serving, had laid the groundwork for modern anti-Jewish prejudice. How deeply did their ideas affect the ordinary German citizen? Certainly, liberalism did not vanish but the rational concept of the equality of all men ran counter to the irrationality of the idealized and idolized state. Obedience to the state was tantamount to obedience to a higher spiritual power. From the unification of Germany in 1871 to the rise of the Nazis in 1933, the forces of modernism, that is, progress through material advancement, would be challenged time and again by advocates of a return to the past. It is not surprising that the barometer of antiSemitism rose and fell in tandem with political and economic tensions. Jews, who could never belong to the world of German blood and soil, were held responsible for socialism, for capitalism, for stock market failures, and for labor strikes. Politicians from the ultraconservative right could always count on considerable public approbation when they targeted the Jews for the painful economic dislocations that are part and parcel of industrialization. AntiSemitism had become a cohesive political issue around which political organizations could be centered.

At the core of Nazi policy stood hatred of the Jews. Hitler could call upon the past for instruction. He merely intensified and broadened the attack; history supplied the essential components. Every crudity of Nazi misrepresentation had antecedents. For example, had not Theodor Fritsch, in his *Handbook of AntiSemitism,* asserted in the 1880s that Jesus was not a Jew but was of Aryan descent? Jews as a species were intrinsically vicious and irredeemable. If Germans valued their own survival, they must destroy the accursed race.

The division of peoples into races—black, white, Asian—originated as a system of classification unrelated to any value judgments. Race became racism when innate characteristics were assigned biological attributes by pseudoscientists. The fact that science does not recognize the existence of either a German or a Semitic race was ignored and a new nationally correct biology was created. Eighty years before Hitler became chancellor, the English son-in-law of Richard Wagner, Houston Stewart Chamberlain, influenced millions of readers with his treatise entitled *Foundations of the Nineteenth Century.* He wrote as an oracle, not as an historian or a scientist; his analyses were not the consequence of research, but of insight. He "knew" intuitively that he had discovered nothing less than the mechanism shaping the historical process. According to Chamberlain, the essential traits of a people were determined by the proper or improper racial components of their biological heritage. Creativity, moral fiber, character, and so on, were fixed by the interplay of specific racial strains. The Jews, of course, were a hopelessly bastardized race, while the Germanic people were the inheritors of inevitable greatness. Once the theory had been stated, Chamberlain had no difficulty in corroborating it with many hundreds of pages of selected evidence.

The racist writers of the nineteenth century did not advocate mass murder, yet their theories played an important role in the coming disaster. Perhaps they hoped to inspire nationalism strong enough to defeat the particularism that delayed unification until 1871. Whatever the motivation, they fostered the conceit that destiny had placed the German people on a separate course from the rest of the world.

Without Hitler, biological racism may have amounted to nothing more than a footnote in the history of modern Europe. The theory of an innate, unalterable

Children behind a barbed wire fence at the Nazi concentration camp at Auschwitz.   (Photo courtesy of Tony Stone ImagesSSS.)

Jewish malignancy would have remained the purview of quacks. But hatred for the Jews was at the core of Hitler's obsession. The claim that Jews were the bearers of a genetic flaw enabled the Nazis to rationalize their nearly successful genocide. If Jews were despicable merely because they did not accept Christ, then conversion or emigration were possible options for their survival. If Jews could not share the enigmatic ethos of the Teutonic past, the German *Volk,* they might be excluded from official positions or be subjected to social discrimination. But if the taint was congenital, if by their presence alone Jews contaminated society, then only their obliteration could make the world safe. And that delusion underlies the tragedy of the Holocaust.

CHAPTER 2

The World That Was Annihilated

Although it was strictly forbidden, some members of the SS took pictures of concentration camp arrivals. The images are heartbreaking, not because the men, women, and the children look so dreadful but because they look so ordinary, so familiar. Indeed, they resemble the photographs in the albums at Grandmother's house. The families by the railroad tracks had been told they would be resettled in the East. Their luggage was carefully packed with items most precious and most needed after the expected resettlement. They look bewildered, confused, and weary rather than frenzied. How could they suspect that they had arrived at a death camp? That in hours, or days, they would die? The officers of the SS Deathhead Squads who were charged with the execution of Hitler's Final Solution to the Jewish Question were quite successful in their efforts to create a reassuring atmosphere. There might be an orchestra playing, beds of flowers, and orders to pile the luggage over here, they would need to find it after the delousing procedure.

Indeed, the arrows on the windowless building they were approaching assured them that the disinfecting showers were just ahead. You knew the Germans and their fixation on cleanliness. Of course, there were rumors, rumors simply too dreadful to believe, rumors of death. Wasn't it terrible, what some people would say? As if the prospect of resettlement were not frightening enough. So they looked at the flowers, and heard the music, and the Nazis were pleased with their deception. It would not do at all for hysteria to disrupt the smooth working of the death factory.

Most of the families waiting their turn are Polish, some are Germans and Austrians and Czechoslovakians. As Hitler's armies defeat one nation after another, the variety of victims mirror their conquests. Indeed, by 1943 a microcosm of European Jewry assemble at the death camps. Some are better dressed, they had been held in transfer camps in France, Belgium or Holland; others, coming from many months in Polish ghettos, are undernourished and wear patched clothing. Mothers and grandmothers carry the babies and hold the hands of the older boys and girls. It is very quiet. Only the children whimper but there is no food, not even a sip of water for them. Some men pray, perhaps God will hear them?

Who are these people? Or, more precisely, who were they? We know that they had no future, their present was compressed into hours or days, but what of their past? Unless we can give them some human dimensions, their deaths will remain mere statistics. To understand the meaning of the Holocaust, its victims must be more than entries in German ledgers. The dehumanization of the killing process must be reversed and the faces on the old photographs brought back to life, even if just for a moment.

THE VICTIMS

These men, women, and children were the Jews of Europe. With the exception of Finland, every country defeated by or politically linked to the Germans, contributed to their numbers. They had been caught in a vast net the Germans spread over most of the continent. In the east, it reached from the outskirts of St. Petersburg to the Ukraine, and spread south across the Balkans. Exempting Switzerland, (which the Germans preferred to leave neutral), France, the Low Countries, Denmark and Norway complete the encirclement. Italy, which had resisted German pressure to surrender its small Jewish population, was caught in the mesh in 1944 when German troops moved into the peninsula.

Jews had lived in Europe since before the birth of Christ and had adopted, in varying degrees, the customs and mores of their host countries. Surely, there had been intermarriages as well. How else could one explain the great differences in physical appearance among them? There were blue-eyed blondes and dark-eyed brunettes, and freckled redheads. Some men were over six feet tall, others under five. High cheek bones, so common among the Slavic peoples were represented as well as oval faces from the North.

The two thousand years of the dispersion of the Jewish people from their ancient homeland, the diaspora, also evolved into two major forms of worship. Jews who settled in central and eastern Europe are called Ashkinazim while the exiles who found refuge around the rim of the Mediterranean basin are known as Sephardim. Over the millennia of their separation they developed variations in ritual and liturgy although the essence of their faith remained similar. The most notable difference concerns their vernacular language. In central and eastern Europe, the spoken and written language was Yiddish, a lingua franca that crossed many borders. Related to medieval German with a generous sprinkling of Hebrew as well as the vernacular of the host nation, Yiddish journalists, poets, and novelists created a literature of great beauty. Isaac Bashevis Singer, a Nobelist in literature, is but one representative among many

Map 2.1 *Europe under Nazi occupation before June 22, 1941.*

eminent writers. Sephardic Jews, whose numbers are much fewer, developed Ladino. This too became a spoken and written language, rooted in Latin, Hebrew, and whatever was the native tongue of a particular area. Ladino thus might be enriched by Turkish, Spanish, Greek, or North African vocabulary.

Most Western European Jews effected a greater degree of assimilation to the culture of their homeland than Eastern Jews. This was largely due to the availability of greater opportunities. Although antiSemitism never disappeared, here the Jews were citizens, they spoke the prevailing language and participated in every aspect of national life. It must be remembered that in Germany, France, Holland, and Belgium as well as Italy and England Jews constituted a small minority, one percent or less, of the total population. Considering their small numbers, their achievements were great. In science, the arts, and literature they contributed to the national honor and, in turn, began to feel themselves as part of their communities. Social acceptance lagged behind economic and political admission but was also growing as the continuing process of industrialization broke down ancient class barriers. Many Jews were clearly part of the rising middle classes. Often, they became fervently nationalistic. They fought in the uniforms of both the Allies and the Central powers during World War I. At the turn of the twentieth century they confidently expected that their religious faith would not block full integration. Surely, the achievement of complete equality was merely a matter of time.

The majority of Jews, however, did not live in western Europe, they made their homes in Russia, Poland and the southeastern parts of the Austro-Hungarian Empire. Obviously, European Jewry did not share a single culture. Any attempt here to re-create its diversity, country by country, within the context of a single chapter would serve to confuse rather than clarify. It is more sensible to concentrate on a narrower aspect of the life that vanished, namely Polish Jewry. This choice is justifiable for two reasons: first, because 3 million Polish Jews were murdered. No other country sustained such losses. Second, their once thriving culture no longer exists. Whereas pockets of Jewish life remain in Western and Southern Europe and a revival of Jewish culture is emerging in Germany, Poland is barren. How strange indeed that Hitler, who despised the Poles, achieved his greatest success there. It is Poland, not Germany, that is nearly *Judenrein* ("cleansed of Jews").

BRIEF HISTORY OF POLISH JEWRY

The term *Polish Jews* requires definition. The three partitions of Poland in the eighteenth century divided the land and its people among Prussia/Germany, Russia, and Austria. However, even without a political homeland, the Poles continued to foster their native culture and did not blend into the fabric of their conquerors. Poles, and that included Polish Jews, lived for almost 150 years under the flags of Russia, Germany, and Austria. Thus, it is possible to speak of Polish Jewry even when such a designation might refer to Galicia in the South, to Pinsk in western Russia, or to Posen, which sometimes was part of Germany.

According to German sources, of the approximately 6 million Jews killed, 4.3 million came from occupied Russia and Poland. In percentages, 85 percent of Polish and 71 percent of western Russian Jews were murdered. Their civilization has vanished. The few thousand Polish Jews who survived the Shoah were met with hostility when they made their way back to their hometowns. The Polish people who occupied their former homes and places of business often greeted them with hatred, even pogroms. Clearly, the remnant could not reestablish itself on Polish soil. Emigration to Israel, to the United States and Canada and even to Germany was preferable. Cities, towns, and hundreds of villages that once sustained a distinct Jewish life, today have little or nothing left to remember the past. Only traces remain: a half-ruined cemetery, a former synagogue now used as a civic center, perhaps a defunct Talmud-Torah school where Polish poetry is recited.

Holocaust survivors from western Russia were also unable to revive Jewish cultural life in their former homes. During the more than seven decades of Communist control, the government followed a policy of Russification. Similar to Czarist aims, the Soviets wanted to homogenize their various people. Under the guise of equal aversion to all religious worship, Jews were treated with either outright persecution or merely discouraged from maintaining their cultural distinctiveness. That policy did not change after the war. In fact, Soviet authorities refused to acknowledge that Jews specifically had been singled out for total destruction by the Nazis. Their commemorative World War II monuments pay homage to Russian victims only. Since the disintegration of the Soviet Union into separate nations, however, some changes have taken place, and the revival of some Jewish religious institutions is now taking place in several of the former USSR member states. However, the economic uncertainties which beset the region and the occasional outbreaks of antiSemitism have encouraged emigration.

Jewish history in Poland has deep roots. In the twelfth and thirteenth centuries the Crusaders attacked Jews with the same zeal they brought to the conquest of the Holy Land. The scream "God wills it," accompanied the burning, looting, raping and murdering and many of the victims fled eastward. They carried with them the medieval German vernacular. From this base, Yiddish developed, which became the universal language of Central and Eastern European Jewry. The kings of Poland, eager to foster a mercantile middle class, welcomed the refugees. The most enlightened of the Polish medieval kings, Casimir the Great (1333–1370), granted them complete freedom to work, to worship, and to prosper, despite objections from the church. Even when less enlightened monarchs restricted the economic and social life of the Jews, medieval Poland offered them more promise than other European states. Throughout the Middle Ages, when Western European rulers persecuted and expelled their Jewish populations, Polish Jews could work and pray in relative peace. Not restricted to peddling and money lending, they could live decently in villages and towns. From the thirteenth century to the eve of the Nazi invasion, they satisfied many of the economic needs of a predominantly agricultural society. From blacksmith to goldsmith, tanner to cobbler, miller to baker, weaver to tailor, merchant to banker, they met the requirements of the rich and the poor. Manufacturing of goods was usually done in homes and small workshops, although some larger establishments, particularly in the textile industry, were set up. Some Jews plied their goods from village to village; others opened stalls in the town square and sold to the peasants on designated market days. Because some Jews had financial skills, they found employment as tax collectors for kings and nobles. This was not an unmixed blessing. During periods of famine, they were identified with the hated oppressors of the poor and subject to pogroms.

AUTONOMY OF JEWISH COMMUNITIES

The Jews of Poland were granted a charter by King Sigismund Augustus in 1551. In accordance with that document and others written with similar intent, they could govern themselves by means of an elected council of elders. These local assemblies organized themselves into regional conventions that, in turn, chose a supreme council. Thus, a sophisticated, well-ordered administrative machinery was set into motion. Jews were designated a separate social group because they did not fit into the established hierarchy. They were neither serfs nor free peasants nor members of the nobility. Most important, they were not part of the Christian world. Rulers simplified the potential difficulties of governing an alien people by allowing them a great deal of autonomy. Jews chose their own leaders annually, usually from among their prominent citizens. They lived in ghettos, sometimes by choice, more often by decree. Their own bureaucracies established and regulated such social services as education, made decisions on proper religious observance, gave relief to the poor, and provided orphanages, and hospital care. The councils also regulated the local economic life by implementing laws concerning trade and manufacture. When disputes required settlement or crimes had been committed, the councils' courts adjudicated both civil and criminal law. It is interesting to note that many of the biblical and Talmudic laws were adopted to fit the needs of legal cases many hundred of years later. Of course, the Elders collected taxes, for the need of their own communities and for the lord or king who ruled the land.

The word *shtetl* is derived from the German and can be defined as a small town. Its Yiddish definition, however, evokes much more then a geographic dot on the map. A shtetl was a community within a Russian or Polish town with a relatively large Jewish population. Within its confines life was governed by a different calendar, a different language, a different set of values than existed on the other side, the Christian side.

Contemporary descriptions of life in the ghettos and small towns, the shtetl, strike us as grim. But it must be remembered that life for everyone was grim. Calamities such as frequent infant mortality, young mothers dying of child-bed fever, an insufficient and deficient diet, commonly polluted water, the dangers of overcrowding, lack of sanitation, and the absence of privacy were the norm for all but the aristocratic few. Life was short and harsh, wars devastated the countryside, and natural disasters were accepted as God's will. Birth usually determined your place in society, and very few could move above their predetermined station. The concept that human beings, simply because they were human, could expect the rich and powerful to care about their misery had not yet risen on the Eastern European horizon.

THE END TO PEACEFUL COEXISTENCE

It is estimated that half a million Jews lived in Polish lands by the middle of the seventeenth century. Depending on the precarious balance of power between king and church and the influence of German merchants who disliked competition, Jewish life fluctuated between prosperity and subsistence. Despite periodic outbursts of anti-Jewish violence, the number of Jews increased. The most devastating attacks occurred in the decade between 1648 and 1658 when the Cossacks revolted against their Polish oppressors and included the Jews in their fury. These massacres in the Ukraine were followed by a Swedish invasion from the north and Russian incursions from the east. In the Polish counterattacks, the Jews were accused of complicity with the enemy and thousands were killed.

From the seventeenth century on, the promise of peaceful coexistence between Poles and Jews was marred by officially sanctioned and privately enforced restrictions. Without the protection of the authorities, prejudice became increasingly open and extreme. Christian hostility was met in kind by the Jews, but since they were virtually defenseless, their insecurity deepened into apprehension. Thus, fear of the Gentile world came to live permanently among the Polish Jews. Each generation found it more difficult to live decently than the previous one. The Gentile world was either indifferent to or gratified by their distress. When rulers issued decrees that forbade them to live outside of certain designated areas, the ghetto was created. The Jews were now legally and physically separated from the rest of the inhabitants. The gulf widened and the immediately recognizable Jew came into being. He spoke a different language, wore odd clothing, and kept his eyes downcast in the presence of Christians.

SHTETL LIFE

The word *shtetl* means small town, but actually these were market centers where the local rural population came to buy, sell, and trade. The farmers sold wood, grain, and potatoes and bought shoes and salt and oil for their lamps from the Jewish residents. It might be wholly Jewish community, have a Jewish majority, or a strong Jewish minority. Most shtetls were scattered over the Russian Pale of Settlement, the region of Western Russia where Jews were permitted to live. On a contemporary map, the area is about a thousand miles long and three hundred miles wide and includes Lithuania, Byelorus, the Ukraine, and eastern Poland. The typical shtetl was a dreary looking place. The houses were constructed of unpainted wood, jammed together along unpaved and unlit streets. A well or two provided an often unreliable source of water for the entire community. Family life revolved around the kitchen stove, the only warm spot during the long, cold winter. There were beds or mattresses everywhere, the floors were usually packed earth, and the rooms virtually unventilated. The furnishings were sparse, a table, some chairs, perhaps a hope chest, and a real bed for the parents. Nevertheless, it was a moot question who was better off, the shtetl dwellers or the nearby peasant whose animals might share his hut with him and his family.

Jewish life consisted of a rhythm in which the religious and the prosaic functions were interwoven into a single pattern. The rabbi was generally the most important member of the community because God and his commandments were part and parcel of every activity. Torah and Talmud provided the basis of laws, religious as well as secular. Hundreds of prayers were uttered, not merely during synagogue services but as part of such mundane activities as washing one's hands or eating the first apple of the season. The search to understand the holy texts was a sacred obligation for those able to cope with the intricacies of commentaries piled upon commentaries. The Almighty of the shtetl was not an unknowable deity who dwelled on high but one who lived among His people.

Family life was the paramount source of happiness. Children were treasured long before Western civilization discovered the child-centered family. The Sabbath was a joyful celebration, even in the poorest household. Fathers headed the family but mothers were honored and respected. She made it possible to observe the holy days with special foods, with white tablecloths, and Sabbath candles. Grandparents, in-laws, uncles, aunts, and cousins lived with the family, or down the street, or a few miles away in the next town. Relationships were close, often quarrelsome but supportive in times of need. When persecution intensified, families and communities sought security from among their own; it was pointless to hope for help from the world outside.

CULTURAL ACHIEVEMENTS

The fact that during the late Middle Ages many generations of Poles and Jews had lived more or less amicably side by side has been obscured by nineteenth and twentieth century antiSemitism. The modern history of Poland, with its institutionalized and grassroots hatred of the Jews, has overshadowed the earlier centuries of coexistence. But it was Polish soil that nourished several vital and enduring elements of Jewish culture. Among these achievements we can point to the following: the study of kabbalah, the preservation of rational orthodoxy, the development of Hasidism, the advocacy and promotion of Zionism, and the modernization of many religious practices.

KABBALAH

The quest for God's blessings is as ancient as man himself. Speculation on the mysteries of creation, of man's role in the universe, and the ways that might lead to an understanding of the creator are time-honored traditions in Jewish thought. Side by side with the philosophical and devotional search for God, the allure of mysticism has also endured. The most abiding form of Jewish mysticism is called kabbalah. Although the invoking of magic symbolism can be traced to the very roots of Judaism, its medieval and modern formulas were largely based on the *Zohar.* This thirteenth century book was attributed to Moses de Leon but based on revelations of a second century sage named Simeon ben Johai. From the Zohar emanated centuries of occult conjecture and cosmology.

The kabbahlists sought to pierce the mystery of life and death and all the unanswerable questions by discovering some secret meaning in the holy texts. Magical powers were assigned to the individual letters of the Scriptures and it was believed that their specific arrangement concealed some shrouded significance. By manipulating the words and letters, reading them upside down, superimposing one upon another, even reading them backwards, their truth might be revealed. Months and years of scrutiny, of poring over every stroke, obscured the simple truth of the holy books. A form of numerology developed, wherein letters were given numerical value which were arranged and rearranged to extract their secrets.

The concept that the universe can be made understandable through mathematics strikes a sympathetic chord in the age of space exploration, but Jewish mysticism had no scientific basis. The numbers from one to ten were believed to have radiated directly from God and were assigned supernatural qualities. The longing to penetrate the mystery of God all too often turned into superstition. In times of great suffering, the need to understand God's seeming indifference to human anguish grew especially strong. After the expulsion from Spain, the devotees of kabbalah increased rapidly. Like medieval alchemists, men spent their lives in search of the right formula, and like astrologers they consulted their books to do God's will.

Events in European history during the sixteenth and seventeenth centuries provided a seedbed for the growth of superstition and delusion. Natural and man-made calamities—floods, famines, the Protestant upheavals, and the Thirty Years' War—created chaos and terrible suffering. If only it was found, then the right incantation might appease the wrath of God? This fever to influence fate through magic was echoed in the Jewish population of Poland. Here, civil and foreign wars had caused great anguish. The degeneration of kabbalah into occult numerology was one aspect of the desperation; another was the appearance of a number of false messiahs. These men, some charlatans, others self-deceived, were supported by hundreds of thousands of followers. The most excessive claims of imminent redemption found disciples only too eager to be deluded. Men and women gave up their livelihoods and their homes and embarked for the Holy Land in the expectation of messianic deliverance. Had not the Holy Books prophesied that great evil will precede the day of salvation? Had they not remained faithful to God's commands and still lived in wretchedness? Surely their suffering was the prologue to redemption. And each time that a pseudomessiah turned out to be either a fraud or a fanatic, the despair of his believers grew deeper.

RATIONAL ORTHODOXY

Jewish learning of the eighteenth century consisted largely of pedantic, formalized repetition. The teacher, usually the rebbe (rabbi), accepted boys into his school who were as young as four or five years of age. They studied Hebrew, the language of prayer, while Yiddish was their mother tongue. Instruction was largely a matter of rote memorization. Although it was permissible to question the meaning of the text, one did not dispute the explanation of the rebbe. Usually, the boys were confined all day in cheerless rooms without an outlet for youthful exuberance. A boy's pale, earnest face was deemed handsome, and the excelling student was the joy of his parents.

Advanced scholarship was equally uninspired. Endless recitation and argumentation over minutia were the norm and ritual was exalted over philosophical, even theological discussions. And yet, the spark for the love of learning remained. Able young men were encouraged to study all their lives. Because learning was valued above all other attributes, a bright student could hope to make a good match. It was entirely acceptable that he never earn a living for his family. He was sustained either by his proud father-in-law or by his supportive wife.

Both Jews and Gentiles neglected to educate their girls. Their future role as wives and mothers was fixed. Jewish women accepted their roles as home makers and obedient wives. The fortunate man was blessed with a wife who filled his home with children, sons were valued more then daughters, kept a well ordered house, was a good cook and devoted mother. Women could earn communal respect for kindness and wisdom, but they performed few religious rites. In the synagogue, the sexes were separated, and Orthodox men avoided touching, even looking at women who were not close relatives in order to curb any inappropriate desire. Jewish women were probably less subjugated than their Christian contemporaries. Judaism does not acknowledge the concept of original sin. Eve is viewed as the mother of mankind rather than the temptress. The connection between sin and sex, which has rested so heavily on Christian women, does not exist in Judaism. God commanded man to multiply, and sexual urges were the God-given means to that end.

The sterility of the intellectual life of the Polish Jews in the eighteenth century was alleviated by the reforms of Elijah, the Vilna Gaon (wise man). Elijah sparked a revival of Jewish learning by widening its inquiry to include new fields of knowledge. His approach to study corrected long-existing deficiencies. He urged the cultivation of scholarship rather than memorization. Among his own accomplishments were a translation of Euclid into Hebrew and a treatise on astronomy. His influence left a permanent imprint on the evolution of Eastern Jewry. Fine minds were now able to find within Orthodoxy the challenges of a wider education.

Elijah established in Vilna, the capital of Lithuania, a model center of study. His Talmudic academy cracked open a window to the world beyond the confines of shtetl mentality. Under his leadership and that of his followers, philosophy, science, theology, and Hebrew were added to the curriculum. The rabbis who graduated from his school brought a more modern outlook to their congregations.

Jewish boys entering school in Vilna, 1929.   (Courtesy Yivo Institute for Jewish Research.)

The breadth of the Gaon's mind was, however, not suitable fare for the masses. The work he required could be mastered by the intellectual elite but was beyond the common man. The laborer, who had to work so that his family could eat, nonetheless sought the divine presence in his life. How could he reach God? Serve God? The question was answered for many Polish Jews by the appearance of Baal Shem Tov and the development of Hasidism.

THE HASIDIC CHALLENGE

In recent years, Hollywood has produced several movies that depict Hasidic life in the United States. Certainly, many residents of large cities have seen the bearded men in black suits and their modestly attired women. Hasidic veneration of their leader, the rebbe, is celebrated and/or decried by Jewish and Christian observers. Sometimes hailed as committed fundamentalists or condemned as religious fanatics, Hasids have carved for themselves a conspicuous and worldwide niche. Their devotion to each other and to their form of Orthodoxy is impressive and so are their almost crime-free, drug-free communities. Although often located in the midst of old and crowded inner cities, Hasidic enclaves are models of the spirit of neighborliness. In several ways, the modern adherents of Hasidism vary from the intent of the founder of the sect, the Baal Shem Tov ("Master of the Good Name"), but these differences are not part of this discussion. It should be understood, however, that rather than declining in numbers, Hasidism is strong and still growing.

The Hasidic movement overcame two insufficiencies within Jewish life in Poland. First, increased persecution caused greater insecurities, which, in turn, intensified the search for spiritual consolation. Second, the unlearned had no access into the tight circle of Talmudic scholarship. Hasidism began as a revolt of the unschooled against the aristocracy of the academics. To serve God was the nearly universal goal of ghetto and shtetl Jewry. Those who could not spend years in intensive study of the Scriptures and its numerous commentaries felt, and were made to feel, inadequate. The fact that the scholars were part of the social elite could only add to the frustration.

The charismatic founder of Hasidism freed the unlettered from the inadequacy caused by the aristocracy of scholarship. Israel of Moldavia, the Baal Shem Tov, believed that devotion to God is rooted in the emotions, not knowledge. Prayer was joy and joy was prayer. Worship could be expressed through music and dancing. The beauty of nature, seen as a distraction by the Talmudists, was deemed a manifestation of the love bestowed on mankind by the King of the Universe. The Baal Shem Tov elevated faith over ritual, not by discarding the holy books but by interpreting them in an unconventional way. To the Hasids, the presence of God is everywhere in the universe and one may communicate with God anywhere and at any time. This approach to religion was essentially democratic, since wealth and distinction avails one nothing in the eyes of the Almighty. The emotions of optimism and exultation replenish the whole man, body and soul. Rituals are necessary, but the essence of religion is faith, expressed from the depth of feeling. In enthusiasm, ardor, and communal spirit, the Hasids resemble the religious zeal exhibited by revivalist churches.

The Baal Shem Tov wrote no instructions for his followers. His personality was the center of the community he created. After his death, the administration of Hasidic life continued to revolve around the figure of a leader. As the movement spread throughout Eastern Europe, it split into several groups. Each chose its own rabbi, a position that developed into a dynastic seat of power. Although such a rabbi reigned without a constitution, without an army, without any but moral force, he had a great deal of power. His word was law, his decisions final, the loyalty of his followers absolute. His sphere of jurisdiction was greater than that of any monarch. His disciples awaited his judgment on all questions affecting their lives, be they of an economic or personal nature. The source of this authority was based on the conviction that their rabbi stood in a special communion with God which allowed him to intercede on their behalf.

HASKALAH

Haskala, a Hebrew phrase meaning "Let there be light," was a Jewish philosophical movement. Its aim was three-fold: to renew Hebrew learning, to bring European culture into Jewish life, and to break down the walls separating Christians and Jews.

The philosopher Moses Mendelssohn, a friend of the great dramatist Gotthold Lessing, was the very personification of the spirit of tolerance and liberal thought. Both men devoted their considerable talents and fame to teach their contemporaries the meaning of humanity. Mendelssohn struggled against both Jewish and Gentile bigotry. His philosophy challenged the narrowly circumscribed beliefs and practices of both Jews and Christians. His devotion to the cause of mutual understanding and his forbearance opened the door through which German and Jewish intellectuals were able to enter each other's realm. Jews began to take part in the mental world of Germans thinkers while some non-Jews acknowledged that Jewishness and Germanness might be compatible. Mendelssohn remained a devout Jew and saw no conflict between Jewish values and Western humanism. With his heart, mind, and powerful pen, he attacked the strictures of empty rituals and the binding confines of rabbinical power. As he sought to widen the world of his people, so did he also fight for their economic and political emancipation, a goal he did not live to see fulfilled. Predictably, his work earned him the opposition of the Orthodox who feared that exposure to a Gentile environment would dilute the traditional visions of Judaism. The fact that his children converted to Christianity obviously provided grist for the mill of enemies of Haskala. Mendelssohn's insistence that his daughters' education equal that of men certainly marked him as a man far ahead of his time.

Mendelssohn's impact was not confined to Central and Western Europe. Gradually, his concepts moved eastward, where a segment of the largely urban strata of Polish Jews fell under the influence of Haskala. To whatever degree the reluctant Polish authorities permitted, these were the Jews who learned to speak Polish, attended Polish schools, and tried to become part of every aspect of Polish national life. Many entered the middle class, were active in the professions, and owned medium-sized businesses. Others entered the urban proletariat, operated the sewing machines in small factories, delivered goods by horse and wagon, and finished textiles in their homes. Most were patriotic Poles who chose to live outside the walls of actual or spiritual ghettos, even though they rarely cut their Jewish cultural ties. In hundreds of organizations they transplanted the closeness of shtetl life to the city. They united into associations to serve every human activity, from birth to burial, so that no one need be alone. Some went to synagogues where they prayed from the time-worn books of the Orthodox; others hoped that the Reform movement of Germany would take root in Poland. Still others did not pray at all. Nevertheless, all were Jews.

ROOTS OF ZIONISM

The two major events in Jewish history in the past century were the Holocaust and the creation of the state of Israel. The 1948 vote by the United Nations that sanctioned the formation of a national homeland for the Jews has been linked by some observers to the Holocaust, but political Zionism had begun much earlier. In the struggle to create a national homeland for the Jews, Polish Jewry played a vital role.

The passionate nationalism of the nineteenth century touched the long buried longings of many subjugated peoples. Several waves of revolutions engulfed Europe, reaching from France to Poland and culminating in the uprisings of 1848. The Poles had dreamt of liberation from the heavy hand of Russia, but like Italy, Prussia, Hungary, and Austria, the moment to realize the ideal of self-determination had not yet come. Among those Poles whose dreams and hopes were shattered when the uprisings of 1830 and 1848 failed were a number of urban Polish Jews. They had chosen the path of Haskala, the enlightenment, and expected to enjoy full equality with Christian Poles. The largest component of Polish Jewry, however, was still confined in their nearly autonomous enclaves. They did not believe that their conditions would be improved by the efforts of Gentiles. Their poverty, insecurity, and well-founded fear of pogroms were, after all, inflicted on them by the Gentile world. Nor could anyone deny that most Catholic Poles were very reluctant to accept Jews as equals. Assimilation of Polish Jews was discouraged by the Orthodox rabbis on the one hand and opposed by the church on the other hand. Life in the Diaspora was tenuous, and the Jews needed to find another answer to their dilemma.

The hope of going back to the land of Israel had been kept alive for nearly 2,000 years, ever since the Romans exiled the Judeans. Hundreds of generations had uttered the words "next year in Jerusalem" at the end of the Passover meal. But such hopeful expressions implied an abstract longing, not a blueprint for action. Political Zionism, that is, the organized effort to bring about a national Jewish state, evolved from the confluence of several historic streams. Many Jews recognized that the spirit of enlightenment had not halted antiSemitism. Even a secularized Europe had been unable, perhaps unwilling, to stop prejudice. Instead, new forms of the old plague had arisen. The Dreyfus trial in 1894 in France demonstrated that in the very birthplace of liberty, equality, and fraternity, bigotry still flourished. The Dreyfus case was the most sensational trial of the century. Alfred Dreyfus, a Jewish captain in the French army, was falsely accused of treason. AntiSemitic conservatives connived to commit this injustice and it took twelve years to vindicate the captain. The efforts of the great French writer Emile Zola played a primary role in reversing a patently prejudiced decision.

Toward the close of the nineteenth century, a new form of bias attracted the xenophobes. The allegation was made that Jews were racially and ethnically different. The modern nation-state could not integrate the ever alien Jew. (A further discussion of the racial aspects of Hitler's hatred will follow in the next chapter). Despite the success of the American experience, the notion that diversity could be a source of strength had not taken hold among many Europeans.

The search for an answer to the persistence of antiSemitism was accelerated by the policies of czar Alexander III. His father, the Great Emancipator, had freed the Russian serfs and eased the most repressive measures against the Jews. His tragic assassination in 1881 was blamed on the Jews and was followed by years of officially condoned, perhaps instigated, pogroms. The death toll of those riots in the Pale of Settlement, the southwestern region set aside for Jews, was appalling. Once more, the physical survival of Russian and Polish Jews was in question.

During the final decade of the nineteenth century, the hope to create a Jewish homeland in Palestine had the support of growing numbers of young Jews. When the English government expressed interest in such a scheme, the dream took form. Considering the fact that at this time the Holy Land, the focus of the Zionists, was under Ottoman rule and not part of the British Empire, this was merely a gesture. Nonetheless, a number of young Russian Jews actually translated the concept of creating a homeland by taking up plowshares and settling as farmers on the barren Palestinian land. They made up the first small trickle of pioneers. A nation, however, was not built by the earnest efforts of a vanguard. It required massive support, political negotiation, and excellent leadership. It required, in other words, the ability of Theodor Herzl.

THEODOR HERZL

Theodor Herzl (1860–1904) was a Jewish journalist from Vienna who had been assigned to cover the Dreyfus trial in Paris. Captain Dreyfus' prosecution unleashed an upsurge of antiSemitism that astounded and dismayed the young journalist, as well as many of the supporters of assimilation. Herzl concluded that only a Jewish state could solve the Jewish problem. The nations of Europe, he argued, should support this agenda because continued antiSemitism would undermine their internal peace. Persecution of the Jews would deliver them into the ranks of revolutionary socialists and even the most liberal governments would be thrown into turmoil. Herzl devoted the remainder of his life to effect legitimization of the concept of nationhood for the Jews.

Herzl's book *Der Judenstaat* (*The Jewish State*) outlined the practical steps by which his vision could be realized. The work created a sensation, although much of the response was negative. Many Orthodox Jews protested that the ingathering in the Holy Land could occur only when the promised messiah appeared. Herzl was not an observant Jew, how dare he suggest conventional statehood for the chosen people? Other critics contended that Judaism was a religion, not a nationality. Leaders of the assimilated communities held that integration into the society of the various countries would take place eventually. Patience was called for, not demands for separateness. And then there was the segment of the Jewish population that wanted only to remain invisible, who feared any publicity lest it give rise to more persecution. Among many Eastern European Jews, however, particularly the young, the idea of a homeland met enthusiastic support. Here, the ideal of returning to the land of the Scriptures had already taken tentative root. Now a man of action had emerged from the West to provide the essential political leadership.

The First Zionist Congress met in Basel in 1897. For the first time in 1,800 years, Jews from throughout the Diaspora gathered to plan their future, rich and poor, capitalist and socialist, orthodox and liberal. They spoke many languages, but their voices were unified in their aim to establish a national home for their people. They marveled at the white flag with the blue star of David, wept upon hearing a Jewish national anthem, and came away believing the impossible dream. They elected Herzl as the first president of their World Zionist Organization. Thus, they laid the foundation for the future state of Israel.

Meanwhile, difficulties mounted. Palestine was Turkish, and land sales for proposed settlements required the sultan's consent. That consent was never given. Herzl believed in diplomatic solutions to the deadlock and tried to enlist the rich and the powerful to promote his plans. He played on the Kaiser's egotism to win his good offices to intercede with the sultan. In vain, he faced the palpable hatred of the Russian foreign minister. He even applied to the Pope for help. All was fruitless. Only Great Britain showed a sympathetic interest by offering Herzl a haven in Uganda, East Africa. Should Uganda be accepted? Perhaps as a temporary refuge for the suffering Eastern Jews? Or was Zionism unshakably committed to Zion, that is, Palestine? The organization was split by this controversy when, suddenly, just forty-four years old, Herzl died.

Theodor Herzl did not live to establish a Jewish state. In terms of concrete accomplishments, nearly all his diplomatic missions failed. Nevertheless, he is a founder of the state of Israel. His spirit ushered in a dramatic change in the self-perception, and in much of the world's perception, of what it means to be a Jew. The organization he founded spread from village to town and from West to East. The greater the oppression, the greater the impact of the message: We shall be as other peoples with a national state of our own. Young Jews, mostly Russian and Polish, prepared themselves for a future in Palestine. They studied Hebrew, thus making vital contributions to the transformation of a dead language to one that could serve the modern world. They learned to farm, to irrigate, and to apply practical knowledge to practical problems. Instead of the Talmud or law or medicine, they read treatises on soil erosion, reforestation, and horticulture. They split rocks, built roads, sang and danced and rejoiced in the cooperative kibbutz life. The older generation often disapproved, particularly because often their children's devotion to religion wore thin; but these young people were done with the meekness of their parents. These new Jews had no faith that assimilation would win them equality within the Gentile world. They would not accept the misery of persecution and poverty with docile hopelessness and look only to God for deliverance.

It was difficult for their elders to condone this new activist youth. Religious education had been idealized for hundreds of years, while physical labor was seen as the lot of the intellectually barren. But now their children turned these ancient values upside down. In addition, though the focus of the family had always been the hope for grandchildren, these young Zionists planned to go to far off Palestine. They chose their own mates and resented interference in their private lives. Often, the political views of the future pioneers made the older generation uneasy. The creation of a Jewish homeland required a cooperative spirit that was expressed through democratic socialism.

The religious attitudes of these young men and women ranged from liberal to orthodox, each group creating its own cooperatives. They trained in collective agricultural camps in Poland and Russia and upon completing their preparatory course were expected to live in Palestine, to make *aliyah,* a word that means return to the biblical homeland. Some emigrated legally, others illegally, to become the forerunners of the massive immigration that would follow the First and Second World Wars.

THE REBIRTH OF POLAND

The twentieth century opened with unprecedented optimism. Western Europeans fully expected to expand their domination over the political and economic life of much of the globe. They predicted an end to such anachronisms as war and poverty. Even disease would surely be conquered in the foreseeable future. Science and logic would triumph over all the ills that had escaped from Pandora's box. But then the fantasy was shattered by the catastrophe of World War I. The madness of this devastating war was followed by a hypocritical peace.

After American idealism had raised hopes too high, disillusionment and disappointment were inevitable. Woodrow Wilson was the man of the hour, but many of his expectations were unrealized. The promise of general armament reduction, of free trade, and border adjustments based on nationality were broken by his wartime allies even before they met at Versailles in 1919. One of the promises that was kept concerned the restoration of Poland.

The new Poland had a bloody beginning. From north to south, its plains had been turned into battlefields during the First World War. Already exhausted by the Great War, Poland's newly constituted sovereignty was challenged by its neighbors. Fierce border disputes with the Soviet Union, with Lithuania, with Estonia, and with Czechoslovakia disrupted Poland's attempt to establish an economically viable and politically stable government. The entire interwar period, that is the twenty years between the rebirth of Poland and its defeat by Nazi Germany in 1939, was an era of tension and limited progress. The anticipation that political liberty would be accompanied by economic well-being was not fulfilled. The euphoria sparked by independence turned to bitter frustration in the face of a difficult reality.

The Polish nation held some 27 million inhabitants, 70 percent of whom were ethnic Poles; the rest of the population consisted of minorities, with Ukrainians and Jews comprising the largest percentages. The ordinary Pole could not understand the complexity of the problems his nation encountered. City workers struggled with unemployment; capitalists lacked money to widen the industrial base; an unstable parliamentary system composed of too many political parties had too little administrative experience. Patience and endurance were needed but both were lacking. Millions emigrated, relieving the pressure to some degree. The democratic constitutional government adopted in 1921 was overthrown by a coup in 1926. For the next few years, Poland experienced some economic growth, but just as the recovery gave encouragement to investors, hope for further economic gains was dashed. The Great Depression of 1929 caused severe hardships to the newly established industries of Poland. The origin of the collapse was beyond the comprehension of the masses, and a scapegoat needed to be sacrificed. The Jews were the obvious choice.

Business courtyard on Nalewki Street in the Jewish quarter of Warsaw, Poland. (Courtesy United States Holocaust Memorial Museum.)

Even before the economic disaster, the Polish government between the two World Wars had been a moral failure. The treaty that had reestablished Polish sovereignty had specifically stipulated that the rights of ethnic minorities must be protected. But the pledge was not kept. The minorities were oppressed as the government sought to undermine non-Polish culture and force the minorities to abandon their distinctive way of life. For 150 years, the czars had attempted to turn Poles into Russians without success. How quickly that prolonged and painful lesson was forgotten.

THE INTERWAR DECADES

Politicians of the right and left became more radical and, although these extremists agreed on little else, they were as one in their embrace of antiSemitism. The Jews were held responsible for every calamity that beset the nation. The government sanctioned and encouraged such prejudice and used its legal powers to institutionalize the most irrational scapegoating. Laws were passed to restrict the Jews' economic freedom until fewer and fewer means to earn a livelihood remained. With the exceptions of the textile and some food refining factories, Jews were denied industrial employment. The job security of wage earners was already precarious as mechanization was introduced into growing numbers of industrial establishments. Added to that difficulty, Jewish workers were usually the last hired and the first fired. Higher educational opportunities were severely limited by a quota system. Jewish students who managed to be accepted into universities were forced to sit on special "ghetto benches" placed in the back of lecture rooms. The social services of the impoverished Jewish communities tried desperately to prevent outright starvation, but only the charity of foreign Jews kept a large percentage of the 3 million Polish Jews from pauperism.

The impact of this renewed persecution resulted not only in the growth of Zionism, it was also expressed in the organization of the *Bund*. This was a socialist political party, founded in 1897 to promote the welfare of the Jewish proletariat. It mirrored other socialist parties in its goals: better wages, improved working conditions, and promoting the election of a socialist government. Jewish workers established their own organization because the conventional socialist parties could not or would not meet their needs. Among the special demands of the Jewish workers were their request to keep their holy days, including the Sabbath, equal educational opportunities for their children, and cessation of the government's official anti-Jewish stance. Unlike most of the proletariat, Jewish laborers were well informed, avid readers, and active in a variety of social and cultural activities. In most societies, only the upper and middle classes patronized the arts, but these working people loved literature, art, theater, and music. In western Poland many Jews spoke, read, and wrote Yiddish, Polish, Hebrew, and German, while in the eastern provinces the Russian language replaced German.

Despite their oppression, Polish Jewry was remarkably creative during the interval between the two great wars. Odessa and Warsaw became centers of Hebrew literature. Isaac Leib Peretz became the master in poetry, drama, and the short story. Authors such as Sholem Asch, Isaac Bashevis Singer, and his brother Israel Joshua Singer continued the genre. Theater developed from amateur status to professional productions, and popular performers achieved fame as the darlings of their audiences. Libraries, trade schools, religious education, and magazines and newspapers to satisfy every political leaning flourished in spite of the tenuous economic and repressive antiSemitic atmosphere. Concerts were performed in simple rooms with wooden benches or in gilded halls with plush seats to give pleasure to rich and poor. Jewish composers and musicians were in the forefront of Poland's musical resurgence. Even photography and film making were fostered by Jewish artists. Endless philosophical and political disputations were, of course, accompanied and enhanced by uncounted cups of tea and mountains of cake.

While Polish urban Jewry discovered its great diversity, the shtetl, where God ruled without challenge, still existed in great numbers. Clearly, any attempt to speak of Polish Jewry as homogeneous springs from a flawed premise. The world that vanished had many different faces. A Polish Jew might be Orthodox or atheist, socialist or capitalist, Zionist or patriot. In their dying, however, all differences disappeared. Young or old, healthy or ill, wise or foolish, honest or corrupt, it did not matter. The eyes looking back at us from the photograph of Polish Jews lined up outside the lethal showers of the death camps were the eyes of Everyman.

CHAPTER 3

The Nazis' Rise to Power

The media carry frequent news reports concerning the resurgence of neo-Nazi groups, both in Europe and in America. The swastikas smeared on walls and gravestones send a shiver of fear and revulsion along the spines of the older generation, the generation that fought or experienced Nazism. Invariably, these hate crimes raise some difficult questions: Can a Holocaust happen again? Can it happen here? Should the skinheads and their ilk be ignored or punished? Where is the shadowy line that separates overreaction from disregard of danger?

Some of the answers may be found in the history of the Third Reich. The Nazis were able to reverse the path of Western civilization when three conditions converged that made possible the killing of millions. First, the unthinkable had to appear to be not only doable, but desirable. Persecution, even murder, had to be cloaked as a commendable ideal. "For the good of the many, some few must suffer." (This topic will be explored in the next chapter.) Second, the government must be a dictatorship and exercise total power over every aspect of the life of the people. When the slogan *Die Juden sind unser Unglueck* ("the Jews are our misfortune") became government policy, the Nazis were able to muster the psychological and the physical power to remove said *Unglueck*. Hitler's authority radiated outward from his will—even from his implied wish—to the ranks of his obsequious vassals. No effective resistance remained after the destruction of all opposition. The third prerequisite is the existence of an overt and/or latent prejudice directed against the targeted minority. This writer does not agree with Daniel Jonah Goldhagen's thesis that the German people were ingrained with a special, distinct, murderous form of hatred that made them *Hitler's Willing Executioners*, but clearly many Germans looked upon Jews with suspicion and antipathy. Hitler's control over communications made it possible to create the impression that this minority was representative of all Germans.

The Holocaust required the unqualified commitment to make Germany *Judenrein* (cleansed of Jews) by a totalitarian government controlling a largely passive population. The notion that decent folk mind their own business served millions of Germans very well; it allowed them to justify doing nothing in the presence of evil. Also required were the men and the means to carry out murders on such a massive scale. The logistical problems of transporting and killing millions of people while fighting a war were tremendous. The work and cooperation of many people coming from many areas of expertise were essential. Racial "scientists" had to determine who was a full Jew, a half Jew, a quarter Jew. Economists were used to work out the dynamics of driving Jews from business, industry, and the professions without interrupting the economy. A veritable army of SS, Gestapo, police and the regular armed forces were needed to hunt down and imprison Jews in ghettos. Transportation experts pored over timetables of trains to the camps. As Christopher Browning in *Ordinary Men,* analyzed so ably, civil servants had to be trained to machine-gun naked Jews in open fields. The construction and operation of concentration and death camps demanded many willing hands and minds. The process of dehumanizing the killers and the attempt to reduce the victims to the level of subhumans was an important part of the work of the propaganda ministry. All these operations were possible only in the absence of even the most basic civil liberties and in the presence of a general population who, by and large, chose to see nothing, hear nothing, and know nothing.

THE TOTALITARIAN PREREQUISITE

The German people had opted for a dictatorship. They had relinquished to their government the right to make all political, economic, and many personal decisions. They had handed their individual and public liberties to Hitler like an unwanted gift they wished to return. Many Germans believed that noninvolvement in the actual process of murder absolved them of all responsibility. Those nebulous "others," who were in charge, who had the power, they alone were guilty. As long as one did not order or participate in the mass killings, one's hands were clean. The Reichstag had abdicated its power to become a rubber stamp for Nazi decrees. The principle that resistance to evil was a moral duty did not exist for the vast majority of Germans. Not until the end of the war did men like Martin Niemoeller and Elie Wiesel arouse the world's conscience to the realization that the bystander cannot escape guilt or shame.

An understanding of the Shoah necessitates a comprehension of the theory and practice of Nazism. However, before discussing what it meant to be a German during the Third Reich, we must remember the circumstances that allowed Hitler to take control. The Fuehrer (leader) did not forcibly overthrow a legitimate government; he was the rightful successor to the Weimar Republic. There was no coup d'état, no revolution. The Nazi party won a plurality, which resulted in the selection of Hitler as the chancellor. Those who voted the for NSDAP, that is, the National Socialist German Workers Party—the Nazis—could not claim ignorance of Hitler's true aims.

The press and radio had reported his promises and tirades for years. His book, *Mein Kampf,* (*My Struggle*) was, in fact, a blueprint for his intentions to create a personal dictatorship. Both his enormously well-received speeches and his writing were punctuated by a loathing for a great many things: democracy, communism, peace, and Jews. Historians still debate just when Hitler's hatred of Jews escalated to annihilation, but it was always clear that their persecution was a cornerstone in his program.

The question of why a literate, well-informed electorate chose to throw away its freedom puzzles Americans. Why did so many Germans decide to renounce democratic government and vote for a man who had no formal education, never held a responsible job, was not a German at all but an Austrian? Were the circumstances that led to the demise of the Weimar Republic so exceptional, so singular, that their recurrence is unlikely? Or, might history repeat itself? Is it possible that the conditions prevailing in Germany in 1933 could be duplicated somewhere else at some other time? If the answer is yes, or even possibly, then it is our obligation to study the German situation with self-interested concern.

The difficulties experienced by Germans in the early 1930s were not so singular that they have no parallel; other nationalities faced comparable distress. History, since the fall of Hitler, gives its own evidence that genocides still can and do happen. Other dictators have arisen whose mass murders were carried out to accomplish different objectives but with similar brutality. Each instance is unique in its specifics but several general preconditions remain: a population that is looking for a quick fix for its difficulties, a dictatorial government that exacerbates a longstanding fear or prejudice and blames that group for every calamity.

If a holocaust were perpetrated today by an industrially advanced nation, the resulting tragedy could not be overstated. The consequence of such a disaster would be multiplied by the effects of recent technological and biological advances. The Nazis killed 11 million civilians and plunged Europe into economic, political, and social turmoil. The idea that such carnage could be, would be surpassed staggers the imagination.

THE TREATY OF VERSAILLES

The government that preceded that of the Nazi Party was called the Weimar Republic. After four years of exhausting warfare, the Allied armies defeated the Germans in 1918 and the monarchy of Kaiser Wilhelm II ended. The emperor abdicated amid violent political agitation and fled to Holland. The negotiations of the armistice and peace treaty were the unhappy responsibility of the new government. The German people wanted an end to hostilities and expected terms to be based on Woodrow Wilson's promise of peace without victory. The actual treaty that the German representatives were forced to sign was, in fact, punitive and hardly designed to give the fledgling Republic a much needed vote of confidence. The war guilt clause, placing the blame for the war solely upon Germany, infuriated every level of German society. Many Germans never absolved the signatories for their "betrayal." As a matter of fact, the German representatives were not permitted to participate in the negotiations; the first Republican government resigned rather than sign the treaty. But the German people were near starvation. Shipments of food were withheld until the signatures were affixed. None of this made any difference. "Treason" was the epitaph that followed the men who signed the Versailles *Diktat*. Field Marshall von Hindenburg, hero of the war, refused to represent the nation at the signing ceremony in the Hall of Mirrors. The civilian head of the Catholic Center party, Matthias Erzberger, led the hapless delegation. Within three years, that valiant man was assassinated in payment for his courage. The German army was never held accountable by the public for losing the war or for standing aloof at Versailles or for its failure to support the new government.

The treaty was harsh (that is, unless one considers the severe terms of the agreement the Germans had forced on the defeated Russians in 1918 at Brest-Litovsk). One may well wonder, though, whether Germany would have adhered to President Wilson's Fourteen Points if she had been the victor. The Versailles settlement cost Germany one-eighth of her land along the eastern and western borders, her colonies, and her overseas investments. The German army was limited to 100,000 men; her navy was drastically curtailed, and the German people were obligated to pay an enormous, as yet unspecified reparations bill. In light of today's understanding of international economic linkage among nations, the treaty was bound to obstruct and delay the process of German, or even worldwide, recovery.

THE WEIMAR REPUBLIC

The government of the Weimar Republic consisted of a legislature, the Reichstag, which was elected by universal suffrage and whose members represented the German people as a whole. A president, also chosen by the voters, served a seven-year term. Unlike his American counterpart, the president was not involved in the day-to-day running of the government but stood above political parties. Following national elections, he usually appointed the leader of the majority party in the Reichstag as chancellor. The chancellor then chose his cabinet and thus created the executive branch of government. Because it was difficult for any one party to have a clear majority in the Reichstag, all the Weimar governments were coalitions. The constitution also provided for representation from the eighteen states to sit as the Reichsrat, but that body played a secondary role in the interwar period. Article 48, a constitutional provision sometimes referred to as the suicide clause, permitted the president to suspend the constitution during emergencies. As will be seen later, this stipulation played a critical part in the final destruction of the republic.

As a document, the Weimar constitution was an admirable achievement. It provided for the civil liberties of the people, equality before the law, free elections of a representative government, education guaranteed for all, and safeguards for religious freedom. Despite such a commendable instrument of government, the problems faced by the administration were grave. With the caveat that classifying such difficulties may oversimplify some very complicated situations, the following summaries provide an overview.

Since the political designations right, left, and center vary in time and place, an understanding of their significance during the first half of the twentieth century is in order. These definitions indicate the aims, though not necessarily the practice, of political parties. Members of the extreme or radical left were generally Communists or Marxists. They had broken with the more moderate socialists and worked toward the abolition of private property and the redistribution of wealth. Their supporters were mainly factory workers seeking greater economic and social equality. They accepted riots and revolution as a legitimate means to achieve their ends. Supporters of the moderate, or liberal left, called themselves Socialists. They advocated government control and ownership of all major public services, raw materials, and the means of production and distribution. Their doctrine called for state support from the cradle to the grave for all citizens. Despite such radical declarations, they valued stability and domestic peace. The major Socialist parties of Germany expected that ballots, not bullets, would bring them to power. On non-economic issues, their views often coincided with the policies of the political center. The Catholic Center Party consisted mainly of middle-class Catholics. Its members favored gradual, constitutional changes that assured national stability and prosperity. Obviously, they also wished to protect the large Catholic minority within the Reich. Democrats organized themselves into a party but its membership was never large enough to become a major player in Weimar politics. Among the conservatives were royalists, militarists and some of the old nobility. They were overshadowed by the radical right of ultra-nationalists, the Nazis and other Fascists who thought that only a totalitarian dictatorship could save Germany. According to their credo, it was necessary for a single political party to use every means, including terror, to attain conformity and obedience from the citizens. National glory, war, and conquest would be achieved under the leadership of the Fuehrer. Democracy was judged a hated failure, the consolation of the weak. In addition to these major political divisions, several splinter parties moved in and out of the spectrum, forming and discarding coalitions according to the demands of practical politics.

The Communists were disappointed that German socialism was not modeled after Soviet communism. Communist support came from the urban workers who favored revolutionary methods to bring down the middle class that dominated the Weimar regime. In order to prevent a Leninist revolution, the ruling Social Democrats, under President Friedrich Ebert, made a fateful deal with the German army. Generals Wilhelm Groener and Paul von Hindenburg agreed to support the Republic against any danger of a Communist insurrection. When, in fact, this threat materialized, the army crushed the Communists. From this moment on, German democracy was unable to make itself the master of the armed forces. Weimar's civilian government was under constant pressure from its conservative, ever-critical, and still highly esteemed military. Swelling the ranks of the disillusioned were returning veterans. Unable to find work, they joined the *Freikorps,* a disruptive, often vicious volunteer corps notorious for street fighting for rightist causes. The organization participated in the defeat of the Communists. The use of these men by President Ebert alienated many of the workers and radicalized their politics from socialism to communism. The murders of two Communist leaders, Karl Liebknecht and Rosa Luxemburg, by former cavalry officers, merely intensified their mistrust. To the upper- and middle-class German, however, communism was the dreaded specter haunting Europe. This resulted in a rather sympathetic, almost forgiving attitude, toward political assassinations which was reflected by the leniency of the courts toward political assassins.

Members of the parties on the right glorified all things German. The misery and shame resulting from the loss of the First World War was the source of their anger and hatred. They would not accept the truth that their armies had been defeated. Instead, they covered their humiliation with half-truths and outright lies. The "stab in the back" theory, that civilians, mainly Jews, had sold out the army, was particularly popular. The fact that no foreign soldiers were on German soil when fighting ceased gave this falsehood the appearance of feasibility.

In 1920, members of the old military–aristocratic alliance were secretly joined by industrialists in an attempt to overthrow the government by a coup d'état. Known as the Kapp putsch, it was a total failure. The ill-conceived plan misfired because the workers in Berlin staged a general strike. This time the military refused to respond to the call to defend the republic, but the labor unions united to crush the rebellion. The strikers refused to provide the city with basic services: no power, no mail, no transportation. Within five days, Wolfgang Kapp found that he could not establish a government in a paralyzed city. This fiasco, however, did not spell an end to rightist politics. Other, ever more extreme parties emerged. Among these was the Nazi Party, whose actual name was NAtionalsoZlalistische Deutsche Arbeiterpartei (National-Socialist German Workers' Party).

The Center's major objective was the protection of religious and civil rights of Catholics in a nation dominated by Protestants. In national elections the number of centrists was usually second only to the number of Socialists. Seen as moderate, centrists actually furnished more chancellors than any other party during the Weimar years. Without their cooperation and/or leadership, no government could effectively function. Trying to meet the needs of all Catholics meant that the party tried to serve opposing interests beneath a single umbrella. Workers were courted to join Catholic trade unions, while their Catholic employers and members of the Catholic aristocracy feared and opposed major industrial reforms. Agricultural, military, and commercial concerns also were frequently at odds. Only on the issue of communism was there unanimity; here, the Center party was absolute in its opposition. Obviously, it was difficult to find a conductor to harmonize so many diverse voices. The brilliant Mattias Erzberger was an outstanding leader of the Center. He had seen it as his duty to sign the Treaty of Versailles, thus sparing the army and Marshall von Hindenburg the disgrace of doing so. In the eyes of violent nationalists, that act sullied Erzberger's name. He was murdered by young rightists in 1921.

The Social Democrats suffered from the brutal politics of the 1920s as well. One of their most gifted statesmen, Walter Rathenau, head of the Foreign Office, was assassinated in 1922. The fact that Rathenau was a Jew and that his religion became a point of antiSemitic inflammatory rhetoric was a bad omen. He incurred the hatred of the extreme right because he believed that the signature of German delegates on the Treaty of Versailles obligated the nation to honor its provisions. His murder was hailed by the nationalists as a victory despite the fact that Rathenau had earned international renown when he concluded the Treaty of Rapollo with the Soviet Union. This 1922 rapprochement of two pariahs in the family of nations benefited both participants; it ended their isolation. Germany gained an outlet for her industrial output which was needed by the Soviet states which were pushing to greater self-sufficiency.

The death of the first president of the republic, Friedrich Ebert, might be called murder by defamation. This man who so richly deserved the gratitude of the German people, was hounded to death in the poisoned atmosphere of the era. He was vilified by the right and the left who opposed him for doing his duty, namely trying to make German democracy function. While working people accused him of catering to the middle class, conservatives despised him for his humble beginnings as a saddler. He was publicly denounced as a traitor and went to court to defend his name. Ebert sued the libeler and won the verdict. But the court also found that since Ebert had taken part in an illegal strike in 1918, he was technically guilty. The action and counteraction cost Ebert his life; he delayed a necessary operation for too long and died in 1925 at the age of fifty-four. His successor was the elderly Marshall von Hindenburg, the man fated to hand the government to Adolf Hitler.

ECONOMIC PROBLEMS

While the questions concerning payment or nonpayment of the huge reparations bill caused intense debate in the Reichstag, the French declared Germany in default over a rather minor delivery deficit. No doubt, bitterness over of their defeat during the Franco-Prussian war and the German attack in World War I still festered in France. Supposedly to assure future payments, the French sent troops to occupy the industrial German Ruhr region. This action escalated the longstanding enmity between Germany and France. The German public was incensed at this insult to German sovereignty. The former Allies opposed the French move, yet they did nothing. The inability of the Weimar administration to exercise full control within its own borders emphasized its weakness. But more serious still was the terrible inflation triggered by the occupation of the Ruhr.

The German government urged the workers of the occupied Ruhr to strike rather then work for the French. When they complied, they required financial support. Thousands of miners and industrial workers had to be paid from the national treasury. This burden accelerated the decline of German fiscal health. In order to deal with the debts incurred during the war, to pay for the expenses of demobilization, and the huge penalties demanded by the Treaty of Versailles, the government resorted to printing more and more paper money, which was not backed by gold. The limited quantity of goods on the shelves were bid up by buyers who had money to spend on far too few products. The continued effects of a lost war, the economic dislocation, and the losses of territories all contributed to the problem of inflation. Debtors obviously like to get rid of their obligations with inflated currency, but as the problem intensified, the whole monetary system was undermined. Each rise in prices activated higher wages and the resulting spiral drove the economy to ridiculous extremes. People rushed with their wages to stores lest prices double within the next hour. In 1918 at the end of the war the mark had been valued at 8.4 to the dollar; in 1922, the ratio was 70,000 marks to the dollar; by December 1923, the rate of exchange was astronomical, trillions of worthless marks for a single dollar.

This wild inflation ruined the German economy. Savings intended to provide for the needs of old age suddenly bought a single loaf of bread. Investments quite literally were not worth the paper on which the certificates were printed. Labor unions were nearly destroyed. They could not provide their members with job security or a living wage. Large segments of the middle class were ruined financially. Some of the industrial giants, on the other hand, profited mightily. Their debts melted away, paid off with cheap money. Real estate speculators increased their holdings. The political reverberation of the economic chaos resulted in the further polarization of right and left. As will be noted in the following chapter, the newly organized Nazi party attempted and failed in its premature Putsch to use this crisis to commandeer the Bavarian government.

Finally, beginning in 1923, the administration was able to control the runaway inflation by placing the mark on a par with its prewar currency. The medicine was strong and many of the already weakened businesses collapsed; the standard of living declined further as unemployment and low wages demoralized the breadwinners. But the bitter pill was swallowed and digested and resulted in a partial economic recovery.

MOMENTARY RECOVERY

The international community, somewhat belatedly, made an effort to support Germany's struggle to recover. The Dawes Plan and later the Young Plan, both formulated by Americans, provided for an orderly reparations schedule. Payments were adjusted, gradually reduced, or altogether forgiven. The French troops withdrew from the Ruhr and a major international crisis was averted. The ensuing recovery expanded as foreign investors acknowledged the fine performance of German industry and labor. German companies extended their organizations into giant vertical trusts. These were conglomerates that brought together every process of manufacturing, from extracting raw materials to the distribution of finished goods. Among such successful, monopolistic international combinations, I.G. Farben Industrie was probably the best known. By concentrating vast business and technical power in the hands of its managing directors, they were able to compete successfully in domestic and foreign markets. Prices and profits were controlled, competition eliminated, yet the quality of their output was high. The Weimar constitution provided for greater freedom for the labor unions and under its legal protection collective bargaining secured higher wages and improved working conditions. Unemployment fell and optimism rose. It is fair to say that in the mid-1920s, despite political uncertainties, the German people were rebuilding their economic life. If this trend had continued, political stability might well have followed. But, disastrously, the period of revival was short-lived. Conditions outside the control of the German people plunged the nation into new danger. This time there would be no last minute reprieve.

THE GREAT DEPRESSION

The shaky foundations of the German Republic were subjected to an unexpected shock by the worldwide depression. The Wall Street crash of 1929 destabilized the American economy and, driven by a domino effect, the European economies were pulled down one after another. The Great Depression slashed production, employment, and the purchasing power of individual as well as corporations. Many banks struggled in vain to remain viable, but when debtors were unable to meet their obligations, the number of foreclosures and bankruptcies multiplied. Farmers were the first to suffer economic decline and the dreaded forced sales deprived thousands of their homesteads. Hunger once more undermined the physical and mental health of many Germans. Despair and rage competed within the hearts and minds of men and women who had worked hard all their lives and now faced a daily struggle for mere survival.

German recovery had relied heavily on foreign loans and exports. Financial institutions from the United States had been the most generous creditors but now they were forced to call in their outstanding loans. American importers who had bought German products were forced to shut down these markets, thus deepening the downturn of the economic cycle. No wonder doubts were voiced concerning the ability of a capitalistic free-market system to provide industrial societies with economic safety. The wide swings of the boom and bust cycles obviously hurt a great many people. The opinion that centrally planned economies which were free of foreign interference or dependence found new supporters. The tycoons, of course, wanted no part of Communist or Socialist state planning. The mere suggestion of a possible nationalization of their companies pushed the conservative barons of industry to search for alternative remedies. Even the rhetoric of the Nazis won supporters because they promised to place no restrictions on private property and vowed that they would manage the nation's business life without dependence on foreign support.

The Weimar Republic could not cope with the destitution of millions of its people. The unemployed who were affiliated with labor unions received a small payment social security, but the self-employed and unorganized workers were reduced to poverty. Once more, the middle class, barely emerging from the chaos of inflation, was victimized by economic disaster. No wonder the quick-fix solutions offered by the Nazis appealed to these groups. The Social Democrats, in power since 1928, were unable to alleviate the problems. The voters replaced them with the Center Party under the leadership of Chancellor Heinrich Bruening. The new chancellor, however, was unable to get several of his projects through the Reichstag, so he persuaded President Hindenburg to invoke Article 48 of the constitution. According to that provision, the nation was declared to be in a state of emergency and the parliamentary system was suspended. The measure was to be temporary, but in effect, marked the beginning of the end of the republic. Officially, the takeover by the Nazi Party did not take place until 1933, three years later, but the democratic process ground to a standstill as the nation tottered from crisis to crisis. The conviction that democracy could not work in Germany attracted many voters to the parties of the extreme right and left.

ART OF DEFEAT

The rise of Hitler to national prominence is best understood within the context of the prevailing hopelessness in Germany. World War I had begun with expectations of a quick and easy victory and ended with disillusionment. The search to escape the stark reality of a world gone awry gripped many Germans. Some people comforted themselves by placing all blame for their misfortune on any of the several available scapegoats. It was much more satisfying to denounce the Communists, the Jews, the war-time Allies, or the Treaty of Versailles. Others sought to bury their despair at the bottom of the bottle and engaged in excesses of every kind. The nightlife in Berlin clubs was notorious for its depravity. The craving for entertainment was inexhaustible. Long-held sexual mores broke down in an atmosphere of "anything goes except boredom." The pleasure seekers, of course, were condemned by the conservatives, who shook their heads and recalled illusory versions of the good old days when people knew how to behave decently.

The arts, particularly literature and painting, mirrored the turmoil of the generation. Several great literary figures, among them Erich Maria Remarque (*All Quiet on the Western Front*), Thomas Mann (*The Magic Mountain*), and the poet Rainer Maria Rilke distilled the pessimism of the age. Had the suffering of the war changed nothing? Were militarism and materialism the new gods of German culture? Like so many other writers in the Western world, German authors reflected the age of the lost and angry generation.

German artists were among the leaders using new forms of expression. Dadaism signaled that life and art have no meaning when millions are senselessly slaughtered on battlefields. Jean Arp, Max Ernst, and George Grosz painted shapes and contours, angles and distortions that pointed expressionism toward new directions. Dreams and nightmares, disjointed human forms and non-representative abstracts depicted a world where nothing was beautiful in the traditional sense. These paintings may have disturbed the viewer, but they are glimpses into the artists' anguished conception of this world.

THE NAZIS ENTER HISTORY

The soil in which the Nazi party took root and grew powerful had been well tilled. Since their defeat at the end of World War I, the German people had experienced international humiliation, political convulsions, economic disasters, and cultural escapism. Every calamity left a trail of discontent which fueled the hope that something new, something extreme, would come along and set the world right. Conservatives remembered the past in ever more glowing shapes, extremists on the left looked with yearning and rose-colored glasses toward the Soviet Union, and rightists lent their ears, their conscience, and their money to the several ultra-nationalist parties. The success achieved by Hitler and the Nazi party were the result of a historic convergence of a man and his time.

By any measurement, Adolf Hitler's career was phenomenal. Technically, as an Austrian citizen, he was a foreigner in Germany. His education was incomplete, he had not graduated from high school, nor did he ever hold a paying job. Hitler's appearance, except for the power of his eyes, was ordinary at best. In a nation where family background is highly valued, his *Kinderstube* was surely commonplace. His qualifications for any work were minimal. If ever he had filled out a job application, it is unlikely he would have been granted an interview except for the most menial of jobs. Yet this man held sway over millions and was idolized by many Germans, a people long admired throughout the world.

Adolf Hitler was born in 1889 in Lower Austria, the son of a minor customs official and his third wife. The boy showed no special promise, and he failed the entrance examination to attend the Vienna Academy of Fine Arts. It appears that this rejection turned the young Hitler into a homeless vagabond. For four years he tried to earn pennies peddling the picture postcards he painted. The Vienna interval was also associated with the development of his violent antiSemitism. Vienna, the capital of the Austro-Hungarian Empire, had been a magnet for many poor Jews from the eastern provinces and from Poland. As is usually the case, the newcomers, often with odd customs, unfamiliar religious practices, and a strange mode of dress, were resented. Between 1895 and 1910, the political life of the city was dominated by its Christian Socialist mayor, Karl Lueger. To stay afloat in the caldron of Austrian politics, Lueger tied himself to the hopes and frustrations of the lower classes. Among his formulae for retaining the support of the masses was anti-Semitism. The young destitute Hitler seemed to be deeply impressed by Lueger's simplistic solution of ascribing all calamities to the evil influence of the Jews. Lueger was popular and powerful. He was also an eloquent speaker; all in all a striking model for the future dictator.

World War I gave Hitler's life the direction it had lacked. He moved to Munich in 1913 and volunteered for the German army when the war broke out. From all accounts, he was a good soldier. The fact that he only achieved the rank of corporal would indicate that although he was awarded an Iron Cross first class for bravery, he did not impress his superiors as outstanding. When the armistice was reached, Hitler, by his own admission, was devastated. He returned to Munich where he joined a small political party, the German Workers' party. Its membership was comprised of nearly penniless veterans who held some rather vague positions of extreme nationalism. Although Hitler was their seventh member, he very quickly reshaped this company of malcontents into an effective organization. Here he discovered his exceptional powers as an orator. His words, his gestures, his blazing eyes had an almost hypnotic effect. Time and time again his own inner conviction transfixed his audience. He spoke with certainty when others equivocated; he offered simple, bold solutions with an air of absolute assurance. His world was black and white, he wooed his listeners with his love for Germany and indulged their self-deception by absolving them of guilt and shame. He was, he avowed again and again, destined to rescue the Fatherland from the clutches of Communist and Jewish depravity. His appeal was emotional, not logical, but his words moved his audiences.

THE PARTY PLATFORM

In 1920, the party, soon to be renamed the National Socialist German Workers' party, or Nazi party, drafted the program designed to attract money and members. There was something in this agenda to appeal to nearly every discontented or frightened German. Among the twenty-five enumerated principles, the following are of particular interest in light of future events:

1. We demand on the basis of the right of national self-determination, the union of all Germans in a Greater Germany.

2. We demand equality for the German nation among other nations and the revocation of the peace treaties of Versailles and Saint Germain. (The latter was concluded between the Allies and Austria.)

4. Only a racial comrade can be a citizen. Only a person of German blood, regardless of religious denomination, can be a racial comrade. No Jew, therefore, can be a racial comrade.

5. Non-citizens shall be able to live in Germany as guests only, and must be placed under alien legislation.

6. We therefore demand that every public office, no matter what kind, and no matter whether it is national, state, or local, can only be held by citizens.

8. Any further immigration of non-Germans is to be prevented. We demand that all non-Germans who entered Germany after August 2, 1914, be forced to leave the Reich without delay.

10. It must be the first duty of every citizen to perform mental or physical work. Individual activity must not violate the general interest, but must be exercised within the framework of the community, and must be for the general good.

25. To implement all these points (these also included confiscation of war profits, mandatory profit sharing of large business enterprises, old age insurance, land reform, death penalty for many criminals, educational and health service, newspaper censorship, and circumscription of religious freedom), we demand the creation of a strong central power in Germany. A central political parliament should possess unconditional authority over the entire Reich.

Considering the fact that most party platforms contain empty verbiage rather than a plan for governing, this document came close to being a blueprint for the conduct of the Nazis in office. The need for union with Austria was cited, along with scrapping the treaties ending the First World War. Discrimination against the Jews was clearly delineated, although the specifics of persecution remained vague. Hitler's preoccupation with so-called German blood, so vital in his Aryan superiority ideology, was given several references. Article 10 asserts that the citizens exist for the nation, not vice versa, a concept of central importance in the Third Reich. The last proposition alludes to dictatorship by the party and is just short of endorsing totalitarianism.

THE SA

In 1921, Hitler created the SA, (*Sturmabteik*, storm troops) a semi-military band of men to protect Nazi party meetings and to harass rival organizations. These troopers wore brown shirts, pants, and boots and were often referred to as the Brownshirts. Most were unemployed toughs; some had seen military service. Their antisocial behavior was glamorized as heroic acts in defense of the Fatherland. In fact, they brawled in the streets with the militant members of opposition parties, threatened voters near the balloting places, and beat up Jews and other targeted civilians. Under the leadership of Hitler's friend Ernst Roehm, their numbers swelled to 400,000 in 1932. When Hitler became chancellor, he enhanced the SA's powers by converting it to a national, political police force. While ordinary policemen were expected to enforce the law, the SA was beyond and above the law. But Roehm's ambitions for the SA were greater than Hitler's. Roehm aspired to create a truly military force, one to rival and equal the regular army. As will be noted later, the feud between the *Wehrmacht* (regular German army) and the SA was decided in 1934 during the Night of the Long Knives in favor of the traditional army. After the eclipse of SA power, the function of terrorizing the public was taken over by the SS, the better-trained, better-schooled elite of Hitler's private army.

THE FAILED BEER HALL PUTSCH

Hitler's first attempt to attain political power was a local affair. He planned to unseat the Bavarian administration with a coup d'état in 1923 in Munich. Named after the beer hall where the attempt began, its scenario resembled a comic opera performance rather than a serious political strategy. Act I opened in the cellar where some

3,000 Bavarians, including several political, military, and social leaders, had gathered to hear a speech by Gustav von Kahr, the state commissioner. Outside, 600 members of the semi-military units of the SA surrounded the building. They set up a machine gun with its muzzle pointed toward the door of the building. In the beer hall, in the meantime, there was shock and high drama. Von Kahr was droning on when suddenly an excited man with a mustache jumped on a chair, fired a shot toward the ceiling, and shouted that the national revolution had begun. Hitler, in the company of a few followers, then exclaimed that the SA had already taken over the police and army barracks and that soldiers and police had joined the revolution. That was a lie. Several of the dignitaries hustled Hitler into a back room. There a very tense Hitler informed them that the new head of the German nation was the renowned General von Ludendorff. The stunned circle of officials recovered enough to tell Hitler to stop his nonsense. The enraged leader of the Nazis screamed that tomorrow would find Germany with a new government or he and his comrades would be dead. Neither prediction was accurate. One by one the heads of the Bavarian government managed to escape the beer hall and prepare for the coming showdown with these would-be revolutionaries.

Ludendorff, the war hero turned right-wing eccentric, arrived in time to lend his considerable prestige to the coup. Meanwhile, news of the Bavarian uprising had reached the head of the national army. Its leadership promised to stand by the republic and declared its willingness to commit troops to quell the insurrection in the event that Bavarian authorities needed help. As it turned out, such assistance was not required.

The next scene was enacted on the streets of Munich. The SA, led by Ludendorff and Hitler, marched toward a confrontation with Bavarian police. Three thousand Nazis were stopped by a barricade of 100 policemen. Hitler's demand that they surrender was answered with bullets. The line of Brownshirts melted away. Neither Hitler nor Ludendorff were injured, but the putsch was over. The sixteen Nazis who were killed that November morning became the glorified martyrs of the movement; their praises were sung many thousands of times in the "Horst Wessel Song," the Nazi anthem.

The last act of the putsch was played out at Hitler's trial. Indicted for treason, he did not stand as a penitent at the bar of justice. Quite the opposite, he used the public prosecution as a propaganda platform and turned failure into a publicity success. The whole nation suddenly knew who he was. He was found guilty and sentenced to five years' imprisonment. Actually, he served less than two years and used that interval to further advance his cause. While rather comfortably confined, he dictated the holy writ of Nazism, *Mein Kampf* (*My Struggle*), to his friend and secretary, Rudolf Hess. The lesson of the failed takeover was not lost on Hitler; he was now certain that although he was fated to resurrect Germany, it must be done through legitimate means. In other words, the way to victory was ballots rather then bullets. The acquittal of Ludendorff, so obviously a conspirator against the republic, was a clear indication that the judicial system remained unduly awed by the military. Hitler's brief sentence and comfortable incarceration was another example of the indulgence with which the judicial system viewed the extreme right.

It is difficult to judge the actual impact of Hitler's book. During the Nazi era it was found in most German households; it replaced the Bible as an almost mandatory wedding present. Every student could quote passages from its pages. Hitler became a millionaire from the number of copies sold. (He placed the profits in Swiss banks.) How much of the volume was actually read and understood by the general public one cannot guess. The first edition was almost unreadable. It was a jumble of Hitler's racial and administrative notions, of his admonitions for the German people, of his economic and political aspirations, and of love for his mother. It was so poorly organized and contained so many grammatical errors that subsequent editions had to be cleaned up by the editors. In retrospect, the German people, in fact, the entire world, would have done well to pay greater attention to Hitler's stated objectives. Those who actually bothered to plow through the volume had few surprises when Hitler ultimately achieved power.

Among the major propositions postulated in *Mein Kampf* are the following:

1. Unconditional authority belongs to the leader. This concept, often called the *Fuehrer Prinzip,* regards democracy as a despicable form of government and the Weimar Republic one of its most depraved examples.

2. The Germans are a superior race. As Aryans, they are the bearers of the highest expression of racial fulfillment. Aryan racial purity must be maintained at all cost. No diseased or weak people must be allowed to have children.

3. The Jews are the essential enemy in Hitler's pseudo-Darwinistic concept of survival of the fittest. Jews endeavor to ruin Germany and all civilization; they have no culture, and Jewish men desperately seek to seduce Aryan women.

4. All life is a struggle for survival; war is the natural and honorable expression of that struggle.

5. Marxism is the other great enemy of Germany. Often the Marxist and Jewish menace are depicted as one and the same.

6. Germany's economy must become self-sufficient. Dependence on foreign loans and trade was designed to keep the nation enslaved to interest payments.

7. Nationality and race are a matter of blood and soil. Only birth and heritage can bestow the German birthright, not language or religion or cultural imitation.

8. Large economic complexes must be broken up and all businesses must share profits with their workers.

With the exception of the last item, most of the ideas expressed in the book became Nazi policy after 1933.

THE ARYAN SUPERIORITY MYTH

At the center of Hitler's beliefs was the racial doctrine. Since it was the theoretical basis and the rationale for the destruction of so many millions deemed unfit to live in the Nazi universe, it requires further elaboration.

Who was the Jew according to Nazi doctrine? No logical answer emerges from the thousands of pages dedicated to the topic. The Goebbels' propaganda machine and the pages of Julius Streicher's *Stuermer,* a weekly newspaper dedicated to Jew baiting, reveal the Jew to be an enigma: powerful enough to threaten every civilization but also cowardly and servile; racially pure (although totally evil), yet lusting after Nordic women. He was the capitalist with an insatiable appetite for money but also responsible for organizing labor into hated unions; he was responsible for that religion of meekness, Christianity, nonetheless Christ was depicted as a Nordic chieftain. In other words, the Jew was whatever the Nazis needed him to be at any given moment.

How did the German people manage such confusion? It seems that they divided their judgment into two categories. First, there were their Jewish neighbors, the ones they knew in flesh and blood. They were viewed as ordinary people, no better or worse than most Germans. And then there were the other ones, the despicable ones. They lived somewhere else, in some vague sphere beyond their horizon. Because it was quite unthinkable that the authorities would lie, this must be so.

Herbert Spencer had theorized that Charles Darwin's survival of the fittest was a concept that could be applied to human societies. Might makes right; that is nature's way. Nazi "racial philosophers" adopted the theme. It dovetailed with their doctrine of the warrior as the highest expression of mankind. From this assumption and the pseudoscientific pretensions of other exponents, the theory of Aryan superiority was advanced. The fact that there is no Aryan race was no deterrent. The term Aryan is the designation of an Indo-European language group. By virtue of skillful manipulation, a lie was elevated into a so-called science. From kindergartens to universities, racial studies were presented to students as objective truth. Aryan superiority was "proven" with concocted data of biological measurements and historical "evidence" of past greatness. The ideal men and women were blond, blue-eyed, tall, straight-backed, with high foreheads and straight noses. Side by side with the physical attributes of the Aryans were their spiritual qualities: courage, honesty, intellect, inventiveness, and artistic excellence. These traits were genetically embedded in the bloodline. The superiority of the Nordic race permitted, no, demanded, the right to subjugate less advantaged people, such as the Eastern European Slavs. Thus, counterfeit biological factors were given momentous significance in this perverted form of Darwinism. The race most fit to dominate had the natural right to mastery over lesser races, the nation able to subdue the weak is endowed by nature with the right to conquest.

The spurious scientists of the Third Reich elevated the theories of the fertile minds of Houston Stewart Chamberlain and Alfred Rosenberg to the level of dogma. Chamberlain (1855–1927) was born an Englishman who turned his back on his native country. He married the daughter of composer Richard Wagner and became fanatical in his admiration of all things German. His mental acrobatics were astounding. He admired Galileo, Dante, Michelangelo, and Leonardo da Vinci, and insisted that these historic figures were racial Teutons. In fact, all benefactors of mankind, all gifts enjoyed by humanity, stemmed from the Nordic race. Even Jesus was given an

Aryan heritage. The Teutonic/Germanic people stood in direct opposition to the destructive power of the only other pure race, the Jews. In his lofty, metaphysical style, Chamberlain rewrote history. Racial impurity was blamed for the fall of ancient Rome, and the Jews had inherited the ethnic disorder that felled mighty Rome. It is difficult to believe that such nonsense found so many advocates; nevertheless, his books were best sellers and won critical praise in Germany.

Alfred Rosenberg (1893–1946), a Lithuanian by birth, was the chief ideologist of the Nazi party. After a stint as editor of the Nazi newspaper the *Voelkische Beobachter*, Hitler awarded him several political positions. His final post was as Reichsminister for the Eastern Occupied Territories, where he promoted the brutal Germanization of conquered Poland, supervised slave laborers, and aided in the mass murder of Jews. His dreadful career ended on the gallows upon his conviction by the International Military Tribunal at Nuremberg.

Chamberlain's influence on Rosenberg's thinking was obvious. His best seller, *The Myth of the Twentieth Century*, reiterated the claim of Nordic racial superiority but added a new concept—namely, a virulent anti-Christian element. The Catholic church was held responsible for accepting and spreading the destructive spirit of a Semitic/Latin faith. In pseudoscientific terms, Rosenberg reshaped Christ into an Aryan warrior who, with sword in hand, fought rather than preached a message of love, pity, and meekness. From this convoluted reasoning, Rosenberg leaped to the conclusion that not only were the Jews answerable for their own crimes, but also for all evil, past and present, committed by the Christian world. His attempts to return to the ancient pagan faith, called rather paradoxically, Positive Christianity, was cut short by the war. One must seriously doubt that the god Wotan of Norse legend could have replaced Jesus even among ardent Nazis. Rosenberg's theories sounded confused and even deranged. Nonetheless, Hitler allowed him a great deal of power. Just how many Germans actually shared his vaporous imagination is impossible to tell.

LEGITIMIZING HITLER

The depression had given the Nazi movement the opportunity to increase its strength dramatically. The disillusioned electorate turned to radical parties in increasing numbers. City workers found their way into both the Nazi and the Communist parties. The radical left and its *Rotfrontkaempferbund* (Red Front Fighter Group) and the SA of the Nazis fought pitched battles on city streets. Speakers representing every political point of view harangued the public with their rhetoric. Every sort of uniform was resurrected from attics and cellars. Prominent among these was the gray worn by the *Stahlhelmers* (the Steel Helmets), a paramilitary umbrella organization of nationalistic ex-servicemen. Their smart marching ranks accommodated most monarchists as well as other assorted enemies of the Weimar Republic. However, the Steel Helmets only rarely clashed with the Nazi militia; Hitler had forbidden such conflicts; the connection between the *Stahlhelm* and the regular military forces was too close for comfort, and Hitler had no wish to alienate the army.

Political warfare was expensive, even in the 1930s. The Nazis campaigned hard in every local and national election. The SA, the propaganda campaigns, the sea of swastikas on flags and posters, the uniforms, all these trappings necessitated fundraising. Hitler needed money, or preferably, he needed support from people with money. But would members of the financial and industrial establishment take him seriously? Could their snobbish attitude toward an Austrian upstart be overcome?

Fear of communism gave Hitler a passport into the world of power and money. He was seen as a possible champion, a counterweight against the dreaded Red Menace. When the number of Nazi Reichstag representatives rose from 12 to 107 in the 1930 election, it became the second largest party in the parliament. The Communists, too, had made dangerous gains, from 54 to 77 seats. In the absence of a better candidate, Herr Hitler, so the magnates believed, would have to do. Indeed, he was a little uncouth, not from the background they preferred, but he would be useful as their tool, their means to fight communism. No doubt, this Austrian corporal would be malleable in their experienced hands, a man to be molded to their will.

Two events contributed to the improved standing of the Nazis among the upper classes. The first occurred in 1931 when a conclave of political rightist party leaders allowed Hitler into the vaunted company of important, well-established nationalists. In attendance were the *Stahlhelm's* chief, Franz Seldte; the director of the United Steelworks, Fritz Thyssen; the renowned banker and economic wizard, Hjalmar Schacht; and the head of the Nationalist Party, Alfred Hugenberg. The meeting took place in the small town of Harzburg and was thus dubbed the Harzburg Front. Hitler, always an impressive speaker, made a good impression on the assemblage. Acceptance, endorsement, and financial support by the mainstream of rightist organizations allowed the Nazis to take a giant step up the ladder to power.

During the following year, Hitler was invited to address the members of the elite Industry Club. Here, in Duesseldorf at the center of German manufacturing, Hitler again worked his oratorical charm. He spoke for two and a half hours, shouting much of the time. He persuaded his audience that his party would safeguard capitalism, protect private property, end the communist danger, and keep the trade unions in check. This was music to the ears of the coal and steel barons of the Ruhr. Hitler was given a standing ovation, and more importantly, his future political campaigns were well financed.

THE END OF THE REPUBLIC

The moderate parties of the Weimar Republic had been unable to solve Germany's economic distress and relieve the political morass. At this juncture, in 1932, Hindenburg's first presidential term ended. Hitler decided his time had come and ran against him. It was an election campaign characterized by frequent violence, particularly between Communists and Nazis. The voters at the polls were threatened by the Brownshirts who swarmed around the polling places. Hitler won 30 percent of the vote; this necessitated a run-off election with Hindenburg. The aging war hero was returned to office but his was a hollow victory. Later that year, in the Reichstag elections, the Nazis won 230 seats. They had become the largest single party.

By tradition, Hitler should now have been appointed chancellor, but the venerable president of the republic could not bring himself to hand the government to this ex-corporal from Austria. Hindenburg was eighty-four and his mind and body had lost much strength, yet he had an almost instinctive mistrust of this gesticulating man with the black mustache. So, he tried to give Germany a government without Hitler.

Chancellor Bruening had been dismissed. Who could fill the post? The Machiavellian role played by General Kurt von Schleicher underlined the continuing deterioration of German politics. Schleicher (his name in German means "the sneaky one") had been at the periphery of power for years. He now suggested that Hindenburg proffer the chancellorship to a mediocre member of the aristocracy, Franz von Papen. The debonair von Papen sought to curb the power of the Nazis by bringing Hitler into his fold. The maneuver failed; Hitler did not want to become vice-chancellor. He was certain his time to realize complete power was near at hand. Von Papen took note of the latest political straws floating in the wind and decided that a new election would reduce the Nazi vote. He was only partially correct. The number of NSDAP members in the Reichstag was cut by thirty-four seats. A small victory, but it changed nothing. Von Papen resigned, and Schleicher moved up into the chancellor's office. His was the last administration of the Weimar Republic.

Schleicher tried to check the Nazi menace by creating an anti-Nazi coalition between the army and the trade unions, but even fear of Hitler could not hold together such an awkward pairing. Finally, the chancellor tried to convince Hindenburg that only a military dictatorship could save the Fatherland, but the old Fieldmarshall had sworn to uphold the constitution and would not sign such an order. Schleicher had no choice but to offer his resignation. Hitler never forgot nor forgave Schleicher's attempt to obstruct the Nazi attainment of power. In 1934, during the Night of the Long Knives, also known as the Blood Purge, six Nazi murderers entered Schleicher's home and killed him in front of his family.

The curtain fell on the republic when Hindenburg was finally persuaded to ask Hitler to form a government. Von Papen, still under the illusion that his titles, his background, and his experience would impress Hitler, had a hand in the machinations. He took the vice-chancellor's office, certain that he could keep Herr Hitler in check. The Fieldmarshall's son, Oskar, also pressured his father to submit to the inevitable, namely turning the government over to the Nazis. It must have been a bitter pill for the old soldier to swallow. On several occasions, Hindenburg had stated that never, absolutely never, would he ask Hitler to be chancellor. Hitler's response was tragically prophetic when he replied: "Hindenburg is eighty-five years old, I am forty-five. I can wait." Actually, he did not wait very long. Within a year he would occupy the president's office as well.

CHAPTER 4

Masters of the Third Reich

The Holocaust was implemented by men, not mechanical robots or spineless puppets. Men planned, executed, and exulted in the commission of modern history's most despicable crime. The more we learn about the methods used to realize Hitler's vision of a world without Jews, the more insistently the question recurs: What kind of people could have committed these unspeakable crimes? The answers are as haunting as the questions. Visiting Berlin and sitting in a cafe some fifty years after the liberation of the concentration camps, I found myself staring into the faces of older Germans, wondering, wondering, wondering. . . .

HITLER AND THE JEWS

Hatred of the Jews was Hitler's central passion. The man and the Shoah cannot be separated. The suggestion that the Fuehrer did not order, in fact did not know of the mass killings flies in the face of all we know about the administrative apparatus of the regime. No one would have dared to execute such a momentous scheme without Hitler's actual or implied order. Even though a written directive for the Holocaust has not, as of this writing, been uncovered, veritable mountains of research indicate that Hitler's elite vied with one another to do their master's will. Often, the heads of agencies dealing with Jewish issues anticipated Hitler's wishes and converted them to action. The dictator's expectations took on the shape of directives. But while his orders were often cloaked, those responsible for the Holocaust always stayed within the boundaries of established policies. It would have been suicidal to act in opposition to the Fuehrer's order or his implied intentions. The men who operated within

Hitler's inner circle would have denounced one another if any one of them stepped outside the prescribed perimeter of action. The disappearance of a rival could lead to advancement of one's own career.

In *Mein Kampf* Hitler gave little indication of how his early personality was shaped. He created the impression that upon passing a group of religious Jews on the street during his stay in Vienna, he realized with mystical insight that these bearded, black-garbed men were a cancer upon Germanic life. Actually, during the period of 1907–1913, the young Hitler adapted his racial and political concepts from ideas promulgated by others. For example, an ex-monk who called himself Lanz von Liebenfels wrote extensively on Aryan superiority and flew a flag with a swastika over his castle. Liebenfels insisted that Jews headed the list of inferior races who must make way for the superior Aryans. His notion of "making way" included deportations, slave labor, sterilization, and killing, methods later used in the Third Reich. Another precursor of Nazi theory was Georg Ritter von Schoenerer. He was the leader of the Austrian pan-German movement which urged the union of all Germans into a single nation. He, too, exhorted his followers to recognize Jews as a national menace. The previously mentioned mayor of Vienna, Karl Lueger of the Austrian Christian Social Party, became Hitler's mentor in two areas: First, his accusation that the Jews engaged in shameless financial exploitation was accepted by the adult Hitler; and second, Lueger's manipulation of the masses was a prototype for masterful use of dramatic and emotional propaganda techniques. Karl Lueger's effectiveness in haranguing crowds amid a display of symbols and finely tuned pageantry was not lost on the young Adolf.

Few of the methods Hitler employed during his war against the Jews were new. Anti-Jewish malevolence was practiced in the ancient, medieval, and modern world. These antecedents foreshadowed the Nazis' program rather explicitly, only the death camps were an innovation. Clearly, Jews have a history of persecution, of usefulness as scapegoats. The Christian Church had institutionalized abhorrence of them, kings had treated them as chattel and had shut them into ghettos. Yet none of these antecedents help to explain the Holocaust. The persecutions of the past were based on objectives or motivations which made sense to the persecutors; something profitable was expected to result. Today's students are trained to examine the causes, events and results of historic events in order to reach conclusions but the Holocaust does not fit that formula. There is no answer to the essential Why? Why did Hitler's vision of a Europe without Jews take priority over all economic, political and military consideration? We can agree that Hitler himself was the source of the Shoah, only he had the power to implement the mechanism of destruction. But what motivated this lethal hatred? Here, we fail to supply an answer. A number of scholars have proposed some provocative theories and we will make note of several. However, we must understand that the mind of Hitler cannot be examined post mortem with any scientific certainty. He and those who knew him best are dead and culling facts from anecdotes and from deliberate distortions becomes more and more difficult.

Hitler, the orator. (Courtesy AP/Wide World Photos.)

THE IRRATIONALITY OF THE HOLOCAUST

Before we attempt to understand Hitler's *Weltanschauung* through the eyes of several of his interpreters, some misconceptions need to be dispelled. Governments, we know, have killed segments of their own people since the dawn of history. But atrocities were committed with the expectation that some gain, some advantage, some profit would result from the slaughter. It is rational therefore to infer that this concept should hold true for the Nazi era as well. But such a supposition is not born out. As will be explained in greater detail below, killing six million Jews did not benefit Germany. The Holocaust rendered no political, social, economic or military advantage to the Nazis. In fact, killing the Jews was detrimental to Hitler's domestic and foreign policy goals. Then why was it done? Before we examine that question, it is necessary to dispel some of the erroneous concepts which are still noticed in American classrooms.

NO ECONOMIC BENEFITS

Among the incorrect explanations for Hitler's determination to make Europe *Judenrein* is the view that Hitler's motives were economic; he needed the wealth of the Jews to fuel his military plans. But theft of Jewish assets was a long way from the gas chambers. Hitler seized the Jews' properties and bank accounts and all valuables, from jewelry to wool coats, and then, when their considerable skills could have advanced his objectives, he had them murdered. He wasted an important resource to satisfy some destructive imperative within his own mind.

To place Aryans in jobs and businesses held by Jews was simple enough and done efficiently wherever German armies established dominion. One can assume that the newly enriched Germans became grateful supporters of the Nazi party. But again, this expropriation was sufficient, it did not need to lead to the Shoah. Indeed, the equipment and manpower required for the killings exacerbated the critical labor shortages on farms and in factories. As German men, including many skilled and semiskilled workers, were called into the armed services, a severe labor shortage resulted. During the war, as the military casualty lists grew longer, the need for workers intensified. Keeping the Jews alive and utilizing them as unpaid slaves would have made economic sense. Instead, their annihilation cost the Germans many millions of working hours.

NO POLITICAL BENEFITS

Were the Jews killed for political reasons? Hitler once stated that if there were no Jews he would have needed to invent them. In other words, they were needed as scapegoats for every setback suffered by Germany. How does that statement translate into their destruction? It does not. Dead scapegoats have no value. Once gone, they can no longer absolve the living of their failures. A new scapegoat would then be required, but the Jews would be difficult to replace, historically they were unsurpassed as objects of blame.

Did the Jews at any time pose an actual political danger to the Third Reich? Again, the answer is no. Joseph Goebbels, Minister of Propaganda and Public Enlightenment, denounced them as Marxists, Communists and saboteurs, as greedy capitalists, and as traitors in league with the enemy, but he furnished no evidence to substantiate his words. The Jews of Germany, at most one percent of the population, never constituted a political bloc. They did not support any single political ideology or candidate. A diverse group, they included urban workers, lower and upper middle class artisans, businessmen and a wide range of professionals. Not even the minister of Public Enlightenment thought it expedient to accuse them of conspiracy to usurp either the economic or the political order. His assertion that the Jews were both greedy capitalists as well as organizers of subversive labor unions, undermined both allegations. His revival of the rather well-worn accusation that Jews planned to overthrow Christian civilization, a claim made in that old czarist forgery known as

The Protocols of the Elders of Zion, was not believable. The *Protocols*, published in 1903, had been written at the behest of the Russian secret police and purported to be the minutes of a secret meeting of the leaders of international Jewry. The alleged aim of the cabal was the domination of the Christian world. Here the pathetic Jew of the middle ages was being replaced by a new version, the sly, powerful, brilliant and very dangerous modern Jew. The old scapegoat was dressed in new clothes.

Hitler often coupled Jew and Communist to form a single word, a device that played on the fears of the German middle and upper classes. Capitalistic Jews in league with the Communists? That made no sense. Actually, Jews were no threat to the government; they had no political power. The very success of the Holocaust demonstrates their weakness, their inability to exert any influence in Germany or internationally.

We have already dealt with the phenomena of religious, nationalistic, and racial antiSemitism. The hostility created by this ancient and modern antagonism provided the groundwork upon which Hitler built the organization of annihilation. Some scholars assert that German philosophers during the past two centuries prepared a unique Teutonic predisposition for the Holocaust. Their arguments are not convincing. It is questionable how much influence was exerted by the learned professors from Kant to Fichte, Hegel, and Treitschke over the minds of ordinary Germans. Until the rise of Hitler, the ebb and flow of antiSemitism had washed the shores of Spain, France, Germany, Poland, and Russia without partiality. More authoritative research is needed before it is possible to accept the existence of a distinctly German and particularly vicious form of antiSemitism. One could make an equally dubious case for the opposite *Weltanschauung* (conception of the world) by quoting from the works of Germans who urged tolerance and acceptance of differences among people. Finally, we must not assume that Hitler's racial ideology was derived from reading the works of philosophers whose theories were often unintelligible to most Germans. Neither Hitler nor the men who sat at his feet were philosophical thinkers. They took pride in action, not debating, and they often sneered at the intellectuals whom they considered useless baggage.

OTHER THEORIES

Clearly, economic, political, and intellectual rationales do not explain why Hitler hated the Jews with such an all-encompassing rage. What are the thoughts of some of the scholars who have grappled with the subject? We will ignore such aberrant theories as Hitler, the supposed victim of syphilis or the equally insupportable opinion that Hitler became deranged because he had only a single testicle. Can psychiatry provide some answers? Perhaps, but it must be remembered that at best, psychological analyses of Hitler result in theories, in probabilities, or presumptions. As social scientists, historians prefer to place emphasis on the term *scientist,* and seek hard evidence rather than rely on conjecture. Any attempt to discover a dead man's motivation cannot yield measurable, conclusive data. Nonetheless, as students of the Holocaust we cannot evade the central question concerning the state of Hitler's mind and thus we are compelled to step into these uncertain waters. Always, however, we must remember that these theories are open to interpretation. We may accept or reject them, wholly or in part. The book *Explaining Hitler* by Ron Rosenbaum (Harper Collins, 1998) is particularly helpful in this inquiry.

The individual who views all human events as the will of God is able to accept man's inability to penetrate the mystery of His ways. Jews and others who have unshakable faith in God's presence in human affairs may have a silent, inactive, and hidden God in Auschwitz. However, the notion that God used Hitler as his tool in order to accomplish some enigmatic purpose, must present great difficulties, even for the orthodox believer. Emil Fackenheim, often called the theologian of the Holocaust, conceded that there will never be an adequate explanation of Hitler. He urged that instead of trying to understand God, we accept the 614th commandment (there are 613 rules of worship in Judaism). Fackenheim's additional commandment forbids Jews to grant Hitler a posthumous victory. Hitler triumphs when Jews lose their faith and when they fail to support the state of Israel. The highly controversial Hannah Arendt spoke of the banality of evil in her book on the trial of Adolf Eichmann in Jerusalem. She developed the concept that the Nazi leadership created a wall, an emotional separation between themselves and the reality of their crimes. Her Eichmann, and by implication Hitler as well, dealt with the suffering they inflicted by shutting off their capacity to feel empathy. They were impervious to the suffering they inflicted; they committed crimes without emotional involvement. Evil became a banality, a matter of entries in a ledger. The English historian Alan Bullock who is best known for his *Hitler: A Study in Tyranny,* concluded that Hitler knew exactly what he was doing. But he also stated in an interview with Ron Rosenbaum that he believed that the Fuehrer was the consummate actor, always performing, always on stage. Did the role he played become his reality? The answer is not clear.

When the Nobelist Eli Wiesel wrote his memoir of Auschwitz in his famous *Night,* he engraved an unforgettable scene into the mind of the reader: the Germans were hanging three prisoners. One of the victims was a mere boy and he was swaying, grotesquely dancing, at the end of the rope. The rest of the prisoners were forced to witness his slow dying. One of the men asked: Where is God? And another replied: there, on the gallows. Although later in his life Wiesel's faith was restored, the depiction of God swinging to and fro in deadly agony is at the heart of an awesome question.

People who are persuaded that Hitler was mentally ill, perhaps a psychopath lacking a concept of good or evil, are able to judge Hitler as not guilty by reason of insanity. But do we have a standard measurement for madness? The confusion of psychiatric and legal insanity remains unresolved. Every American court of law would consider Hitler legally sane and able to stand trial. And then there are several historians who maintain that the Holocaust was not the work of one man, no matter how charismatic, but was the inevitable culmination of centuries of hatred of the Jews; Hitler merely implemented a foreordained certainty. And again, proof for this theory is too thin to be convincing. This writer lived her childhood years in Germany and never felt estranged from her Christian friends until Nazi ideology reached her school.

WHY DID HITLER HATE THE JEWS?

Can psychology explain Hitler? Perhaps. Adolf the child probably lived in an unhealthy family environment. The father may have been a nasty brute and the mother pious in the extreme. Even these previously accepted impressions have been challenged in recent years, but let us assume that Hitler had a miserable childhood. As miserable as the Jewish children who spent years in hiding to save their lives? As miserable as the orphaned and impoverished boys and girls in Africa whose parents died of AIDS and now they are left with no one to care for them? Of course not. No doubt, early childhood traumas play a role in the development of one's personality, but that is not analogous to producing a Hitler. Surely, the world would be a place of unremitting savagery if frightful childhood experiences produced destructive, depraved adults.

Among the several psychological analyses offered, the most compelling account, in this writer's view, was written by Robert G. L. Waite in his book *The Psychopathic God: Adolf Hitler.* Waite and others maintained that the paradoxical, irrational, sexually aberrant Hitler was reared in circumstances that were destructive to proper maturation. For Waite's Hitler a number of abnormalities came together to form a neurotic, and toward the end of his life, a psychotic man. But here, a word of caution is on order: Even if we accept the premise that certain childhood and adolescent traumas twisted and deformed him, Hitler knew that killing the innocent would heap the condemnation of the civilized world upon his head. The SS units who carried out the murders were sworn to absolute secrecy; the site of killings was in the east, Poland and Russia, away from the eyes of German civilians. Hitler understood that his actions were criminal. No matter what problems young Adolf may have encountered, nothing can absolve the adult.

A MAN OF PARADOXES

Biographies of Hitler delineate his personality as paradoxical. He was brutal, but also capable of kindness, particularly to children and animals. Sometimes his honesty could be disarming, but lies served him with equal ease. His grasp of reality was a matter of timing; sometimes it seemed firmly based, at other times his fantasies seemed to overpower his mind. His life was marked by acts of courage as well as of cowardice. In public, he exhibited superb self-assurance; in private, he worried about the impression he made. He saw others only in two diametrically opposing shades, black or white, blind supporter or dangerous enemy. His moods could swing from rage to gentleness in a moment. His capacity for hatred, coupled with his conviction that destiny had singled him out for a messianic role, made him the most dangerous man in a perilous century.

Hitler glorified the concept of the perfect Aryan specimen but he hardly met his own criteria. Furthermore, his inner circle included a number of misfits. When facts contradicted a concept in his mental world, Hitler did not change his mind, he altered the facts. Thus, for example, it became Nazi lore that Jesus was not a Jew, that Jews were infectious vermin, that Franklin D. Roosevelt and most of the English nobility were Jewish, that Judaism was a race not a religion, that only Aryan blood was creative, and non-Aryans were merely fit for enslavement. The determining factor of good and evil, right and wrong, was blood and blood alone. His preoccupation with blood, and Jewish blood in particular, ran like a refrain through his mind. One cannot but wonder why.

THE PARENTS

Hitler's father, Alois, was the illegitimate child of Anna Marie Schickelgruber and Georg Hiedler. The father's brother Johann adopted and reared the boy in his home. Later, Alois changed the spelling of his name to Hitler. The uncertainty of his ancestry may have contributed to his son's fixation on genetics and raised questions concerning his own bloodline. Austrians have a long history of antiSemitism and it is not unreasonable to presume that young Adolf heard anti-Jewish comments during his childhood. Such early indoctrination, when coupled with insecurity concerning his ancestry, may have caused Hitler's fascination with blood. If he feared that his own blood could be tainted, then his many references to poisoned blood, his refusal to father any children, and his strange eagerness to endure leeches as part of medical treatments become more understandable. Whether consciously or not, doubts regarding his Aryan purity may have resulted in some strange personal habits. For example, he was obsessively clean (Jews are dirty); he drew attention away from his nose with a mustache (Jews have large noses); in 1935, just two years after he became chancellor, he banned Gentile females under the age of forty-five from work in Jewish households (his grandmother had been a maid, although not in a Jewish household); and sexual intercourse between Jews and Gentiles was declared a capital crime. The razing of the entire village where his father was born was certainly bizarre. Surely, there were other sites where an artillery testing ground could have been installed without moving the residents to new homes. Did Hitler hope that the disappearance of the village would cause his father's memory to go up in smoke as well?

Robert Waite is not alone in his allegation that Alois Hitler was a mean and cruel man. He had risen from peasant stock to become a minor customs official on the Austro-German border. Clara, Adolf's mother, was his third wife. She was twenty-three years younger than her husband. It would not be unusual if Alois expected, and usually was given, total and silent obedience from his family. Nor would it have created any stir, if he beat his wife and children, either drunk or sober.

The adult Hitler rarely mentioned his father. As a matter of fact, he did not commonly refer to Germany as the Fatherland. It is the Motherland he promised to save, the Motherland he extolled endlessly.

Alois seemed to interpret the duties of fatherhood to consist of either ignoring or browbeating his son. Erik Erikson, the renowned psychologist, used the term negation in just such a context and stated that a child who is negated develops the desire to destroy.

Hitler's mother was pictured as a deeply troubled, pious Catholic. She had lived with her husband Alois before they were married, and the sin seemed to consume her conscience. She probably interpreted the death of two of her children as God's punishment for her weakness. If Waite is correct, then Adolf was not only the object of her maternal love, he also represented the possibility of God's forgiveness. So she clung to him, doted on him, adored and spoiled him. She hoped the boy would enter the priesthood, but Adolf was expelled from the religious school he briefly attended when he was caught smoking. While there is no doubt that the boy loved his mother, he surely must have hated her as well. Why did she allow herself to be beaten? Why was she so powerless? And even more tormenting was her inability to protect her children. How could she love them and do nothing when the father abused them? Why did this wide-eyed, pale woman work so hard to please her despicable husband? What secrets did the mother and the father share when they closed their bedroom door?

Growing up with a brutal, all-powerful father and a loving, indulgently permissive but weak mother does not bode well for the future of any child. The resulting confusion is commonly identified by family counselors as receiving "double messages." Hitler's mother died when he was nineteen. By then the ingredients for future neurosis may already have been in place.

A PSYCHOSEXUAL VIEW

According to Freudian analysts, the personality of the adult Hitler reveals behavior that points to unresolved problems in his psychosexual development. The Fuehrer was a compulsive talker; he was given to uncontrolled tantrums (German anti-Nazis called him *Teppichfresser,* one who chews on carpets). The line between imagination and reality often blurred in his mind; his sniffing of his own body and repeated washing were neurotic. His personality was rigid, and he was unable to change his mind. He spoke about the "granite foundation" of his philosophy and prided himself on his inflexibility. He never admitted to any mistakes; failures were never his, others had to bear the blame. Unable to be a friend, he had no friends.

Nor did Hitler resolve his Oedipal conflict; his relationships with women were never normal. There is general agreement that the most important woman in his life was a young niece, Angela Raubal. Hitler kept her a virtual prisoner until she succeeded in her efforts to kill herself. His most lasting attachment was to Eva Braun. She was his mistress for twelve years; during this time she too attempted to end her life.

Eva was Hitler's wife for one day, April 30, 1945. She was Hitler's partner in death when she and Hitler committed suicide in their Berlin bunker. Eva matched Hitler's concept of the ideal woman: quiet, loyal, disinterested in politics, undemanding, and shallow. Hitler commented to Albert Speer, his personal architect and wartime production chief, that a highly intelligent man should *take* a primitive and stupid woman. The wording is revealing not only in connection with Eva, but that a man should take a woman. This contemptuous statement was made in Eva's presence.

Was Hitler mentally ill? Unfortunately, a simple yes or no is not possible. Within the legal context, he would have been pronounced sane. He knew right from wrong and chose wrong. Had he lived to face the judgment at Nuremberg, he would have been hanged because he understood the consequences of his actions. Could the psychiatric community have argued the legal findings? Possibly, because Hitler was a borderline personality, neurotic but not consistently psychotic. In other words, as Robert Waite construed, he was able to function effectively despite certain obsessive and sado-masochistic traits. In the early years of his regime his very pathology, his certainty that heaven itself had mandated his mission to save Germany, gave him the appearance of commanding authority. As Fuehrer, he brushed aside all opposing opinions in favor of the dictates of some inner voice only he could hear. After the German armies had failed at Stalingrad, his behavior was described as aberrant. Like a demented man, he ordered armies about that no longer existed, had uncontrollable fits of rage, and saw treachery everywhere. Defeat may have pushed him from the realm of neurosis into madness.

While German soldiers were freezing to death from the rigors of a terrible Russian winter and supplies were urgently needed at the front, the German railroad system delivered trainloads of victims to German death camps in Poland. On April 29, 1945, one day before Hitler's death, while Berlin turned into blazing rubble, he wrote his so-called political testament. The final sentence reads as follows:

> Above all I charge the leaders of the nation and those under them to the scrupulous observance of the laws of race and to the merciless opposition to the universal poisoner of all peoples, International Jewry.

We return now to the original question. Why did Hitler hate the Jews? Our response, largely based on Waite's analysis, is a theory, well reasoned, but nonetheless a theory. To this observer it seems the most acceptable of the various attempts to explain Hitler. Perhaps some day another study will replace these perceptions, but in the meantime the following speculations appear the most valid.

Hitler was subject to various mental and emotional problems. Because he did not fit in, he felt isolated, inadequate, and at the same time, vastly superior to others. It is possible that the ferocity of Hitler's hatred of the Jews may have stemmed from a latent sense of self-hatred. No one can map the unconscious mind, but the damage done by his parents, his early anti-Jewish environment, his failure as an artist, and his happiness followed by desolation during his stint in the army all may have contributed to his warped personality. The possible role of genetic factors must be left in abeyance; future researchers in this field may add additional pieces to the puzzle.

What emerges at this point is a hypothesis that the troubled child and unhappy teenager grew into a man who despised himself. His rather disgusting sexual deviations could only increase this sense of worthlessness. But the human ego is very fragile; it protects itself from unpleasant truths and builds elaborate defenses. Among such defensive mechanisms is scapegoating, the transfer of guilt and shame to the shoulders of others. Hitler's self-hatred, constantly fed by his dreadful crimes, may have turned outward. Individuals who despise themselves, whose spirits are awash with vague guilt and free-floating anxiety, seek an outlet for their destructive, often suicidal, conflicts.

Since the dawn of history, scapegoats have been used actually and symbolically to shed evil and misery. The greater the offenses, the greater must be the suffering of the sin-offering. If we accept the premise that Hitler needed a scapegoat, not merely as a political convenience but also as a result of a deep-seated personal neurosis, then the Jews were well suited to play that role. The sacrificial offering must be docile, without powerful friends or allies, and have a past that marks them with a long established burden of culpability. This description fit the majority of European Jewry between 1935 and 1945.

The theory of Hitler's self-hatred externalized into anti-Jewish hatred opens a glimpse into the irrationality of the Holocaust. In Hitler's mind, the death of every single Jew may have destroyed some atomic particle of the self he wished to obliterate. Thus it may be possible to understand why a million victims could never be enough, nor 10 million. All Jews everywhere had to die, but even then, he could not be satisfied. Other scapegoats would have to be driven to their death. A terrible image strikes the inner eye: a picture of Europe if Hitler had won the war. . . .

THREE EXECUTIONERS OF THE FUEHRER'S WILL

If we accept the explanation that Hitler tried to extinguish the fire of his self-hatred with the burnt offerings of European Jewry, the insatiability of his destructive impulses becomes comprehensible. This, however, leaves the historian with the still unanswered questions concerning the motivations of the men who so willingly carried out the orders to commit genocide. Excluding the officials who "merely" expedited the paper trail that ended in mounds of human ashes, the thousands of SS troopers, organized into the special killing squads of the infamous *Einsatzgruppen,* were involved in the physical execution of men, women, and children who were guilty of nothing at all. What do we know about members of these special task forces? Their work was not abstract, their own eyes met those of the victims, their hands held the guns that killed an estimated 1.5 million Jews. What did such men say to their wives, their children, or their parents at the end of a day's work? It is inaccurate to dismiss them as brutes or savage animals outside the perimeter of civilized society. The commanders of the four individual detachments of mobile killing units, the *Einsatzkommandos,* were professional men with many academic degrees who were quite at home among Germany's cultural elite. Some members of the

Einsatzgruppen were volunteers; others had been conscripted into this ghastly duty. A few objected to the assignment of supervising and participating in mass killings and were given other duties, as far as we can determine, without penalty. Once again, students of the Holocaust must face the fact that morality and education may march to different drummers.

It is not within the scope of this book to examine the motivation of all or even any of the Nazis. We cannot comfort ourselves with the view that the torturers and killers, demented, in some way different than we are. That is not true. Christopher Browning's *Ordinary Men* is recommended to the student interested in further exploration of this topic. The writer's own research into the life and death of a small town, *Winzig, Germany, 1933–1946,* disclosed that roughly 20 percent of the towns-people were Nazis. According to their recollections, most joined the party in the early and mid-1930s in the hope of economic gain. Apparently only a handful had enrolled because they shared Hitler's ideological convictions. It would be a mistake, however, to generalize from this or any other narrow study because the actual and the stated motives are not necessarily one and the same.

It will have to suffice to discuss, albeit briefly, three criminals at the top of the Nazi hierarchy. The choices of Hermann Goering, Joseph Goebbels, and Heinrich Himmler are based on their importance in carrying out the Final Solution, the Nazi's euphemism for the annihilation of the Jews. Did they hate the Jews? Why? How did they achieve the personal and political power that enabled them to climb to the heights of Hitler's world? Were there similarities in family background, in neurotic behavior, in education, in attitude toward religion, in ambition, in failures in earlier enterprises? Should a pattern emerge, could it help future generations to identify and reject men and women who cover their criminality with honeyed words? Unfortunately, at this point we cannot identify a Nazi archetype. Perhaps further study will be more fruitful; for now, it seems clear that evil comes in as great a variety of packaging as does the rest of humanity.

HERMANN GOERING

Life is struggle. Hitler, in the very title of his book, proclaimed this to be his concept. The leaders who operated in the upper realms of the Nazi hierarchy shared that *Weltanschauung;* in fact in their climb to high office they had to exhibit their ability to remove men who could impede their ambitions. Goering's appearance, overweight, with a charming smile and his fondness for flamboyant uniforms, could easily lead the observer to the impression that the man was a dandy. That would be a mistake. Although he liked to call himself a Renaissance man, he began his rise to power as a soldier. Goering, who was never burdened with ideological scruples, was a mercenary who found his war, first during the campaigns of World War I and later in the Nazi movement and its continuous warfare. He craved power and the adulation of the masses who saw only a whitewashed version of his character—the avuncular officer who combined the attributes of a hail-fellow-well-met with that of a war hero. His ridiculous vanity, his appetite for luxury, and his megalomaniacal cruelty were unknown to the public. In the end, Hitler called him his greatest disappointment and deprived him of all honors and authority.

Hermann Goering (1883–1946) was born into a "good" Bavarian family. Among the political and social nonentities of the Third Reich, he stood out as the welcome exception to the rule. His father, a distinguished colonial official, had been the first governor of the German protectorate of West Africa. Hermann's first wife, Karin von Katzow, came from a well-connected background. Young Goering's career before he discovered the Nazi party in 1922 had been in the military. He was a much decorated fighter pilot in the infant *Luftwaffe*, the German airforce. After the death of the famed World War I ace, Baron von Richthofen, Goering took his command. At the end of the war, Goering, like so many of his contemporaries, found it difficult to adjust to civilian life. He joined the fledgling Nazi party in 1922, and thus qualified as an "early fighter." Hitler was delighted with this supposedly wealthy, famous new recruit and made him commander of the SA. Goering was by his Fuehrer's side during the Beer Hall Putsch, the failed Nazi attempt to overthrow the Bavarian government. In the melee, Goering was severely wounded but managed to escape from the country. Apparently, these injuries launched his addiction to morphine. When a declaration of political amnesty cleared the way for his return, he was assured of high rank in the Nazi party.

Goering's Rise and Fall from Power

Goering's rise was rapid indeed. Among the positions he held were president of the Reichstag, Reich's minister without portfolio, commander in chief of the *Luftwaffe*, minister president of Prussia, and Prussian minister of the interior. He created the Prussian Political Police, which was soon (1934) incorporated into the Gestapo. These were not empty titles. Goering enjoyed the exercise of personal power. If ever he had scruples, they did not prevent him from directing the execution of old comrades. During the assassinations of the SA leaders on the Night of the Long Knives, (also called the Blood Purge, see Chapter 5), he was in charge of the Berlin region. It was Goering who established the first concentration camp at Oranienburg. To the delight of many Germans, "our Hermann" was made a full general in 1936 and shortly thereafter he became the czar of the Four Year Plan for economic development. In that capacity he directed German industry and its effort to achieve self-sufficiency and military preparedness. As chief executive of the state-owned *Reichswerke Hermann Goering,* a huge mining and industrial complex, he amassed enormous personal wealth. He became an avid collector of great works of art, sometimes by purchase, sometimes by forced gifts, and finally by theft from the great collections of defeated nations. He built a small palace, Karinhall, named after his deceased first wife but presided over by Emmy, his second wife. Emmy had been an actress who continued to perform in style as Hitler's official hostess during state functions. The Goerings became notorious for the exorbitance of their parties—so lavish were they, so outrageous, they rivaled the circuses of the emperors of ancient Rome.

Hermann Goering.   (Courtesy UPI / Corbis.)

Goering did not advocate Hitler's policy of expansion through war, although he played a central role in the annexation of Austria and Czechoslovakia. The day before the attack on Poland, Hitler, never at a loss to take advantage of a dramatic moment, declared that in case he, the Fuehrer, died in the fighting, Goering was his designated successor. A new title, chairman for the Reich Council of National Defense, was added to the many he already held. Within the year he was named *Reichsmarschall,* a high military rank.

The mantle of success did not suit Goering very well. His love for the decorative aspects of power was not in tandem with his disinclination to work. Although he relished his titles, he did not enjoy the performance of the accompanying duties. The search for wealth in order to enhance his personal pleasures occupied much of his time and energies. His rivals for Hitler's favors, such as Goebbels and Himmler, used every opportunity to whittle away at his authority. Although the *Reichsmarschall's* tailors created fantastic costumes and uniforms in every color, it was impossible to hide his ever-increasing girth. Not only did he change his wardrobe many times a day, with each new outfit, a different set of jewels adorned his fingers and glittering waistband. By the 1940s, the ace of World War I had grown gross and grotesque.

Some early doubts notwithstanding, once Germany was committed to war, Goering gave it his full public support. In fact, the *Reichsmarschall's* power and popularity reached their greatest heights during the Polish and French campaigns. The blitzkrieg, or lightning war, (adopted from the theory of mobile warfare suggested by a French officer named Charles de Gaulle and rejected by the French General Staff!) depended largely on the air force. After the fall of France and Poland, the German media used every word of praise in its vocabulary to laud the *Luftwaffe* and its chief. But unexpectedly, the promised quick defeat of England did not happen. First, Goering's pilots were unable to prevent the escape of British and French troops from Dunkirk. Then the English Royal Air Force would not yield its domination of the skies over the English Channel. As a result, the invasion of the British Isles had to be delayed again and again and finally it had to be abandoned. Goering's inability to protect the Fatherland from Allied bombing raids further diminished his popularity. Hitler turned cool toward his erstwhile comrade. Perhaps, if the *Reichsmarschall* had boasted less and paid more attention to his duties, his star might not have descended so rapidly. He even neglected to keep his darling *Luftwaffe* abreast of new developments in the field of aviation. By 1943, it was clear that Goering was a shell, left standing with empty titles and a chest full of medals but no authority.

Despite the fact that Goering was not a fanatical antiSemite, he played an important role in the persecution of the Jews. His participation in almost every aspect of the destruction of European Jewry was not born from conviction but from subservience to the stronger will of the Fuehrer, coupled with utter greed. In 1938, he played the major role in international negotiations between the German government and an intergovernmental committee proposing to speed up the emigration of German Jews to foreign countries. Nothing came of the negotiations, but Goering's action refuted the claim that he had always been convinced that the annihilation of Jews was necessary to secure Germany's future. His personality seemed to have no inner core. Self-gratification masqueraded as principle. If others had to pay a price, any price, to assure his obscenely grandiose lifestyle, that was his due. Thus, he joined and often took charge of the crusade against the Jews, a crusade which included the appropriation of their possessions.

Whenever, wherever Nazi policy presented possibilities of increasing his personal wealth, Goering was certain to be in the picture. As head of the economic Four Year Plan, he controlled the profitable Aryanization campaign. Aryanization was the euphemism for the legalized theft of Jewish assets. Jewish-owned property was taken over by ethnically correct buyers at a fraction of its actual value. The state withheld from the seller whatever price the state dictated by having the payment deposited in specified banks. This money was doled out in small monthly installments. If the former owner emigrated, that bank account was confiscated by the state. Obviously, Aryanization was replete with opportunities for private bargain hunting by Germans with the right connections.

In 1938, Goering commented that it might be necessary to place Jews into ghettos at some future time. Within two years he called for the physical separation of the Jews from the Aryan Germans. The idea of using Jewish work brigades also germinated in his mind, a concept that was issued as an order in 1938. After the destruction of Jewish property during the *Kristallnacht* pogrom, (see Chapter 6), it was Goering who proclaimed that the insurance companies must compensate, but the payments were to be made to the state and not to the policy holders. The wrecked stores had to be repaired at the owners' cost, while insurance reimbursement went into the national treasury. Always eager to cloak theft with justification, the Nazis proclaimed that the Jews were responsible for causing the pogrom in the first place.

Goering hoped to maintain permanent control over the Jews, but he was outmaneuvered by Himmler. It is doubtful, however, whether the Jews would have fared better if Goering had retained command. In 1939, he appointed Reinhard Heydrich, one of the Jews' most deadly enemies, to head the Reich Central Office for Jewish Emigration. The selection of this man to positions of ever-expanding power was in itself a crushing blow to Jewish survival. Before Himmler and his SS usurped mastery over all the Jews within the Nazi grasp, Goering had directed Himmler's activities. Thus it had been the *Reichsmarschall* who ordered the emptying of the ghettos and the deportations of its inhabitants to concentration camps in Poland.

Despite these blows against the Jews, Goering did not share Hitler's fanatical views on the super race theory. He never accepted the Fuehrer's assessment that the Jews, by their very existence, threatened Germany. Jews had usefulness, first, by virtue of their possessions, second, as slave laborers. But whatever their value, their destruction was vital to Hitler and one did not argue with Adolf. In July 1941, Goering asked Heydrich to prepare a final solution to the Jewish question. Although he did not attend the fateful Wannsee Conference of January 20, 1942, he shares responsibility for the death of 6 million Jews.

Goering brought on his own collapse. The war was going badly for the Germans, yet he paid less attention to his work than to his tailor. His behavior grew increasingly bizarre; even Hitler lost patience with him. At first, the Nazi leadership merely bypassed him in their decision-making processes, but that did not make an impact on Goering's lethargy. His drug addiction and regression into infantile theatrics intensified. Shortly before the end of the war, he was dismissed from all his posts. Hitler believed that his old comrade had conspired to replace him and ordered him to be shot. In the chaos of the final days of the Reich, however, there was no opportunity to carry out that order.

For a few belated moments, at the moment of the German collapse, some of the old vitality seemed to surge again in that bloated body. He claimed, upon hearing of Hitler's suicide, that he was the new Fuehrer, the one and only man to represent the German government in dealing with the Allies. He actually demanded a meeting with General Eisenhower. Instead, he was captured by American troops and placed before the International military tribunal at Nuremberg. During his incarceration while awaiting the judgement he was cured of his addiction. His body regained some shape, and he defended himself with considerable vigor. Nevertheless, he was found guilty of crimes against humanity. In the end, his flair for theatrics prevailed. He swallowed a vial of poison two hours before his scheduled hanging. The mystery and drama of his final exit gave him the attention he had craved all his life.

JOSEPH GOEBBELS

Among the intellectual lightweights at the top of the Nazi elite, Goebbels was an oddity. He was well educated, had attended several renowned German universities, and earned a doctorate in literature. He was often called brilliant, even by people who despised him. Under his stewardship, propaganda, once merely the art of persuasion, became the medium for mass manipulation. He combined applied science and technology with total ruthlessness to create a mental vacuum for his audience. At any precisely timed moment, he could create an emotional frenzy of either Fuehrer worship and/or rage against the supposed enemies of the Fatherland. Among all of Hitler's henchmen, Goebbels was the most able and the most cunning. He did not fit in among the dullards who surrounded the Fuehrer, neither in mind nor body. His appearance was ill suited for leadership in the Reich, which valued brawn over brain.

Goebbels could not live up to the image of the Aryan he so relentlessly acclaimed as perfect. He had neither the long, sturdy legs, the slim waist and wide chest, nor the fair skin, blue eyes, and blond hair of the idealized German. His importance to Hitler had to be great indeed to forgive his puny frame, the large head sitting atop a spindly body, the brown hair and eyes, and swarthy complexion. Worst of all, he walked with a distinct limp and had to wear a special shoe and brace. His left leg was several inches shorter than his right. This was the result of an operation he underwent as a boy when he was ill with osteomyelitis, an inflammation of the bone marrow. Even the most touched-up photos could not erase his physical shortcomings. Goebbels was well aware that behind his back he was called "mouse general" and "malicious dwarf." Many Germans believed he was born with a clubfoot. Among his enemies, gossip was spread that he was partly Jewish, and the clubfoot was cited as evidence.

Goebbels' body and mind were at odds with Aryan doctrine; that he rose to great power nonetheless demonstrated the strength of his will. Ashamed of his physique and reluctant to display his intellect, he forced himself to live a cynical lie. He often pretended that his lameness was due to a war wound; he appeared at public meetings in SA uniform at the head of a contingent of SA troopers. In order to appear "one of the boys," he expressed distaste for intellectuals and erudition. His diaries were filled with adulation for Hitler, whose private conversations were notoriously long-winded and boring. Whether these entries revealed his true feelings remains questionable; after all, he was a professional liar.

Goebbels was born in 1897 into a devoutly Catholic Rhineland family. His father had been a manual laborer who rose to a lower middle-class position. The young man, already painfully aware of his handicap, was desolate when other youths went to war in 1914 and he was rejected. He never came to terms with his inability

Joseph Goebbels.   (Courtesy UPI/Corbis.)

to serve as a soldier. Success at university life gave him status, but it could not mend the anguish over his deformed leg. He was awarded a doctorate at Heidelberg and from then on insisted upon being addressed as "Herr Doktor." The attempt to win fame and fortune as a writer floundered when his book *Michael* and two plays were received with critical scorn. His career as a journalist was short-lived. His keen and restless mind was searching for a calling, for a way to show the world his brilliance when in 1922, quite accidentally, Goebbels heard Hitler speak in Munich. The die was cast; the Austrian with the black mustache and the hypnotic voice was the means by which his own star would rise.

Goebbels' first propaganda campaign served his own objective—to sell himself, to penetrate and become part of Hitler's inner circle. The Fuehrer responded to his flattery, despite such nasty comments about the Doktor as "Wotan's Mickey Mouse" whispered behind his back. This particular insult implied that while Hitler was Wotan, chief of the Norse gods, Goebbels was his funny rodent. The Nazi party, nonetheless, could use a man who was not only an impassioned speaker, almost as intoxicating as Hitler himself, but was also a master of the written word. The fact that this new recruit combined a cunning mind with a complete absence of integrity increased his value. Goebbels edited a newspaper, *Der Angriff* (*Attack*), to promote National Socialism and did so with total disregard for the truth. Even his detractors were awed. Thus, before the Nazis came to power, he had developed the concept of "the big lie," that is, a lie so blatant, so outrageous, and repeated so often that the public could not conceive of anyone so daring to tell a falsehood on such a scale.

When Hitler appointed him Gauleiter (district party leader) of Berlin, Goebbels created the highly effective political theater that would later dazzle all of Germany and beyond. He was credited with the great gains of the Nazi party in the Reichstag elections of 1932. "Herr Doktor" cheered when some 20,000 books were burned in bonfires across the nation, leaving much of the cultural heritage of Europe in ashes. Among the volumes thrown into the flames by university students and some of their professors were a number of revered classics and the works of Jewish, communist, and pacifist authors. Goebbels had an instinct for judging the mood of the masses and fed their appetite with slander, rumors, and personal attacks. Some of his SA Brownshirts walked the streets with bandaged heads, reddened with dye for more dramatic effect, to simulate injuries suffered during street fights with the communists. He wrote articles under an assumed name in which he lauded Dr. Goebbels as a man of extraordinary valor. After the death of a contemptible SA rioter named Horst Wessel, Goebbels fabricated martyrdom for the street brawler. For a dozen years Germans sang the Horst Wessel Song as their second national anthem. One of the lines in this Nazi hymn ran, "Yes, when the blood of Jews spurts from our knives, then things go twice as well."

In 1928, five years before Hitler became chancellor, Goebbels became propaganda chief for the party. This assured his appointment as National Minister of Public Enlightenment and Propaganda in 1933. The title did not indicate the dimensions of power that he wrung from his position. He built an empire that encompassed jurisdiction over the cultural life of the nation in which propaganda was but one of many facets of his activities. His commitment to Hitler was total. He never abandoned his mission: to glorify the Fuehrer and his vision of the new Germany.

KING OF PROPAGANDA AND CULTURE

As cultural czar, Goebbels had the authority to dictate the literary, artistic, journalistic, and musical tastes of a nation. He decided which sports were proper for school children, which films the movie houses could show, and what theatrical productions could be produced. His censorship extended to the written and the spoken word; he masterminded and managed the spectacular rallies that imitated the pomp and solemnity of religious ceremonies. He was the arbiter of painting and sculpture and decided what was acceptable Aryan artistic expression. Propaganda, he stated, had no relationship to truth, only to effectiveness.

The outbreak of the Second World War caused Goebbels' fortune to lapse for several years. He was jubilant over the early victories, but his public assurances of a quick end to the struggle were proven wrong. The public felt deceived by his pronouncements. He further blundered when he treated the Allied forces with contempt rather than with the respect due a worthy adversary. He seemed unaware that victories over an ignoble foe earn no glory. His pledge that German civilians would be safe in the fortress the Fuehrer had built around them flew in the face of reality as, night after night, Allied bombers delivered a message that belied his words. Goebbels' enemies within the party believed the little man was finished.

But when the possibility of defeat, though unspoken, was no longer unthinkable, Goebbels' services were again in great demand. The nation must be readied to fight to its last breath. Now his approach was to instill fear and hatred for the enemies of the Reich: the Jews, of course, but also England, the Soviet Union, and the United States. If defeated, he warned, the German people could expect no mercy. Rape and pillage, particularly at the hands of the "Asiatic hordes," would be their fate. In an effort to reverse the spirit of weariness and hopelessness, he promised them a marvelous secret weapon that would turn the tide of the war. His glee at the death of Franklin D. Roosevelt was obscene. Hitler was still the child of destiny, so Goebbels assured the public, with the cursed "Rosenfeld" gone, the American war effort would wither away. But German defeat was inevitable. Goebbels' appointment in 1944 as general plenipotentiary for the war effort was, in effect, a gesture. Germany had no reserves left to prevent the invasions from either direction, the east or the west.

In his early life, young Joseph seemed indifferent to the so-called Jewish question. As soon as he realized that such an attitude would prevent his rise in the ranks of the party, he conformed to the required, politically correct antiSemitic stance. Whether he believed what he said and wrote is debatable, but it hardly matters. His portrait of the Jew was a dehumanized caricature that was effective in persuading millions of Germans that there "must be something to it." The assassination of a German official in Paris by a Jew (these events will be more fully explained in Chapter 6) gave Goebbels the opportunity to demonstrate the sincerity of his anti-Semitism. He turned the shooting into the provocation for a nationwide pogrom from which German Jewry never recovered. With his talent for brutal, often satanic exaggeration, he thus answered those who claimed he did not hate the Jews enough. All the media under his control attacked the supposedly all-powerful, international, conspiratorial Bolshevik Untermenschen (subhumans), the Jews who controlled the economic world from New York to Moscow. The pogrom known as *Kristallnacht* was of his making. To the Germans and the foreign press, the devastation of German Jewish life was presented as a spontaneous reaction by an enraged public.

MURDER AND SUICIDE

Certain aspects of Goebbels' life and death bore a resemblance to Hitler's. Both men appear to have been driven by self-hatred. In Hitler's case, Jews became his personal sacrificial scapegoat; for Goebbels, all of humanity was the enemy. Only Hitler was exempt from the sharpness of his pen. He was a homely man, small and lame; the antithesis of the Aryan superman he so masterfully glorified and so consummately envied. Although the details differ, both men had difficulty in their relationships with women. Goebbels had many affairs, before and after he was married. As a politically powerful man, he had no difficulty in proving his virility with ambitious starlets eager to further their careers. His wife, Magda, was ready to ask for a divorce when his philandering became a public scandal. Only Hitler's personal intervention prevented the breakup of the marriage.

In their suicides, the similarities between Goebbels' and Hitler's personalities were striking. Goebbels actually orchestrated Hitler's death. He urged his Fuehrer to die like a hero portrayed in German mythology, a godlike superman who leaves this world in a blaze of destruction. Only suicide and flames could feed the future legend of his greatness. The drama must end like a climactic scene from Wagner's *Goetterdaemmerung*. Afraid of capture by the Russians, Hitler agreed. He paid the faithful Goebbels a final tribute. In his last testament, Hitler appointed him to a leading role in a future German government, a nomination that can only be characterized as bizarre.

But Goebbels had decided to play out his own drama. In his last words he apologized for refusing, for the first and only time, an order from the Fuehrer. He had decided to die because life no longer had any value. His wife, he wrote, had chosen to die with him. Joseph and Magda had brought their six children to Hitler's underground bunker and refused to have them flown out to safety. Goebbels' final crime violated the most basic norms of humanity. He claimed that if his children had been old enough to speak for themselves, they too would rather die than live in a world without Hitler. The picture of the mother and father, going from bed to bed, handing their children a lethal drink, was the penultimate scene of Goebbels' life. The curtain came down on May 1, 1945. With Russian tanks entering the chancellery garden, his wife took poison and Goebbels shot himself.

HEINRICH HIMMLER

Himmler is often called the architect of the Holocaust. The epithet denotes more than theoretical planning: Himmler supervised the day-to-day reality of the killing process. He did not conceive of the Shoah, Hitler did, but the efficiency required to murder such great numbers in less than five years was largely Himmler's work. Some writers have called him the perfect bureaucrat, the man who carried out orders with the mechanical efficiency of a robot. But that characterization does not take into account the man's fanaticism nor his political acumen. The smooth implementation of the Holocaust required the resources of a master of deceit. Everything about Himmler, including his appearance, was deceptive. It must also be remembered that the threshold leading to Hitler's office was always crowded with ambitious men jostling to get nearer to the seat of power. Himmler's success in that perilous arena indicates that the man cannot be reduced to a single, simple caption.

Himmler was the most feared and hated man of the Third Reich. He inspired terror not only among Jews, but also in the general population. The arm of his Gestapo, his SS, and the police forces he commanded seemed to reach into every home and workplace. Germans and the peoples in the conquered lands were silenced by fear. Himmler deliberately cultivated the perception that no word, no action escaped his knowledge. The slightest criticism of the regime, even a political joke, might result in arrest. It was better to keep quiet, trust no one. There were whispers of terrible tortures inflicted during Gestapo interrogations and of unspeakable conditions in concentration camps. In the center of this atmosphere of dread was Heinrich Himmler.

Hannah Arendt, the author of *The Origins of Totalitarianism* and *Eichmann in Jerusalem,* could have identified Himmler along with Eichmann as subjects who confirmed her theory of the banality of evil. The man was so ordinary, so conventional, it is very difficult to see him as a fanatical mass murderer. His upbringing was comfortably middle class; a devout Catholic home, the father an educator with connections to Bavarian nobility, the mother attentive to her home and her three sons. Psychiatrists cannot point to cruelty or abnormality in the workings of this family. Heinrich was the middle child, born in 1900. The young boy was already unattractive, though not repulsively so; his small eyes, thin lips, and weak chin gave him a ratlike expression. He attended a technical college and was awarded a diploma in agricultural studies. He married a nurse with whom he shared his interest in such parascientific subjects as herbalism, mesmerism, and homeopathy. We know little of the marriage. Heinrich was not a faithful husband and fathered several children out of wedlock while neglecting his own family. After he achieved great power, he exhibited an affinity for mysticism and superstition which often bordered on the absurd. During his boyhood his schoolmates noticed none of these oddities; they described him as methodical, hard working, attentive to detail, utterly without charisma. He was a plodder, adequate but not outstanding.

Heinrich Himmler.   (Courtesy AP/Wide World Photos.)

When the First World War erupted, Heinrich was in school. At age seventeen he served for a year in a Bavarian infantry regiment without duties at the front. The end of the war and the politics of the Weimar Republic disappointed young Heinrich. Like so many others, he joined a rightist paramilitary organization. He met Hitler and joined the National Socialist Party. At the Beer Hall Putsch of 1923, Himmler stood next to SA Commander Ernst Roehm and therefore could claim the vaunted "early fighter" designation. During the six years following the failed Putsch in Munich, Himmler functioned in various capacities in the Nazi party while earning a living as a chicken farmer and fertilizer salesman. Up to this point his career was in no way distinguished. His subservience and slavish loyalty had made an impression on Hitler, and the "faithful Heinrich" was assigned to head the SS, or *Schutzstaffel* (Defense Echelon) in 1929. With this appointment, a new chapter opened for Himmler, for Germany, and tragically, for the Jews.

His State Within the State

Himmler's advancement cannot be separated from the evolution of the SS. The Blackshirts, as the SS members were called, consisted of a mere 300 men when Himmler became their chief. The troop's original duty was to protect Hitler during public appearances. Taking a page from the praetorian guards of ancient Rome, virile, handsome men were selected to enhance the Fuehrer's presence. Their emblems were symbols rather than decorations, the double lightning, a stylized form of the letters SS, the skull or death head on collar and ring of certain battalions, the dagger in the belt, the black tunic, trousers and boots, all were calculated to instill awe among civilians. Their appearance was no mere facade. It represented careful training, a specific code of conduct, total dedication to Hitler personally—as opposed to service to the nation—and readiness to perform any assignment no matter how repulsive. Since the SS became the instrument of the Holocaust, its development will be detailed elsewhere; at this point, suffice it to say that the SS as a cult and an instrument of terror was Himmler's work. He created a state within the state where ordinary rules of morality and law did not apply. He brought a businesslike approach to fanaticism that made mass murder a product to be manufactured with all the efficiency of modern technology.

Himmler had the opportunity to show Hitler his loyalty during the massacre of the SA leadership, the Night of the Long Knives. By committing the blood purge murders of a number of the veteran leaders of the Nazi movement, the fidelity of the SS could never be questioned again. The organization's job description expanded to include the identification and elimination of all alleged internal enemies of the regime.

Master Race Mania

Himmler was obsessed with Aryan racial purity for Germany. He made the SS the instrument to turn his fixation into a blueprint for his own version of a brave new world. The *Reichsfuehrer* (National Leader) of the SS had been a student of agriculture who envisioned the use of selective breeding to produce the master race. He was convinced that genetics, or blood as the Nazis called it, determined all the characteristics of a people. Valuable Aryan blood must be nurtured; inferior blood, such as Jewish, Gypsy, or Slavic blood, must be prevented from further polluting the Nordic race. Himmler not only believed this, but devised plans to implement this fantasy.

The SS was at the center of his plan; these were the men and their carefully selected wives who would validate his theory. Candidates for membership in the SS were required to trace their racial purity for three generations; they took an oath to marry only "qualified" and approved Aryan women and promised to father many children. Out-of-wedlock offspring were welcomed and became the financial obligation of the SS organization. Land taken from Poland and perhaps western Russia was to be awarded to this new caste of super-Germans. They would own the land and the dispossessed Slavic underclass would work the farms. "Surplus" Poles had to be eliminated, moved eastward, or killed; it was immaterial which method was employed. Such Aryanized land was to Germanize in perpetuity the *Lebensraum* conquered from Poland. In order to prevent the native peoples from rebelling against this new order, potential leaders among them, such as the university educated, army officers, priests, and communists, would have to be eliminated.

Poland had a large Jewish population of over three million. Himmler believed Jews to be the most dangerous enemy of the Reich, thus their destruction was an essential. The SS played the vital role in the execution of the Final Solution and thus the obsessions of Hitler and Himmler dovetailed into one operation. Himmler planned also to save, in his words, to harvest the genetically superior material carried in the genes of those Aryans who lived in the eastern lands. A monumental process involving the transfer of hundreds of thousands of so-called ethnic Germans was well on the way between 1940 and 1944. Called *Volksdeutsche* (belonging to the German people) their resettlement was halted when the German army suffered reverses. Meanwhile, the Poles and Jews who had been dispossessed were killed or enslaved. Himmler exhibited similar cruelty when he directed the murder of Germans whose physical and/or mental imperfections made them unworthy of life. His so-called euthanasia program sanctioned the killing of children and adults whose progeny could pollute the racial integrity of the nation. Only the fit were allowed to survive and only he could determine who was or was not fit to live in his German world.

At the height of his power, Himmler commanded an empire. In 1939, he became the Reich's Commissar for the Consolidation of the German Nation. The title was grandiose but so was the power it yielded: commander of an enormously expanded SS, including control over the "racial degenerates"; commander-in-chief of the concentration and death camps; chief of the *Einsatzgruppen;* political administrator of the eastern occupied territories; head of the Gestapo and all police organizations; minister of the interior; and supreme commander of the People's Army, the *Volksturm,* or Home Guard, and of the Werewolf troops of teenagers who had sworn to defend the Fatherland when all else was lost.

Himmler's power emanated from the single source of Hitler's will. But every-thing depended on winning the war, and the Fuehrer could not order that miracle. Finally, when even the faithful Heinrich realized that all was lost, he tried to approach the Allies with peace feelers. Apparently, he had no idea that he was the very last man with whom the victorious commanders would deal. Hitler was furious with the last-minute desertion of his paladin and ordered his arrest—a futile gesture reminiscent of Goering's fate.

The personal files of the *Reichsfuehrer* were destroyed at his orders. Nevertheless, enough evidence remains from other sources to give succeeding generations a portrait of a man who was slavishly devoted to Hitler, who was totally indifferent to the fate of millions, and whose unrealistic racial theories bordered on the demented. His rise to power from obscurity confirmed his stamina as an in-fighter and his skill as an administrator. His character was devoid of any ethical code save that of loyalty to his Fuehrer.

Himmler tried to escape in disguise after the German surrender. He was captured by the British and while undergoing a physical examination, he bit down on a vial of cyanide hidden in his mouth. He had made the mistake of masquerading as a low-ranking Gestapo agent, unaware that that entire organization had been declared criminal. He died almost instantly, thus he, like Hitler, Goering, and Goebbels, slipped out of the hangman's noose.

CHAPTER 5

Germans Under the Nazis

The once popular assessment that the Nazis ran Germany with clockwork precision has been rejected by historians. The uniformity of marching feet, of arms outstretched at a precise angle for the Hitler salute, the vaunted punctuality of the trains, and the conformity of the faces of Hitler Youth beneath the swastika banners all created the myth that these appearances mirrored German life. The facts, however, paint a different picture. Nazi German politics were muddied by conflicts, uncertainties, and unclear lines of authority. Hitler worked sporadically, often his orders were vague hints rather than commands, and he encouraged interservice rivalries among his deputies. As long as the men around him vied with each other for a scrap of his power, his own position was more secure. The fact that no serious contender ever challenged Hitler's authority indicated that this approach produced the desired results.

DESTRUCTION OF THE REPUBLIC

On January 30, 1933, Field Marshall von Hindenburg, president of the Weimar Republic, reluctantly agreed to the appointment of Adolf Hitler as chancellor of Germany. Thus, the government was now headed by the former corporal who achieved power in accordance with the Weimar Constitution. The choice of Franz von Papen as vice chancellor had finally convinced the old President that Hitler could be reined in if necessary. The elegant Franz was a man from the old school of diplomats, a man the aged president could understand who had helped to assure him that Hitler could be managed. After all, the Nazis held only three other cabinet posts out of eleven, and the important ministries were in the hands of conservatives. The fact that the Nazis had attained their greatest popularity in 1932 but attained only 32 percent of the votes, gave this reasoning the appearance of logic. Nazi election rhetoric had emphasized nationalism, a rather nebulous form of socialism, vicious anti-communism, and the promise of relief from economic woes. The old guard was opposed only to the socialist allusions. AntiSemitic tirades had been muted because they proved an ineffective election tactic.

In retrospect, we see that Hitler began his political career with deceptive conformity to the Weimar Constitution. Within two years, he had transformed Germany into his personal dictatorship. Civil rights disappeared, long-established institutions became unrecognizable, and conventional social and cultural mores were successfully challenged. The myth of Jewish debasement and its obverse, Aryan supremacy, came to play central roles. One of the most totalitarian governments in history was established, and only defeat on the battlefield would dislodge it. This was Hitler's work. No matter how abhorrent the man and his crimes, his extraordinary ability must be acknowledged. The caricature of the mustached buffoon distorts the truth as much as the heroic image created by Goebbels.

The Nazification of the nation was a process, not an event. As processes go, the transformation was implemented at breakneck speed. It is not possible to assess exactly who is to blame for the destruction of the German republic, there is lots of guilt to go around. Three factors played major roles in the fiasco. First, the opposition parties in the legislature, the Reichstag, were unwilling or unable to put aside their differences and present a united opposition to the Nazis; second, the leaders of the Weimar Republic had been unable to convince the German public to cherish their democratic freedoms; and third, in their narcissism, the conservative upper class overestimated its own power and underestimated the Nazi party and Adolf Hitler.

THE LAST ELECTION

Even before he took office, Hitler asked for and was granted new Reichstag elections. He hoped to win a majority so that he could reshape the government with the endorsement of the legislature. This desire to disguise every procedure with the veneer of legality was apparent throughout his political life; perhaps as a result of the failed and unlawful *Bierhalle Putsch* in Munich. The election date was set for March 1933. With the resources of the government behind him, the new chancellor could run a very effective, often coercive, campaign. But politics cost money, lots of money. Hitler addressed a conclave of Germany's industrial magnates and pledged to the heads of such giants as Krupp, I.G. Farben, and United Steel Works that the coming election would be the last one. He vowed to preserve private property and hinted broadly that regardless of the wishes of the voters, he would stay in power, he would find a way. It seems inconceivable upon reflection that such a speech was actually applauded. When Goering passed the hat, he collected 3 million marks. One may wonder if Hitler intentionally played upon the vanity of these men; he created the impression that he would be useful to them as a front man, a puppet whose strings they held.

Hitler kept his word; this would be the last German election until 1949. The Communist and Socialist parties were unable to present their candidates to the public effectively. The Nazis saw to that; their meetings were frequently disrupted or shut down by the SA; many of their leaders were arrested or went into hiding; and their printing presses were smashed. In Prussia, Hermann Goering had become the state's Minister of the Interior. He urged his police to shoot anti-Nazi suspects. Although the words "Socialist Workers" were part of the proper name of Hitler's party, trade unionists were beaten regardless of their political affiliation. Street fights escalated into killings, and still neither the German people nor any of their institutions rose in protest. The churches, professional and labor organizations, university faculty and students, civil servants, and most importantly, the armed forces remained passive. By their moderation (or was it cowardice?), they further encouraged the street gang methods of the Nazis.

Hitler had hoped to provoke the Communists into acts of violence that would provide him with an excuse to destroy their organization once and for all. In the Reichstag, the Communist party held 100 seats out of a total of 600, and if these delegates could be dislodged, then the Nazis would have a clear majority. They were the Nazis' most committed foes and had to be eliminated. How this problem was solved reads like the plot from a B movie.

THE REICHSTAG FIRE

The word Reichstag, similar to the U.S. House of Representatives, denotes both the legislative body and the building. On February 27, 1933, just a week before the elections, the Berlin Reichstag building was torched. Without question the blaze was the result of arson. The large amount of incendiary material found on the premises left no doubt on that issue. But who set the fire remains unclear to this day. The Berlin police arrested a mentally impaired young Dutchman, Van der Lubbe, at the scene. Hitler and his team seized the moment they had probably created themselves when they accused the Communists of hiring Van der Lubbe to commit the crime. Most of the Communist legislators were arrested; the rest went into hiding. The Nazi press shouted Red conspiracy and declared the illegal seizure of the duly elected Communist Reichstag members a triumph of law and order.

There was a trial. Five men—the incoherent Dutchman, a former Reichstag deputy, and three Bulgarian Communists residing in the Reich—were charged with arson and intent to instigate a rebellion. The world was watching; possibly this saved all but the pathetic Van der Lubbe. No one who knew this confused and obviously disturbed young man believed him capable of high treason. Nevertheless, that was the verdict, and his life was cut short by the guillotine. The other defendants were acquitted.

Did the Nazis set the fire and use the unfortunate Dutchman as their dupe? Was it coincidental that a retarded person who had a predilection for pyromania was in the building just in time to be observed by members of the SA? The truth will never be known. It was obvious, however, who benefited from the crime. The day after the fire, Hitler succeeded in persuading von Hindenburg to sign a decree "for the protection of the people and the state." The otherwise liberal and progressive Weimar Constitution contained a clause, Article 48, whereby in times of crisis the President may temporarily suspend the fundamental rights of German citizens. By invoking this article, supposedly to prevent a Communist coup d'état, Hitler was given temporary dictatorial powers. Thus, on February 28, 1933, the freedom to speak, to write, to assemble, to have privacy in one's home, and the guarantee of due process of the law were all swept away. The great majority of Germans cried no tears over the disappearance of the Communist leadership; many believed that even an abuse of power was laudable if it rid Germany of communists. Of course, once Hitler had the opportunity to rule without the restraints of constitutional government, he found a way to seize absolute and permanent power. The device to achieve this was the Enabling Act.

The election that followed the Reichstag fire was tainted by many abuses. Uniformed SA men confronted voters at the ballot boxes and "persuaded" many to vote the Nazi ticket. Despite these tactics, however, Hitler did not win the victory he expected. When the ballots were counted, the Center party and the Socialists held

Hitler addressing a giant Nazi demonstration, 1933. (Courtesy AP/Wide World Photos.)

their own; even the leaderless Communists lost fewer votes than anticipated. Instead of a landslide, just 44 percent of the votes went to the Nazis; only in conjunction with another ultra-rightist party, the Nationalists, did they achieve a simple majority.

Hitler intended to nullify the Weimar Republic by revoking its constitution. But he wanted to achieve dictatorial powers by legal means. His regime must always appear to act within the law of the land because most Germans would oppose an unlawful seizure of power. The drastic changes he intended had to originate from a legitimately constituted source. A way had to be found to persuade the democratic Republic to vote itself out of existence. The constitution provided that during a national emergency, the Reichstag, by a three-fourths vote of its membership, might suspend the organic law of the land.

THE ENABLING ACT

The hysteria created by the Reichstag fire had prevented the Communist representatives from taking their seats in the legislature. Other anti-Nazi members were "detained" by the SA. The passage of the so-called Law to Remove the Distress of the People and the State, better known as the Enabling Act, required a 75% majority. This required a large bloc of votes from parties that were not on the extreme political right. Two days before the vote on this important legislation was to be cast, Goebbels created a most disarming, seductive scenario. The ceremonial opening session of the Reichstag was held in the Garrison Church at Potsdam. This church was connected with everything dear to von Hindenburg and the Prussian military establishment. Hitler, all sincerity and humility, paid homage to the spirit lingering in these hallowed walls, and the old President wiped a tear from his eye.

On March 23, 1933, Hitler requested a four-year suspension of the constitution. A cowed Reichstag voted as the Nazis asked: 441 in favor and 94 opposed. Hindenburg signed the order. When the Center party voted yes, the constitution was doomed. The Catholic delegates justified their support of the bill with the argument that their endorsement would allow them to exert some influence over the Nazis, an argument we have heard before. Only the Social Democrats resisted but they could not prevent the passage of the Enabling Act. And so the Reichstag had signed its own suicide note.

The consolidation of political power, the *Gleichschaltung* (Coordination) took place during the next several months. One by one the separate strands of authority were pulled together into Hitler's chancellery. All political parties except the NSDAP were outlawed. The fact that this was accomplished without serious opposition might be attributed to fear of Nazi terror, as well as to widespread bitterness over the failures of the Weimar Republic. Many Germans were willing to give Hitler a chance; perhaps dictatorship would succeed where democracy had failed. State governments were reorganized. A unified, highly centralized administration replaced the previous federal system of government. Local legislatures were deprived of their autonomy. A single individual, the political *Gauleiter,* usually a reliable Nazi who took his orders from Berlin, headed each of the political units within the Reich. Bureaucracies were Nazified by means of a purge that was camouflaged as The Law for the Restoration of the Professional Civil Service. All Jews and many anti-Nazi bureaucrats were ousted from their positions. It was not possible to remove all "unreliable" officials and keep the government functioning, but whenever and wherever possible, they were supplanted by party members. It must be remembered that teachers, including university professors, were also civil service appointees.

On May 1, 1933, Hitler celebrated the working man and his contribution to the past and future greatness of the Reich. With laudatory speeches and parades, the working class was lulled into wishful thinking about the importance of its future role. That was the calm before the storm. On the following day, all trade union headquarters were raided, their assets confiscated, and their leaders sent to concentration camps. Within the week, labor unions were dissolved, and strikes were declared illegal. Without a choice in the matter, workers were enrolled in the German Labor Front headed by Robert Ley. The actual purpose of the Labor Front was the suppression of the German workers' time-honored and hard-won rights. In due time, the Nazis forbade workers to leave their jobs without permission, they were prohibited from bargaining for better wages, or complaining about poor working conditions. Some historians have referred to this relationship as the "enserfment" of labor. The National Socialist German Workers' Party (Nazi or NSDAP) clearly had expunged the Socialist component of its identification.

THE LEADERSHIP PRINCIPLE

The *Fuehrerprinzip,* a theory that total power must be confined to a single leader, had already been delineated in *Mein Kampf.* Hitler called parliamentary government irresponsible and he never revised his position. Every aspect of his dictatorship was organized so that departmental leaders derived their authority from him alone. This concept was carried through the party organization as well. For example, the head of the *Frauenschaften* (womens' organizations), Gertrud Scholtz-Klink, was entitled to call herself the *Fuehrerin,* the female Fuehrer. Implementation of the principle was well underway within a year of Hitler's appointment as chancellor. During the next decade, the grip of the Nazi party would grow tighter until party and government functions were indistinguishable.

Not all Nazis approved of Hitler's ultra-rightist shift of their original goals. Clearly, Hitler was willing to sacrifice the needs of the working class to benefit the industrialists. Some early supporters disapproved this repudiation of the needs and hopes of German labor. They wanted to keep the promise of "national socialism" and challenged Hitler's policy of favoring the capitalists. This protest did not come from the workers whose leaders had disappeared, but from within the party itself. The showdown is known as the Night of the Long Knives and/or the Blood Purge, two melodramatic designations for a melodramatic event.

THE BLOOD PURGE

Hitler's flirtation with the conservative, even reactionary elite—namely the generals and the barons of industry—created problems. In the center of discontent was the SA and its chief, Ernst Roehm. No doubt, this swashbuckling adventurer and his Brownshirts had contributed greatly to his friend Adolf's victory. Roehm had been remarkably successful in attracting young men to the ranks of his troopers. In 1933 they numbered 2 million strong. Despite his past contributions, Roehm was becoming a liability. He had taken seriously the socialist pronouncements of the Fuehrer and urged a second revolution to bring about the promised shift of the nation to the political left. Obviously, the regime had no intention of curbing the profits of the powerful few in order to promote the interests of the workers. In addition, Hitler and Roehm differed in their view of the role of the SA. Hitler wanted the corps to function as a political army, the paramilitary strong arm of the party. Roehm was ambitious and demanded a greater arena for himself and his men. He wanted his units incorporated into the regular army, a suggestion the generals found totally unacceptable. The officers of the high command were appalled at the notion of a "people's army" under the personal command of Roehm, whose homosexual lifestyle raised eyebrows. It was no secret that he and other leaders of the SA engaged in all sorts of debauchery. This alone made the SA leadership unacceptable to the great majority of Germans.

Faced with the choice of appeasing either the regular army, which had the power to topple Hitler if it had the will, or Ernst Roehm, Hitler made his decision. Goering and Goebbels agreed that the old comrade and his cronies had to be sacrificed. The fact that Heinrich Himmler's SS was willing, perhaps even eager, to carry out the assassinations removed any practical difficulties. With one blow the power of the SA would be broken, the generals would be appeased and grateful.

The arrests and most of the executions took place on June 30, 1934—the Night of the Long Knives or the Blood Purge. Hitler himself participated in the arrest of Ernst Roehm. Some SA leaders were murdered immediately, others, like Roehm, within a few days. The liquidation of the chiefs of the SA also served as an excuse to settle some old scores between rivals. The exact number of victims has never been firmly established, perhaps as few as 100 or as many as 1,000 were killed. No indictments were filed; no due process of the law was ordered. After the assassinations were carried out, the public was told that Roehm and the SA had planned to usurp the government in a counterrevolution and for the sake of public peace and order, the authorities had been obliged to strike quickly. Actually, nearly all of the alleged plotters were surprised in their beds, thus no credence can be given the official justification. The SS, of course, earned the Fuehrer's gratitude and its growing importance can be traced to this moment marked by the murder of old comrades.

As usual, the Nazis attempted to mask their crimes as legally sanctioned acts. An obedient Reichstag passed a law that retroactively legitimized the assassinations. There would be no other challenges to Hitler's power from within the Nazi party during the life of the Third Reich.

GOVERNING THE THIRD REICH

In totalitarian Germany, the line between officials of the Nazi party and government administrators was blurred. Loyalty to the Fuehrer and the rank in the hierarchy of the party were crucial in obtaining a position in the government. In other words, politics were the most important criteria for bureaucratic appointments. This was true for the file clerk in a village town hall as well as the foreign minister in Berlin. Obviously, many good workers who did not have the right connections or had not joined the Nazi party, lost their positions. Men and a few women who had displayed their swastika armband early on, were given preference as a matter of course. Their qualifications may or may not have been adequate for their assignments. Such blatant patronage raises the question "How could, how did the Nazi government function?" Those who lived these years in Germany are likely to reply: "Not very well."

Hitler's personal power was the overriding force in the administration. No institution, and certainly no individual, not the churches, not the aristocrats, not tradition, not the working classes nor the industrialists curbed his authority. His pronouncements became the law of the land in all political, economic, and even cultural affairs. The rather ineffectual challenges to his personal rule were overcome quickly and he was obeyed even when the nation lay in rubble. Hitler's style of governance was rather haphazard. It suited him to encourage rivalry among his administrators, and he often gave vague orders that required interpretation by his subordinates. This lack of preciseness and clarity was used by his subordinates to interpret the Fuehrer's will so that what Hitler implied could have the effect of an order.

Like the emperors of ancient Rome, Hitler retained a façade of the old political institutions. Ministries continued to exist, even the Reichstag met to rubber stamp his decrees. Cabinet members continued to meet, but Hitler was not interested in supervising their affairs and did not participate in their sessions. A state secretary of the chancellery ferried papers between the ministers and the Fuehrer. The difficulty in carrying on the business of state was further complicated by Hitler's nepotism. He appointed certain favorites to powerful posts and granted them the privilege of riding roughshod over other bureaucrats. For example, Fritz Todt, who built the famous German road system, the Autobahn, was responsible to no one but Hitler and received his funds directly from the chancellery. Thus, Todt could ignore the established ministry of transport and do as he saw fit. This sort of dual authority existed in many departments and created personal and interdepartmental controversies.

The Nazis could not fill all administrative jobs with their own people and, therefore, some offices remained in the hands of experts. The hope was to oust "unreliable" officials as soon as politically dependable replacements could be found. To prevent a collapse of the governmental functions, some non-party members remained at their civil service posts. This was principally true during the first several years of the regime. Many of the old employees of such departments as the foreign ministry, the national banking system, the economics ministry, post office, railroads, police, education, courts, and public health were needed to conduct the nation's business. But their future was uncertain. The more responsible the position, the more eager were the *Gauleiters* (highest ranking regional Nazi party officials) to install their comrades. Many of the older bureaucrats found that their duties were hampered by the constant interference from party officials but fear of losing status and pensions kept them at their desks.

The framework of the Nazi party resembled a pyramid; Hitler stood at the apex, below him were the *Gauleiters,* the functionaries whose territories roughly matched that of the old German states. Further divisions, from provinces to counties to villages, were headed by party men. As noted earlier, lines of authority were often confused, and the judge, the school principal, the museum director, the postmaster, and so on worked in a morass of conflicting directives. Many civil servants solved their dilemmas by becoming active members of the Nazi party. Then they needed only to follow orders issued by the party and could ignore the directives coming from other authorities.

Von Hindenburg was eighty-seven when he died on August 2, 1934. Hitler used this opportunity to declare that the office and functions of the presidency were henceforth merged with those of the Fuehrer. Members of the armed forces were required to swear a new oath of obedience, not to the Fatherland but to the Fuehrer

Adolf Hitler and Paul von Hindenburg, Potsdam, 1933.   (Courtesy UPI/Corbis.)

personally. The generals, by virtue of this submission, lost the independence they claimed to hold so dear. When the voters were asked to legalize the dictatorship by means of a plebiscite, 90 percent gave their approval. No doubt, many votes cast for Hitler were expressing fear rather than political conviction. Nevertheless, Goebbels could proclaim that the nation had spoken; the Weimar Republic ceased to exist and was replaced by the personal rule of the Fuehrer.

Hitler had no patience with and no understanding of the intricacies of economics. He simply wanted to realize certain highly visible objectives, regardless of any long-range implications. Foremost was his goal to reduce the unemployment rate. When he came to power, some 6 million Germans were out of work. Within the next four years that number was reduced to 1 million. Production rose more than 100 percent in this period and a sense of hope and expectation for the future kept the rather poorly paid workers acquiescent. Public works, from grandiose construction schemes to the innovative *Autobahn* road system, were partially responsible for these gains. Also, the revival of the armament industry played a major role. Hitler's ambitions for Germany were in the arena of foreign affairs; the expansion and glorification of the Reich sooner or later would lead to war. To create the necessary war machine required money, but the details of financing his aims were other people's concerns.

Hitler was fortunate to have the wizardry of Hjalmar Schacht at his disposal. Hjalmar Schacht was brilliant and opportunistic. He claimed to be a monarchist, but was a founder of the German Democratic Party. In 1931 he declared that he was not a Nazi but he enabled Hitler to achieve important economic success. During the Weimar Republic he had earned fame for his genius in finance. At age thirty-nine he became a director of the National Bank of Germany. Within seven years he was appointed director of the *Reichsbank,* the foremost monetary institution in the nation. He had been largely responsible for curbing the runaway inflation of 1923. Because he opposed the financial policies of the Weimar Republic, he resigned his post. Within a year of Hitler's appointment as chancellor, he accepted the post of *Reichsminister* of Economics. He masterminded the early economic successes of the Reich despite his objections to some Nazi policies, including the violent anti-Semitism. Claiming opposition to Hitler's military aggression, he nonetheless readied the German economy to prepare for war. He printed money and manipulated currencies. When foreign creditors feared that they might lose their German investments, Schacht convinced them to invest more money in order to recoup a shaky debt. Hitler, of course, was delighted to have such a renowned banker in his service.

Schacht became disillusioned with Nazism and secretly flirted with opponents of the regime. At this point he was no longer the economic czar; much of his authority had been usurped by Goering who was in control of the Four Year Plan. This plan, devised in 1936, attempted to make Germany self-sufficient and independent of foreign imports. Despite the creation of various synthetics and ersatz fabrications, Germany was never able to free itself of the need for certain imports. Only conquest could provide the nation with the petroleum and food products it lacked. But the foundation upon which the German war machine was created sprang from the mind of Dr. Schacht.

After the attempt on Hitler's life in July 1944, Schacht was arrested and spent the following year in several concentration camps. He was one of the defendants during the postwar Nuremberg Trials and was acquitted by the international tribunal.

FARMERS AND WORKERS

In his campaign speeches, Hitler promised land reforms to small farmers. Among these pledges were the breakup of the huge estates held by the Prussian Junkers, (landowning nobility), the abolition of interest on farm loans and of land speculation. Such assurances of aid were welcomed by a deeply indebted peasantry. Their fear of foreclosure was justified as thousands of farmers were evicted from their ancient holdings. Not only did the farmers lose their livelihood, but their social status dropped from landowner to land worker. This was a serious matter even to the titleholder of the poorest few acres.

The Nazis' promise to ease their condition had won the party much support from the agricultural community. Hitler charged Walter Darré to head the Reich's farm and food ministries. Darré believed that the Aryan race sprang from some mythical interaction of German blood and German soil and thus the preservation of the small farmer was a racial as well as an economic necessity. He instituted price controls and production quotas; the former enabled farmers' incomes to rise; the latter deprived them of their freedom to grow what they wanted. The Reich's Hereditary Farm Law was, at best, a mixed blessing. To ensure that farms of less than 308 acres remained intact, the owner could not sell his property but was forced to pass it on to a single heir, the oldest or youngest son according to local custom. The heir was then obligated to provide for the basic needs of his siblings. Such inherited farms could not be divided, mortgaged, or be foreclosed. While this legislation provided security, it also tied the farmer to the soil. Siblings of the firstborn son often became farmhands on their brother's property. A certain similarity to medieval serfdom is an inescapable observation.

As was noted earlier, the working class lost its right to organize, to bargain collectively, and to strike. In place of independent unions, the German Labor Front was proclaimed the successor to the so-called, "Marxist dominated", labor unions. Hitler appointed Dr. Robert Ley to head the Workmen's League, which was designed to assure the submission of labor to the nationalistic goals of the regime. The Nazification of the trade unions was carried out with a carrot/stick approach. Germany's more than 20 million workers were promised better pay, an end to industrial strife, emergency financial assistance, greater educational opportunities, and stable wages. These assurances were repeated over and over and never fulfilled. But cosmetic changes were made. For example, factory managers were urged to make working conditions more pleasant. Ley instituted "Strength through Joy," a program of recreation for outstanding workers. Highly publicized and financed by the state, participants might go on luxurious vacations, visit theaters, and participate in various sports. The Volkswagen scheme was a unique proposition to promote greater productivity. Laborers by the hundreds of thousands permitted the government to make deductions from their wages toward ownership of a Volkswagen. It must be remembered that very few German factory workers boasted possession of a car, an important status symbol for the middle class. Goebbels' propaganda press waxed ecstatic about the respected status of workingmen and issued posters depicting the well-muscled laborer as the indispensable counterpart of the soldier.

But Germany was not the new Eden for the working class. No Volkswagens rolled off the assembly lines for the men; the money withheld went into the production of tanks instead. Wages remained low as civilian productions were subordinated to the rearmament demands of Hitler's quest for *Lebensraum* (space to live). After 1939, the requirements of war determined employment policies and workers not inducted into the military were pushed to the limit of their endurance. There were no pay raises, only the declarations of gratitude from the government. No longer could a worker choose his occupation freely; a state agency had the right to approve or disapprove changes of employment and residence. As a good soldier must do his duty without complaint, so must the German laborer. The effectiveness of that appeal may be judged by the fact that workers remained at their tasks until the Allies destroyed their factories.

BUSINESS INTERESTS

The gulf between election rhetoric and the actuality of governing was further exemplified by the Nazi attitude toward small businesses. The craftsmen and small shop owners had been promised the breakup of their giant competitors, such as chain and department stores. Large numbers of the lower middle class had voted for the NSDAP, expecting protection for their vulnerable businesses. Such help was never given. The small business associations were dominated by Nazi party members who discouraged political action among their membership. Even when the Jews had been driven from the economic life of the nation, the plight of small enterprises did not improve. The economic welfare of individuals was never a concern of the Nazi hierarchy; the emphasis was always on doing what must be done to assure Germany's victory in the coming war.

The subordination of domestic needs to foreign policy goals, however, enabled the great manufacturers and industrialists to thrive. During the first six years of the Third Reich, they increased their profits from 1.75 million marks to 5 billion marks. Although the government issued innumerable rules and regulations dealing with production, import and export, prices and wages, allotments of raw materials, and the size of the work force, the great corporations flourished. No attempt was made to break up the giant corporations or curb their profits. Hitler knew that their productivity was a vital component of his plans of conquest. If, in the pursuit of his larger goals, the hopes of the workers for a better life were sacrificed, so be it. Without unions, without the right to strike, the workers were powerless against the linked strength of employers and the government.

The re-arming of Germany was to be carried out with a maximum of self-sufficiency and a minimum of imports. The manufacture of substitute products, the ersatz materials, resulted in various synthetics. However, they could not meet the nation's fuel and food requirements. The people could drink coffee made from grain, but tanks and planes could not operate without gasoline. What Germany needed must be taken by force as soon as that force was irresistibly strong. Meanwhile, no matter how eloquent Dr. Goebbels' homage to the virtue of labor, the gap between rich and poor grew wider. It was the soldier, splendid in his uniform, whom children mimicked in their games, not the well-muscled worker on the assembly line.

PUBLIC EDUCATION

"How could the Holocaust have happened in the land of Goethe and Beethoven?" This often-asked question implies a connection between culture and ethics. In this context, the term *culture* refers to a people's art, music, literature, institutions, and prevailing attitudes. These values are passed from one generation to the next and may be accepted, questioned, or altered. Ethics, on the other hand, denotes principles of morality and behavior. The long-held assumption that educated people have higher ethical standards than uneducated people was challenged by Nazi Germany. University degrees and an appreciation for the classics, for example, did not influence the well-educated commanders of the *Einsatzgruppen* as they carried out their bloody business.

As noted above, the Nazis viewed education of the young as an important vehicle for the perpetuation of the nation which they frequently called the Thousand Year Reich. To insure this rather ambitious goal, education became—to a large degree—indoctrination. It is not an exaggeration to state that schooling underwent a revolution at the hands of the Nazis. Before 1933, in conformity with other European institutions of learning, Germans were taught that intelligence was an excellent quality and that degrees from universities opened the way to successful careers. Good students justified their parents' pride and hope. The Nazi ethos, however, adopted an anti-intellectual posture that flew in the face of tradition. The strong body was valued above the brilliant mind, obedience above critical thinking, patriotism above family loyalty, and conformity above individualism. German youth was to be recast in a new image.

The man appointed to Nazify the educational system was an old friend and supporter of Hitler, Bernhard Rust. He had not been a successful pedagogue; his teaching career had ended when he was fired for molesting a schoolgirl. Nonetheless, Rust supervised the centralization of the educational system and the dissolution of local school boards. All professional decisions, including teaching appointments, were under his jurisdiction. He promised to do no less than effect a transformation of German education. To a rather frightening degree, he succeeded.

Rust was able to rely on the enthusiastic support of faculty members who were already committed Nazis. Many were veterans of the Great War, nationalistic to the point of chauvinism, and conservative to right wing in their politics. Even before membership was mandatory, the percentage of educators in the party was considerably larger than the 20 percent of the general population. Remarkably, the proportion of university professors was highest of all. The partnership between school and parents, so familiar to Americans, rarely existed in Germany. The teacher was in charge, period. Most educators fell in line with Rust's new directives; some conformed merely to keep their jobs, others left the profession. Parents did what they had always done: told their children to mind the teacher.

The needs of the state, not the welfare of the child, was the basis of Nazi pedagogy. To guarantee classroom application of this philosophy, only the politically reliable were permitted to teach. Jews were excluded immediately. Teachers with records of democratic or socialist sympathies were dismissed as soon as replacements became available. All academic associations were automatically incorporated into the National Socialist Teachers Organization and, in effect, became extensions of Goebbels' propaganda network. Eventually, all teaching staff were required to enroll in the party and swear an oath of obedience to the Fuehrer. Faculty, from kindergarten to graduate school, was obliged to attend intensive training courses on the new education goals.

Rust initiated some fundamental changes in order to transform German youth into zealous, antiSemitic, obedient Nazis. Physical education was given top priority; usually, it was scheduled for five hours per week. Students who did not complete their PE requirements, regardless of any physical handicaps, could not receive their graduation diplomas. Girls were also compelled to participate in the rigorous body building programs. As the Fatherland needed healthy soldiers, so it needed strong, fertile mothers. Curricula were rewritten to conform with the national ideology. Particular emphasis was placed on changes in history, biology, and German literature. Aryan racial theories were accorded the pretensions of scientific study, and students were required to trace their personal racial inheritance as far back as possible. Readings were purged of the works of Jewish and liberal authors. Every field of instruction was twisted to follow Nazi ideology. For example, a geography lesson emphasized Germany's need for *Lebensraum;* an ancient history class instructed students that the culture of the Germanic tribes was superior to that of the Romans; the physical sciences became a vehicle to demonstrate the biological inferiority of the Jews; and mathematical problems related to the number of bullets needed to kill Germany's enemies. If Jewish children were present, they often were called to the front of the class to have their subhuman features analyzed. The racial superiority of Germans found expression in almost every topic, and a pupil could not spend a single day without learning something about the perfidy of all Jews. Questioning the lesson was discouraged. Students who came to class wearing the uniform of the *Hitler Jugend,* the Nazi youth organization for boys or that of the *Bund Deutscher Maedel,* the girls equivalent, were especially welcome. Physical punishment, usually caning, was not discouraged. Boys and girls who wore glasses, were physically weak, whose parents were not members of the Nazi party, or were serious about scholarship found the atmosphere to be hostile.

TRAINING THE NAZI OF THE FUTURE

The most intense ideological indoctrination of German youth took place within the Nazi Youth movement. The young Baldur von Schirach, a poet by avocation and professional Nazi by vocation, was Hitler's choice to head the Hitler Youth organization. In 1936, all other youth organizations, including church groups and the Boys and Girl Scouts, were outlawed. Membership in the Hitler Youth movement was made compulsory and the state, rather than the party, became its sponsor and financed its budget. Most of the youngsters enjoyed the activities and the bonds of comradeship the groups fostered. The programs included camping, hiking, day and night marches, and many sport competitions. Some groups offered instructions in flying model planes, participation in marching bands and singing contests. Indoctrination into Nazi concepts of race and reverence for the Fuehrer were included at every opportunity. Parental complaints that their children had so little time at home merely assured the troop leaders that they were doing a good job.

Large amounts of money were expended to mold the next generation in the Nazi image. From the ages of six to nineteen and often beyond, the greatest influence on the development of German youngsters was not the parents, not the schools, but the *Hitler Jugend.* Six-year old boys were inducted and called *Pimpfe.* Usually around ten years of age, they advanced to the status of *Jungfolk,* having demonstrated their physical fitness and shouting Nazi slogans. Within three years the youngsters were eligible to be installed in the *Jugend.* Acceptance was not automatic; it depended on passing some highly competitive examinations that tested strength, courage, and the ability to follow orders without question. Some youngsters demonstrated their competence by completing such tasks as laying telephone wire and reading semaphore; preparation for army service was always one of the goals of the organization. Graduation at eighteen promoted the young man into the NSDAP and/or the SA.

Girls were subject to similar regimentation. According to Nazi ideology, the natural sphere for women was the nursery and the kitchen. Members of the *Bund Deutscher Maedel (BDM, Union of German Girls)* were ordered to braid their hair into two pigtails, wear blue skirts and white blouses. When they marched in parades, they usually created a stir of admiration. They too underwent rigorous physical training in order to become healthy mothers of healthy children. Advancement up the organizational ladder depended on enthusiasm and mastery of the tasks tested. There were, however, only three schools to train leaders in the Nazi women's movement. Older girls received instruction in cooking, childcare and homemaking. The view of girls entering the workplace was denigrated; the role of the ideal woman was that of a mother and as an adjunct to her man. Any ambition for independence and equality was characterized as a Jewish-Bolshevik plot.

Even at the age of nineteen, young Germans' commitment to the state was not over. Both men and women were required to give six months of labor service to the nation. Called the *Landjahre,* the supposed theory behind this innovation was that city and country people should know about each others' lives. Urban youths went to work on farms, country youths to the cities. After completing this obligation, men entered the military for their compulsory service. Women were not accepted into the military, they were expected to marry. However, out-of-wedlock children were fully accepted by the party. Pregnant girls were offered the opportunity to deliver their babies in cost-free maternity homes. If they wished, they could rear their children and receive help from the government, or could offer them for adoption. As one would expect, all university enrollment declined during the Nazi era, but that of women dropped most sharply.

The Nazis established three types of schools to train the leaders of the future; the *Adolf Hitler Schulen,* (Adolf Hitler Schools), the *NAPOLAS,* (National-Political Training Institutes), and the *Ordensburgen* (Order Castles). The *Hitler Schulen* selected students of promise from among the *Jungvolk.* Racial background, particularly blond hair and blue eyes were of the greatest importance. Their training emphasized military ideals with five periods of physical training and one-and-a-half of academic study per week. Nonetheless, after completing the course the young men were considered ready to enter universities.

The second of the training institutions, the *NAPOLAS,* aimed to educate officials for important posts in the Third Reich. Although under the direction of the Nazi party, the old Prussian academies which had offered academic and military instruction, served as models. Of course, the sons of loyal Nazis were given preference in the enrollment. By 1938 there were 23 such schools but few cadets were able to fulfill their ambitions; the war pulled the graduates into the army.

Candidates who had been judged fit for future roles in the highest echelon of the party might be placed into one of the four *Ordensburge.* These students were older, alumni of the Adolf Hitler schools, usually in their mid-twenties when they were offered the chance to be among the elite. They lived in castles amid medieval settings and ceremonies that created a mystique of brotherhood and service. The philosophy underlying their training is best summed up by their motto: "Believe, Obey, Fight." The SS ran these institutions and expected that its graduates would join their officer corps. The war, however, absorbed most of them as well before they could reach their intended goal.

Anyone visiting Germany in the prewar Nazi years would be charmed by its polite, goodlooking youth. Healthy, respectful, and active, they compared favorably with children of other nations. That was one side of the coin. The other side involved the rapid decline of the intellectual standards in German schools and universities. Everyone was overtaxed with rounds of endless activities that had no connection to studies. One might assume that juvenile delinquency had disappeared inasmuch as young people seemed to live in a perpetual, albeit highly regulated, summer camp. The facts refute such assumptions. Gangs were still active, and juvenile lawlessness continued to exist—an interesting puzzle for the sociologists.

THE CHRISTIAN CHURCHES

Much has been written about Hitler's campaign against the churches. But this battle did not destroy the major Christian institutions. While no church was burned down or turned into a museum, it was the spirit of Christianity that was under siege. Even though the official philosopher of the NSDAP, Alfred Rosenberg, denounced Christianity and tried to promote a cult of pagan worship, the German masses rejected his *Mythus*. Rosenberg's claim that Jesus was an aggressive, revolutionary Nordic whose essence was perverted into a faith of Christian meekness fell on deaf ears. Few Germans accepted his Aryan creed of a gospel of racial purity. Not even the Protestants accepted his denigration of Popes as mere merchants of snake oil.

Hitler wanted no confrontation with the churches. It was enough to bring them into line by restricting many of their functions. The Nazis closed most religious schools and outlawed religious fraternal organizations. Freedom to teach the tenets of the faith was severely curtailed. But persecution is a relative concept. The doors of the churches remained open. Some individual members of the clergy, both Catholic and Protestant, suffered greatly for preaching anti-Nazi sermons. The vast majority of priests and ministers, however, went about their business as best they could and kept clear of dangerous topics. That list included such essential ideals as love thy neighbor, turn the other cheek, and the concept that obedience to God takes precedence over obedience to man. Thus, the churches continued to function in the observance of rituals while the spirit of Christianity was deeply tarnished.

Individual members of the clergy who spent years in concentration camps for resisting the Nazis deserve the accolades of their congregations, but their heroism was personal. German religious institutions did not battle the Nazi anti-Christ; instead, by their silence they permitted the perpetration of terrible wrongs. Hymns were sung, masses said, and baptisms celebrated, but the doctrines of mercy, love, peace, and equality before God were suspended.

HITLER AND THE PAPACY

The Catholic Center party had opposed the Nazis even after the *Gleichschaltung* (bringing into line) of all political parties. Hitler appreciated the potential opposition of the Centrists. Although the Fuehrer did not practice the faith of his parents, he never underestimated the power of religion. He not only wanted to avoid an all-out conflict with German Catholics, he courted their support. Shortly after coming to power, in 1933 he concluded a concordat with Pope Pius XI. This agreement guaranteed the free exercise of the Catholic religion in Germany, the right of Catholic children to receive religious instruction in public schools, and the protection of church institutions. The Vatican, in return, recognized the regime and promised to dismantle its church-sponsored social and political organizations.

Hitler derived immediate benefits from the treaty. His reputation for diplomacy was considerably enhanced. Before long, however, the Nazis violated many provisions of the agreement, and the hope to safeguard the Catholic institutions in Germany ended in humiliating failure. The Catholic Youth League was dissolved, classroom religious instruction was banned, and religious publications were prohibited. The Center Party had, of course, met the same fate as other political parties, it was abolished. During worship the Nazis intimidated congregations by the presence of uniformed SA and SS men in the churches.

The ideal of a perfect race ran counter to the Christian obligation to love all the Lord's creations, no matter how impaired. When the Nazis actualized their plan to sterilize those Germans judged too "defective" to have children, the churches objected strongly. Nevertheless, the medical procedures continued. By 1937, some 200,000 people had been sterilized for reasons such as schizophrenia, alcoholism, and a range of physical problems. The objective of creating the master race took an even more heartbreaking turn when it was decided to stop feeding "useless eaters." So-called misfits were quietly, secretly murdered. When Cardinal/Archbishop Clemens von Galen of Muenster became aware of these "euthanasia" killings, he declared from the pulpit that this practice was a grievous sin. Fear of public reaction brought an end to the use of lethal injections and gassings of children and adults. This victory came too late for an estimated 100,000 victims. Von Galen's success raises the inescapable question: What might have been the Nazi reaction if the churches had protested the disappearance of the Jews?

The persecution of Catholics grew more pronounced over the years. Arrests of individual members of the clergy were carried out in public, and the press published stories of the alleged immorality of the accused. Priests and nuns suspected of trying to save Jews were sent to concentration camps, sometimes after a trial by a Nazi court, the so-called *Volksgericht* (Peoples' Court), and sometimes without any trial. Pius XI issued an encyclical in 1937 entitled "With Deep Anxiety" in which he deplored Hitler's breach of the concordat, the illegal persecution of Catholics and the Nazi promotion of a cult of race and blood. Upon his death in 1939, Pius XI was succeeded by Pius XII. Several of his messages expressed concern over the fate of the non-Aryans, mainly Jews who had converted to Catholicism, but he declared that he could offer no other succor than prayers. The Jews and their fate were never mentioned. The Vatican was later censured for its silence by Jews and gentiles, individuals and institutions. Defenders of the Pope responded that his protests would have harmed Catholics without benefiting the persecuted Jews. Obviously, the entire question of the official reaction of the papacy to the Holocaust remains a painful issue to this day. It should be noted that Pope John Paul II has asked for forgiveness for the sins of omission in an encyclical in 1998.

PROTESTANT RESPONSES

The relationship between the Nazi state and the Protestant communities failed to develop into a consistent policy. Neither the government nor the religious groups found a satisfactory method of dealing with the other. The official stance was to reduce the influence of traditional religion without causing serious opposition. Several different approaches were tried, sometimes at the same time. The attempt to crush the independence of the churches by placing them under the control of a synod of pro-Nazi ministers was not successful. The Nazis were unable to unify or completely control the church federation they established under the Evangelical theologian Ludwig Mueller. Mueller was given the title of Reich Bishop, but the so-called German Faith Movement failed to attract mass support. The notion of joining Christianity with Nordic paganism revealed the muddled thinking of Alfred Rosenberg. The great majority of Protestants resisted this Nazi version of their faith. Hitler himself kept aloof; he knew that pushing the people too far and too fast from long-established tradition would cost him popular support. Finally, the Nazis had to settle for weakening the churches by the tactics they had found most successful: intimidation, harassment, and even terror. Protestant ministers, like priests, were arrested during services in front of worshipers. Both the fear and the reality of imprisonment in concentration camps stilled all but a few voices of protest among the clergy.

German Protestants, numbering about 45 million out of a total population of some 60 million, were not a homogeneous group. The majority were Lutherans, followed by Calvinists, with smaller representations of Methodists and Baptists. The several thousand Jehovah's Witnesses deserve mention because the Nazis persecuted them relentlessly for their steadfast adherence to the doctrine of the superiority of God to man and for their dedication to peace. Further divisions occurred within the denominations over the issue of cooperation with the Nazis. It is important to remember that Martin Luther, the towering figure of the Reformation, was fiercely antiSemitic. His unrestrained verbal attacks on the Jews were not equaled until Goebbels' rhetoric. The Nazis, of course, invoked these denunciations to fortify the concept that it was possible to remain a devout Protestant while becoming an equally devout Nazi. The great reformer had been an ardent German nationalist, who exhorted his followers to give unquestioning and complete obedience to civil authority. Thus, Nazi aims dovetailed with Lutheran doctrine.

Most of the reformed churches tried to avoid running afoul of the authorities by preaching "safe" sermons. In the process, essential Christian doctrine was watered down to observance of rites and rituals in an atmosphere of disquiet. Some Christians, however, raised their voices in opposition. The best known among these was the Reverend Martin Niemoeller. A highly decorated U-boat captain of World War I, he had described his wartime experiences in a best seller, thus his name was familiar to most Germans. A fervent nationalist, he had supported the rising Hitler. But the actuality of Nazis in power and their racial and anti-Christian policies offended and disillusioned him. An activist by nature, he became the leader of a religious resistance movement. His confessional church was a counterweight, albeit an ineffectual one, to Hitler's German Faith Organization.

Niemoeller was the guiding spirit of the Pastors' Emergency League and the Confessional Church. In 1934, its members drafted a statement declaring their opposition to Nazi interference in church affairs and to the doctrine that might makes right. They also declared that Christianity was irreconcilable with the Nazis' German Faith Movement. At its height, Niemoeller's organization included some 7,000 of approximately 17,000 Lutheran ministers. The Gestapo responded swiftly. More than 700 ministers were arrested and usually sent home after a brief but highly "educational" imprisonment. Pastors who were deemed unlikely to fall into line, numbering about fifty, were sent to concentration camps. Hitler was concerned that the voices raised in favor of the arrested clergy could harm national unity. He preferred a gradual rather than an abrupt weakening of the power of the church. Direct pressure was eased. Niemoeller, however, was seen as the spark of the movement. In 1937, after preaching a sermon on obedience to God, not man, he was arrested. He was tried in a special court on charges of "abuse of the pulpit." Since his sentence was shorter than the time already served while awaiting trial, the court ordered his release. As he left the courtroom, however, he was arrested by the Gestapo and placed under "protective custody." He survived seven years in various concentration camps until, in 1945, he was finally liberated by the Allies.

It would be misleading to see Pastor Niemoeller as spearheading an army of righteous Christians. During the seven years he endured the Sachsenhausen and Dachau camps, he was almost forgotten by the German people. The brief candle of protest, the Confessional Church, was quickly snuffed out by the Gestapo. Only after the German defeat did Pastor Niemoeller become a hero once again. He had been a "good German," a symbol of German decency and courage, in the face of the general submission of the Protestants to the repression of religious freedom. It also needs to be said that he had no interest in the fate of the Jews.

NAZI JUSTICE

Every sphere of life in the Third Reich was subordinated to the ideal of the *Volksgemeinschaft,* that is, the ideological and organizational unity of the German people. Individual rights had to give way to communal rights; individuals and institutions were measured only by the new criteria established by the Nazis: Did this person or institution promote the Nazi *Weltanschauung* of blood, race, *Volk,* and conquest? Those who failed to advance Nazi ideals were deemed useless; those who stood in the way had to be rooted out. Ruthlessness, even cruelty, became a virtue in the battle to destroy the real and imagined enemies of the new order. Concepts of justice were no exception. The regime was based on the decisions of men, not the rule of immutable laws designed to secure lives and property in a civilized society.

The Third Reich did not issue a new legal code. The existing system was reinterpreted to suit the contemporary realities. Most of the sitting judges were already nationalistic and conservative, and some were committed Nazis. With the exception of Jewish jurists, there was no wholesale dismissal of judges. The courts continued to function. New harsh laws poured forth from Berlin in a constant stream, mainly in connection with safeguarding racial purity and protecting the regime from opposition. By 1945, there were forty-three crimes punishable by execution, including *Rassenschande*—defilement of race by sexual intercourse between Aryan and non-Aryan. Crimes committed by juveniles were tried in adult courts. The criminal justice code sanctioned beating of prisoners during questioning—but not more than twenty-five blows delivered to the buttocks. This practice was officially approved as was the use of torture by the Gestapo and SS.

It was still possible to get justice in a German court in some civil and criminal cases, but that was by no means a certainty. If a party member sued a nonmember, the verdict was likely to be tainted; if an individual hoped to win against the community, his case was doomed. Those sworn to uphold the law became accomplices in crimes against humanity; judges signed the orders for sterilization and euthanasia. The preservers of law had become its despoilers.

The Nazis were unceasingly preoccupied with the possibility of political counteraction. The Gestapo alone employed thousands of informers whose identity was unknown to the public. Remarks implying the slightest criticism, even a joke, could be interpreted as a political crime under the Law Against Malicious Attacks on State and Party. To deal with the spate of accusations, special courts were established whose judges were fiercely loyal to the regime. Cases involving so-called treason were heard by the Nazis' *Volksgericht,* the People's Court, which consisted of a combination of party jurists and high-ranking Nazi officials. The proceedings had little resemblance to our understanding of justice. Defendants were threatened, denounced, and shouted down by the judges. There was no appeal of the verdicts. When an attempt on Hitler's life misfired on July 20, 1944, the highest *Volksgericht* ordered the execution of between 180 and 200 accused conspirators. Cases involving party members were tried by yet another innovation, *Parteigerichte* (the "Party Courts"). These tribunals were generally used to discipline members of the NSDAP and punish administrative irregularities.

The most tragic perversion of justice was the Holocaust. The criminals, that is the SS, were empowered to act as judges, juries, and executioners. The question of wrongdoing by the victims was irrelevant; to be a Jew was a capital crime. Himmler had become the master of the Jews and other "enemies of the state," and the SS had the right to take their possessions, their liberty, and their lives without the formality of accusation, trial, and verdict. The Nazis' civilian victims are reckoned to number 6 million Jews and 5 million non-Jews.

CHAPTER 6

German Jews to 1939

The term antiSemitism originated in Germany. It was first introduced into the vocabulary in the 1870s by Wilhelm Marr in his book *The Victory of Judaism over Germanism* and popularized by the diverse factions that opposed the integration of Jews into the life of the German Empire. The fact that hatred of Jews was given a new designation in the recently unified nation confirmed that a new dimension had been added to an ancient prejudice. No longer was the age-old aversion based solely on its Christian antecedents, but the taint of racial inferiority was now superimposed on the long-accepted religious bias. AntiSemitism became the catchword that sanctioned the notion that an inherent incompatibility existed between Jews and Gentiles. Thus, the theory evolved that a number of supposed negative "Jewish characteristics," ranging from avarice to zealousness, were inborn and inbred. As a result, Jews could never be part of the Germanic people, even if they converted to Christianity. Nor would their residency on German soil, be it of hundreds of years in duration, alter their inability to be part of the *Volk*. The acceptance by some Germans of such sophistry in the nineteenth century marked a reversal, perhaps a conservative reaction, of the generally more liberal attitude of the era.

EMANCIPATION

The medieval persecution of the Jewish people in Europe had been deeply rooted in the deicide (God-killer) myth. The refusal of the Jews to accept Christ was viewed as an unforgivable perversion. The miserable state of Jewish life, though caused by severe economic restrictions, was explained in religious terms: This was God's punishment for their rejection of the Savior. All past sins, however, could be absolved through conversion. Beginning with the Age of Reason (also called the Age of Enlightenment), during the eighteenth century, Christian control weakened and some of the old assumptions concerning the Jews were challenged. The great writers of the era, the *philosophes,* men such as Jean Jaques Rousseau, Voltaire, and Montesquieu, who agitated for fundamental political and social changes, paved the way for the coming French Revolution. They insisted that human institution must be based on logic, not tradition, not religious doctrine. They attacked the political abso-lutism of the French government and its compliant sister, the church. In the process the prevailing anti-Jewish prejudices were questioned. The course of the French Revolution would have amazed the *philosophes,* though the slogan, Liberty, Equality, Fraternity might have pleased some of them. When Napoleon made himself the ruler of France and beyond, his soldiers carried these revolutionary ideals into central Europe. Although liberty was slow in coming and fraternity is still a dream, the concept of equal treatment before the law had significant effect and influenced the treatment of the Jews.

By the end of the eighteenth century, Jews in Central Europe, France, and England had been granted most civil rights. As the ghetto walls fell, its former occu-pants were grateful and hopeful that the forces of rationalism would allow them to live peacefully as citizens in the Gentile world.

In Germany the Jews lived on a roller coaster of hope and despair for more than a century. The pull of the old conservatives and the push of the Enlightenment contracted and advanced their hopes of acceptance. The achievements of Moses Mendelssohn (1729–1786) had raised their expectations of entering into the full rhythm of German life. Mendelssohn, the "German Plato," exhorted the Jews to emulate educated Germans; speak their language, read their literature, and study the natural sciences, history, and philosophy. In the intellectual salons where men and women of learning came together, Jews and Gentiles met as equals. The eagerness of German Jewry to be accepted inspired them to embrace German culture enthusiast-ically. The voices of admonition raised by the Orthodox rabbinate could not hold back the desire of most German Jews to join the mainstream of national life. They hoped that cultural conversion could accomplish what religious conversion had done in the past, but without the loss of their Jewish faith.

CAN JEWS BE GERMANS?

Germany was not unified into a single nation until 1871. Bismarck's political achievements were followed by rapid economic growth, as German industry com-peted to manufacture goods for international markets. German Jews eagerly partici-pated in these expanding economic opportunities. As they entered and succeeded in various business and professional pursuits, voices of opposition grew stronger. Even though this renewed anti-Jewish agitation rested upon the old overt and covert reli-gious antipathies, now the claim of ethnic incompatibility opened a new anti-Jewish front. The indictment alleged that Jews were ethnically and culturally different, "aliens in our midst," who could never be true Germans. Modern German anti-Semitism had found a new theory to support an old resentment.

The second half of the nineteenth century was a period of great economic, social, and political upheaval. Power was shifting from the landowners to the middle class; factories replaced farms as the nation's preeminent workplaces; scientists and philosophers confronted and questioned many long-accepted articles of faith. The unpropertied classes were no longer quietly grateful for the opportunity to work; instead, they organized to gain some political influence. These displacements were accompanied by stress and confusion and, as in bygone eras, some people held the Jews responsible for their loss of status and security.

ECONOMIC ANTISEMITISM

Throughout the Middle Ages and beyond, Jews had been subjected to severe economic restrictions. The rulers of the more than 300 German principalities regulated the activities of "their" Jews for centuries. A few "court Jews" found favor and employment, usually in the management of money, at the courts of the petty states, but they were few in number. For the most part the Jews lived in ghettos and in their ability to make a living they were not permitted to compete with Christians. Generally, they were limited to petty trading, horse and cattle dealing, and money-lending. Some few Jewish artisans provided for the needs of fellow Jews within the ghetto. In southern Germany, the law provided that only one son could enter into the business or occupation of his father. Permission for craftsmen, such as tailors, carpenters, shoemakers, furriers, goldsmiths, and the like to sell to the world outside the ghetto was rarely authorized. Generation after generation of Jews competed with one another in the narrow economic perimeters allotted to them.

During the first half of the nineteenth century, the door to economic opportunity opened a crack. The Napoleonic wars (ended in 1815), were followed by the gradual emancipation of Western and Central European Jews. Most German states (their number was reduced to thirty by Napoleon) permitted Jews to do business with the Gentile world on a more equitable footing. The unification of Germany and the ensuing industrial expansion gave Jews entry into growing trade and manufacturing activities. The revolution in production required modernization of business methods, particularly in finance and banking. Now the middlemen, the traders, the storekeepers, the men who understood investments and the raising of capital, were in demand. Workers were needed to man the machines. Factory owners were not interested in the religious affiliation of their labor force.

For the Jews, such economic changes were not obstacles; rather, they were opportunities. Many took full advantage of these new possibilities and often they succeeded. Within a generation or two, many poor Jews had entered the middle class and a few became rich and powerful. As they embraced bourgeois economic values, they usually adopted the prevailing German moral and cultural standards as well. With an enthusiasm often typical of newcomers seeking acceptance, they plunged into German art and literature as admirers and as contributors. The German language replaced Yiddish, modern dress was substituted for the somber traditional garb. The process of change permitted Jews to live less isolated and restrictive lives. For Jewish intellectuals the bounty of European culture, its literature, scientific and artistic accomplishments, were a feast for the senses.

German Jews, by and large, espoused emancipation and acculturation. Their successes, however, reawakened a barely dormant antiSemitism. The economic upheaval that accompanied the development of German industry frustrated those who did not or could not benefit from it. Social and political power was no longer limited to the landholding nobility as money challenged old and respected family position. The cycles of boom and bust, the hardships caused by recurring periods of unemployment, the emergence of new wealth and new poverty—all were factors in creating insecurity and anxiety. Who could be blamed for ushering in this new and, for some, frightening state of affairs?

Because there is no connection between prejudice and reality, it was not difficult to target the Jews. Capitalists, unhappy with the growing Socialist movement among their workers, noted that some of the labor leaders were Jews. Factory workers, protesting the avarice of the owners, pointed to the few Jews among manufacturers. When wild speculation resulted in the crash of 1873, the press singled out Jews for condemnation. Monetary inflation and deflation can cause economic hardships and Jews were held responsible for both. Although the name of Rothschild was held in high esteem in financial circles, it was the opinion of the anti-Jewish establishment that the banking house had become entirely too rich and powerful.

POLITICAL ANTISEMITISM

Expansion of suffrage in national and state elections in the German Empire stimulated the development of political parties, ranging from the reactionary to the radical. The majority of German Jews supported liberal politicians. This fact aroused the antagonism of some factions within conservative and reactionary circles. Even Otto von Bismarck, the architect of German unification and venerated chancellor until 1890, was willing to use the convenient Jewish scapegoat. Bismarck the politician had lost two major battles in his long and usually successful career; he was unable to reduce the influence of Catholicism (*Kulturkampf*) in Germany, and he could not stem the tide of socialism among the working class. Jewish leaders had supported him in both these battles and when he failed to win them, he blamed the Jews.

German conservatives discovered that antiSemitic propaganda had vote-getting power. In courting the blue-collar middle class, shopkeepers, craftsmen, and petty officials, the promise to restrict Jewish competition was effective ammunition. Many of the recently enfranchised factory workers joined socialist parties that were not apt to include antiSemitism in their platforms. But other parties, too, vied to enroll them into their ranks. Among these was the Christian Social Workingmen's Party.

Founded in 1878 by Adolf Stoecker, the official court chaplain of Emperor William I, this organization made vilification of Jews its centerpiece. Stoecker, like Hitler, was an eloquent speaker, a rabid antiSemite and a good organizer. Several international anti-Jewish congresses were convened in Germany with his endorsement. For the first, but certainly not the last time, a delegate from an overtly anti-Semitic party took his seat in the Reichstag. Stoecker demanded the revocation of citizenship for Jews and their removal from certain professions. But his diatribes were too regressive even for Bismarck, who declared that the nation would not permit religious affiliation to intrude on the rights of citizenship.

AntiSemitism had considerable political appeal. The Catholic centrists joined with the Conservative Party to include a pledge in their platform to combat the so called "oppressive and disintegrating Jewish influence on our national life." Ambitious politicians gave assurances that Jews would be "kept in their place." They promised their constituents that only Christians would teach their children and serve them as magistrates.

The phrase, so often repeated by the Nazis, "the Jews are our misfortune," was given legitimacy, even respectability, when used by the renowned historian Heinrich von Treitschke. So forceful were the accusations coming from the extreme nationalists, from certain members of the clergy and from the ever-present clique of opportunists, that antiSemitic violence broke out. During the last quarter of the nineteenth century these disturbances resulted in the destruction of property and physical injury to Jews. With the exception of the Socialists, no civil authority took these riots seriously. Many German Jews, however, recognized that they needed to exert themselves on their own behalf. What forms their self-defense should take remained a divisive question until Hitler supplied the answer.

JEWISH REACTION: THE REFORM MOVEMENT

The Jews of Imperial Germany, citizens under the law but attacked by powerful forces, were facing a dilemma. The great majority continued to await complete acceptance by their Christian fellow nationals. They believed that it was possible to serve two masters, to be patriotic Germans and retain their religious attachment to the ancient faith. There were Catholic Germans, Lutheran Germans, why not Jewish Germans? *Deutschtum* was not incompatible with *Judentum.* For theological and philosophical reasons as well as the desire to facilitate the process of acculturation, German Jews initiated the modernization of religious practices. Rites and beliefs that were obsolete or considered contrary to the judgments of modern science were discarded or changed. Dietary prohibitions, the use of phylacteries in prayer, and the separation of men and women in synagogues were held to be outdated. Choirs and organ music were introduced to enhance the service. Sermons were preached in German. Prayer books were revised, and German translations of Hebrew texts were provided. Predictably, Orthodox Jews who remained the most numerous, were appalled and accused the reformers of abandoning Judaism for Germanism. The fact that members of Reform congregations were more likely to marry outside their faith and were often lost to the Jewish people gave substance to their fears.

But there was more to the Reform movement than the search for public acceptance. It was a revitalization of the faith. The need to bring harmony to Jewish civil and spiritual life was real. The foremost advocate of reform was Abraham Geiger, a noted scholar and critic who became chief rabbi of the synagogue of Breslau. He believed that the outward forms of Judaism must not be dictated from antiquity, but as a vital living faith. In his view the ethical essence of the religion was not altered by the elimination of archaic ritual. To the distress of the Orthodox rabbinate, prayers for the coming of the messiah and the Jews' return to Zion were eliminated. The rationale was that German Jews must look upon Germany as their one and only homeland. It should be stressed that Reform Judaism removed none of the moral requirements from the Judaic faith. The command to act with righteousness and the struggle for social justice, two concepts rooted in the Torah, remained central in the Reform movement. The very success of the reformers widened the gap between the traditionalists and the modernists and theological debates sometimes disintegrated into factious quarrels.

IS ZIONISM THE ANSWER?

The desire of the German Jews to be treated as equals with their Christian neighbors was not generally shared by the Gentile world. No matter how sincerely the Jews proclaimed their patriotism, how eagerly they embraced German culture, how successfully they advanced German economic progress, antiSemitism did not disappear. Although most German Jews continued to hope that time and education would work on their behalf, many Jews were forced to face the obvious. Most painful was the unwillingness of the German government to protect their legal rights during riotous antiSemitic outbursts. What more could they do? What more should they do? One reaction, indeed an ancient one, was to flee. The modern equivalent of flight, that is emigration, caused large numbers to seek asylum beneath the outstretched arm of the Statue of Liberty. By 1880 the United States had opened its doors to 250,000 German-speaking Jews. They were literate, many had skills, and they were hard working. Town and cities on the East Coast, the West Coast, and the vast areas in between were enriched by their contributions to the cultural and economic life of the United States. Although statistically their numbers were soon overshadowed by the influx of Eastern European Jews, the mark they left on American Jewish institutions was indelible.

The majority of Jewish Germans remained in the Reich. They continued to anticipate and advocate their complete integration into the fabric of German life. Through their achievements, they hoped to convince the government and their fellow citizens that they constituted an asset to the nation. Every friendly gesture on the part of the politically and socially powerful was hailed as evidence of their acceptance, every setback characterized as temporary.

But not all German Jews shared this optimism. A gradually increasing number believed that only a Jewish homeland could solve the so-called Jewish question. Zionism was the movement that called for the reestablishment of a Jewish nation in the Holy Land. Its modern beginning was the work of Eastern Jews. The czars of Russia had persecuted the Jewish people for generations and idealistic young men and women chose to exchange Russian despotism for a return to the ancient homeland. The life they chose in the Jewish enclaves of Turkish Palestine and its barren and malaria-infested soil was backbreaking and dangerous. In Western Europe, however, Zionism was in direct conflict with assimilationism, and its appeal was very limited; that is, until the emergence of the remarkable Theodor Herzl.

Herzl, born in 1860 in Budapest, grew up in a home where Reform Judaism was practiced. He worked in Vienna as a writer and journalist, barely affected by his occasional brushes with antiSemitism. He was working as a newspaper correspondent in Paris when the trial of Captain Alfred Dreyfus, a Jew, aroused widespread interest throughout the western world. There he was, in the cultural center of Europe, among the people who had declared liberty, equality and fraternity a national motto, who nonetheless practiced blatant discrimination. Dreyfus's alleged guilt was transformed into public shouts of "Death to the Jews." Herzl not only came face to face with an ancient problem, he was challenged to find solutions and devoted his life to their realization.

His Zionism centered around three concepts: 1) AntiSemitism is a permanent, fixed condition; 2) the Jews are like any other nation but for the lack of a homeland; 3) Palestine should become the national territory for the homeland of the Jewish people. Jews had been at the mercy of the Gentile world for nearly 2000 years and nowhere were they secure. Only through the establishment of a state of their own could they achieve peace and equality. Despite the fact that relatively few German Jews actually settled in that neglected and impoverished Turkish province, the Zionist movement won considerable financial and ideological support. The ZV or *Zionistische Vereinigung* (Zionist Union) combined separate chapters into a single organization which enhanced its strength and voice. Its members contributed monetarily to the establishment of some of the earliest Kibbutzim (collective agricultural settlements) in Palestine.

THE CV REACTION

The assimilationists protested vehemently against the idea of a Jewish homeland. Their efforts had been directed toward convincing their Christian neighbors that Jews were citizens whose patriotic devotion could not be challenged. Now the Zionists asserted that integration into the national life of the Diaspora was at best unrealistic. This, they claimed, played into the hands of anti-Semites. Their own union, the CV, or *Centralverein deutscher Staatsbuerger Juedisches Glaubens* (Central Union of German Citizens of the Jewish Faith), exerted pressure on the German government to end all remaining discrimination. The CV considered it a point of honor to combat antiSemitism, not submissively, but as their right as German citizens. Its legal arm fought bias in the courts while its educational efforts stressed the timelessness and significance of Jewish values. Although fearful of political activity, the organization represented 60,000, or 12 percent, of German Jewry. They expected that the problem of *Deutschtum* versus *Judentum* would be resolved and soon Jews would practice their faith as comfortably as did the German Protestants and Catholics.

But antiSemitism has no rational basis and is not open to sensible approaches. Heinrich Class's book *Wenn Ich Kaiser Wer* (*If I Were Emperor*) made that point emphatically. Published in 1912, Class fanned the old fires of anti-Semitism and kindled some new ones. He urged the enactment of laws forbidding Jews from voting, removing them from public service, banning them from the armed forces, prohibiting them from owning land and excluding their service as directors in some institutions. He further suggested that they pay double the ordinary taxes. When the Nazis came to power they found these suggestions inspirational for their own legislative actions.

WORLD WAR I AND THE WEIMAR YEARS

The rift between the Zionists and the assimilationists was temporarily healed by the outbreak of the First World War. In a paroxysm of patriotic fervor all differences were buried, not only among Jews but former political opponents rallied enthusiastically round Kaiser and flag. German Socialists, for example, dropped all pretense of solidarity with workers in other nations; the fact that the soldiers facing them on the battlefield might be French socialists ceased to be important. Clearly, nationalism had overwhelmed internationalism.

German Jews donned the uniforms and fought side by side with their Christian neighbors. As long as German victories fed the national ego, antiSemitism was given a respite, albeit a short one. When the war ended in 1918, four years of carnage had destroyed much more than lives, property and empires. The optimistic view that human progress was the destiny of Western man had been invalidated in the trenches. The post-war generation was born to cynicism, to economic and political turmoil, and to pessimism. Alienation was the catchword and the good old days were recalled as having been much better than they actually were. In the bitterness over a lost war and the ensuing disorder and revolutions the familiar scapegoat was again hauled to the surface. The trauma of defeat needed justification and once again guilt was placed at the accustomed doorstep.

Between 1919 and 1933 Germany tried democracy. The fundamental laws had been drafted in the city of Weimar and that city gave its name to the following fourteen years of German history. The Weimar Constitution established a democratic republic which was modeled in part after the English and United States systems. Most German Jews who numbered about 1 percent of total population of 60 million, supported the liberal, pro-republican parties. The Republic granted total equality to all citizens, regardless of religious affiliations. For Jews it seemed the attainment of all their hopes. Their children graduated in increasing numbers from universities, entered the professions, worked in financial institutions and became active in politics. Their contributions to the arts and the entertainment industry made Jews more visible to the general public. Many went into their own business; forty-six percent were self-employed. Intermarriage with Christians reached an extraordinary 60 percent.

But, as was noted in Chapter 3, the Weimar years were turbulent. The German people did not easily adapt to the uncertainties of democratic politics. The Treaty of Versailles, always referred to as the *Diktat,* continued to fester in the national consciousness. Many were incensed by the unseemly abuse of freedom that frequently resulted in violence. Fanatics on the right and the left of the political spectrum short-circuited the election process by assassinating government officials. Among the casualties was Walter Rathenau, the Jewish minister of foreign affairs. He was killed by men who thought his death would somehow avenge the German defeat. The comment made by Rathenau's mother reveals the extent of the delusion which gripped Jewish society: Referring to her son's murderers, she said that if only they had known him, what a fine man he was, how totally devoted to the Fatherland, they would not have killed him.

Attempts by extremists to overthrow the government shook the republic but did not topple it. It survived for fourteen years, led by coalitions of Socialists and Centrists who tried to cope with mounting internal and external pressures. The Nazis on the political right and the Communists on the left were as one in their hope to overthrow the young Republic.

The Weimar years were also a period of startling contrasts. Never before had Germans enjoyed such freedom of expression nor had they been subjected to such political and financial instability. It was an age of great artistic achievements in architecture (the *Bauhaus* School), in film making (Marlene Dietrich's *Blue Angel*), in modern art (Dadaism), and in literature (Erich Maria Remarque's *All Quiet on the Western Front*). The seamy side of the liberated spirit was seen in the cities. License translated into licentiousness. Excesses of every sort from pornography to gross exhibition of opulence made headlines that disgusted the struggling majority of Germans. Advocates of tradition collided with these new currents and blamed the amorality of the decade on the overindulgence of artistic and personal liberties. Some Jewish artists and playwrights were in the forefront of modern expression. Not unexpectedly, some Germans chose to blame them for all the evils that had befallen the nation.

Although the Jews had complete legal equality, most of the established bureaucracy of the defunct German Empire of William II had been left in place. They were the members of the old guard who viewed the republic with something between distaste and hostility. Their continued authority guaranteed that anti-Semitism remained in public institutions. Nor did hatred of Jews abate in the private sector. German Jews were represented in disproportionate numbers in areas most visible to public view, such as the entertainment industry, the press, the legal profession, and as owners of large department stores. Their achievements energized the old antipathies. Hitler was not the only politician to realize the vote-getting power of antiSemitism; he was, however, by far the most successful.

EARLY RESPONSES TO THE NAZI DANGER

Why didn't the German Jews see Hitler's handwriting on the wall? Why did they not flee while there was still time? These questions are often asked but they are based on the wisdom of hindsight. For those living in the early 1930s, the choices were not so clear.

Most German Jews loved their homeland and felt emotionally and culturally tied to it. Their attachment blurred their vision. Even though the increase of Nazi delegates in the Reichstag was worrisome, emigration was viewed as unnecessary, even unpatriotic. In the years preceding 1933, many political observers believed that Nazi antiSemitic venom was merely a vote-getting tactic. If Hitler ever came to power, so ran the argument, such rhetoric would cease and certainly would never be enacted into law. It was unthinkable that any German government would revert to the methods of medieval absurdity. Although debates concerning the wisdom of emigrating echoed in every Jewish home, the general consensus was to sit tight, wait, don't panic. The few who had pursued political careers and some of the highly visible stars in the entertainment business left the country. For the majority, "Let things settle down" was the motto. Not even in their nightmares could they imagine the Shoah. Yes, they suffered indignities at the hands of those hooligan Brownshirts; yes, there was destruction of property and even several murders. But these were illegal acts, and the courts were bound to reestablish the rule of law. After all, this was Germany, a nation proud of its civilization.

Let us suppose that a family decided to leave Germany in 1934. Where could they go? To places with unpronounceable names that one could hardly find on a map? What would happen to parents and grandparents who would not or could not go? Or the sickly ones whom no country wanted? What of the businesses, built up over many years? How can one just walk away? For the rich and famous, the doors opened wide; for families of middle-class means or the Jewish poor, the choices were few or none. The Western world had not yet recovered from the Great Depression; every nation was struggling to keep the number of its unemployed from increasing. It was not a time to take in strangers.

"Be strong, be patient, it will pass"—such was the reassuring advice offered by Jewish newspapers. The leaders of the CV urged the Jews to react with dignity and self-respect, with helpfulness toward each other and with perseverance. Since these were the words the Jewish community wanted to hear, they were heeded. There were, however, some warning voices. Realists who carefully studied the Nazi leadership, the mood of the people and the indifference of other nations to the rise of Nazi power, tried to sound the alarm: Leave, run for your lives. But where to? The United States State Department urged its German consuls to issue visas sparingly.

Other nations would only admit refugees who could support themselves without going to work. In other words, the immigrants could not add to the number of jobless natives. So, the wishful thinking drowned the warnings of the realists. Only Hitler's increasing terror tactics and the *Kristallnacht* pogrom awakened the majority of German Jews to their perilous situation. Then, when every corner of the globe was considered a possible refuge, they waited patiently outside the gates of embassies, hoping for a visa to anywhere. More often than not, their petitions were denied. Approximately half of the German Jews waited too long or could find no nation to accept them in time to save their lives.

ORGANIZING FOR SURVIVAL

Before the implementation of the Final Solution, German Jews organized themselves for mutual aid. As their persecution accelerated, so did their need to help one another. Step by step the government robbed them of the necessities of existence. First, Jews were ousted from political life, then they were cut off from their economic bases and then from cultural and educational participation. With each loss, they created their own organizations to try and fill the void. They closed ranks, supported one another, and tried to provide for their spiritual and economic needs. Many rediscovered their religious heritage; the synagogues had never been so well attended. Despite great difficulties, national organizations provided entertainment by Jewish artists, which included some first-class musical and theatrical performances. Unemployed professors gave lecture series and adult education classes offered occupational re-training that could be helpful for future emigrants. When Jewish children were expelled from public education, Jewish schools tried to close the gap. Aid for the poor, free soup kitchens, and clothing were provided until the death trains took the final remnants to the East.

As long as the Nazis deemed it to their advantage, such self-help was encouraged by the authorities. They welcomed the establishment of technical and agricultural training programs for young people hoping to settle in Palestine. The government permitted Jewish agencies to furnish counselors to aid prospective emigrants in wading through the morass of paperwork. The remarkable cooperation of Jewish parents and English families enabled thousands of Jewish children to survive. Youngsters barely out of diapers up to their early teens were taken into the homes of English volunteers. By 1939, when the onset of the war ended the rescue mission, ten thousand Jewish children had been brought to the railway station in Berlin by their parents; ten thousand traumatic good-byes had been said by mothers and fathers who waved their handkerchiefs long after the trains had rolled from sight. Only a small percentage of the children on these *Kindertransports* saw their parents again.

Jewish self-help associations tried to find work for the growing number of unemployed but only Jewish businesses were permitted to hire Jews. The resulting idleness of so many young people was a problem without a solution. Organized sports competitions tried to create an atmosphere of normalcy. Language instruction, particularly English, was offered to the hopeful emigrants. Two Jewish newspapers kept their subscribers informed of the latest dictates of the government and urged the people to stay calm and to remain optimistic.

The local religious congregations, the *Gemeinden,* bore the burden for some of these activities, but on the national scale the RV, the *Reichsvertretung der Deutschen Juden, (National Agency for German Jews)* played the major role. Until he was arrested and sent to Theresienstadt concentration camp, the renowned liberal rabbi Leo Baeck led the struggle to preserve a semblance of German-Jewish life. By the winter of 1938, German Jews were impoverished and received financial help from overseas, particularly from Jewish organizations in the United States. Shortly after the Japanese attacked Pearl Harbor, Germany declared war on the United States and it was no longer possible to send direct aid. At that point the isolation of European Jewry was nearly complete.

The Nazis had welcomed the activities of the RV because it was convenient to use the organization as a conduit for their orders. The leaders were called to the offices of the Nazi officials to receive and promulgate their latest decrees. Later, as we shall see in Chapter 8, this procedure evolved into the *Judenraete,* the Jewish Ghetto Councils. A cloud hangs over these organizations, but there can be no question that for as long as it was possible, Jewish self-help extended material and moral assistance to their fellow victims.

THE HOLOCAUST: MASTER PLAN OR EXPEDIENCY?

The Nazi commitment to make Germany *Judenrein* (cleansed of Jews) is not questioned by students of the Holocaust. Events occurring even before Hitler launched World War II left no doubt that he wanted to purge Germany of its Jews. His later conquests extended this passion to a wider arena. A persistent question, as yet unresolved, concerns the timing employed in order to achieve their pure Aryan state. Was genocide the aim from the inception of Hitler's ideology, or would emigration have satisfied his objectives? Some historians, known as the Intentionalists, are convinced that the actual physical destruction of the Jews was already outlined in *Mein Kampf.* Opposing views are held by the Functionalists. Their research led them to conclude that the annihilation strategy evolved rather than followed a preset blueprint. The conquest of Poland and war against the Soviet Union provided the opportunities for the *Endloesung,* the Final Solution. In the confusion of battle great crimes could be committed and covered up. Himmler, obedient to implied, verbal, or possibly written instructions from Hitler, initiated the mass murders because an expedient moment had presented itself.

The controversy between the Intentionalists and Functionalists remains unresolved. We do know that the conquest of Poland initiated new Nazi policies. Previously, the killing of Jews was incidental to the tactic of making their lives so wretched that they would flee to anywhere. The laws enacted before 1939 became progressively more brutal and were always accompanied by obscene propaganda campaigns. But there were no death camps. Not until the fall of Poland were the murder factories built. The sequence of events that began with "You may not work among us," led to "You may not live among us," and escalated to "You may not live at all." In the lands conquered by Germany after 1939, this sequence of persecution was greatly accelerated. Confiscation of property, expulsion from homes, and physical annihilation could, and often did, occur on a single day.

It is the view of this writer that during the early years of his regime, Hitler merely wanted a Germany without Jews. Physical destruction was not part of his first blueprint. (This point will be further explored later in this chapter.) The systematic annihilation of Jews began after the defeat of Poland. It may well have resulted from an amalgamation of three factors. First, the acquisition of Poland brought 3.5 million Jews under German authority; such numbers could not possibly be driven out of the country. Second, the war offered the opportunity to commit great crimes under the cover of patriotism. Third, and perhaps most importantly, was the progression of Hitler's neurotic hatred of the Jews into a mania.

The following personal experience may serve as a support for the Functionalist view:

> In the Spring of 1939, my parents, brother and I had been promised visas to emigrate to the United States. A visa is merely a stamp placed into a passport. For his own sadistic reasons, the mayor of Winzig, our little Silesian hometown, refused to issue the necessary passport. When, in December of that year, the American consul was made aware of this fact, he telegraphed the mayor: "Your denial of passports directly opposes your own government's policy to promote emigration. If this family is not given their passports immediately, I will notify your superiors of the fact that you are obstructing your own policy." The passports were ready the next day.

WHO IS A JEW?

Nazi genetic experts had great difficulty in deciding on a legal definition of who was to be considered a Jew. Serious people engaged in lengthy and weighty debates on the subject. Precisely to whom did the increasing number of anti-Jewish laws apply? Particularly perplexing was the status of the children of mixed marriages. Dr. Bernard Loesener of the Department of the Interior was recognized to be an expert on Jewish Affairs, and he was instructed to clarify the issue. The Law for the Restoration of the Professional Civil Service, enacted in April of 1933, set forth the official definition: A person is a non-Aryan if his parents or grandparents were Jewish. This applied to children having one Jewish parent or one Jewish grandparent or if one parent or grandparent practiced the Jewish religion. In other words, Jew and non-Aryan were interchangeable terms because both and religion and ethnicity determined racial status. Christians were regarded as Jews/non-Aryans if they had one or more Jewish ancestors. But this definition required further refinement. Did the prohibitions applicable to Jews have equal validity in the case of a Christian who had the misfortune of having one Jewish grandparent? Was the valuable German blood flowing in that individual to be squandered? In 1935, the question was taken up again and a new category was created, the *Mischling* (one of mixed race). The revision maintained that

1. a full Jew had three or four Jewish grandparents;
2. a *Mischling* was a half-Jew who had two Jewish grandparents, practiced Judaism, and/or was the child of a three-fourths Jew;
3. a *Mischling* of the first degree had two Jewish grandparents, but did not practice Judaism and was not married to a Jew;
4. a *Mischling* of the second degree had one Jewish grandparent.

It seems inconceivable to us here and now that officials and so-called genetic experts spent months working out this absurdity. But there was a deadly aspect to the application of these classifications. Although *Mischlinge* were designated non-Aryans and prohibited from many activities, most German *Mischlinge* survived the Holocaust. Wilhelm Stuckart, State Secretary of the Interior, made this bizarre observation to explain his opposition to the deportation of *Mischlinge:*

> I have always considered it dangerous biologically to introduce German blood into the enemy camp. The intelligence and excellent education of the half-Jews, linked to their ancestral Germanic heritage, make them natural leaders outside Germany and therefore very dangerous. I prefer to see the *Mischlinge* die a natural death inside Germany.

It must be noted that although all Jews were non-Aryans, not all non-Aryans were Jews. For example, children of Polish-Jewish parents were treated as fully Jewish; Poles did not belong to the Aryan race, and their blood was not worthy of salvage.

During the period between Hitler's rise to power and the events known as *Kristallnacht*—the Night of the Broken Glass, November 9–10, 1938, anti-Jewish laws were issued in intermittent spurts. During each lull, many German Jews and their sympathizers—yes, there were some—hoped that the worst was over. That optimism lasted until the next series of decrees was promulgated. The years 1933, 1935, and 1938 were particularly prolific. Jews were legally barred from enjoying the rights of German citizenship, they were deprived of their freedom to work, and they lost the privilege of owning real estate.

THE BOYCOTT

In order to have an overview of the persecution of Jews before the Final Solution, we need to step back to 1933. Hitler lost no time in proving that his government's anti-Jewish rhetoric should be taken seriously. By decree, April 1, 1933, was declared a day of boycott of all Jewish businesses. An Action Committee of the NSDAP coordinated the efforts "to teach the Jews a lesson." On the first of April and for several days thereafter, Jewish stores, institutions, industrial concerns, and offices found SA troopers stationed at the entrances to their places of business. Customers or clients who tried to enter were stopped, harangued, and sometimes beaten. The message was clear: Don't deal with Jews. This measure was also useful in testing the reaction of Christian Germans and that of foreign nations. The behavior of Germans on this occasion foreshadowed the conduct they adopted throughout the regime. With few exceptions, they complied with the boycott. When prevented from entering they were at first confused, momentarily annoyed and then retreated: No sense getting into trouble with the Brownshirts. Certainly, some Christians were privately angered, perhaps even ashamed, but the nation remained quiet and Hitler had his answer.

The foreign press, however, in editorials and news stories, demonstrated its repugnance. The Nazi leaders rather adroitly turned this criticism to their advantage. Was this negative press from abroad not proof of the existence of a Jewish international conspiracy against the Gentile world? Did this not corroborate that *The Protocols of the Elders of Zion* was based on truth? Furthermore, the leaders of German Jewry were instructed to urge their counterparts in Europe and America to stop any adverse portrayal of Germany. Unless these "misrepresentations" ceased, German Jewish interests would suffer further. Although these threats were not usually taken at face value outside of the Reich, they initiated a dilemma: Will our protests against the Nazi tactics harm or help the Jews? Will our efforts to help incite reprisals against the very victims we wish to aid? On the other hand, will our silence be interpreted as indifference and thus encourage further outrages? Well-intentioned foreigners were never certain of how best to respond.

In 1933, Jews were ousted from the civil service and the legal professions. The Orthodox community suffered a distressing blow when kosher butchering was outlawed. The ratio of Jews permitted to attend public schools and universities was reduced. Thousands lost their livelihoods when banned from working or participating in the cultural and intellectual life of the nation, such as the press, radio, the arts and the sciences. Frightening scenes of terror and humiliation became commonplace, when, for example, elderly men were forced to scrub sidewalks or the beards of religious elders were cut amid the jeering laughter of the SA. Though the government frowned upon such freelance operations because they might undermine party discipline, it was useless for Jews to seek redress through the judicial system. The courts were not interested in such cases. Nevertheless, it became clear to the government that a systematic approach to the Jewish question was needed.

THE NUREMBERG LAWS

The so-called Nuremberg Laws of 1935 stripped Jews of their citizenship; they were now intruders and unwelcome subjects. Further, the laws prohibited marriage and sexual relations between Jews and Gentiles. For the Jewish partner, such an offense was punishable by death. Employment of Aryan female servants under the age of forty-five in Jewish homes was forbidden. The edict also barred Jews from service in the armed forces. The realization that they no longer had any legal recourse dismayed the German Jewish population. Those who had connections overseas made ready to leave. At this point it was still possible to take some assets out of the country. An unease that often progressed to fear engulfed the German Jewish community. The hope of the assimilationists that respect for justice would protect them was dashed. Instead, the law had been turned into an instrument of persecution. It was time to send one's children out of harms way and begin to look into the possibility of escape.

During the 1930s, the Germans did not enact a uniform policy concerning the emigration of its unwanted subjects. Officially, their policy encouraged their exodus. A flight tax of 25 percent of the emigrant's assets was imposed and until the middle of the decade it was possible to transfer some money out of the country. Two special banks were established that shifted Jewish assets to Palestinian banks in a rather elaborate scheme designed to ease the German need for foreign currency. Local authorities throughout the Reich were advised to permit, even to assist, in the flight of the Jews.

But no golden door, nor any door, opened to receive them. The lines in front of foreign legations grew longer but the number of visas issued remained scarce. The year the Nazis took power, 1933 saw a considerable exodus. Jews whose public image made them vulnerable, businessmen who had foreign affiliates, men and women whose political astuteness was exceptional, and young Zionists were among those who left the homeland. Although their number, 37,000, was larger than that of any following year, they represented a mere 6 percent of the total. Some families crossed the borders into neighboring countries, but they were not permitted to work. Only the philanthropy of American Jews sustained many of these émigrés. However, when the Nazis marched into Poland, France, Belgium, and Holland, many of these semi-legal émigrés were among the first to be given up by their host countries and shipped to concentration and death camps.

The Nuremberg laws were appended many times. Eventually, over 400 provisions dealt especially with the "Jewish problem." Jews were forbidden from entering parks, zoos, hotels, theaters, sports events, or any public building. They could not sit on public benches or use public transport. The early restriction of the number of Jewish children permitted to attend public schools was increased several times until a total ban was enforced. Jews could not own radios, furs, or woolen items. When food and clothing were rationed, Jews received ever-decreasing amounts of life's necessities: no milk, no eggs, no meat. Restrictions on economic activities mounted until Christians and Jews could not work side by side in any establishment.

Ever reluctant to have any action appear illegal, the courts decided that those employers who had long-term contracts with Jewish workers could abrogate the agreements. The justification: Jewishness was interpreted as the legal equivalent of death; thus such agreements were null and void. The Nazification of the courts guaranteed that legal challenges would be decided in favor of the government. For example, when the drivers' licenses of Jews were canceled, appeals brought before the courts failed. The decrees issued became increasingly Kafkaesque. Minor infractions were punished with long terms of incarceration in Dachau, Buchenwald, or

Sachsenhausen concentration camps. Those prisoners who could prove that they were about to leave Germany were freed. Eventually, the Nuremberg laws were further amended to include an array of dehumanizing and degrading prohibitions: A yellow star had to be worn when appearing outside the home; Jews could not own phones but neither could they use public telephones; curfews kept Jews off the streets when others shopped; food rations grew constantly smaller. How can one comprehend the ban against white canes used by the blind and badges identifying the deaf? The law forbidding Jews to own pets, even birds, created scenes of tearful leave-taking as beloved companions were left at designated depots.

JUDEN RAUS (JEWS GET OUT)

Until the attack on Poland in September 1939, the Nazi government used every means at its disposal to force the Jews to leave. Major cities actually provided government offices to speed the exodus along. Jews were without professional and economic status; they were socially ostracized, and newspapers such as Julius Streicher's pornographic *Stuermer* were unrelenting in their attacks. There were arrests without charges and beatings in the streets. Each time there was a let-up the Jews breathed easier. The year 1936 was often misinterpreted; because the Olympic Games were played in Germany and the government wanted to make a good impression on the hundreds of thousands of visitors. Signs in stores warning that Jews would not be served disappeared temporarily; park benches no longer advertised that these seats were for Aryans only; even Goebbels and the press restrained their abusive rhetoric. But the lull merely forecast a more violent storm.

The persecution of German Jews shifted into high gear during 1938. A *Kennkarte* was issued and had to be carried at all times. This was an identification card which included physical description, fingerprints, and photo. Males of all ages were required to add "Israel" as their the middle name and females were ordered to affix "Sara" to their given names. The government argued that these internal passports helped the state control its enemies. Goering ("guns, not butter") had taken charge of preparing the national economy for the coming war. His control of the Four Year Plan gave him enormous power. As long as he could claim to be acting in the interest of military preparedness, he could counteract the decrees issued by every other agency of the Reich. He demanded that all present and future traitors must be neutralized before the nation could fight a foreign war. That category included all Jews from age one to one hundred.

With increasing speed the remaining economic opportunities were eliminated. Jewish doctors were officially designated as medical orderlies and were forbidden to treat Aryan patients. Thousands of Jews who were not born in Germany were suddenly expelled. Despite the increased pressure, the Nazis complained, the exodus of the Jews was not proceeding fast enough. The problem, of course, was not their reluctance to go but that they could not find nations willing to grant them asylum. Only between 150,000 to 170,000 German Jews, that is one-third of the pre-Nazi number, had left by 1938. Goering decided to speed up the process by removing them completely from the national economic life.

The method was not new. It was called Aryanization and involved the forced sale of Jewish businesses and property to Aryans. Of course, favorite members of the Nazi organizations were the recipients of this boon. The price for the real estate was determined by a Nazi functionary at a fraction of the actual value. But even that amount was not handed over to the sellers. The money was deposited into a special bank account and, depending on the size of the Jewish family, a sum was doled out every month. In case of emigration the remaining money was confiscated by the government. The rationale for this action was based on the legal interpretation that, ipso facto, all Jewish wealth had been acquired through fraud and the state was entitled to reclaim it all.

It could hardly be a coincidence that in 1938 the government required every Jewish household to itemize their possessions. Questionnaires were mailed which directed the recipient to list all his remaining resources. German and Austrian Jews (the *Anschluss,* or union with Austria, had taken place in March, 1938) were required to acknowledge and describe in detail their ownership of such items as silver candlesticks, paintings, radios, furs, furniture, cut glass, heirlooms and jewelry. When the time came, and that was very soon, to expropriate these personal effects, the authorities knew exactly who had what. All that was needed to deprive the Jews of everything of value was some sort of justification. And that was provided by a Polish teenager living in Paris who had no idea that his actions would serve as the excuse for a pogrom.

KRISTALLNACHT POGROM

If any doubt remained concerning the intentions of the Nazis to make Germany *Judenrein* (cleansed of Jews), they were removed by the events generally called *Kristallnacht,* the Night of the Broken Glass. Neither Christian nor Jew could ever again claim that they did not realize the seriousness of the Jewish plight. The terror of November 9, 10, and beyond was played out in full view of the German people. The scenes of beatings, screaming women, and arrests of men took place on the streets and in public places throughout Germany. Spectacular fires and widespread destruction of property were inescapable confirmation that a pogrom, an outbreak of violence against Jews either sanctioned or carried out by the government, was in progress.

The first scene of the drama was played out between the German and Polish borders. In October 1938, the Gestapo executed an order to forcibly expel all Jews born in Poland. Even those who had become German citizens were included. Some 7,000 men, women and children were declared to be stateless. They were forcibly assembled and placed into sealed railroad cars. In an eerie portent of future transports to the east, they were shipped into the no-man's land between the German and Polish frontiers. The Poles, however, refused to accept them and attempted to drive them back into Germany. The misery of these exiles, living in makeshift shelters between the borders, was obvious. Eventually, under pressure and with financial support from worldwide Jewish organizations, the deportees were reluctantly admitted into Poland.

A young man, Herschel Grynzpan, knew only that the Nazis had deported his family from Hanover. He was living in Paris, hoping to emigrate to Palestine. Unable to get in touch with his parents and sister, he became distraught. He decided that he must exact revenge from the Germans. He managed to purchase a revolver and went to the German embassy. There he was admitted to the office of a minor functionary, a third secretary named Ernst vom Rath. Shouting that he was avenging his people, he shot the German who died the following day, November 9.

The shooting took place during the weeklong commemoration of the *Bierhall Putsch*. The Nazi leaders had gathered in Munich to celebrate the fifteenth anniversary of that fiasco when they were informed of the Rath murder. Goebbels, ever mindful of the sensational value of a Jew killing a German, received Hitler's approval to turn the event into an excuse for a major pogrom. The *Gauleiters* (provincial party chiefs) and heads of the SA, SS, and Gestapo were notified to go into action by Himmler and Goering who feared that Goebbels might reap too much benefit from his coup. All rushed to the telephones and ordered the destruction of all Jewish businesses and communal institutions. The arrest of all Jewish men between the ages of 16 and 60 and their confinement to concentration camps was to accompany the vandalism of property.

The pogrom has been called *Kristallnacht* because thousands of windows were smashed, and the broken shards glittered in the streets like crystal. All of Germany's 275 synagogues were destroyed; those that did not burn were dynamited. Places of business owned by Jews were demolished by arson, ax, club, and crowbar.

In areas where many Jewish-owned shops were clustered together, the streets resembled a combat area. The destruction was carried out by the light of burning buildings; the air was acrid from the smell and smoke of scorched cloth and wood; the sirens and bells of police cars and fire equipment added to the hellish image. Sidewalks were impassable with goods strewn everywhere: Here, wine from the liquor store ran like a red river on which floated puffs of feathers from the bedding store. There eyeglasses and radios, candy and typewriters, merchandise of every sort, were trampled underfoot. Regular police and firemen were under orders not to interfere except to protect the property of Aryans.

Each town and city had variations of the scenario as local commanders of the SA, the Gestapo, and the Nazi party interpreted the orders to "teach the Jews a lesson" with their own ideas. In some cities, private homes were ransacked, furnishings thrown from windows, and Jews were beaten. Where the SA was encouraged to give vent to frenzy, murders were committed—100 Jewish men were killed and an uncounted number injured. In other areas, words such as JEWS DIE were smeared on steps and doors of homes. Some Jewish schools were torched, others left alone. Placards were hung from many destroyed shops, which read: THIS IS THE PEOPLE'S REVENGE FOR THE MURDER OF VOM RATH,

DEATH TO INTERNATIONAL JEWRY. The Nazis tried hard to convince the German public that this pogrom was a spontaneous riot, caused by the wrath of the people. Never was spontaneity so well planned and systematically organized. In forty-eight hours a total of 7,500 businesses were demolished. The public at large did its best not to see, hear, or know anything and rarely participated in the attacks. Looting was forbidden and here again, local circumstances determined the observance or disregard of that order.

The *Judenaktion,* that is anti-Jewish riot, of *Kristallnacht* was not restricted to the destruction of commercial establishments. For two days and nights the Gestapo, the internal security police known as the SD (*Sicherheitsdienst*), and regular police combed the country in search of Jewish men. With prepared lists of names and addresses, they swarmed through the villages, towns and cities. Streets, bus stations and railroad terminals were turned into tragic theater as men were pulled from screaming families. Many of the arrests were accompanied by beatings, although very few of the men resisted. For the most part they were completely bewildered. They asked: "What have I done?" "Where are you taking me?" but were answered with curses. Suicides reached a new peak.

There were no indictments, no trials. The crime committed by Herschel Grynzpan required retribution from all the German Jews. Thirty thousand men were shipped to concentration camps. Officially, they were removed from German society to prevent the German people from venting their "justified revenge" upon them. The camps Goering had set up were filled to capacity; depending on the region, the men were sent to Dachau, Buchenwald, or Sachsenhausen. There the prisoners were marched in circles, stood endlessly at attention in order to be counted, did calisthenics, and tormented themselves with fearful pictures of the fate of their families. Eight hundred of them did not survive the hardships of the beatings and the stress of their "protective custody." In contrast to later incarcerations, these prisoners were released. First to go home were men who could prove that their emigration was imminent. Later, the others were permitted to leave if they claimed that they would leave Germany as soon as possible.

A Case in Point: Bremen

On the fiftieth anniversary of *Kristallnacht*, the city of Bremen commissioned an investigation into the events of the pogrom. The result of this research was intended to be used as teaching material in their schools. The following are some excerpts from that document:

> In Bremen . . . resided about 900 Jews whose homes were scattered all over town. When, during the night of November 9 to the 10 the order to "let loose" arrived at SA headquarters, the first reaction was to reach for the so-called Jews list. In Bremen this had been prepared as early as 1935. The list was copied and distributed that same night to the secondary SA facilities located in various districts.

. . . SA troopers were summoned. They roamed the city without giving a thought to the nature of their orders and dutifully performed their mission.

The results were recorded in the police archives. For example: In seventeen Jewish businesses and residences, windows were demolished, and, in part, furniture and shop fittings were destroyed.

. . . With total success we completed the incineration of the Synagogue on Garten Street and we also destroyed the living quarters of the Rabbi. We were also successful in laying waste the chapel in the cemetery and damaged the grave stones. The visitation to the old age home at . . . was carried out by particularly diligent SA men. Here windows were broken, doors splintered, mirrors shattered, the old people were stomped on and driven from the premises.

Two women and three men were murdered during the pogrom in Bremen. When this news reached the SA commander, the killers were told that they had gone too far. However, the men were exonerated when they claimed that they were following orders. Eventually, after the war, these crimes were investigated and the surviving murderers were brought to justice and sentenced to long prison terms.

THE AFTERMATH

No matter how blatantly the Goebbels press corps tried to assure the German public that the pogrom was an impulsive reaction by an enraged nation, the public response was negative. Too many people had seen and recognized the men with the torches and axes and knew they had come from the ranks of organized Nazis. A more serious complaint concerned the terrible waste of perfectly usable merchandise. What purpose was served by the destruction of so much property? The cost of replacing the windows alone drew millions of foreign exchange marks from Germany and kept the Belgian glass factories running at full speed for many months. Were there not many Germans who could have made good use of the furniture, the clothing, the very buildings that had been rendered useless?

Within the party hierarchy, the nights of violence and vandalism against the Jews reverberated at the highest level. Goebbels had obviously tried to take charge of the Jewish policy and that was not to be tolerated. Goering and Hitler, still in Munich, inspected the damage in that city and the *Reichsmarschall* convinced the Fuehrer that such outbursts must not be tolerated. As a result, the conduct of Jewish affairs was assigned to Goering and Himmler and the ambitious Goebbels was not permitted to meddle again. On November 12, Goering convened a meeting to review the recent events and discuss the future management of the Jewish problem. The principal functionaries in attendance were Himmler's emissary Heydrich, Economics Minister Funk, Justice Minister Guertner, a representative from the foreign ministry, and a member of the insurance industry. Goebbels was also invited but received no thanks for his role. In fact, when Goering was finished denouncing the pointless destruction, the propaganda minister made no rebuttal.

The representative from the insurance companies' association estimated the losses at 25 million marks (3 million marks for broken glass). Goering directed that the insurance companies must pay the claims, but since the Reich had suffered the real damage, the money was to go into the national treasury, not to the insured claimants. The immense cleanup of the streets was the responsibility of the Jews. Goering then ordered Minister Funk to create legislation that would once and for all drive Jews from all economic participation in Germany. The Aryanization of businesses that had been more or less voluntary was now made compulsory. In addition, as retribution for the crime committed by Grynzpan, the German Jews were fined the enormous sum of 1 billion marks. At the very time when the greatest demands for aid were made upon the Jewish community, when food, clothing, and housing were needed desperately, its funds were expropriated and German Jews became paupers.

During the debate, Heydrich was complimented on the success of his methods in driving the Jews from Austria. Heydrich's reply augured ill for the future: Despite all his efforts, the exodus of the Jews was still entirely too slow. At the present rate it would take years to get rid of them all.

The foreign press of the Western world reported the events in their respective newspapers. In headlines and editorials, Germany was condemned. Ambassadors from many nations delivered protests to the German Foreign Ministry. The law faculties of ninety-seven foreign universities remonstrated against such racial-political terrorism. Pope Pius XI issued a rather vague statement of sympathy for the victims. Franklin D. Roosevelt recalled the American ambassador and declared that he found the actions of *Kristallnacht* to be utterly abhorrent. An attempt, however, to boycott German goods from coming into the United States was not effective. Thus, the Nazis were convinced they could do as they pleased and they would not be condemned with any weapon stronger than words. And words could never harm them. Had not a League of Nations commission on refugees met at Evian in October 1938 without reaching any conclusions? No doors were opened to admit the thousands of potential German Jewish refugees. Hitler interpreted this lack of action correctly: No country would actually help the Jews.

Yet somehow, after the November catastrophe, 100,000 German Jews managed to escape. They fled to Shanghai, South America, Africa, Asia, and places they could hardly find on a map. A Nazi official was present when they packed their bags; their passports were stamped with a large red J (Jew), and about ten dollars per person was the amount of money they could take with them into their uncertain future. But German Jews knew they must flee, go anywhere to save their lives. The friends and relatives they left behind could only hope that they too could escape the land they had loved too well.

CHAPTER 7

Hitler's War

When historians discuss the causes of wars, they often use the term multiple causation; only rarely is war the result of a single determining factor. But it is accurate to call World War II Hitler's war. He planned it, directed it, and worst of all, he wanted it. The theory that both world wars were really one single event, interrupted by a twenty-year truce, underestimates the essential role of the Fuehrer. It was his power, his leadership, his concept of Germany that plunged the world into its most devastating conflict. Two passions dominated Hitler's mental world: hatred for the Jews and the lust to dominate Europe. These two compulsions were joined into a war of aggression. German conquests provided the SS with the opportunity to annihilate Jews from the regions between the Pyrenees to the Russian steppes and from the shores of the North and Baltic Seas to the Mediterranean. The cost of Hitler's war in human lives has been estimated at 35–55 million of military and civilian deaths. The Holocaust accounted for 6 million non-combatants' deaths, a figure equal to two-thirds of the Jews then living in Europe. The theory that the Second World War was an inevitable consequence of the First is based on the view that the Treaty of Versailles left the German people so hostile and so vengeful that they were merely waiting for the opportunity to vindicate their defeat. While the Versailles *Diktat* was perceived as terribly unfair, it was not the burning question on the minds of the German people. The period following the Great War presented grave problems much closer to their everyday concerns. The memory of the human and economic losses of the Great War was still fresh and had blunted the desire for military adventures. This observer was a child watching the mobile army units streaming toward Poland in late August of 1939. Though the townspeople stood on the street, there was no cheering, only glum faces and muttering. When the German press announced the news of the "necessity" of the Polish invasion, the public reacted almost entirely with stoic silence. Furthermore, ascribing to the provisions of the

Treaty of Versailles the responsibility for causing the war ignores the manifest willingness of the victors to moderate certain aspects of the treaty. That process was already underway during the 1920s. Additional adjustments to ease Germany's burdens were clearly feasible. Unless one believes that all historical events are ordained by a force beyond human power, Hitler and his militant supporters must bear the major responsibility for turning Europe into a charnel house.

HITLER'S FOREIGN POLICY

Hitler believed that war was a natural imperative. He based his theory on a twisted interpretation of several highly questionable hypotheses. From social Darwinism he concluded that all life was a struggle for survival, for men and nations as well as for plants and animals. The strongest state had the right to subjugate weaker states and the battlefield was the ultimate arena where Aryan superiority would be confirmed. So-called Nazi philosophers such as Alfred Rosenberg borrowed freely from Frenchman Joseph Arthur Comte de Gobineau's (1816–1882) four-volume *Essay on the Inequality of the Races.* Gobineau asserted that only Aryans are creative, and the purity of the race must be guarded as scrupulously as life itself. On the lowest rung of his racial hierarchy were the Jews, who were usurpers and contaminators. A misinterpretation of the philosophy of the renowned Friedrich Nietzsche (1844–1900) was also useful to the Nazi theorists. In *Thus Spake Zarathustra,* Nietzsche portrayed the ultimate man, the *Uebermensch,* as beyond ordinary humans in spirit and not subject to the accepted moral values of the masses. Nazi propagandists perverted Nietzsche's Superman by giving him Nordic features and dressing him up in an SS uniform. Actually, the philosopher had been rather contemptuous of his own countrymen and he had never condoned antiSemitism. But such truths were concealed from the German people. They were offered quite a different *Weltanschauung:* Life itself is struggle; war is the supreme test of superiority; notions of meekness and mercy have no place in the contest for power; and the end justifies the means. How many mature men and women accepted this chilling version of national purpose is impossible to say, but impressionable youths may have found these theories appealing.

LEBENSRAUM

There was never any secrecy concerning Hitler's foreign policy aims. He outlined his intentions in 1923's *Mein Kampf* and reiterated them in many speeches. By virtue of its superior Aryan race and the fact that Germany needed space to live, the expansion of German borders was inevitable. This need for living space, or *Lebensraum,* was not to be satisfied through colonies on foreign shores but in the broad and underpopulated regions of Eastern Europe. Large areas of farmland were vital to the development of a Nazi hegemony in Europe and the establishment of German autarchy. The Slavic inhabitants now in possession of these lands were racially inferior and must be forced to give way to the Aryans. They would be removed from their soil and in the process many would be killed. The survivors would be useful as labor to toil for their German masters.

To realize these goals would require armed conflict, that was a certainty, in fact, a desirable certainty. Thus, the end and the means of Hitler's foreign policy were determined from the beginning. Once that premise is understood, the vacillations of Nazi foreign affairs become comprehensible. The making and breaking of treaties that appear contradictory were actually within the policy parameters set by the Fuehrer. Peace with Russia, war with Russia; peace with England and France, then war against them; a treaty with Poland, the invasion of Poland; the actions seem inconsistent but the agenda never changed.

Hitler, who seldom took any interest in the details of domestic affairs, was personally involved in the pursuit of foreign aims. During his first week in office in 1933, he summoned his top generals and told them of his vision to conquer Eastern Europe. Since the Revolution of 1917, so the Nazis asserted, the Soviet Union was ruled by mere *Untermenschen:* Jews/Bolsheviks. (In Hitler's mind, Jews and Bolsheviks were interchangeable terms.) Russia was ripe for conquest because its former czarist/Germanic leadership had been replaced by a racially inferior dictatorship. No doubt, the need for eastern territories would lead to war. Until Germany was ready for conquest, a period of peace was required. During that interval the military and the civilian populations must prepare and be prepared for the coming conflict. Diplomacy in foreign affairs and strengthening the popular resolve at home would buy the necessary time. The army, Goering's economic plans, and Dr. Goebbels' press would speed that process.

Hitler's domestic policies also become clearer when viewed as components of this strategy. Schemes such as the proposed settlement of racially perfect SS men and their families in the Ukraine, the preparation of the young to bear arms or bear children, the misnamed euthanasia killings of those deemed mentally and/or physically unfit, Dr. Mengele's bogus research in Auschwitz, which sought to increase the number of twins born to German mothers, the brutal and wasteful treatment of defeated peoples—all these activities were parts of Hitler's comprehensive scheme. Even the Holocaust, that is, the destruction of the most dangerous and despicable race, was necessary to the establishment of Hitler's brave new Nazi world.

THE INTERNATIONAL ATMOSPHERE

The United States withdrew from the center of European affairs during the decades between the two great wars. France and England should have accepted the role of international leadership, but neither was willing or able. The war had weakened them, and their people were disillusioned because victory had brought them no appreciable rewards. French and English politicians could not present a united front against the rising Fascist states of Italy and Germany. Fear of communism at home and of the Soviet Union abroad dominated their policies, while wishful thinking colored their perception of Hitler and Mussolini.

While France feared a revival of German aggression, its government lacked the power and resolve to lead Europe in preventing the military resurgence by the Nazis. The Third French Republic had suffered much during the Great War, and her political party system was unable to operate as a cohesive whole to forestall another assault from her neighbor to the east. Extremists from the right and left could not reconcile their differences, and crisis followed crisis. France wanted a Germany economically strong enough to make reparations payments but too weak to become a threat. Obviously, these were conflicting aims. Traditionally, France had relied on help from Russia to prevent German expansionism, but the Communist revolution had created a gulf between democratic France and Soviet communism. French diplomacy tried to compensate by concluding alliances with the newly established eastern nations: Poland, Czechoslovakia, Romania, and Yugoslavia. These, however, were small, struggling countries. The French derived little satisfaction from these treaties and decided to build an elaborate defense line along its German frontier—the Maginot Line. From Switzerland to Belgium the fortifications ran north and south in eastern France. The line consisted of a series of underground forts connected and serviced by railroads, power stations, elevators, food and munitions depots, hospitals, and immense defensive installations. Three hundred thousand men could be assembled in its underground stations while above ground cannons sprouted from casemates which pointed toward the German border. The existence of such a modern, extensive as well as expensive, defensive system gave Frenchmen a false sense of security that would prove to be costly beyond all expectations.

The British hoped to maintain control over their empire despite the increasingly independent stance of their dominions. They had no desire to enhance French ambition to play the European superpower. The First World War had turned many Britons into pacifists, and military expenditures were unpopular. Unemployment figures were high, and disillusionment with the lack of spoils from victory was rife. As long as her naval power was superior, the British lion wanted to sleep without interference from the continent.

EARLY NAZI DIPLOMACY

Hitler inherited a number of international obligations from the Weimar Republic. Most significant was the Treaty of Versailles. The 1919 convention, concluded without German participation, was humiliating to the Germans. They lost considerable territory to newly reestablished Poland in the East and to France in the West. Germany's colonies were taken away; the Rhineland was demilitarized, and the German army was reduced to 100,000 volunteers. Of the huge reparations assessment, however, only a small portion was ever collected. Allied statesmen had not been indifferent to the protestations that the treaty provisions were unfair, a *Diktat*, coerced upon a prostrate people. The practical application of such consideration had resulted in adjustments of the original terms. The Locarno Pacts of 1925 removed the French armies from the Rhineland in return for German guarantees to respect the

French and Belgian frontiers. In 1926 Germany was admitted into the League of Nations, ending its international pariah status. League membership also required that Germany was now pledged to uphold the organization's peacekeeping responsibility. In 1928, the Weimar Republic was one of twenty-three nations to sign the Kellogg-Briand agreement that bound the signatories to the outlawing of war as an instrument of national policy. The Dawes Act of 1924 and Young Plan of 1929 had provided some relief of the reparations debt and eased the schedule of payments. If Hitler had been satisfied to govern Germany in peaceful coexistence with its neighbors, further revisions of the Versailles provisions would have been feasible, even likely.

When Hitler became chancellor, the first order of business was to secure his own and his party's internal power. Within two years all political and most individual opposition had been eradicated, and he became the unchallenged master of Germany. Now his foreign ambitions could be given maximum attention, however, without disturbing the image of the diligent, peace-loving caretaker of the German people. The great sacrifices he would demand from them in the coming war must be made obediently, or better yet, willingly. It was vital that the German people

Adolf Hitler and Prime Minister Neville Chamberlain in Munich, 1938. (Courtesy AP/Wide World Photos.)

identified their well-being, their future with the dreams and goals of the Fuehrer. In order to maintain the illusion that the regime cared about them, their basic needs and expectations had to be met. Hitler frequently reminded his audiences of the promises he had kept: reduction of unemployment, restoration of law and order in the streets, rebuilding of the infrastructure, and respect from other nations. No doubt, their children would have a brighter future and inequality between the upper and lower classes would continue to be diminished.

Until Germany was militarily strong, Hitler was careful to assume a circumspect attitude in foreign affairs. He spoke of his desire for peace with great conviction while plans to rearm Germany were progressing in secret. He claimed that all he sought was parity with other European nations. Toward this end he retained conservative ministers in his foreign, defense, and state departments. Not until 1938 was the servile Nazi Joachim von Ribbentrop given the official title of Minister for Foreign Affairs. Hitler went so far as to shrewdly offer demobilization as soon as Germany's neighbors did the same. The proposal was a sham; he knew very well that this proposition would not be accepted. But the appearance of peaceful intentions was maintained and some members of the foreign services of Europe and the United States declared what a fine fellow Herr Hitler was. Fear of the Soviet Union played a considerable role in the deception that the Nazis were not so bad; the Western world was nervous because Communist political parties were getting support from the Soviet government. Since the Nazi party was the implacable enemy of Russia, it was tempting to overlook the alarming features of Hitler's policies. It seemed wise to prevent a possible rapprochement between Nazis and Communists by making concessions to the Germans. Even when Hitler withdrew Germany from the League of Nations and from the Geneva Disarmament Conference, no alarm bells were sounded in London or Paris. After all, so ran the argument of the appeasers, Herr Hitler had to satisfy German public opinion, such was nothing more than the nature of politics.

In 1934, Hitler signed a treaty with Poland. The agreement stipulated that both countries would maintain peace with one another for ten years. The pact startled the Western world. The Weimar government, in its search for allies, had sought good relations with Russia. How could Germany befriend Poland, the nation that was created out of deep cuts into western Russia and eastern Germany? The Treaty of Versailles had separated East Prussia from the rest of Germany, and every German believed the loss of the Polish corridor was a scandal to be rectified in time. Thus, the newly recreated Poland existed between two nations who resented its very existence, both of which hoped to regain their lost territories. Adding to Poland's insecurity was the lack of geographic barriers along its borders; her flat terrain left the country open to invasion from east and west. Naturally, the nonaggression pact with Germany was welcomed in diplomatic circles and seen by many observers as another indication of Hitler's intentions to be a good neighbor.

The treaty also sent a clear message to the Soviet Union (established under Russian leadership in 1924) that the Weimar government's policy of cooperation was over. Evidently, the anti-Communist propaganda coming from Goebbels' press was not just window dressing and should be taken seriously. Russia and her associated states must look elsewhere for friends. The truth that Hitler had no intention of honoring the Polish agreement was simply not grasped by the foreign offices of the diplomatic world of the 1930s. Hitler was buying time in order to advance his military and psychological preparations for the war to come. Poland, of course, was invaded in 1939, and became the first victim of his obsession for eastern *Lebensraum.*

INERTIA IN FRANCE AND GREAT BRITAIN

During the period between 1933 and the outbreak of the war in 1939, Hitler tested the diplomatic waters again and again. How far could he go in ignoring the Versailles covenant before the former Allies would stop him? His foreign policy decisions required a careful reading of the resolve of France and England. Would they go to war to prevent the resurgence of a powerful Germany? Would the restoration of military conscription, ordered in 1935, give rise to alarm? The inadequate responses to the contravention of the Versailles Treaty revealed the ineffectiveness of the League of Nations. At this point, Germany was still weak, but Hitler masqueraded as a champion of peace, a reasonable man who demanded only justice for his people. Behind the façade, the Nazis were forging a mighty military machine. Only when his soldiers were the best trained, best equipped in Europe would Hitler's goals become clear. By fright or by fight he would achieve his great Thousand Year Reich and the *Lebensraum* it required.

At this point decisive action by France and England could have delayed, perhaps halted the Nazi thrust. France wanted treaty compliance from Germany, but without English support its voice was muted. Great Britain hoped to return to its traditional isolation from the quarrels of Europe and needed time and peace to recover from the effects of the Great War. Its dominions were loosening their ties to the mother country; trade dislocations and budget crises required resolution and labor unrest beset the government and the people. Great Britain hoped to safeguard its island by means of a naval agreement whereby the German navy was to remain at one-third the size of the English navy. German submarines, however, were permitted to constitute 60 percent of their English counterparts, a decision the English would live to regret. France was anxious and continued to pour money into the Maginot Line. Alone in its demand of German compliance with the Versailles Treaty provisions, the French overcame their reluctance to deal with the Communists and concluded a defensive alliance with the Soviet Union in 1935. Each agreed to support the other in case of German aggression.

The maintenance of peace by common action, so optimistically pledged by the League of Nations, proved to be an empty promise. France and England, the backbone of the League, did not have the necessary spine to prevent the rise of renewed German aggression. International cooperation collapsed in the face of domestic problems. The United States, never a member of the League, exerted only limited influence. Congress would have opposed more direct participation in European affairs even if the president had wished it. Hitler was free to advance his goals.

BLOODLESS VICTORIES

Hitler's foreign policy reflected the inertia of the nations that might have opposed him. Each victory he achieved without resorting to war encouraged him to pursue further adventures. Germany's neighbors were unwilling to read the danger signs and today, with the advantage of hindsight, we are perplexed by this blindness. In the 1930s, however, the opinion was widely held that the German people would not support a war if some of their reasonable objectives were realized. If that meant the abrogation of some provisions of the Versailles treaty, that seemed a fair price to pay for peace.

The Treaty of Versailles barred any German military presence in the Rhineland and in the highly industrialized Ruhr region near the French border. Most Germans found that prohibition insulting to their national honor. When Hitler moved troops into the forbidden zone in 1936, the League of Nations protested with words, not action. Predictably, Hitler's popularity increased greatly. In the same year, Germany officially withdrew from the League and from the Locarno Pacts. These treaties had been signed by Germany, France, Czechoslovakia, and Poland in 1925 to ensure peaceful adjudication of disputes. Italy and England had agreed to act as guarantors of its decisions. Once again, German conduct, so clearly in contrast with Hitler's peace-loving oratory, did not arouse serious concern in Paris or London.

In 1936, the leftist republican government of Spain was under attack by the followers of the Fascist general Francisco Franco. Mussolini and Hitler had just concluded a military alliance with the Spanish Fascist and sent massive aid to Franco's forces. The Spanish Civil War served as a proving ground for Hitler's soldiers, tactics, and weaponry. The Soviet Union, in turn, sent support to the opposition until the losses sustained by the Republican army caused Stalin to withdraw his aid in 1939. England and France declared their neutrality but thousands of young men from the western democracies, including the United States, volunteered for the anti-Fascist forces. Their efforts, however, could not turn the tide, and Franco was victorious. The joint Spanish venture of Hitler and Mussolini strengthened the relationship of the two dictators. In 1939, the Rome-Berlin Axis was formed when they signed a formal alliance of aid and friendship. Both men could now proceed with new confidence in pursuing their grandiose plans.

AUISTRIA: FIASCO AND VICTORY

Hitler, who was Austrian by birth, was bent upon the unification of his actual and adopted homelands. The annexation, specifically forbidden by the treaties ending the Great War, was known as the *Anschluss*.

Hitler first attempted to gain control over Austria in 1934. The German Nazi party supported a growing number of Austrian Nazis and incited them to attempt a coup d'état against the government of Chancellor Engelbert Dollfuss. When the Austrian SS employed political terror tactics against Dollfuss, a right-wing dictator in his own right, he responded with mayhem and murder. In retaliation, the Austrian

Nazis broke into his office and shot him in the throat. In the style of a gangster movie, the Nazis refused to allow him any medical attention, and Dollfuss bled to death on the sofa of his office. But the plot to topple the government failed nevertheless. The loyal Austrian army, under the leadership of Dr. Kurt von Schuschnigg, then the Minister of Justice, routed the Nazis. In 1934 the Rome-Berlin Axis was not yet anticipated and the Italians feared German domination of Austria. While the Austrian Nazis attempted their coup, Mussolini mobilized his army on the Italian-Austrian border to prevent the fall of the legitimate Austrian government. Hitler had to acknowledge that the *Anschluss* would have to wait.

Schuschnigg became chancellor and remained in office until 1938 when German troops marched into Austria and consummated the *Anschluss*. By then Mussolini's neutrality was assured, while the politicians of France and England continued to delude themselves that this breach of the Versailles Treaty would finally satisfy Germany. Great numbers of Austrians greeted the Fuehrer in an ecstasy of jubilation as he entered Vienna. Schuschnigg was sent to a concentration camp where, astonishingly, he survived and outlived Hitler by more than thirty years.

THE SUDETEN GERMANS

The Austro-Hungarian Empire which was composed of peoples adhering to many different nationalities, had been Germany's ally during the First World War. When the Central Powers were defeated, the Austrian hegemony was broken up. Hungary, Yugoslavia, and Czechoslovakia became independent nations and Austria was left a small, landlocked German-speaking country. Among the newly established nations, Czechoslovakia was the showpiece of success. Its parliamentary democracy functioned well. Czech industry was balanced with Slovak agriculture, and the solid leadership of its president, Thomas Masaryk, enabled the young republic to thrive. But there were difficulties due to the ethnic diversity within its own borders. The Czechoslovakian population of 14 million people was composed of Czechs, Slovaks, Germans, Moravians, Hungarians, Austrians, Poles, and Ruthenians. Among these, the German minority caused the most severe problems. More than 3 million so-called Sudeten Germans lived mainly in the Bohemian northwestern mountainous regions. They would have preferred incorporation into the German Reich. Although the government in Prague tried to accommodate their grievances, they remained dissatisfied.

A Bohemian politician named Konrad Henlein founded the *Sudeten Deutsche Partei*. The stated aim of the party was regional autonomy. Henlein was actually a Nazi in Sudeten clothing. His ideology mirrored Hitler's and his relationship with Berlin was mutually beneficial. Henlein accepted substantial financial support and in return he provided Hitler with the excuse to demand the annexation of the Sudetenland. Henlein's organization represented 60 percent of the Sudeten Germans and his deputies in the legislature in Prague were instructed to be totally uncooperative. On orders from Hitler, they demanded virtual independence for their region, expecting, perhaps hoping, to be refused.

Encouraged by the easy success of the Austrian annexation, Hitler decided to take over the Sudetenland. In February of 1938, he tested international reaction by sending troops to the border. The Czechoslovakian government responded by massing a well-trained, well-equipped army of 400,000 along the disputed area. When France and the Soviet Union indicated their willingness to uphold their treaty obligations and support Czechoslovakia in case of attack, the Germans were called back. But not for long, indeed, not for long.

The plan to attach the Sudetenland to the Reich and subjugate the rest of the Czech nation was set for October 1938. Henlein was ordered to step up his agitation, to demand nothing less than autonomy. The Prague government under Eduard Benes tried desperately to prevent the dismemberment of the nation and offered Henlein a semi-autonomous state, modeled after the Swiss cantons. But Hitler did not want concessions, he wanted the dissection of Czechoslovakia. For the Benes government, the loss of the northwestern area would be a disaster. The mountains provided the country with a natural defense line, and the loss of the region would seriously damage the viability of Czech industry. The survival of the republic had been guaranteed by treaties with France, the Soviet Union, and England. The question was: Would these promises be kept in the face of German demands? The lack of assurance by the British government under Prime Minister Neville Chamberlain was the decisive one; France and the Soviets would not act alone to protect Czechoslovakia. As Henlein and his Nazis created chaos, the Benes government tried to cope with the disorders by invoking martial law. On the twelfth of September, Hitler made a speech in which he accused the Benes government of atrocities against the German minority. Germany, he shouted, would not stand by while such crimes were committed. Europe was faced with a full-blown diplomatic crisis.

APPEASEMENT AT MUNICH

The dread of war impelled Prime Minister Chamberlain to approach Hitler directly. As an English gentleman, he was going to speak to his German counterpart and by a shake of hands secure tranquillity in Europe. He made the first airplane trip of his life to meet with Hitler in his mountain retreat at Berchtesgaden. Hitler's demands remained unaltered: immediate possession of the Sudetenland or there would be war. Chamberlain, after consultation with his divided cabinet in London and the French Premier Edouard Daladier (but not with Benes), informed the Prague government that it must cede the areas inhabited by the German speaking majority. The Czechs had no choice but to accept the ultimatum. Believing he was the bearer of good news, Chamberlain returned to Hitler with the Czech reply. But instead of gratitude, Hitler was furious. He had decided to raise the stakes, he now presented the British Prime Minister with a map that indicated new territorial demands. Chamberlain agreed to submit the map to the Benes government. The French responded with equivocation but Benes replied with an explicit NO. Millions of people all over Europe remained glued to their radios, hoping for peace but fearing war.

Benito Mussolini suggested the convening of a four power conference to ease the tension. Chamberlain, Daladier, Hitler, and Mussolini met on September 29, 1938, in Munich. Neither Czechoslovakia nor the Soviet Union was invited despite the fact that any decision would affect their vital interests. In the long run they may well have been grateful for that affront; future generations could not blame them for participating in the ensuing shameful events.

The Munich Conference has become a metaphor for appeasement. It was there that Czech independence was handed to Hitler in the vain hope that this sacrifice would prevent war. Once again, Hitler raised the prospect of peace so ardently hoped for when he declared that the Sudetenland was his final demand. Whether or not this fiction was actually believed hardly matters. The impotence of European powers was revealed for all to see: First, it was obvious that the League of Nations was a paper tiger; second, France and England were militarily and psychologically unprepared to take on Hitler; and third, Hitler had been utterly misjudged.

The Munich Pact stipulated the Czechoslovak government cede to Germany the larger area that had been demanded. In effect, this left Czechoslovakia defenseless. Slovakia was given federated status; Poland and Hungary annexed small border districts. Benes resigned, and the proud achievement of Versailles, a prosperous, democratic Czechoslovakia, was doomed. Nonetheless, upon his return to England, Chamberlain waved a copy of the agreement and told his countrymen that he had brought them "peace in our time." The gift of prophecy, however, belonged to Winston Churchill, who warned that this was not the end but only the beginning of the reckoning, the first sip of the bitter cup to come.

Munich was a great success for Hitler and encouraged him to proceed toward further adventures. His generals had been fearful of military confrontations, but he had judged the irresolution of the West correctly. It is possible that at this time he began to be convinced of his own infallibility. An ironic footnote to these events was the fact that a group of German officers under the leadership of the chief of the general staff, General Franz Halder, had plotted to remove Hitler by a coup d'état. When Chamberlain appeared in Munich, hat in hand, the planned resistance within the officer corps, which included several of its highest-ranking members, was aborted.

THE CZECH FINALE

The dismemberment of the Czechs' territorial remnant was accomplished in the following spring. Hitler ordered the president of the truncated republic, Emil Hacha, to Berlin. The scenes enacted at that meeting concluded the Czech tragedy. Hacha begged Hitler to allow his people to retain their national life. Hitler responded with threats that for every Czech battalion there was a German division ready to march. Czechoslovakia, he warned, was about to be invaded, with or without Hacha's consent. How much blood it would cost the Czech people was entirely in his, the president's hands. Unless his signature was affixed to the prepared document inviting the

German troops to restore order in his country, squadrons of bombers would raze Prague. Hacha, who suffered from a heart ailment, fainted. Hitler's doctor revived him. Hacha pleaded for permission to telephone his cabinet but was refused. Finally, at 4:00 in the morning, physically and emotionally exhausted, he signed the document that permitted German troops to enter his homeland. (See map 7-1)

Hitler's armies marched into Czechoslovakia unopposed. This, however, was Hitler's last cheap victory. From here on, the German people would have to pay a

Map 7-1   *Germany's Expansion, 1933–1939.* (From Jackson J. Spielvogel, *Hitler and Nazi Germany: A History*, 2E. Upper Saddle River, NJ: Prentice Hall, 1996.)

price for his foreign exploits. France and England, even the Soviet Union, began to make military preparations. No longer was it debatable if Hitler would strike again; the question was merely where and when. During the summer of 1939, the world had its answer. The German propaganda ministry directed its full attention to the alleged suffering of the German minority living in Poland. There was an ominously familiar ring to the claims of atrocities committed against hapless fellow nationals. The next victim of Hitler's aggression had been identified.

THE STARTLING HITLER-STALIN PACT

From its inception, Nazi doctrine had emphasized its total opposition to Communism. The Goebbels press spared no adjective to reduce the Soviet leadership to the level of brutes. Often they were characterized as Jew-Bolsheviks, *Untermenschen* (sub-humans), and Mongols. The Nazi *Weltanshauung* induced a policy based on three concepts: Communism was an evil form of social organization; Jews, due to their racial defects, were destroyers and parasites; the Soviet Union, ruled by Communist-Jews, was the proper arena for German expansion. Thus, the annihilation of a hated regime and a hated people, and the conquest of coveted territory dovetailed neatly into a single approach. Hitler had consistently denounced Stalin as the enemy of civilization, while Stalin referred to him as the Nazi beast. No wonder the political world was astonished when unexpectedly it was announced that an agreement between the Soviet Union and Germany had been signed on August 23, 1939.

The two foreign ministers, Joachim von Ribbentrop and Vyacheslav Molotov, had worked out an accord that stipulated that for ten years neither country would support any third country if it attacked either Germany or the Soviet Union. That much, at any rate, was revealed to the public. There was also a secret protocol providing for the division of Poland and giving Stalin a free hand in the Baltic States. These arrangements were disclosed only after the Polish defeat by German armies. In light of the fact that neither dictator had any scruples, the astounding Berlin-Moscow entente was not nearly as bizarre as it seemed at first glance.

Stalin's intentions were probably twofold. The Munich appeasement of the previous year had caused consternation in Moscow. Was it possible that the four signatories in Munich might combine their forces against the Soviets? Stalin had been diplomatically rebuffed by the Western democracies and the nation's isolation caused much concern. The treaty with Germany relieved the anxiety about a combined Western assault. A second reason for the alliance was Russia's need for time to build up its military power. Stalin probably expected that sooner or later Germany would launch an attack. Both dictators approved the agreement in order to develop their own hidden agendas. If the planned conquest of Poland was merely the first step for further *Lebensraum* in Russia, Stalin, who had decimated his own officer corps because he distrusted them, required a period of peace to repair his country's defenses.

Hitler, on the other hand, dreaded the possibility of a two front war. With Russia neutralized, he could conquer Poland easily and—if it became necessary—then turn his attention to the western front. He was hoping, though not certain, that the appeasement mentality of Munich would continue and that he could wage "a little war" against Poland. Should France and England wish to spill their blood for the Poles, however, he would teach them a lesson in warfare—but on one front at a time. There had been no change of the basic plan; Russia, with its vast farmlands, its wealth in oil, and other natural resources was the proper place for planting the roots of the Thousand Year Reich.

Once again the world was holding its breath and Hitler did not keep the anxious millions waiting very long. As always, he sought a justification for his actions. Preliminary to the attack on Poland, a piece of absurd drama was enacted. The Poles must seem to be the aggressors for purposes of domestic and foreign propaganda. Himmler's aide, Reinhard Heydrich, chief of the Gestapo, wrote the script. SS men were dressed in Polish uniforms and simulated an attack on a small radio station in the German town of Gleiwitz, one mile from the Polish border. The men who staged the fictitious attack provided "proof" of Poland's treachery when they left behind the dead body of a German civilian. The victim, actually an inmate from a concentration camp, had been shot to provide reality to the theater. With cameras rolling, this supposed evidence was presented to a shocked public. Hitler, whose armies were already massed at the border, marched into Poland on September 1, 1939. Within two days France and England honored their defensive treaties with Poland and declared war on Germany. World War II had begun! It started with a farce but it ended in a tragedy of momentous dimensions.

THE WAR AT A GLANCE

This brief account cannot detail the complicated ebb and flow of battles fought on four continents. A few generalities have to suffice in order to explain the international composition of the 6 million Jewish Holocaust victims. Our interest, therefore, is confined to the European arena of the conflict (see Map 7-2). The Pacific and African operations, although vital in the defeat of the Germans and their Japanese ally, require no attention here.

The two coalitions of belligerents became known as the Axis and the Allied powers. Germany and its original Axis partner, Italy, were more or less reluctantly joined by Hungary, Romania, Bulgaria, and Finland. The military aspects of the Axis in the European theater of war were completely dominated by Germany. The alliance of Poland, France, and England evolved into the Allied powers which eventually included the Soviet Union, the United States, Canada, Australia, New Zealand, and most of the remaining Western world. Spain maintained its official neutrality but had close ties to Germany. Sweden, Switzerland, Portugal, Ireland, and Turkey were able to stay out of the conflict probably because Hitler decided they were more useful to him as neutrals.

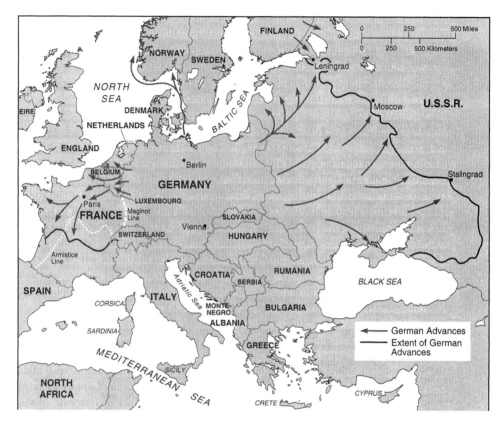

Map 7-2 *Military Operations of World War II: The German Offensives, 1939–1942.* (From Jackson J. Spielvogel, *Hitler and Nazi Germany: A History,* 2E. Upper Saddle River, NJ: Prentice Hall, 1996.)

During the first two years of the war, Germany was astonishingly success-ful. Its military tactics, the *Blitzkrieg,* (lightning war) utilized mobility to an extent hitherto unknown in the manuals of any general staff. Hitler recognized that in manpower and resources his enemies were superior and if the war lasted long enough their superiority might result in his defeat. Thus, speed was the essential factor, armies had to move like lightning. German mobile columns appeared deep in enemy territory long before their opponents thought it possible. The German offensives were usually initiated by heavy bombing aimed at the destruction of the enemy's air force, the communication and transportation sys-tems. These attacks were followed by divebombers hitting hostile troop concen-trations to inflict heavy casualties and create chaos. Before recovery was possible, assaults by all types of mobile artillery, from light tanks to motorcycle companies, caused further losses and heightened the confusion. Heavy tanks secured the rear and prevented escape and reorganization. Aerial assaults on fleeing civilians produced panic and frenzy. It is curious indeed that *Blitzkrieg* strategies had first been advanced in 1934 by a French colonel named Charles de Gaulle. But his superior officers rejected this approach.

The war lasted six years. In the European Theater of operations it ended on VE Day, May 8, 1945. It had been fought with new weaponry and new tactics on land, at sea and in the air. Civilians were involved in every aspect of the efforts of the belligerents. Bombs killed them, invading armies put them to flight, food rationing left them undernourished. Worldwide, the dead numbered between 35–55 million. The devastation and military expenditures have been estimated to cost the incomprehensible figure of $2 trillion. To a much greater degree than the war in 1914–1918, this was global war and a total war. Aerial bombardments brought unparalleled destruction to cities and the introduction of atomic weapons in the Pacific Theater of operations threatened the very existence of all life on earth.

During the war the Nazis had expanded their dwindling labor force by the use of slave labor. Men and women from their conquered territories had been forced to supply their war machine and they had helped to grow food on German farms. At the end of the armed conflict there were 7 million foreign workers in the Reich. They became known as displaced persons. As Soviet armies marched westward, they established Communist regimes in eastern Europe and the Balkans. Many of the slave laborers from these regions refused to go home to live under Communism and they roamed across Europe wondering where and how to rebuild their lives. (See the Epilogue)

The United States and the Soviet Union emerged as rival superpowers. Their competition for political and economic predominance was called the Cold War. For the following 45 years this conflict dictated the policies of both nations. On several occasions the cold war boiled over into military confrontations. The division of Germany into Democratic and Communist parts, West Germany and East Germany, was part of this struggle of the giants. Not until 1989 was Germany reunified into a single nation. A new peacekeeping organization was created, and since hope does spring eternal, the world prays that the United Nations may eventually accomplish its mission.

The fighting was over but only then did the world learn of the fate of the Jews of Europe. When Allied soldiers liberated the death and concentration camps, battle weary combat soldiers cried. All speculation, all rumors, all denials came to a halt. A Shoah, a genocide of 6 million Jews had been carried out during the chaos of war. German conquests had enabled the Nazis to locate, trap, and kill their victims. Even in areas where German occupation was of short duration, such as in Italy and Hungary, Nazi organizational skills and fanaticism had assured the annihilation of hundreds of thousands of Jews. It seems absurd to call killers dedicated, but the label does apply. Complete dedication to their task was required to identify, round up, isolate, and massacre so many people in so many countries in so brief a time. Just how many German civilians knew the truth about the "resettlement of Jews" is impossible to tell. No official announcement ever admitted the truth. But certainly the Polish people knew, the death camps were located on their soil and to that country we must now return.

THE DEFEAT OF POLAND

The conquest of Poland was completed in one month. Hitler's *Blitzkrieg* strategies caught the Polish army in a huge vise between the Baltic States and Slovakia. The Poles, whose forces still included horse cavalry, tried bravely and pathetically to defend their country against tank units and aerial attacks. Warsaw was bombarded relentlessly and held out for four weeks. The Soviets invaded Poland from the East to claim their share of territory as stipulated in the Molotov-Ribbentrop pact. The statistics of men killed in action speak for themselves: German losses were 11,000 compared to Polish losses of 120,000. Seventy thousand of these casualties occurred in battles against the Germans and 50,000 against the invading Russians. Although the French and English governments honored their treaty obligations and declared war on Germany, they were unable to supply any aid in time to prevent the fall of Poland. The campaign was over before they could ship arms or men to support the Poles.

The Nazis occupied western and central Poland, a region that in 1939 had a population of 20 million. The eastern territories and its 12 million people, which had been occupied by the Soviet Union, were overrun in 1941 when Hitler launched his attack on Russia. Thus, many of the refugees who had fled eastward to escape the Nazis were overwhelmed two years later. Among these, a fortunate minority made its way deeper into Russian territory, some traveling as far east as Siberia. The hardships they endured were grim but most survived, whereas life under Nazi occupation was a nightmare from which 5 million of Poles never awoke.

Hitler had resolved to destroy Polish national life. He considered its Slavic inhabitants as racially undesirable and its farmlands suitable for Aryan expansion. To secure the subjugation of the defeated people, the annihilation of the entire Polish elite was ordered. With stunning ruthlessness, most members of the aristocracy, military officers, political leaders, priests, and the intelligentsia were murdered. Pre-war prominence in any field of the nation's political, economic, or cultural life was a death sentence. Like the proscriptions of ancient times, these murders were carried out to eliminate the possibility of organizing any anti-German resistance. (Actually such ruthlessness gave rise to opposition). The SS and Gestapo followed the German armies and carried out this dreadful objective. The people of Poland were totally unprepared for such savagery. Those members of their government who eluded the Nazi murderers and escaped to England left behind a people in chaos and despair. The Poles did not expect a merciful occupation, but nothing in modern history enabled them to anticipate such barbarism.

Poland was cut in two. The western provinces, which the Germans called the *Ostgaue,* were annexed to the Reich. Largest within that region was the district called *Warthegau.* South-central Poland, now referred to as the General Government, became the private kingdom of Hans Frank, Hitler's friend and lawyer. Frank had risen rapidly in the Nazi hierarchy and held several important legal appointments before he was chosen to be the governor-general of occupied Poland. In that position, he combined the avarice of a Goering with the ruthlessness of a Himmler. For example, he declared German the official language of his Polish speaking realm, he confiscated and stole great art treasures, and sent countless innocent people to their deaths. Life in Poland remained deliberately without any reasonable order, even minimal services to the public were refused. Frank described his function as that of a lord in charge over so many slaves whose value was proportionate to their usefulness to Germany. His lifestyle was royal, his residence in Cracow was palatial. Three major death camps were located in his territory, and he often complained that the constant influx of Jews interfered with his administrative duties.

HIMMLER'S VISION OF POLAND

Hans Frank, to his regret, did not own the Jews; Himmler and the SS did. With yet another title to fit his extended authority, Himmler was named Executor of Purification of the Conquered Lands. In this role he was charged with three mandates: first was the reduction and enslavement of the biologically undesirable population; second, the identification and preservation of any Aryan elements in the population; and third, the Germanization of regions formerly occupied by the native population. The plan called for the establishment of agricultural settlements of SS families so that Polish soil would be tied to the Reich forever. Like warrior knights from the Middle Ages, a new nobility would be created to secure the *Lebensraum* in the East. The SS was to be installed as the lords on their estates and their serfs would come from the decimated Polish population.

Poles had hoped that the German occupiers would act in accordance with the rules of civilized warfare. Such expectations had to be abandoned very quickly. The German armies and the SS which arrived on their heels showed none of the correctness so often attributed to them. Old prejudices and new indoctrination had taught the Germans to ignore, even to take pleasure, in the misery of the Poles. The cruelty of the German occupation in the eastern occupied territories has been thoroughly documented. Hitler's orders were simple enough: Germanize Poland in ten years. The cost to the native people was irrelevant; they were consigned to a life of service and submission. Polish suffering must be acknowledged, particularly in view of the oft-repeated charge that most Poles cared nothing about the fate of the Jews. While anti-Semitism was widespread, it is also true that many of them risked their own lives to save their Jewish neighbors. It should also be realized that the brutality of the German conquerors may have robbed many Poles of the ability to care about the suffering of others. The Nazis held Slavs in humiliating contempt and their lives were expendable. Himmler was granted a free hand to interfere in the already inefficient civilian bureaucracy with a mandate to keep Poland secure. He interpreted that directive as a mandate to terrorize the defeated people.

Polish men and women were at the mercy of individual, often competing, German and collaborating Polish officials. Alleviation from hunger and the winter cold was not considered a responsibility of the occupying forces, indeed they looted their victims' food, goods, and treasures. The confusion of conflicting orders from the SS, the police, the Gauleiters, officers of the German army, and native bureaucrats created continuous anxiety and frustration. The Nazis had no wish to resolve this anarchy. For example: a Pole seeking to obtain a driver's license could not be certain to whom to apply; he was sent from one office to another, waited many hours in long lines until the weeks of interrogation and intimidation made him quit the effort. A rudderless, frightened, and impoverished people were, in the view of the conqueror, more likely to be docile and compliant.

It is not an exaggeration to speak of the enslavement of Polish workers. Men and women were treated as a renewable commodity. They were shipped here or there, to work on farms, in mines, or in factories. Almost a million farmers were uprooted to make way for the Germanization of the land. Workers who were deported to the Reich had a better chance of survival than their families at home; at least they were given some food. But hunger, cold, disease, and punishment for real or imagined acts of sabotage took an appalling toll on civilians. The fact that some of the Poles joined together in secret, usually in the forests, and formed resistance groups is testimony to their tenacity and courage.

The people of Poland were severely afflicted by a particularly vicious aspect of Himmler's *Lebensborn* (fountain of life) program. The major thrust of this scheme was the encouragement of German girls to bear racially desirable children, preferably fathered by SS men. The less-known component of *Lebensborn* was the kidnapping of blond, blue-eyed children from occupied lands. Babies and young children were snatched from their homes and sent to German couples for adoption. Their exact numbers are not known but it has been estimated that several hundred thousand children "disappeared." If the Nazis kept records indicating the specific fate of the *Lebensborn* children, they have not been found. Even now there are aged mothers and fathers searching for a trace of their lost boys and girls.

When the bloodletting was over, after six years of German occupation, Poland lay in ruins and more than 17 percent of its population, some 6 million, were dead. Of this number, about half were Jews and half were Christians. With the possible exception of the Gypsies, only the Jews of Europe suffered a higher percentage of civilian losses.

THE WAR IN THE WEST

The period from the fall of Poland in October 1939 until the following spring has been dubbed the "phony war," or *Sitzkrieg* (sit-down war), because there was no activity on the Western front. Hitler hoped but failed to drive a wedge between the French-English alliance, and his generals advised against a winter campaign. In the spring, the Germans struck again; without the formality of a declaration of war. Denmark was overrun in a single day. The German admiralty had urged the occupation of Norway in order to secure submarine bases in the war against England. The

Norwegians held out for a month. On May 10, the *Blitzkrieg* armies marched into France. By invading the poorly prepared Low Countries, they outflanked the Maginot Line. Holland asked for an armistice in five days; Belgium lasted three weeks. The combined armies of Britain and France were unable to stop the German advance. Only the "miracle of Dunkirk" saved the Allies from complete disaster. This miracle was actually a retreat. British ships rescued 215,000 of their own men and 120,000 French soldiers from the northern beaches of France. In June, Paris was surrendered to prevent its destruction. A demoralized, defeatist French government under Marshall Henri Pétain wanted peace at whatever cost. The official capitulation of France was consummated on June 22, 1940. On that day, at the exact spot in the forest of Compiègne where, on November 11, 1918, Germany had acknowledged its defeat, an ecstatic Hitler turned the tables on France. It was probably the moment of his greatest triumph. At this point, Mussolini added a tainted jewel to Hitler's crown; with France prostrate, he opted to join Hitler's war. Franklin Delano Roosevelt called this action a stab in the back, and the phrase has stuck.

Hitler's terms were harsh. Alsace and Lorraine were annexed to the Reich. The large northern sector, including Paris, was placed under military administration, although Nazi politicians could not keep their hands in their pockets and frequently interfered. The French people were compelled to pay for the cost of the occupation. German aims, quite simply, were to exploit the conquered people and their products to the fullest. By implied and direct terror, the possibility of any opposition to the occupation forces was to be prevented. German ruthlessness in trying to wipe out the French underground resistance organizations cost thousands of French men and women their lives.

The central and southern two-fifths of France were permitted to form a puppet state. Marshall Pétain, hero of the Battle of Verdun in the First World War, now became a German pawn. He always claimed that his compliant attitude toward the Germans saved many lives; however, the problem of cooperation with the enemy continues to haunt the French. When the war ended, Pétain was tried and spent the rest of his life in prison. His Vice Premier, Pierre Laval, was an outright collaborator of the Nazis. He allowed his country to be looted, made no objection when French slave laborers were forced to work in the Reich, and even tried to raise a French army to fight alongside the Germans. In his desire to please his Nazi masters, he not only complied with, but tried to anticipate their wishes. His role in the deportation of French Jews was shameful (see Chapter 9). Laval, too, was tried by his countrymen and met his death by firing squad in 1945.

Not all the Jews living in France were French. Tens of thousands were refugees from other Nazi-occupied lands. Many were illegal residents, thus their number cannot be precisely determined. The prewar native Jewish population was about 300,000, with perhaps an equal number of émigrés. Paris was the magnet; in 1940 it is estimated that more than half of its Jews were from Poland, Czechoslovakia, and Germany. The conquest of Holland and Belgium caused a renewed influx. The possibility of a sudden and disastrous French defeat was totally unforeseen. As in all the conquered countries, foreign Jews were the first to be sacrificed to Nazi demands.

GOVERNING THE CONQUERED NATIONS

The Nazis had no master plan for the administration of their conquests. None of the defeated peoples were given a systematic, businesslike government. All were exploited, but the degree of severity differed. An overlapping of military, civilian, and native authorities was common. In Norway, a native Nazi, Vidkun Quisling (his name is now synonymous with traitor), served as the puppet prime minister. He shared power with the equally hated *Gauleiter* Josef Terboven. Denmark was permitted to keep its democratic institutions as long as the government and people cooperated with the Germans. When that cooperation was sabotaged by an active Danish resistance organization, Reich Commissioner Werner Best and the German army appeared in Copenhagen. Although the German administration of Holland and Belgium differed in theory, the reality of daily life varied little. Belgium was governed as a military district and Holland by Nazi civilians under Artur Seyss-Inquart. Everywhere, native resources and manpower were diverted to benefit Germany; art treasures were plundered from public and private collections. The small size of the Low Countries and their terrain made it very difficult to escape from German surveillance, nonetheless, underground fighters organized and harassed the despised conquerors. Members of resistance groups faced not only the danger of German capture, but also the treachery of their own countrymen who had opted to collaborate with the enemy in order to gain some advantage for themselves.

The Nazis did not view the Western Europeans with the same contempt reserved for Slavs and Jews. Generally, the French and Northern Europeans did not suffer hardships and losses to the same degree as the Eastern victims, although they experienced shortages of everything and lived in a state of constant anxiety.

GREAT BRITAIN ALONE

Only the English remained to deprive Hitler of total victory. That stubborn island people, led by Winston Churchill, refused to see the futility of resistance. Did they not realize that fate had ordained that Nazism must triumph? Although the English stood alone, they spurned Hitler's peace feelers. Hitler believed the English people would demand that their government enter into a rapprochement with Germany if they suffered heavy losses at sea. However, even though German submarines inflicted much damage, they could not stop all of the vitally needed shipments from reaching the island. The British Commonwealth nations and the United States provided the essentials and the English could not be starved into submission. Hitler needed a quick victory; a prolonged war might bring Russia and the United States into the conflict. The Fuehrer decided to invade Great Britain (Operation Sea Lion) as soon as the German air force established its superiority over the skies. Goering promised that his *Luftwaffe* was equal to the task, but the RAF (Royal Air Force) continued to hold its own and eventually dominated in the air. The relentless aerial bombing of English cities strengthened rather than weakened English resolve. This, in Churchill's words, was Britain's finest hour. Hitler's invasion plans were canceled.

THE BALKANS AND OPERATION BARBAROSSA

The failure to force Britain to the peace table had created new problems for Hitler. Germany lacked the raw materials necessary for an extended war. Gasoline propelled the *Blitzkrieg,* and Germany had none. Oil-rich Romania and its Balkan neighbors, Hungary and Bulgaria, had been cajoled and threatened into cooperating with Nazi interests. Hitler would have preferred not to expend any military manpower in the Balkans and continue to dominate the area politically and economically. But there he came into conflict with his ally and erstwhile mentor, Benito Mussolini. The Italians looked upon Southeastern Europe as their sphere of influence. They had invaded and conquered the small Adriatic nation of Albania and now coveted Greece.

Greece, however, was not Ethiopia or Albania. With the aid of British forces, the Greeks routed the Italians. Hitler now had to divert armies to rescue Il Duce from a humiliating defeat and also to safeguard the Romanian oil supplies. His armies defeated the combined Greek and English forces; even the island of Crete was occupied by Germans. It became necessary to secure Bulgaria and Yugoslavia as well. The cost of controlling the Balkans was an ongoing liability, particularly due to the persistent harassment from Yugoslav guerrillas. The Balkan diversion caused a fateful two-month delay in the attack on the Soviets; just how fateful this was would become clear when German armies found themselves fighting the Russian winter and the Soviet soldiers at the same time.

On June 22, 1941, two years after Hitler and Stalin had signed their ten-year non-aggression pact, Hitler attacked the Soviet Union. Thus began the two-front war he so greatly feared. The judgment that England was in no position to land troops on the shores of continental Europe and the expectation of a quick victory on the Eastern front persuaded the Fuehrer that actually he was not fighting on two fronts. The official pretext for the war was so thin that Goebbels need not have bothered to contrive it. The true motivation was rooted in past hatred and present circumstances.

Hitler was unalterably convinced that German *Lebensraum* was destined to be on Polish/ Russian soil. His abhorrence of communism had never diminished. It was only a matter of time before ideology would be translated into attack. Hitler feared that in time British troops might link up with those of the Soviet Union. He was certain that it would be better to strike against Russia before this could happen. Furthermore, Mussolini's attack on Greece had brought the English to the Balkans, threatening Germany's oil supply. The time was ripe. Hitler activated *Fall Barbarossa,* the code name for the Russian invasion. He anticipated victory before the onset of winter. The Soviet armies, Hitler claimed, were dominated by Jews and Bolsheviks and thus would offer little resistance.

Hitler was well aware that Japan and the United States were on a collision course. He encouraged the Japanese to attack the United States because he believed that a war in the Pacific would prevent American forces from playing a role in Europe. Russia, according to this plan, would be crushed in a few months. At that point, even with some aid from overseas, England would be forced to surrender. Germany, then, would be in position to dictate peace terms. The Fatherland would have it all; raw materials, *Lebensraum,* and slave workers to fulfill the destiny of Hitler's vision of the New Order—German domination of Europe.

Hitler miscalculated fatally. Although German divisions penetrated deep into the Soviet Union, they were unable to take either Leningrad (now St. Petersburg) or Moscow. Unprepared, without winter clothing, the cold took a terrible toll among the German soldiers. The Eastern front bogged down along a line reaching from the outskirts of Leningrad to the fringes of Moscow and stretched south to the gates of Stalingrad (now Volgograd). The Battle of Stalingrad, considered a turning point of the war, stopped the German offensive and by the fall of 1942 German troops were on the defensive. Hitler, who had convinced himself that he was a military genius, now took personal command of the armed forces. No doubt, he had some military talent; however, when his strategies failed, he insisted that cowardice and treachery among the generals, not his orders, were to blame. His refusal to permit troops to retreat, even when in an untenable position, was particularly costly. At this time, however, Allied victory was still far from certain. The Germans took the entire Crimean Peninsula; General Erwin Rommel, the Desert Fox, campaigned successfully in Africa; and the German U-boat fleet inflicted heavy losses on Allied shipping.

The population of these areas of conquests had to endure the terrible ordeal of Nazi occupation. As in Poland, absurd racial theories determined policy. Where cooperation might have been achieved, resistance was fostered. Surely, this was the case in the Ukraine where the arriving Germans were welcomed as liberators. But that goodwill evaporated when it became clear that the Germans viewed the Ukrainians with utter disdain. The Baltic States, too, might have collaborated; instead, German severity nullified that potentiality. Soviet officers, and of course Jews, were singled out for the infamous "special treatment." Millions were enslaved, starved, or murdered outright.

The German administration of the conquered Russian regions was a botched operation. The authority of different Nazi officials, the military, the SS, and the private empires carved out by Goering, Himmler, and Albert Speer of the Armaments Ministry collided amid bewildering confusion. Disregard for the needs of the native population was the only point of unanimity. Over 3.5 million Russian soldiers were taken prisoner during the first months of the war. They were labeled subhuman in the German press and were treated with such cruelty that their captors must bear the subhuman label. The Nazis were unprepared to accommodate so many POWs and instituted a deliberate policy of mass starvation in concentration camps and arbitrary shootings in the fields and woods of Russia. Surviving Soviet prisoners of war reported that when starvation drove them to cannibalism, their German guards expressed utter disdain for the victims of their own atrocities. Only when German labor shortages became extreme were they used as slave laborers. At the end of the war, the Soviet Union had lost 20 million of its people, military and civilian. This staggering number is greater than the combined losses of all other belligerents in Europe.

THE TURNING OF THE TIDE

It is impossible to know with certainty why Hitler declared war on the United States just after the Pearl Harbor attack. The fact that he had concluded a tripartite agreement of mutual aid with Italy and Japan was not a decisive issue; Hitler honored his signature quite selectively. Perhaps he believed that President Roosevelt was bound to enter the conflict in any case or that the United States presented little danger because the Americans would be unable to fight in the Pacific as well as in the Atlantic theaters of operation. He may have believed that Europe would be prostrate at his feet before the hated Roosevelt could interfere. How little he understood the Americans; obviously, he did not grasp that such a declaration rallied the American people to a resolute, unified stand against the Germans.

Hitler was right when he stated that Germany could not win a long war. When the quick success of the earlier campaigns could not be duplicated after 1942, Allied victory was simply a matter of time. The courage and perseverance of Britain and the Soviet Union afforded the United States the necessary breathing space to draw upon its great human and material resources. On the seas, in the air, and on the ground the combined effort of the Allies overwhelmed the Germans. The contributions of the United States were essential. Not only did the United States send soldiers and sailors, armaments and medical supplies, but also vitally needed quantities of food. The psychological effect of the American commitment is difficult to measure, but surely it inspired renewed courage to the weary, embattled people throughout Europe. Nonetheless, victory was not cheaply won. To the last day of the war, Hitler's armies inflicted heavy losses, even when the final outcome was no longer in doubt.

Allied forces, under the leadership of General Dwight D. Eisenhower, attacked Germany in a huge pincer movement with Berlin at the center. Russian armies moved westward along a vast front from the Baltic Sea in the north to Bulgaria in the south. They pushed through Poland, took the Balkan countries, and continued their offensive toward the North and West. In the winter of 1944 they were poised on the German border.

The Western Allies invaded Sicily in 1943 and struggled up the Italian boot against heavily defended German installations. Sick of the war, King Victor Emanuel expressed the wishes of his people when he dismissed Mussolini and hoped to make peace. For all intents and purposes, Italian troops were no longer a factor after the summer of 1943. Rome and Florence were taken in 1944. Italian partisan fighters had imprisoned a rather subdued Il Duce. He was freed in a daring German helicopter rescue mission, but in April 1945, Italian anti-Fascists captured and

Air raid on Berlin during WWII. (Courtesy UPI/Corbis.)

executed him. The Allied armies reached Northern Italy, where they remained deadlocked with German divisions until the end of the war.

The successful landing on D-Day, June 6, 1944, gave the Soviets the second front for which they had pressed so long and so urgently. From Normandy, American, British, Commonwealth, and Free French troops fought their way eastward while others moved north from the Mediterranean. The German armies still numbered 10 million men who suffered as well as inflicted heavy casualties. Hitler hoped to halt the Western assault at the fortifications on Germany's Western frontier (Siegfried Line), a defense installation running opposite the Maginot Line. But the fortifications could not check the advance of the Allies into the Reich itself. German cities were bombed relentlessly and as the rubble piled up, German civilians experienced the horror their Fuehrer had unleashed on so many other nations.

Hitler was still directing operations from one of his several underground bunkers. In July 1944, a group of Army and civilian anti-Nazis attempted to assassinate him. Hitler's fury and revenge were maniacal; accusations, some true, some false, condemned men to death by methods of execution that Spanish Inquisitors would have envied.

As Allied soldiers entered Berlin, Hitler, in his bunker beneath the Chancellery garden, directed armies that no longer existed. His scorn for the German people was obvious when he ordered the destruction of everything the enemy might use. If these orders had been carried out, the ruin of the Reich would have been total. Hitler, irrational, perhaps insane, saw treason everywhere. His generals, even Goering and Himmler, could no longer be trusted. Worst of all, the German people preferred peace to death, thus proving their weakness and their unworthiness. Afraid of falling into Russian hands, he shot himself on April 30, 1945. According to his instructions, his body was burned. Goebbels had also remained in the Berlin bunker and had not wavered in his loyalty. He poisoned his six children and then he and his wife committed suicide. One week later, Hitler's designated successor, Admiral Karl Doenitz, surrendered unconditionally to emissaries of the British, French, Soviet, and American forces.

The legacy of the twelve years of Hitler's dictatorship cannot be evaluated in the context of this text. Suffice it to say that from the ashes of the Third Reich a vastly different world was wrought. Every aspect of human life, psychological, military, economic, political, religious, and philosophical, was permanently and deeply affected. There was so much suffering, so many losses, such upheaval, even the balm of time cannot erase the scars. And yet, veterans of many battles, men well versed in the cruelty of war, testified that nothing in their experience equaled the horror they felt upon entering a concentration camp. There they saw the absolute evil that man can do to man.

CHAPTER 8

From Ideology to Isolation

The Nazis were tireless in their efforts to dehumanize both the victims and their killers. They took great pains in a double-edged attempt to demean the Jews in their own eyes and to convince the SS that Jews were dangerous subhumans. Memoirs of survivors and reports from concentration camp records affirm that the psychological bombardments were more successful with the perpetrators than with the victims. Starved and bereft of their families, unable to keep themselves clean, clothed in rags, with shaven heads, and wooden clogs on their feet, deprived even of their names, the vast majority of the prisoners behaved as moral men and women. Some among them were heroes, some were villains, and most tried to stay alive one more day without hurting a fellow sufferer.

The Nazi executioners can be divided into two categories, the officials who propelled the paperwork and the men who murdered the Jews and other "undesirables." Both groups used language to disguise the reality of their work by the use of a deceptive vocabulary. For example, again and again they were told that they were ridding the world of vermin, carriers of infection whose extermination was beneficial to mankind; the word *Endloesung* which indicated the annihilation of the Jewish people, has no ominous connotation in German. In fact, Final Solution might refer to the answer of a mathematical problem. The term resettlement sounds benign but in Nazi-speak it meant imprisonment in ghettos or concentration camps, or the journey to the death camps. The word *Lebensborn* in German translates to well of life, two words that create a charming picture, however, as we noted in the previous chapter, masked the kidnapping of children. The order to use mobile killing units was given the deceptive name *Auszerordentliche Befriedigungs Aktion,* that is special pacification action. When the trains rolled into Auschwitz, their human cargo was greeted with large letters arced above the entrance gate, *Arbeit macht frei,* work will set you free. That promise was kept only for those victims who equated death with freedom.

The objective of "purifying" the Reich by purging it of Jews was clearly a fixed doctrine from the beginning. In due course, Nazi conquests spread the *Judenrein* concept to most of the European continent. Historians do not agree just when Hitler decided to transform his zeal to rule a Germany without Jews into the prescription for annihilation. Some researchers, the Intentionalists, believe that genocide was always the blueprint, always the intent. An opposing view is held by the Functionalists who see the death factories as the result of an evolutionary process. Circumstances, they assert, heightened by the confusion of wartime conditions, the large number of Eastern Jews who came under Nazi rule, and the general indifference of the world to the fate of the Jews resulted in a step-by-step acceleration of persecution.

The Nazis tried to promote emigration during the prewar years, such as the aborted plan to transfer Jews to a designated area near Lublin and the scheme to ship them to Madagascar. Just when the decision was made to change from a policy of expulsion to total destruction remains unclear. A *Schnellbrief,* (urgent directive) was sent by the Chief of Security Reinhard Heydrich as early as September 21, 1939 to his *Einsatzgruppen* commanders. The secret instructions, issued before the end of the brief Polish campaign, ordered the removal of Jews to ghettos but spoke of that action as a preliminary operation to the *Endziel,* the final aim. It seems that the decision to attack Poland coincided with the eliminationist decision of the Nazis.

Lecturers on the Holocaust, within and outside of the classroom, sooner rather than later will be confronted with questions concerning the guilt of the German people. Invariably, some members of audience believe that all Germans must have known that the disappearance of their Jewish neighbors was synonymous with their destruction. From the safety of the lecture room it is not difficult to assert that the inaction or indifference of German civilians in the face of such knowledge makes the whole nation culpable.

WHAT DID THE GERMAN PEOPLE KNOW?

This argument stems from a wrong premise. A personal incident may serve to illustrate the point. When the writer left her small Silesian hometown, several members of the family were left behind. They were murdered in death camps. Years later, at a reunion of former neighbors, I was asked by several of them about the whereabouts of these relatives. I answered with one word: "Auschwitz." The faces of questioners turned from shock to disbelief to sorrow. Obviously, they would not have asked the question if they guessed or knew what the answer would be.

It is not possible to ascertain how many German civilians were aware of the existence and the functions of the death camps. Obviously, many had to know. First of all, there were the participants in the process and their friends and relatives. Others who had access to the truth included members of the regular *Wehrmacht* who assisted in roundups, even in shootings. Certainly, large numbers of bureaucrats were involved in expediting this enormous and complicated undertaking. Railroads were rerouted, financial institutions received and disbursed goods, and funds taken from the Jews had to be disbursed. Thousands of businessmen benefited from the Aryanization process. Employees in the Health Ministry and doctors were frequently concerned with ghetto and concentration camp epidemics; ministers from the foreign affairs section had to be apprised in order to respond to questions from abroad; manufacturers of poison gas and crematoria had to suspect or know of the ultimate uses of their products. Members of police auxiliary troops who were frequently used to augment the SS were partners in the killing process and it is doubtful they complied with the oath to tell no one. Recipients of used clothing from which the Jewish star had recently been removed surely must have wondered or perhaps understood what happened to the original owners. As the Jews disappeared from their neighborhoods, many Germans guessed but did not face the truth about the meaning of the official explanation, that Jews were resettled in the east.

It is noteworthy that the German government tried to prevent knowledge of the genocide from reaching its citizens. The perpetrators of the Shoah, the shooters and gassers, swore to keep their terrible secrets. Does this indicate that despite years of intensive anti-Jewish propaganda, Nazi officials did not believe that ordinary Germans would condone their actions? Himmler frequently spoke of his mission to annihilate the Jews in almost religious terms, but only to his own minions. Hitler, quite literally with his dying breath, consoled himself that he had at least been victorious in the destruction of the Jews. But no public announcement ever set forth what actually happened to the Jews. Thus, it is not possible to determine how many Germans realized that the trains were moving men, women, and children to their deaths. It is likely that the majority of Germans deliberately chose to remain in the dark; that was the easiest path. The war had taken sons and husbands from their midst; destruction by Allied bombing affected millions of families and encouraged an attitude of indifference to other people's problems. Dreadful rumors were whispered, but it was best to deny their possible truth than to deal with yet another emotional burden.

AN OVERVIEW

Before detailing the mechanics of the Holocaust, it is useful to have a general understanding of the framework of the operation. Although there were differences in place and time, once the decision was made to solve the "Jewish problem" by means of total eradication, the road to the gas chambers was but the final step in a series of recognizable, preparatory actions. The ideological basis, that is, the paranoid hatred of Jews, had been government policy since 1933. The agents to carry out the genocide, the SS, had the training, the will, the arms, and the official instructions to commit the mass murders. The Fuehrer needed no approval for his actions. No parliament, no court of justice, no political opposition had survived to challenge the crimes of the state. The voice of the people was stilled; the churches, with minor exceptions, were submissive to secular authority; and the killing mechanisms and techniques either already existed or were devised without difficulty. Members of the medical and the judicial professions, though sworn to support life and justice, in their official posture supported the actions of their government.

The first step toward annihilation was to ascertain how many Jews lived in a designated region. Americans who are accustomed to keeping religious affiliations private are often puzzled about the ability of the Nazis to identify their victims. During the 1940s, it was not difficult to discover the religion of Europeans. Not only did most official statistics indicate faith, but ordinary documents such as licenses, insurance policies, passports, applications for jobs, school records, membership in organizations, etc., commonly recorded religious beliefs. The registers of Jewish congregations and associations were confiscated as a matter of course by the Germans. Thus, it was not difficult to determine the number of Jews, their addresses, their occupations, and even the status of their bank accounts. Several thousand Jews survived by hiding, but that escape from death was very dangerous because it usually depended on the willingness of others to take great risks. Some Jewish women who looked Aryan, blue-eyed blondes in particular, passed as Christians. Their success often depended on their ability to get away from areas where they could be recognized and denounced to the Nazis. While the *Mischlinge* were accorded special consideration in the Reich, such refinement rarely applied to the conquered areas.

The removal of Jews from economic life usually followed the process of identification. In Germany, this procedure took several years, but it was accomplished rapidly in the conquered territories. Through directives for Aryanization and by forcible expulsion, Jews were deprived of their jobs, their businesses, and the practice of their professions. The looting of their possessions was usually accompanied by their removal from their homes and subsequent confinement and murder.

The next step entailed the physical separation of the Jews. Ghettos were established in major cities in the East and Jews from the West were transported into these already overcrowded enclosures. This massing of Jews into designated districts served several purposes. Their physical removal from their homes facilitated the expropriation process; the property they were forced to leave was declared abandoned and acquired by this or that German agency. Ghettos were easily controlled; Jewish councils, the *Judenraete,* were used to run the routine affairs of the ghetto. Since they were enclosed by walls or barricades of some sort, little manpower was required to prevent escapes and smuggling. Both the ghettos and the concentration camps were located at or near railroad depots. Thus, when the Nazis ordered the liquidation of a ghetto, the process of transporting the victims by rail was carried out with minimal effort. Lastly, living conditions within the ghettos also served to reduce the number of Jews by means of starvation and rampant disease.

The final phase of the Holocaust was the outright killing process. At first, the SS squads, the *Einsatzgruppen,* used guns. When shooting was deemed too slow and such direct contact with the victims regarded as psychologically undesirable (for the shooters), new methods had to be found. After a brief experiment using carbon monoxide gas generated from the exhaust of vehicles and diesel motors, the death factory was initiated. Instead of the killers rounding up the victims, the victims were brought to the killing centers. Railroads transported Jewish families to Poland from all of the Nazi-dominated lands. Within three years all the ghettos were emptied; some of their hundreds of thousands were used as slave laborers, but most were killed in the gas chambers.

TYPES AND AIMS OF CONCENTRATION CAMPS

The term concentration camp has several definitions and thus requires clarification. The original, official German explanation stated that the camps were installations for the purpose of re-educating members of the political opposition. Anti-social inmates were to be turned into useful citizens. Under the guise of placing troublemakers into "protective custody for the restoration of law and order," the government had the legal right to imprison suspects without trial. The earliest major camps, Dachau, Buchenwald, and Sachsenhausen, held actual and suspected dissidents such as labor union leaders, Communists, Socialists, members of the clergy, pacifists, and others. Jews were always among the victims, but in the early months after Hitler came to power they did not comprise the majority.

The original educational intent was never put into practice, and the sham was soon dropped. Concentration camps were huge prisons where so-called enemies of the state served sentences at the pleasure of several agencies entrusted with the security of the regime. The system expanded rapidly and developed three distinguishable types. Some sites combined several functions within the same compound. Best known are the death camps of Treblinka, Chelmno, Maidanek, Belzec, and Auschwitz-Birkenau. These were the killing centers that carried out the policy of genocide where the great majority of prisoners were murdered by one of several methods upon arrival.

The second group of some twenty concentration camps were designed to serve the killing process as well. Here, death came more slowly as the result of catastrophic living conditions. These installations were attached to work sites, and the starved prisoners were forced to perform heavy labor. Most of the victims survived for a few weeks, some for a few months. The number of work-related camps was constantly expanded; largest among these were Gross-Rosen, Ravensbrueck, Stutthof, Bergen–Belsen, and Theresienstadt in Czechoslovakia. Jews predominated among the prisoners in most of these camps.

A third type of mass detention facility was designated as labor camp. The inmates were, for the most part, non-Jewish men and women who had been rounded up in the conquered nations. Their work was usually connected to military needs. Some of the factories and mines exploited the skills of both Jews and Gentiles. In such facilities, the Jews were quartered separately, received less food, and suffered greater brutality. A vast network of hundreds of satellite installations was created, which enslaved millions of workers throughout Germany and its conquered territories. Buchenwald alone had 134 subcamps. The Germans treated their slave workers as a renewable resource whose welfare was of no concern to the state. Often toiling in factories and mines below the surface of the earth, men and women saw no daylight, lacked even the most rudimentary hygienic facilities, and received starvation rations. Inevitably, the death toll was high. As noted earlier, upon the collapse of the Reich they became the displaced persons of Europe. Destitute and bewildered, they roamed about as they looked for loved ones. Many were afraid to return to their Communist-dominated homelands, most suffered ill health and deep psychological scars. Their number, estimated at 7 million, presented serious problems to the Allied occupying forces at the end of the war. (See the Postscript.)

THE SS AND EMPEROR HIMMLER

The SS was an elite political army. Since no equivalent force exists in this country, it is not possible to compare it to anything familiar to Americans. In its discipline, the SS imitated the military; in ideology, it was trained to follow the Fuehrer with fanatical loyalty. Depending on the specialty of the unit, the SS was empowered to act as police, as judge, jury, and executioner, as spy and counterspy, as future Aryan settlers in the eastern *Lebensraum* conquests, as enforcers of political correctness, and as liquidators of all people deemed unworthy of life.

The popular image of the neat Germans, devotees of cleanliness and orderliness, was not borne out by Hitler's method of governing the country. As was noted earlier, the newsreels, depicting the perfect cadence of goose-stepping boots, hid the haphazard style of the Fuehrer's governance. Like a medieval liege lord, he preferred to have his vassals vie with one another for their realms as long as their loyalty to him did not waver. It is also a commonly held notion that Heinrich Himmler's domain ran with the precision of a fine clock. This perception also failed to withstand the scrutiny of historical research. The source of Himmler's power came directly from Hitler, but no clear table of organization connected the *treue Heinrich's* authority to his own group commanders. Himmler imitated his Fuehrer's formula and gave his subordinates ambiguous, often overlapping, areas of control. As his authority doubled and redoubled, the most aggressive of his department chiefs amassed the greatest power. To the sorrow of millions, they competed vigorously to impress Himmler with the fierceness of their pursuit of supposed enemies of the Reich.

SS stands for *Schutzstaffel,* or Defense Echelon; its black-uniformed troops were also called the Black Order. From the small band of handsome men, Hitler's personal guards numbering a mere 289 in 1929, Himmler carved out an empire of power and fear. As the circles of SS responsibilities widened, so did the number of collateral organizations. Eventually, all of the Reich's policing power was concentrated in his office of the Reich Security Main Office (RSHA). The parent organization, the general SS, was constantly culled of men to serve in one or another of the spun off groups. One of the early tasks of the SS was to protect the

Nazi party organization. The original function of the of the SD, (*Sicherheitsdienst, or Security Service*) was to ferret out its enemies. These units under Reinhard Heydrich were enlarged until they numbered 100,000 and were responsible for total internal security. Heydrich was a technocrat par excellence. A man without friends, he had been cashiered from the navy for womanizing, an insult he never forgot. His raw ambition and cold-blooded pragmatism were exactly what was needed by the SS. Himmler relied on him to find the practical means to implement his vague visions of an Aryan-dominated Europe. Although Heydrich had no particular hatred for the Jews, this indifference did not diminish his effectiveness in the management of their destruction. A specialist in terror with an insatiable hunger for power, he had the bearing, the blond appearance, and the arrogance of the very model Aryan superman. His meteoric career ended in 1942 when Czech resistance fighters killed him with grenades thrown under his car. Hitler and Himmler reacted to that assassination with a fury that cost 860 Czechs their lives. The entire Czech village of Lidice was destroyed on the unproven charge that the assassins had been sheltered there.

The *Totenkopfverbaende* (Deathshead Units) were SS specialists empowered to guard and administer the concentration camps. The name was derived from the symbol on their uniforms, a human skull. In 1934, Himmler appointed a convicted political terrorist, Theodor Eicke, to the post of inspector of concentration camps. Eicke had served as a commander at Dachau and went about his task with uncompromising hatred for the inmates. He scrapped the pretense that the camps were rehabilitation centers and changed their function to penal institutions. Eicke's directives were clear, brutal, and detailed. For example, he wrote the barbaric rules governing solitary confinement, the method of administering beatings, and instructed his men that pity for the enemy was an emotion unworthy of an SS man.

In 1936, after a successful power struggle with Goering, Himmler acquired control over the regular German police, called Orpo (*Ordnungspolizei*). Its members were uniformed and did such ordinary police work as regulating traffic and patrolling the streets. However, when the need arose, Himmler did not hesitate to simply incorporate entire squads into the SS. The same sort of unwelcome adoption coerced the Equestrian Association into the SS. In fact, Hitler awarded honorary SS command titles to men who had no connection to the SS. Thus, the notion that all of Himmler's men were totally imbued with Nazi ideology is open to question.

The secret state police (*Geheime Staats Polizei,* or Gestapo) had been spun off from the SD and became the Nazi party's most powerful organ for apprehending political dissenters. Its very name was whispered with dread. The use of torture in interrogation of suspects was well known; escape from its grasp was all but impossible, and appeals from its verdicts were futile. The normal limits of common law or common humanity did not apply to Gestapo operations. A network of informers called *Spitzels* tattled on their neighbors, even about such offenses as telling an anti-Nazi joke. Wherever German conquests brought Nazi rule, the Gestapo followed to investigate, sometimes to conduct show trials in its own courts, to imprison, to torture, and to execute. The utilization of fear was intentionally fostered as an effective weapon to discourage potential opposition. The Kripo (*Kriminalpolizei*), or criminal police, was also attached to Himmler's security forces. Its units often participated in the annihilation of Jews. Their role in executing the Final Solution was rationalized by a fine legal point: Being a Jew was in itself a crime, and all Jewish property was the result of criminal activity, thus the criminal police were rightfully involved in the elimination of this element.

The *Einsatzgruppen* (Special Mobile Task Forces) played a particularly dreadful role in the *Endloesung,* the Final Solution, to the Jewish problem. Himmler's trusted disciple Heydrich selected the men from his SD units. Originally they were used as political counterintelligence in Austria but during the Polish and, particularly the Russian campaigns, they were turned into organized killers. Before they were dispatched to the East they received some weeks of indoctrination. They were told that their task would be difficult but essential to the Fuehrer. No further details were revealed. Their number never exceeded 3,000, and how so few men were able to murder between 1.5 million and 2 million human beings will be discussed in the next chapter.

A special branch of the SS was the *Waffen SS,* or military SS. It expanded until it numbered a million men and became the largest of the SS organizations. Hitler was never convinced that the officers of the regular army were completely loyal to him, whereas the special units of the *Waffen SS* could be trusted. The early recruits were thoroughly indoctrinated with Nazi ideology and also received the training of regular soldiers. The Allies found them a formidable foe that combined military ability with the fanaticism of the true believer in Hitler's vision. First used in the Russian campaign and later in France, they earned a reputation for courage and resolve. They served under their own officers but were attached to regiments of the regular army. As might be expected, animosity between their units and the *Wehrmacht* was a common problem.

The *Waffen SS* attracted large numbers of so-called non-German Aryans into its ranks. At the end of the war half of its soldiers were foreigners designated as "racial Germans" and "foreign Aryans." As the war dragged on, the requirements of total commitment to Hitler and ideological training were often cut back. Men who hoped for military glory and quick advancement, which was not available to them in the regular army, were also drawn to these units. After the war, they may well have regretted that the runic SS symbol had been tattooed in their armpits which made it impossible to deny their membership in the SS.

Himmler had created a visible and an invisible empire. As the functions and the personnel of secret police, regular police, and *Waffen SS* expanded, Himmler was in a position to execute the Final Solution of the Jewish problem. This was a plum coveted by others, including Goering, the Foreign Office, Internal Affairs Ministry, the Propaganda Agency, and the Economic Ministry. Himmler, however, had the Fuehrer's confidence and that resolved the matter. The Black Order, with all its various competing yet interlocking branches, became the major instrument of destruction in Hitler's war against the Jews.

MEMBERSHIP AND TRAINING

Himmler's armies were fluid, constantly changing, sometimes competitive forces rather than a centralized, monolithic organization. Commanders changed, functions were altered, methods of recruitment and training were adjusted to fit new circumstances, and rival chiefs of the various subgroups rose and fell in power. Only Himmler's authority remained intact and unchallenged. Considering his and Hitler's personality, it may be assumed that Himmler followed the Fuehrer's orders regarding the final aim of Jewish fate but devised his own approaches and methods of annihilation. To achieve the task of killing so many millions, Himmler was forced to incorporate entire organizations outside the Nazi party system. As a result the psychological and physical membership qualifications became less stringent. With the caveat that the internal gyrations of the SS cannot be addressed in the limited space of this text, we will view its role in the Holocaust.

Not until Germany was defeated did the world (and that includes most Germans) discover the full design of the secret realm of the SS. Himmler had adamantly refused to share with anyone, including other Reich ministries, any information about his Black Order. Even the methods used in his training schools, the so called Adolf Hitler Schools, were wrapped in secrecy. The criteria for enlistment, however, had to be made common knowledge in order to attract the desired types.

How comforting it would be to say that the storm troopers were composed of sadists, misfits, and the assorted flotsam and jetsam of human society. If that were true, we could separate the rest of humanity and ourselves from them and be consoled that these were not normal men. But the facts speak of a different truth. Himmler's men, no doubt, included a small percentage of psychological misfits, neurotics, even psychotics, but it has been estimated that these numbered approximately 5 percent of the total. The great majority were so ordinary, they could be anyone. Researchers have not established any common denominators to distinguish the mass murderers. Yes, many were very ambitious, eager for advancement and recognition, but such generalizations fit most careerists. The Blackshirts came from ordinary families, had varied educational and economic backgrounds, and came from Protestant as well as Catholic homes. Yes, they had been exposed to propaganda manipulation; yes, they had been taught that a show of mercy was a sign of cowardice; yes, their heads had been filled with grandiose assurances about their sacred mission, but nothing, nothing at all can explain their willingness to become mass executioners of the innocents.

Essentially, the SS was a volunteer organization. The credentials required for its officers resembled those of the *Wehrmacht*. Among Himmler's most cherished recruits were the sons of the old aristocracy. Their upbringing had accustomed them to taking command and expecting obedience. They carried themselves with the proud bearing, some might say overbearing manner, that Himmler demanded. No doubt, the carefully fostered notion that the SS represented Germany's new elite appealed to their arrogance. Among the Black Order's senior officers, more than half came from families whose surnames began with the vaunted "Von."

The sons of the upper middle class, that is, successful professional, industrial, and business families, also contributed to the SS membership. These young men were not ne'er-do-wells; indeed the number of academic degrees among this group is surprising. Many were lawyers, some were physicians, and others were economic and technical specialists. Their recruitment often began in the Hitler Youth movement and was based on recommendations from their troop leaders. Many of them were the technocrats who saw career opportunities no other service could offer. Their chances in the regular army were not nearly as promising; in the *Wehrmacht* tradition played an important role in the selection of officer candidates while the SS promoted all qualified candidates.

Most of the noncommissioned SS volunteers came from the farms. The revival of primogeniture left younger sons of small landowners free to seek their fortune in the prestigious Black Order. If they performed exceptionally well, they might have the opportunity to enter SS officer training school. The respect, even awe, afforded the smart black uniform and the secrecy surrounding many of their functions created an aura hard to resist. It was, of course, necessary to meet the requirements: a well-proportioned body, Nordic type features and coloring, excellent physical condition, and a hard-to-define authoritative bearing. Certificates, such as baptismal and marriage records, had to prove the candidates' Aryan ancestry going back to the year 1800. The future German lords who would colonize the eastern *Lebensraum* must look splendid and act masterful.

An applicant's minimum age was eighteen. His initial training lasted six months. The rigorous physical demands were equaled by psychological requirements. Rituals were imperative: midnight oath-taking; a mess hall decked out in medieval flags, swords, and daggers; torch-lit parades; and other imagery of a cult. Upon completion of the initial phase, the novice swore personal loyalty unto death to Hitler. Next, he was obliged to fulfill his *Landjahr,* or labor service. German youths between the ages of nineteen and twenty-five were required to work without pay for one year. At the end of that duty, the hopeful SS recruit owed yet another duty to the state, his military service. If his record in the army was good he was now ready for his inauguration into the SS brotherhood. In yet another electrifying ceremony, he swore that he would not marry without the approval of the SS Reichsfuehrer Himmler. In other words, his future wife had to pass the racial purity muster and her appearance had to be judged worthy to bear an SS man's children. As might have been noted, there were no intellectual requirements at all.

ISOLATION OF GERMAN JEWS

The forced relocation of Jews into closed-off quarters was an intermediate step between expulsion from their homes and the Final Solution. It was Himmler's responsibility to set up ghettos in conquered Poland, mainly in Hans Frank's General Government. Cities with rail junctions were preferred locations. The physical separation of Jews from the rest of the population had been underway in the greater

Reich, that is, Germany, Austria, and Czechoslovakia, for some time before the invasion of Poland. Evictions of Jews from their residences were legalized by the imaginative stratagem that since Jews were not members of the German people's community, the *Volksgemeinschaft,* they could not be members of the residential community, the *Hausgemeinschaft.* The removal of Jewish families to assigned locations was added to the responsibilities of the Gestapo.

Walled or fenced ghettos were instituted in Poland but not within the Reich. German Jews, including those who lived in villages or small towns, were allocated specific houses within larger cities. The doors of apartments into which the Jews were forced to move were marked with a star, black print on white paper. In 1942, it was decided that German Jews over six years of age must wear on their chests a six-pointed star the size of the palm of a hand, with the word JUDE written in black on yellow background. It is difficult to conceive of serious bureaucrats attending numerous meetings to decide on the size of the lettering and the age of the youngest children to be labeled.

The confinement of German Jews within the Reich was an interim measure. Their expulsion from the sacred soil of the Fatherland was never in doubt; only the method and timing had to be chosen. In due time they would join their fellow Jews in eastern concentration and death camps. Mass deportations of Berlin's Jews began in 1941. Most were shipped in cattle cars to the Lodz ghetto. There they shared the life and death of its inhabitants. The German experience gave the Nazis the model for future procedures to be applied in conquered lands. Here the guidelines were established and the legal rationalization determined. However, because the Germans were indifferent to the opinion of Slavic Poles and Russians concerning their actions, anti-Jewish laws were implemented more quickly, more cruelly, and more openly in the east.

The pattern of controlling the Jews through their own elders also had been used first in the Reich. The use of Jewish councils to control the administration of the ghetto was effective and spared German manpower for other tasks. Traditionally, German Jewry had regulated its own religious, educational, and welfare needs. Under the stress of Nazi attacks they had formed a centralized umbrella organization which eventually was known as the RV, the *Reichsvertretung* (the National Representative Agency). Its leader was the renowned Reform rabbi Leo Baeck, a man with outstanding credentials. He was a scholar, World War I army chaplain, and head of Berlin's Jewish community. We can glimpse his character by his refusal to leave Germany while there was time. When he was arrested in 1943 and sent to the Theresienstadt concentration camp, he served there as the head of the Council of Elders. He survived the camp and until his death in 1956 he continued to play a prominent role in Jewish affairs. Although his stature was exceptional, the role he assumed as chief of the *Judenrat* was mirrored in all the ghettos. Rabbi Baeck shared with his Polish counterparts the hopeless task of trying to balance the needs of his people with the increasingly brutal orders of the Nazi masters. His moral courage, his dedication, and his presumption that a Jewish administration was preferable to a German one cannot be doubted. But the results were such that in the future grave doubt would be raised concerning the role of the *Judenraete*. The SS used them to do much of their work, thus it can be said that they functioned as agents of their own destruction.

PURGING WESTERN POLAND

The conquest of Poland brought 2 million Jews under German rule. That number was increased again when Germany attacked the Soviet Union in 1941. More than 1.5 million Jews, many of whom had fled western Poland earlier, now came under Nazi control. Poland's military defeat was accomplished so quickly that neither the government in Warsaw nor the villagers on their farms could comprehend the debacle. Polish Jewry had no illusions about the Germans, but they had no idea that plans for their complete destruction were under consideration.

As early as September 19, 1939, Heydrich met with *Wehrmacht* personnel to explain the policy of cleansing Poland of its Jews, its intelligentsia, clergy, and aristocracy. He claimed such actions were necessary to secure the conquered areas from forming anti-German opposition. With some few exceptions, the army was content to have the rear secured by the SS by whatever methods they wished to use. Heydrich explained that there was to be an end to the amateurish improvisations by the SS. Activities by single or small groups of Nazis, such as beatings, shootings, kidnapping, forced labor, arson, collections of ransom for release of prominent men in the community, public humiliations, and various methods of torture, all such unofficial conduct was to be replaced by a unified, properly organized approach. Since the army hoped to stay aloof—brutality against civilians was bad for discipline and morale—the SS was free to enforce the Fuehrer's wishes. Heydrich availed himself of the ultimate technocrat, Adolf Eichmann. He was the man to implement the expulsion and relocation of millions of people, a task to challenge even his proven talents.

As was noted earlier, the Germans had incorporated three districts in western Poland into the Reich. These newly created *Gaue* of greater Germany were to be purged of Jews at once. Hitler had ordered the "cleansing" of the area. The region of Wartheland, the enlarged territories of the East Prussian and Silesian provinces and greater Danzig (now Gdansk) were to become *Judenrein* as soon as possible. Himmler wanted this massive uprooting of hundreds of communities completed within three months, a goal that even his best effort could not effect.

The new eastern boundary of Poland, previously established by the Ribbentrop-Molotov treaty with the Soviet Union, was along the river Bug. The first expulsions from that region consisted of forcing the Jewish families across the river into Soviet territory. The brutality of this action was exemplified by the fate of the Jews of Chelm. Of the 1,800 deportees, 400 survived. Hundreds were gunned down, and many drowned when forced to swim across the Bug. In some areas, Soviet soldiers on the east bank would not permit them to come ashore, causing the hapless victims to run that gauntlet twice.

Six months after the defeat of Poland, 78,000 Polish Jews had been driven eastward. Although their experiences were horrifying, those who made their way to the Russian interior comprised the largest number of Polish Jews to survive the war.

THE DEPORTATIONS

Himmler had charged Heydrich with the overall responsibility of the Jewish problem, and he turned to Eichmann to solve the logistics of Jewish deportations. Short distance trial runs within Poland prepared his staff for the main task, the mass shipment of Jews from Southern, Central, and Western Europe to Hans Frank's General Government. In effect, most Jews experienced two expulsions, from small Polish towns to the ghettos in larger cities and then from the ghettos to the concentration and death camps.

The forced evacuations carried out during the winter of 1939–1940 served to instruct the Germans on such matters as how to procure the rolling stock from the railway authority, how to set up intermediate camps and how to coordinate the various authorities involved in the mass exodus. Timetables had to be devised and assembly points selected for further transport. Eichmann found that negotiation with the Ministry of Transport required considerable skill. It was never a simple matter to secure the necessary trains and prevail over contradicting demands of the military. The SS was compelled to pay the railroad for transporting the Jews, and the cost was passed on to the Jewish elders and their communities. The fees were based on the number of "pieces" a train carried; how the "pieces" arrived did not matter. The same charge was paid whether they reached their destination dead or alive.

During the early stages of the deportations, lists of the expellees were prepared, but as their numbers grew, compiling these rosters was often neglected. A great deal of paperwork was required to catalogue the properties the Jews had to leave behind. These possessions were declared abandoned and became Reich property. The amount and sort of goods the deportees could take with them was strictly controlled and they were searched for forbidden items.

Eichmann wanted the deportations to progress with a minimum of strain on the SS. The use of deceptive stratagems duped many victims to gather willingly at or near railroad stations. Over and over the Germans assured the Jews that they were about to be resettled farther East, that no harm would come to them, that families would be permitted to stay together, and that the early arrivals would be in the best positions to establish their new lives. The local Jewish elders were persuaded to encourage their charges to make their exodus as trouble-free as possible; resistance to German orders would endanger everyone.

Survivors of the Holocaust shudder as they remember their transport to the camps. The trains were made up of freight and cattle cars and were expected to carry a total of 1,000 Jews. Filling the cars was accomplished by violent pushing until every inch was occupied and there was no room to sit down. The single pail in the corner soon overflowed with human waste. The humiliation of men and women attending to their bodily needs in public was a foretaste of the dehumanization process intentionally designed by the Nazis. People who died on the trains had no space to fall down. There were cases of mothers giving birth in cars so packed they had to squat. Thirst made people delirious, hunger caused fainting and madness. Worst of all was the overwhelming need for a breath of air. The trains were sealed, and many cars had no ventilation.

Initially, deportees were permitted to bring some food and water, but these concessions were canceled as conditions grew increasingly harsh. Families who had traveled just a few days barely recognized each other when they tumbled from the cars upon arrival. Dirty, disoriented, physically weakened, trembling with fear for themselves and loved ones, they were often incapable of absorbing the events that had engulfed them so suddenly. Their confusion seemed to infuriate the SS, and they were met with blows and curses. Those who died during the journey were tossed onto the siding by prisoners in striped uniforms who emptied the cars. As men, women, and children from the lands recently subjugated by the swastika were moved across Europe, the trains that carried them became adjuncts to the killing process.

ESTABLISHING GHETTOS

The first deportations were carried out in western Poland during the final days of the military campaign. But merely shifting the Jews from one place to another did not solve the greater Jewish problem for Himmler. Until a decision was made concerning the future handling of the millions of undesirables now under German jurisdiction, a temporary solution was needed. Taking a page from the history of the Middle Ages, the Nazis decided to create ghettos in the major cities of Poland. The five major ghettos were located in Warsaw, Lodz, Cracow, Lublin, and Lvov. Initially, only Polish Jews were confined, but the process was soon extended to include other nationals. German Jews were added in 1941. During the same year, the conquests in the West expanded Himmler's responsibilities to include France, Holland, Belgium, Denmark, and Norway. All areas were ordered to become *Judenrein*. Hitler's later campaigns in Southern and Southeastern Europe brought additional trainloads from the Balkan countries and Italy. The great majority of these victims, however, did not interrupt their final journey by a stay in Polish ghettos but went directly to the concentration and death camps.

Heydrich was an efficient administrator. Even before the Poles surrendered, he began to expel Jews from western Poland. As a rule, they were given no time to prepare for their final exodus from the villages and small towns where their ancestors had lived for hundreds of years. In some instances they were permitted fifteen minutes to pack some belongings. Those who had relatives in the territories not scheduled for annexation to the Reich were urged to join them. The rest were forced to depart on foot or by train to cities designated by the Germans. The might be permitted to take one or two suitcases per person. The bulk of their possessions had to be

***The Star of David attached to the top of this street car indicates it is in use
for residents of Warsaw's Ghetto.*** (Courtesy Corbis.)

left behind and was immediately confiscated. Goering, personally and as the chief of
the Four Year economic plan, was the designated benefactor of this plunder. Because
the majority of Polish Jews were poor the booty was disappointing.

The physical boundaries of the ghettos were usually marked by walls or high
fences. Gates were locked at night and guarded, thus escape was nearly impossible.
But the difficulties of getting over the wall were only the beginning. Once on the
Gentile side, one needed papers, food and money to survive. Only with the aid of
friends could an escapee hope to survive. Denunciations of Jews to the Nazis were a

constant danger. Although the SS controlled every facet of ghetto life, they had very little direct contact with its population and control over tens of thousands required a minimum of Nazi manpower. For their survival, the inhabitants were totally dependent on supplies from the outside. Food and water, electricity and waste disposal, medicines and telephones, postal service and cemetery space were supplied or withheld at whim by the Germans. The size of the ghettos, the number of blocks, houses and available rooms, were decided by SS decree. Frequent reduction in the amount of space allowed the ghetto residents caused constant anxiety. Overcrowding was intense and occupancy of seven persons per room was common. The situation was exacerbated by the continuous influx of new refugees from all over Europe. The death rate from starvation was in direct ratio to the insufficient food rations and lack of medical supplies. No matter how well-meaning the *Judenrat* administrators, nothing could change the fact that the fate of the Jews was in the hands of their enemies.

LIFE IN THE GHETTOS

The Nazis placed the burden of ghetto management on the Jewish councils of elders, the *Judenraete.* The use of Jewish community leaders as administrators had worked well in the Reich and was readily transplanted to Poland. Not only did that arrangement minimize the need for Nazi personnel, there were additional advantages. Hatred for the almost invisible Germans was deflected to the leaders within the ghetto, on the men who were blamed for the lack of food for hungry children or medicine for an ill parent. The lack of even the most basic necessities could be placed directly on the Jewish elder in charge of distributing goods rather than on a faceless German authority. Furthermore, when prominent Jews urged their fellow victims to obey, to be hopeful, to remain peaceful, the possibility of resistance to the Nazis was greatly diminished. Finally, the Jewish councils were a convenient target for blackmail. At the slightest sign of noncompliance, the threat of killing the ghetto leaders more often than not brought about prompt submission.

The SS and/or Gestapo commanders usually had offices within the ghetto from which they issued streams of orders to be carried out by the Jewish administration. How the elders regulated the day-to-day routine of ghetto life concerned them little as long as all commands were obeyed promptly. Several factors influenced life and death in each of the more than twenty ghettos. Geographic location was important; the presence or absence of swamps, woods, nearby villages related directly to the feasibility of escape. The rivalry between the SS and the military commander in the region could work for or against the survival of the Jews. The military commanders usually demanded workers for the manufacture of war materiel and their influence on the SS could shorten or prolong survival within the walls. Always of immediate impact on the degree of misery were two other variables, namely the personality of the Nazi commander and the make-up of the specific *Judenrat.*

At one extreme were the deluded Jewish leaders with messianic complexes who claimed that God had willed them to save their communities. At the opposite end were the ghettos which were organized to represent, as much as circumstances permitted, the will of the majority of its inhabitants. Some of the elders knew or guessed that their labors mattered little, all would soon be dead no matter what their efforts to appease the Germans. Ghetto elders ran the entire gamut of human nature, from weakness to heroism, from practicality to flights of fancy, from humanitarian to selfish concerns. Perhaps the most common complaint against the leadership was favoritism. Council members often were able to spare their own families and friends some particular degradation, provide them with better quarters, perhaps allot them an extra ration, save them from the heaviest labor or delay their boarding the train that eventually took them all to no man's land. The bitterness engendered by unfair practices of Jews toward other Jews ranged from fury to resignation.

The traditional respect for one's elders confounded many of the young Jews whose efforts to organize for resistance and revolt directly opposed the hope of the *Judenraete* that obedience and compliance would save lives.

Despite the differences among ghettos, a number of similar characteristics were discernible. The German policy of holding many people, even the entire community responsible for the actions of individuals, proved to be very effective. For example, a child went over the wall to try to get some food on the other side. He was caught by the guards and now his entire family, or perhaps all the people living in his house or the entire street on which it was located are executed. And the SS regarded death as the fitting penalty for nearly all infractions. Fear of the wrath of collective guilt and collective punishment enabled the Germans to maintain control with few SS men until it became clear to their prisoners that they were doomed no matter what they did.

Ghetto Jews were subjected to curfews; all were compelled to wear identifying markings, a star on an armband or pinned to the chest or back. All men and women were obliged to report for forced labor in accordance with the quotas set by the Germans each day. Every ghetto was overcrowded and, inevitably, prone to the spread of communicable diseases. Typhus was the most recurrent plague but various illnesses induced by malnutrition and poor sanitation decimated the population. The greatest suffering was caused by hunger. Each month starvation killed an increasing number of people. Children and the elderly died first, but lack of food felled even the once strong and hale. In winter, the shortage of fuel contributed to death by hypothermia; people froze in their beds, in the street, at the workplace.

Terror permeated the air of the ghetto. A Jew could be shot or beaten to death by a German without any cause whatever and the killer went about his business without fear of any rebuke from his superiors. No one knew with certainty what the Nazis planned to do and rumors substituted for information. Each day created another cycle of hope and despair: Jews with skills could work and live; no, the SS was enraged at *Wehrmacht* interference and for spite would kill everyone; resettlement in the East would begin soon; no, only a fiery death awaited those who left the ghetto; the war was going badly for the Germans and the Jews would be liberated; oh, no, defeat at the front would merely incite the SS to further outrages. In this atmosphere, every emotion, envy, selfishness, and animosity as well as generosity, sacrifice and altruism was magnified. There were quarrels about food, water and coal, about medicines and the best place to wait in line at the soup kitchens. Endless discussions concerning the value of work permits and the price of anything available on the black market occupied the idle hours. The wildest rumors found acceptance as people were desperate to get through just one more day.

The number of successful escapes from the ghetto was pitifully small. Getting over the wall, through the sewer pipes, or under the fence was merely the first step; finding a place to hide and survive was much more difficult. The Polish countryside was nearly always hostile. Jews who spoke Polish imperfectly, whose faces looked Semitic rather then Slavic, who were too weak to work or too disoriented to think clearly, were quickly lost. It must be remembered that providing food and shelter for a Jew was a capital offense during the German occupation. Poles who had the courage to aid a Jew not only endangered their own lives but also the lives of their families. The heroism of the children in the ghettos must be recalled; they added significantly to the food supply. Even little ones, as young as five years old, managed to get to the Gentile side. They brought back vegetables bought or foraged from Polish farmers. Some German guards opted not to see or hear these nightly shadows; others beat them terribly or shot them for a couple of beets or potatoes.

FUNCTIONS OF THE *JUDENRAETE*

For as long as possible, and that meant four years at most, the councils of elders attempted to give ghetto life a semblance of normalcy. Bureaucracies were established to provide for schools, hospitals, and orphanages. Officials in charge of sanitation faced the impossible task of preventing human waste from causing deadly contamination. Fire brigades were organized to keep the slum dwellings from burning to the ground. During the early months, when it was still possible to receive packages or money, (mainly from American Jewish institutions), the *Raete* confiscated these donations and then distributed the contents to the most needy in the ghetto. The elders were forced to tax everything imaginable to raise the money required to carry out their functions. In ghettos where the Germans permitted the production of goods needed by their army, a small portion of their value might be made available to the councils.

A Jewish police force kept public order and was used to carry out the most hateful of German commands. They lined up the columns of slave laborers who worked in various installations outside the wall; they met the incoming trains and pushed the new arrivals into the worst housing; during the final stages of ghetto existence, they forced the victims into the cattle cars leaving for the death camps. Survivors have testified that the ghetto police usually attracted the worst elements in a community. Their brutality earned them a loathing that often exceeded hatred for the Germans.

Men and women hoped to get factory work. There survival rates were higher compared to those digging anti-tank ditches and carrying rocks to repair roads. Holding a work permit usually entitled the bearer to larger food rations, thus that blue or pink piece of paper provided the worker with a chance of survival. The hope that those who contributed to the German war effort would be allowed to live, lingered on until the dissolution of the ghettos. But there was never enough work, particularly when the SS forbade laborers to leave the ghetto. Without a source of supplies from the outside, no large-scale manufacturing was possible. Those who still had something to sell stood on street corners, hoping for buyers. The greatest demand was for food, followed by the need for warm clothing and heating materials. After the Nazis requisitioned furs, woolens, leather goods, and bedding, the harsh Polish winters continued to cause acute suffering. Even when the *Judenraete* made an effort to parcel out available supplies with fairness, there was never enough and cries of partiality were inevitable. Eventually, the councils established soup kitchens to feed their starving people.

The population within the ghettos changed constantly due to decimation by deaths and increases from the arrival of non-Polish Jews. The newcomers were not always gracefully accepted. When the ghettos were first established there were considerable differences in the economic standing of the population. In the end, nearly all were paupers, although a gap between the have-somethings and the have-nothings remained. When the Nazis decided to reduce the number of Jews by starvation, those families that had been able to hide something of value found a flourishing black market where a pearl might buy a piece of smuggled horse meat.

The councils as well as individual ghetto dwellers made every attempt to imitate the world that had been left behind. Although suicide rates increased and some people were driven to insanity by the sight of unburied bodies in the streets, by the pleas of beggars in rags and of children too weak to cry, the great majority fought to retain their humanity. They sought and found solace through participation in a variety of cultural and religious activities. Actors performed in makeshift theaters; political parties continued to argue about Zionist, Socialist, and other issues; debating societies disputed philosophy and religion; musicians gathered to play and sing for their own pleasure and that of others. The devout prayed to God and asked for his merciful intervention. Although the Germans forbade the establishment of schools, many teachers gathered pupils in their rooms and hoped to give the children some hours of normalcy. Newspapers were secretly authored, copied, and avidly read. Books had never been more precious. Men, women, and children kept diaries to bear witness to their suffering. In prose, poetry, and with pictures, they described what they saw and felt and hoped that the world would remember them. Some of their manuscripts and a number of drawings and photographs survived the liquidation of the ghettos and allow us to marvel at the vigor of the intellectual energy of ghetto life. Indeed, many of the "people of the book" were sustained by their ancient heritage until death overtook them.

THE LODZ GHETTO: A CASE IN POINT

In 1941 the process of confining Polish Jewry in ghettos had been well underway and in August of 1944, the last major ghetto, Lodz, was emptied. At the Wannsee Conference of January 20, 1942, the Nazi hierarchy in charge of the Jewish question

Jews in front of a well in the Ghetto of Lublin. (Courtesy AP/Wide World Photos.)

had confirmed an earlier decision to solve the Jewish question through mass murder. The fact that most of European Jewry was already concentrated in ghettos simplified the execution of the final step. The Jews themselves would provide much of the required paperwork as well as the personnel to collect the victims and load the trains. The period of ghettoization was brief, but it was important as a link to the Final Solution. It is estimated that one-fifth of Polish Jewry died as a result of ghetto conditions before the Final Solution was implemented. The fact that so many of the victims were already assembled in Poland, site of the death camps, allowed the *Endloesung* to proceed with momentous speed.

The city of Lodz in southwestern Poland illustrates the life and death of a Nazi version of a ghetto. The chief of the Lodz council of elders was named Mordekhai Chaim Rumkowski. He was a childless widower, formerly the director of an orphanage. One can sum up his dictatorial administration as well-intentioned at best, self-serving at worst, and bizarre for sure. He may have developed megalomania, for he was certain only he could save "his" Jews. His eagerness to lead the community during the trauma of Nazi occupation was explicable only in terms of his view of his mission: God had appointed him to do His work. The original members of his council, who might have been unwilling to accept his authoritarian style, had been murdered following a summons by the Germans. Thereafter, the council was composed of men who had no previous standing in the community and were unable to curb Rumkowski's excesses.

The Lodz ghetto existed for four years and four months, longer than any other. It was sealed off in April 1940 and its 160,000 people endured the same misery of starvation, illness, and helpless anxiety suffered by all the other Polish Jews. Compared to other ghettos, however, Lodz had several, albeit temporary, advantages. The enclosed area contained some farmland where a little food could be grown; the overcrowding reached 5.8 persons per room, not over 7 as in other ghettos. Rumkowski preached the doctrine that hard work for the Germans would keep the Jews alive. That shred of hope was as vital as food, until, in the end, the truth of their impending death could no longer be denied.

Surely Rumkowski realized the impossibility of serving two contradictory purposes: saving his people on the one hand and assisting the Germans who planned to kill them on the other. His authority was always a gift from his Nazi masters, to be granted or withdrawn at will. The SS chief charged with the supervision of the Lodz ghetto was named Hans Biebow. It suited his objectives to have a strong administration within the ghetto, to have one man responsible for carrying out his orders. Biebow and the SS profited from the manufacturing carried on in the ghetto, where men and women produced clothing at a feverish pace. He wanted calm and orderliness and never even hinted at the eventual dissolution of the ghetto.

Rumkowski, the "king of the Lodz Jews," had almost no previous administrative experience, yet he organized ghetto life with ruthlessness and skill. He developed not only police, welfare, hospital, judicial, educational, and religious departments, but he turned the ghetto into a giant workshop. Among the Jews of Lodz were a large number of skilled workers, many of whom had been involved in the once flourishing textile industry of the region. There were also cabinet makers, tailors, shoemakers, tinsmiths, and others. Food rations and work production were linked, and Rumkowski permitted no interference with his design: Work and we shall live. He issued ghetto money imprinted with his picture, wrote orders above his personal seal. He appeared at public functions with his retinue and bestowed regal favors upon petitioners. Many of the Lodz work force had been unionized and continued to identify with their associations. When they organized a strike in order to win some concessions to ease their terrible working conditions, Rumkowski refused to back down. He brooked no tampering with his authority, and hunger drove the workers back to their ten-hour workdays at starvation rations.

During the 1941–1942 winter, the ragged thousands in the Lodz ghetto were stunned to receive their first order of evacuation. It was merely the beginning; the last such demand came in August of 1944. The Nazis told Rumkowski to ready 10,000 men, women, and children for "resettlement." The Jews did not know that this was a death warrant to be carried out in the gas chambers of Chelmno. Rumkowski decreed that this consignment should be selected from among the "undesirables" of the ghetto residents. In effect, that meant the expulsion of those who had run afoul of the administration (perhaps for the theft of a potato) along with their families. Those who refused to present themselves for deportation received no food rations. If Rumkowski had any illusions that the Germans would be satisfied with one trainload, he learned the truth within a month. Nearly 1,000 Jews per day made the heart-wrenching trip to the rail station. As Germans repeated their demands to reduce the ghetto population, the next group to be pushed out were the people who were unable to do productive work. The unemployed from age ten and up were shoved into the waiting freight cars. When that category had been exhausted, non-Polish Jews who had been shipped in from other parts of Europe were placed on the death list.

The order for new selections coincided with the arrival of a group of Jews from Wartheland. They knew about the installations of mass murder and removed any doubt that "resettlement" was the euphemism for death. When the Nazis instructed Rumkowski to transport the sick, the 10,000 children under age ten, and all men and women over sixty-five, the terror experienced by the population cannot be described. Now that the truth could no longer be denied, who would be willing to shove the victims into their freight cars? For a promise that their own children would be saved, amid screams and curses of helpless parents and children, the police tried to complete their dreadful task, but Germans, aided by collaborators from the Baltic states and the Ukraine, had to finish the savage roundup.

Rumkowski's authority disappeared along with his Jews. He kept a few of his welfare programs operating and hoped the worst was over. Perhaps he thought he had saved the remnant. During the summer of 1944, some 76,000 Jews continued to work and survive in the Lodz ghetto. But as the German armies retreated across Russia, the total eradication of Poland's second largest ghetto was ordered. The remnant of the men and women who had endured for so long and hoped so fervently to live until Germany's defeat were consigned to die at Auschwitz-Birkenau. Among the last to go was Mordekhai Rumkowski.

THE WARSAW GHETTO: ANOTHER CASE IN POINT

The Warsaw ghetto was the largest. For a time, about a half million Jews from Warsaw, from the surrounding countryside and from Germany and Austria were imprisoned within its ten-foot-high walls. It was organized in October of 1940, about a year after the defeat of Poland. One month later it was sealed off from the outside world. Five hundred thousand people had been crammed into an area of approximately three and one-half square miles. Only by realizing that between seven and thirteen people lived in every single room of the approximately 1,500 buildings is it possible to comprehend the overcrowding. Whatever the suffering in other ghettos, it was duplicated and intensified in Warsaw. It must also be remembered that the Polish capital had undergone extensive bombardments, and much of it lay in rubble.

As was true in all ghettos, only those who worked as slave laborers were issued food rations. The allotment was so meager, less than 200 calories per day, that only smuggling prevented immediate mass starvation. The Germans did not permit any nutritious foods such as fruits, fresh vegetables, meat, milk, or fish into the ghetto. Packages sent from the outside were confiscated, and safe drinking water was at a premium. Malnutrition made the population susceptible to epidemics, which raged within the city with regularity.

The Warsaw ghetto was under the internal administration of twenty-four members of a council of elders headed by the widely respected engineer, Adam Czerniakow. His meticulous diary survived the war and gives convincing evidence of his earnest desire to provide a fair administration. He hoped to preserve Jewish lives and act as a buffer between the SS and his people. From the onset, these goals were unattainable. To the Nazis, he was merely a useful instrument of management and eventually an aid in the accomplishment of genocide. If he hoped that his people would understand his dilemma, he was largely disappointed. He was blamed for every shortage, every cruelty ordered by his masters. The venality of the policemen who enforced German demands were placed at his door. Occasionally, he stood up to the SS, even winning some minor points; but in reality, he was unable to alter German intentions, not even for a day.

Czerniakow tried to be impartial in the distribution of allotments of food, fuel, and services; but there was never enough, and the afflicted people reproached him angrily. Just as the Nazis predicted, the *Judenrat* was held accountable for the misery of ghetto life. The elders, well aware of the Nazi policy of communal guilt, struggled to keep the Warsaw ghetto calm. They supported various institutions designed to alleviate some of the suffering by sponsoring intellectual, educational, and recreational activities. Clandestine, unofficial organizations were equally important in easing the stress of such an unnatural existence. Among their self-help activities were efforts to make the ghetto valued and valuable in the eyes of the Nazis. All types of merchandise were in short supply in Poland and the Jews turned to manufacturing. Ghetto craftsmen literally made something from almost nothing; rags and junk were transformed into useful items. They produced clothing, bed linens, shoes, cutlery, pots and pans, paper, and toys. The vitality necessary to forge such enterprises under such circumstances was in itself a triumph. The workers hoped that the German army would realize that it was to their advantage to authorize ghetto production. For nearly a year some raw materials flowed through the gates of the wall. During the exchange of goods from the Jewish to the Polish part of Warsaw, it was possible to smuggle in some food. Aside from this quasilegal trade, an illegal underground system of manufacture and exchange developed. With luck or pluck, by means of black market ventures or corruption, some Jews actually, though only momentarily, became rich. They lived with reckless abandon, ate in restaurants and smoked cigarettes in cafes. The gap between these few and the starving masses created unbearable tension.

In 1942, Himmler ordered the liquidation of all ghettos; liquidation was the SS euphemism for mass murder. The entire process was to be completed by the end of the year, though the process was not completed until the summer of 1944. The Warsaw ghetto imprisoned at that point an estimated 350,000 people. It was among the first to hear the tolling of the funeral bell. In July 1942, the Nazis began to demand that the *Judenrat* provide "settlers" for the journey to the East. The death camp Treblinka was the usual destination of the Warsaw Jews. The weak and helpless were the first to be dragged to the *Umschlagplatz,* the place of assembly for the deportees. The SS promised that volunteers for the "resettlement" would find better conditions; they distributed precious rations of bread and jam to those who willingly reported to the train station. When the supply of volunteers ran out, ghetto police forced their fellow Jews into the freight cars. The Warsaw ghetto police force numbered about 1,700 and was headed by a hated apostate, Jozef Szerynski. His men handled the roundups with brutal competence. They had been promised that their own families would be exempt from deportation. In fact, nearly all of the police and their families were sent to Treblinka in September 1942, on Yom Kippur, the Day of Atonement.

On July 23, 1942, Adam Czerniakow shot himself. He had been asked to hand over the children and could not do it. He knew where the trains were going, and he could do nothing to stop them. The debate, whether he should have used his gun to kill Germans, whether he should have rallied the people into rebellion, is pointless. His note said that he "could no longer bear all this." We do not know, nor can we ever know, his true state of mind when he made his decision. His death changed nothing. The expulsions continued. The Nazis called in auxiliary forces composed of some 800 Ukranians, Lithuanians, and Letts who were eager to participate in the *Aktion*. Polish historian Emanuel Ringelblum, whose chronicles were discovered after the war, recorded events with laconic accuracy: Yesterday so many disappeared, today, so many more. He lamented the fact that the Jews had not offered active resistance when the number of potential fighters was greater. In his estimation, a mere fifty SS men directed the entire evacuation of the ghetto.

One week after the liquidation order was issued, about 65,000 Warsaw Jews had been sent to their deaths. Each train was loaded with a cargo of 7,000 screaming, crying, silent, praying people. Amid the chaos the march of Korczak's orphans was an unforgettable sight. The internationally renowned educator and pediatrician Janusz Korczak had cared for many foundlings in his orphanage. When he was offered the opportunity to escape, he refused. With two little ones in his arms, he and his staff led their charges, dressed in their Sabbath best, singing and carrying banners, to the *Umschlagplatz*. Even the Germans were stunned. When people were afraid to leave their rooms, the Germans and their accomplices encircled specific streets, stormed the houses, and drove out the inhabitants. By the end of the summer 300,000 men, women and children had been forced out of the ghetto.

The remnant of the Warsaw ghetto population, approximately 65,000, was largely made up of young people. They continued to work in the several factories still operating. Perhaps because their more cautious elders were no longer among them, the idea of forcibly resisting the Nazis became a movement, a reality, a declaration of war against their murderers. Here, the most significant of the armed struggles between Nazis and Jews was fought. But, inevitably, the Warsaw ghetto was razed and turned into ashes and its inhabitants lost to the world. (See Chapter 10).

CHAPTER 9

From Isolation to Annihilation

Could the Holocaust have happened without Hitler? The debate over the specific role of the Fuehrer in the annihilation of the 6 million continues. Whatever conclusion historians may reach, it is clear to this writer that Hitler's hatred for Jews was central to the policy of the destruction of Europe's Jews. That one man can command such power over others, that he is able to call to the surface every evil instinct in the minds and souls of his followers, is a terrifying admission. At this writing, the latest plotter of infamy, Osama Bin Laden, is still in hiding and we continue to try to understand the spell he has cast over his suicidal disciples. Perhaps psychologists will someday provide the answers we seek but for the present we must deal with facts, not speculation.

Hitler's compulsion to destroy the Jewish people was transformed from his mind to the reality of genocide by means of a compliant and dutiful bureaucracy, by modern technology, and by troops of highly disciplined killers. The process required a totalitarian government and a silent or obedient or irresolute population who believed that they were not responsible for their government's crimes. The anomaly of war provided the cover, which, at least in part, obscured the truth from the general public. In every Holocaust history class the question is asked: Can it happen again? To a diminished degree, it already has. Events in the Middle East, in Asia, in East Africa and in the Balkans and even in the United States give evidence that it is not difficult to unleash deadly old and new hatreds. Ruthless leaders have caused the devastation of countless lives as far from us as Asia, East Africa, the Middle East, the Balkans, and as near as the city of New York.

The Shoah, so fully and so precisely documented, so enormous in its scope, remains at the center of the study of man's inhumanity to his fellow man. Although the number of 6 million Jews killed is generally accepted, not all researchers agree on a final total. Probably an exact accounting can never be made, even when the tons of Third Reich papers still in warehouses have been catalogued. Whether we speak of 5.5 million or 6 million or 6.5 million, these numerical discrepancies have no bearing upon the fundamental facts of Holocaust history.

THE WANNSEE DECISION

This infamous meeting took place on January 20, 1942, in a lovely lakeside villa outside of Berlin. Six months earlier Goering had ordered Heydrich, the chief of the SD, the Security Forces, to consult with various members of the government and devise a comprehensive plan to solve the Jewish problem. Invitations to the meeting had been accepted by 15 officials who had an interest in the outcome of the deliberation. They included delegates from the eastern occupied territories, from the Department of Justice, from the Four Year economic plan, from several agencies involved with the occupation of Poland, as well as an undersecretary of the Foreign Office and the Minister of the Interior. The SS was represented by a general and, of course, by Heydrich and Eichmann, both experts on the Jewish question. Although the stated purpose of the gathering was to discuss the fate of the Jews, in actuality there was little discussion. Adolf Eichmann took the minutes which have survived and they reveal that the participants merely confirmed the policy which was already under way. Since the invasion of the Soviet Union, which began in June 1941, mobile murder squads, the *Einsatzgruppen,* had followed the German armies eastward and were systematically shooting hundreds of thousands of Jews.

At Wannsee the euphemism *Endloesung,* Final Solution, was adopted to refer to the annihilation of all Jews within the grasp of the Germans. But Heydrich, who chaired the meeting, did not confine his plans to the regions already occupied. He distributed a chart which enumerated the final total of intended victims. His data were incorrect, he believed that European Jewry numbered 11 million, a miscalculation of approximately 2 million. It is interesting to note that he included the Jews of neutral nations, Turkey, Switzerland, Sweden, Spain, and as yet undefeated England in his projection.

There was some discussion concerning the logistics of transporting so many people from one end of the continent to the other. The fate of the *Mischlinge,* the children of mixed marriages, engendered a debate but no solution was reached concerning their fate. Heydrich reviewed the various measures that had been tried but failed to make German territories *Judenrein*. He informed the conferees that the Fuehrer had authorized the evacuation of all Jews to Poland where they would be used as slave laborers. With barely concealed double talk he stated that it was expected that many would die of natural causes. In the event that the survivors should attempt to rebuild their lives, they would be dealt with subsequently. When Eichmann was tried for his crimes in Jerusalem in 1962, he testified that the men sitting around the table at Wannsee openly discussed various methods of murdering

***Nazis rounding up Jewish men, women, and children during the destruction
of the Jewish Ghetto in Warsaw, 1943.***   (Courtesy AP/Wide World Photos.)

the Jews. No doubt, the assembled delegates knew the true meaning of the Final
Solution and agreed to make it the official policy of the German government. Then
the meeting adjourned for an excellent lunch.

It should be noted that 7 of the 15 delegates attending the Wannsee meeting
were academics who held doctoral degrees.

MOBILE KILLING SQUADS

The original concept of mobile terror units dated back to the annexation of Austria
and Czechoslovakia where they played a minor role in the "pacification" of the
region. During and after the Polish conquest, murder squads were used to decimate
the Polish elite, and, in a rather haphazard way, to kill Jews. In the Western theater of
operations, namely France, the Low Countries, Denmark, and Norway, the army did
not permit SS intrusion, much to Himmler's distress. During the campaign against
the Soviet Union, however, he was given nearly complete freedom to conduct waves
of organized massacres that have no counterparts in history.

Heydrich had begun to prepare for major *Aktionen* in May 1941. He assembled
3,000 men, picked from every organization under Himmler's authority, and told them

that "real men" were needed for a task of special difficulty but of enormous importance. This duty was to be performed in the East, not a place to which volunteers were likely to flock. No specifics regarding their mission were revealed until after weeks of intensive indoctrination. Even then, references to their actual objectives were oblique, cloaked in euphemisms like "political criminals" requiring "special treatment"; "eradication of typhus carriers"; and "elimination of the Bolshevik menace."

The official wording of the assignment of the *Einsatzgruppen* was to follow the German army into the Soviet Union and protect its rear from attack by partisans and saboteurs. In actuality, their mission was the slaughter of innocent civilians on a hitherto unprecedented scale. The *Einsatzgruppen* shot between 1.5 to 2 million Jews, as well as many hundreds of thousands of non-Jews within a period of less than two years. Among the Gentile victims, the number of Russian prisoners of war was particularly high. The standard legal cover for these executions was the small hyphen Hitler placed between two words so that they became one: Jew-Bolshevik. All Jews, per se, were indicted as communists; consequently they were dangerous subversives. Since Jewish children, even the unborn, were genetically destined to become mortal enemies of Germany, they, too, were under a death sentence. When that accusation wore thin, several commanders of the mobile squads told their men that the killings were necessary to prevent typhus, or some other epidemic. These incredible rationalizations seemed to satisfy the perpetual need for a legal cloak for the commission of heinous crimes.

Nearly all the German generals of the regular army accepted the presence of the *Einsatzgruppen* as long as they did not interfere with regular army activities. After the war, the military claimed that it had no hand in the dreadful work of the mobile killing units, but the facts do not bear out those assertions. (See Afterword). The records show that in some regions there was considerable cooperation between the terror squads and the *Wehrmacht* in rounding up victims, even in the actual shootings. The military, as a matter of policy, turned all captured Jewish prisoners of war over to the SS for immediate execution. When Colonel General Johannes Blaskowitz and Admiral Canaris, the chief of the *Abwehr,* the German military counterintelligence, protested to their superiors in Berlin about the savagery of the SS, they were told not to interject themselves into an area outside their competence.

The commanders of the mobile killing squads came from the German middle class. Most were professional men, lawyers, doctors, intellectuals, and even a minister of the Protestant church. Their troops were quite similar to their counterparts in other SS organizations. The *Einsatzgruppen* were organized into four units: Group A, the largest with 990 men, went north to the Baltic states; B operated in the north-central region of Russia; C worked in the south in the vicinity of Kiev; and D, the smallest with a strength of 500, advanced behind the southernmost German army in the Crimea (see Map 9-1). Each battalion was augmented by auxiliary troops of native Eastern Europeans. Among these were ethnic Germans who lived in Poland; another large contingent of volunteers came from the Baltic States, and Romania and the Ukraine were also represented. The murder of 60,000 Jews in Odessa, which shocked even the Germans, was the grisly work of Romanians. These men knew

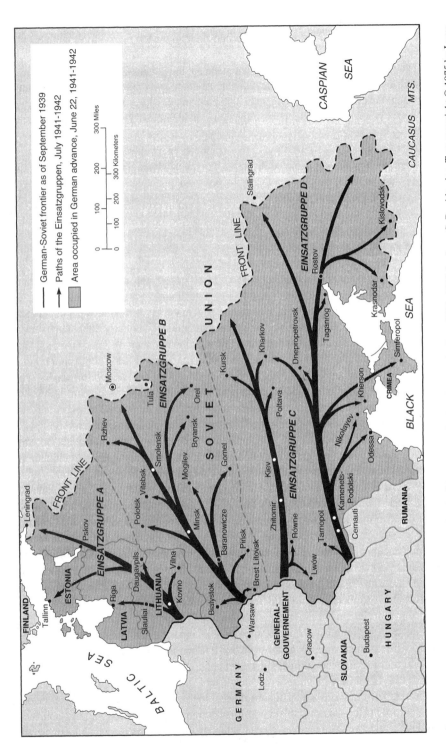

Map 9-1   The Einsatzgruppen, 1941–1942.   (From *The War Against the Jews 1933–1945*, by Lucy S. Davidowicz. Text copyright © 1975 by Lucy S. Davidowicz, maps by Vincent Kotschar, copyright © 1975 by Henry Holt and Co., Inc. Reprinted by permission of Henry Holt and Co., Inc.)

exactly what their functions would be when they signed on, and their deliberate, often enthusiastic participation in these crimes defies rational analysis.

The killing squads were also augmented by the utilization of several reserve police units. These units were generally composed of men who were too old or too young to serve in the regular SS or the armed forces. Many had joined the Order Police in the hope of avoiding service far from their homes. Their training in police work, however, hardly prepared them for their duties in the Soviet Union. Since Himmler was the chief of all police enforcement, he was empowered to order them to participate in *Aktionen* against civilians. The inexplicable participation of ordinary Germans in such butchery was the topic of an excellent book by Christopher Browning. (See the Bibliography).

BOLTS FROM THE BLUE

As the German invasion in the summer of 1941 penetrated deep into Russia, the people in the conquered regions were totally unprepared for the fate that awaited them. They had no idea that Hitler was poised to wage another war, a war that had no bearing on military combat and was aimed against many Slavic and all Jewish civilians. Marked for immediate annihilation were Communist party functionaries, the political leaders of captured towns and villages, and Jews. The Soviet government had utterly failed to warn its people that this invasion was not to be compared to the Kaiser's in 1914. In fact, some Soviet citizens, particularly Ukrainians who despised Stalin and had suffered under the harshness of his regime, actually welcomed the invading troops as liberators. Even the Jews had no idea what to expect at the hands of the Nazis. But the illusion that the Germans were civilized and would respect the accepted rules of warfare did not last long. The ruthlessness of the invaders and their contempt for the defeated population became evident very quickly.

When the first wave of killers swept into Russia behind the German armies, the Jews were easily deceived. They had no reason to question the Germans who offered such comforting words as resettlement, or temporary relocation to move civilians away from the battle zones. The imposing Nazis in their black uniforms, often on horseback, issued orders and they were obeyed. Told to assemble in the town square, Jews assembled; instructed to march to the outskirts, they marched; directed to climb aboard trucks, up they clambered. When the vehicles were filled, some Jews ran after them, hands outstretched, pleading to be lifted on board and join their parents or children. Had anyone told them that they were about to be shot, they would not have believed such an outrageous idea. In many rural areas, the Jews were the only skilled artisans and was it not a well known fact that the Germans appreciated good workers? It was impossible to envision the madness of a government that would destroy its assets.

After the first wave of killings, rumors of the mass shootings flew ahead of the *Einsatzgruppen*. The roundup of the victims became more difficult and more brutal. Many Jews, perhaps 1.5 million, fled eastward, deeper into the vastness of the Soviet

Union, even to Siberia. In fact, they comprised the bulk of Holocaust survivors from Nazi occupied areas. The Jewish population in the conquered Soviet regions was estimated at 3.5 million. This number included Jews from the area of Eastern Poland that had been ceded to the Soviet Union in 1939, refugees from the Baltic States, and 2 million Soviet Jews. Despite the fact that over 40 percent of these intended victims escaped, the numbers killed by the *Einsatzgruppen* were staggering. During the first five months of the operation, it is estimated that half a million men, women, and children were executed.

A second wave of killings was ordered against those who had evaded the first *Aktion.* When this was halted in the fall of 1942, the figure of 1.5 million shooting deaths was reached. It must be remembered that these murders were not the result of bombs delivered from planes high above, or barrages of cannons fired in the heat of battle; these victims stood naked and helpless in front of their killers who shot them, one by one, by one, by one. . . .

METHODS OF MURDER

Although each of the commanders of the *Einsatzgruppen* performed the executions with his own style, some generalities can be noted. To make the task easier, the victims must remain calm. That required skillful lying to the assembled groups. Often the SS used the local Jewish leaders to convince the assembled that no harm would come to them. The killing sites, usually on tops of ditches, were outside of the towns and villages. Once the victims were loaded into trucks, escape was nearly impossible. Screaming their incessant "*Schnell, schnell,*" (quickly, quickly) the killers lined up their prey in assembly line fashion. Some commanders ordered the Jews to kneel in front of their open graves; others shot them standing. A *Gruppen* captain could demand that the Jews hand over their valuables, or he might choose to leave any assets intact until requisitioned by SS economic personnel. None of the killers were permitted to profit in any way from the death of the Jews. All property became the possession of the SS organization. The description that follows is a composite of the testimonies given at the Nuremberg War Crimes Trial and other trials. These accounts were given under oath by survivors and dovetailed with reports from members of the *Einsatzgruppen.* There are also German documents and corroboration from onlookers to attest that the killers usually proceeded in this sequence:

After the German army had rolled through a small Russian town, the inhabitants who had fled into nearby woods to escape the first onslaught filtered back to their homes. Even under German occupation, life took on a degree of normalcy since the battles were fought farther to the East. Depending on location, however, within days or weeks or months, a new and different enemy suddenly appeared. These Germans were dressed in black, not in the army gray. They were members of a unit from a mobile killing squad, the *Einsatzgruppen.* As they fanned across the countryside, their units were usually broken up into smaller squads, *Einsatzkommandos* which may again be subdivided into *Sonderkommandos* composed of fewer than fifty men. The officer in command asked for the rabbi or the head of the town's Jewish council. Having no idea what to expect, the community leaders hurried into the presence of the Germans. Depending on his personality, the officer in charge might use a casual manner to soothe the fears of his victims or speak with authority, to make certain that he would be obeyed. All the Jews must assemble at once in the village square. Within ten minutes, he would conduct a roll call in preparation of their resettlement further away from the scenes of battle. Nothing to worry about, a mere formality, a temporary measure. Leave everything in your homes and make certain that everyone, even babies, were present. Anyone failing to follow orders will be shot.

News of the SS's command spread very quickly. Some of the Jews had heard terrible rumors concerning such roll calls and were frightened. A few of the young people decided to hide despite parental admonition that it was best to comply. They slipped away, hoping to reach some of the partisan groups forming in the woods. The majority suspended their individual judgment and followed the advice of their leaders: Authority must be obeyed. Clusters of families gathered in the marketplace. In minutes, several hundred Jews stood quietly before the Germans.

The blackshirted commander appeared. He was on horseback and looked very imposing. He told the Jews that there was a slight change in his plan; he would explain later. Everyone was to go to a hillside a few kilometers outside the town. Groups of 100 must leave every ten minutes; some of his soldiers would go along. Those who were too weak to walk could go on the truck. The rabbi wanted to ask why this was necessary, but when he stepped forward, the soldiers pointed their guns at him, and he stepped back. While some of the very old, the sick, and the very young were helped onto the truck, the first group left. Gentile neighbors watched them disappear from view. They wondered why the Germans had requisitioned a bulldozer. The noise of its motor could be heard, coming from beyond the hill. What could the Germans be digging?

When the Jewish families arrived at the knoll, they were met by another small squad of SS men, possibly ten or twenty. Their leader shouted at the families to hurry and get undressed. Get undressed? Surely, they did not understand. But when one of the soldiers began to tear the dress and underclothes off one of the women, there could be no doubt. The children were the first to become panic-stricken, some ran about wildly, others clung to their parents. The Germans were shouting, ordering the naked men, women, and children to line up in front of them, on the ridge atop the hill. When several children ran towards the woods, one of the soldiers raised his rifle, and they fell dead. The Jews gasped, the mothers screamed, but the shooter merely reloaded. At that moment, many Jews realized that they were about to be killed. But even though their eyes told them the truth, their brains and hearts could not accept such a verdict. A shocked numbness seemed to roll across the crowd. Many faces lost all expression as they stood naked, with children in their arms, in a row in front of their killers. A beautiful young girl broke away, ran toward the Nazis. In Yiddish, she cried, "Look at me, look at me, I am only sixteen. . . ." She never finished her sentence and fell in a heap. That bullet animated the group. Old men tried to bless their children, mothers clutched their own and other people's offspring, wives and husbands attempted one last embrace, and some called upon God to help them. The men from the *Einsatzkommando* cursed and then the whole squad opened fire, and the Jews plunged into the mass grave below.

Some people were shot but not immediately killed. They lay among the dead and dying, trying to climb out of their grave. But a fresh truckload of victims had arrived. They could hear the cries and terrible moans coming from below and quickly understood their fate. That glazed look of disbelief swept across many faces, unable to comprehend an incomprehensible cataclysm. Some of the children and young people recovered their will to live and made for the woods. Rarely was such an escape successful. An old man with a flowing beard refused to take off his underwear. Religious Jews will not appear naked before their children. He was the first to be killed in his group.

The newly dead and wounded fell upon those already in the ditch. There was a horrible clutching and grabbing among the injured to get to the top, to get air to breathe. Blood, so much blood, mixed with the bladder and bowel contents of the dead and dying. The ditch was heaving with bodies pushing and pulling. And the bodies kept piling up. Only a few, very few, escaped from such mass graves. Even if a victim had the strength to climb out of the pit, it required extraordinary survival instincts to hide when the Nazis brought back the bulldozers to cover up their gruesome work.

THE KILLERS

No matter how thoroughly the brains of the killers had been washed, like Lady Macbeth's damned spot, it was never enough. Their officers repeatedly reminded them that they were instruments in a great historic mission, but the words could not cancel the deeds. These were men with families; how could they separate their own cherished children from the ones they tossed into mass graves, some dead, some still living? Could they accept the burdens of savagery that Himmler placed upon them and remain sane? Even with an unlimited liquor supply at their disposal, could they ever return to a society in which murder is a punishable crime? One also has to wonder why so few of the men requested other duties. Such transfers were possible without penalty. Was fear of reassignment to the dreaded Russian front an overriding concern? Perhaps the sense of accountability blurs after ten, or a hundred, or a thousand murders.

Himmler was aware of the problem, and he was concerned. He toured the *Einsatzgruppen* often and tried to lift the morale of his men. He told them that he knew that their's was a heavy task and somehow they must "overcome themselves." Did he mean that they must suspend their humanness? Their feelings of pity and morality? Even their ordinary intelligence? After all, how great a menace were the Jews? It was known that not a single member of any mobile unit was killed by a Jew. In August 1941, Himmler witnessed an *Aktion*. It was a small massacre, merely 200

Jews. The commander of the squad noted that Himmler was extremely nervous when the executions began. By the time they were over, the chief of the SS was near collapse. He gathered himself enough to make one of his speeches, but the men had seen his reaction. The officer of the unit told Himmler that his men were finished as normal members of society. "What kind of fellows are we training here? Either neurotics or savages!"

A better, faster method for killing Jews was urgently needed. The gas chambers were the result of the search to spare emotional anguish, not of those about to be killed, but of the killers.

SOME GERMAN REACTIONS

Some of the German witnesses to the killings were revolted by the savagery of the SS. The disgust stemmed from two sources. First, the murder of Jewish craftsmen ruined the very industries from which the German war effort could have benefited. The army, in need of everything from winter clothing to bullets tried, and in the long run failed, to prevent the destruction of needed manpower. Second, such massacres could not be kept secret. The special squads combing the sites of the killings, digging up the bodies, burning them, and using special bone crushers to disguise the evidence could not erase the evidence. There had been onlookers who whispered about the sights they had seen. And was it reasonable to expect that all the killers would to go to their own graves without revealing their past? What reaction could they expect, from their families, from the world outside Germany? A case in point was *Gauleiter* Wilhelm Kube, the political head of the occupied territory of White Russia (Ruthenia). Like many other dedicated Nazis, he despised the Jews but disapproved violently of the SS and its atrocities. He was furious that the *Einsatzgruppen* destroyed his work force and shamed the name of Germans. Furthermore, they crisscrossed his domain without consulting with him. In the strange world of Nazism, *Gauleiter* Kube, the antiSemite, worked hard to save Jews. When he heard of planned shootings, he warned the potential victims; he protested to his superiors and found a sympathetic ear in the *Reichskommissar* for the *Ostland,* Heinrich Lohse. Not only were the SS inflicting unnecessary savagery upon the Jews, the mass killings of ordinary Russian peasants were equally self-destructive for the orderly governing of Soviet lands. Kube had become a thorn in Himmler's side and while the *Reichsfuehrer* was considering ways to neutralize him, Soviet partisans solved his problem. In September of 1943, Kube's maid placed a lethal bomb under his bed. Himmler was delighted and called the assassination a blessing.

The use of the mobile killing units was coming to an end in any case. Himmler decided that gas would replace precious bullets and a more impersonal method of ridding Europe of its Jews would result in less trauma for his SS killers. Furthermore, it was not possible to restrict the number of witnesses when the executions took place in the open. It was time to move the killing centers from the eyes of the public.

THE GAS VAN EXPERIMENT

The *Einsatzgruppen* had trapped the Jews where they lived; the next procedure reversed the arrangement and the victims were transported to the killing centers. Midway between these methods was a third course of action, a transitional one, the use of gas vans. Their operation was relatively brief because they failed in two important respects: The numbers killed were too small compared to the effort expended and they did not alleviate the distress of the executioners.

The diesel vans were introduced in Chelmno, a camp the Nazis had established north of Lodz. An old, isolated mansion had been converted into an execution site. Its commander started out with three vehicles which were specially equipped to asphyxiate the Jews of Lodz. Always reluctant to let anything of potential value escape them, the prisoners were told to undress because it was necessary to disinfect them to prevent the outbreak of infectious diseases. No need to get upset; this was a matter of hygiene. The naked Jews were ordered to board the vans which supposedly would take them to the delousing quarters. Actually their clothing was stored for possible use by Germans, although at the end of the war mountains of garments had accumulated.

Fifty or more men, women, and children climbed into each vehicle. They had no inkling that a hose had been attached to the exhaust pipe of the diesel motor so that the deadly carbon monoxide fumes emptied into the sealed interior. If all went according to plan, the driver rode around for fifteen minutes to poison his cargo. Then he stopped near a pit where a group of Jews emptied the van. They removed any valuables not discovered earlier and buried the corpses. Only the promise that their lives would be spared could induce some Jews into the *Sonderkommando,* the ghastly special work detail. The bodies they handled were covered with bodily discharges, horribly distorted by the gas, and yet strangely flexible, as if still alive. The Nazis, of course, did not keep their word; sooner or later the members of the *Sonderkommando* joined the other corpses in the pit.

This, the Nazis decided, was not a good method. The locked-in victims realized what was happening and screamed, banged on the doors, pleaded, and caused the drivers great discomfort. Sometimes it took longer than the prescribed quarter-hour to complete the process. Also, gasoline was in short supply and needed for military purposes. And finally, with so many Jews to be killed, fifty or sixty at a time was simply too slow. At that rate it could take years to finish the operation.

FACTORIES OF DEATH

The solution to Himmler's problem of how to expedite the Final Solution was found in the expertise of Criminal Police Inspector Christian Wirth. Since the abandonment of the so-called euthanasia killings in Germany, Wirth was at loose ends. He had been responsible for the installation of the ostensible bathhouses in which "undesirables," handicapped Germans had been murdered by carbon monoxide.

Himmler commissioned Wirth to oversee the construction of gas chambers in most of the killing centers in Poland. But the Wirth method, which used carbon monoxide gas from fixed diesel engines, was often inefficient. The vermin-killing poison hydrogen cyanide, patented by I.G. Farben known as Zyklon-B, created fumes that were more effective. The blue crystals killed more quickly and were easily dispensed from the roof into openings in the ceilings above the deadly shower rooms. Contact between the SS and their victims was thus reduced to be minimal and Himmler's men would be spared the trauma associated with earlier methods.

The production quotas at the death camps of Chelmno, Belzec, Sobibor, Majdanek, Treblinka, and Auschwitz-Birkenau (see Map 9-2) were measured in the numbers put to death. In the language of the reports submitted to SS headquarters in Berlin, certain criminals had received "special treatment." In a monstrous imitation of the world of ordinary manufacturers, there was competition among the death factories to see which could produce the highest number per day. Auschwitz-Birkenau, the largest of the facilities, could kill 12,000 prisoners a day; a record of achievement no other camp commander could challenge. But then, no other facility could accommodate 2,000 victims at one time and kill them in fifteen minutes or less. Indeed, the name Auschwitz well deserved to be a symbol of the Holocaust.

The machinery of destruction was in place. Now the ghettos were emptied, and the trains from Nazi occupied Europe began to roll toward the Polish countryside. Several officers of the Wehrmacht had made feeble attempts to save the Jews who worked in industry but failed. Himmler, empowered by the Fuehrer himself, had total control. He found in SS Major-General Odilo Globocnik the right tool to take charge of all the death camps. Globocnik's unsavory character combined the hardness and cruelty that this work demanded. Under his supervision, the death factories of Majdanek, Sobibor, and Treblinka were built. When the killing stopped in 1945, the victims numbered approximately 6 million; of these, between 1.5 million and 2 million were children.

In the strange world of Nazi bookkeeping, the names of the prisoners who went directly to their deaths were not recorded, but detailed files were kept on the concentration and slave labor camp inmates. Documentation from the fees the German railroad received for transporting Jews to the death camps as well as other sources allow an approximate count of the victims whose names were not registered. Present research suggests the following totals of Jews killed:

Chelmno	152,000
Belzec	600,000
Sobibor	250,000
Treblinka	70,000
Majdanek	125,000
Auschwitz-Birkenau	2,000,000

The number given for Auschwitz-Birkenau is a minimal figure, other estimates that include non-Jewish victims range as high as 4 million. It is the judgment of some researchers that approximately 4 million Jews were murdered in all of the

Map 9-2   *The German Partition of Poland, 1939/41–1945.*   (From *The War Against the Jews 1933–1945,* by Lucy S. Davidowicz. Text copyright © 1975 by Lucy S. Davidowicz, maps by Vincent Kotschar, copyright © 1975 by Henry Holt and Co., Inc. Reprinted by permission of Henry Holt and Co., Inc.)

death camps. The victims of the *Einsatzgruppen* and additional hundreds of thousands killed in the ghettos and in concentration and slave-labor camps result in the aggregate assessment of 6 million.

In the minds of many students of the Holocaust the words Concentration Camp evokes a single image, namely Auschwitz. Because it was the largest camp and its killing center, Birkenau, was a part of the complex installation, such a metaphor is understandable, but it is also misleading. The Nazi commissioned several types of camps to suit differing needs. The transit or internment camps, such as Westerbork in Holland, Drancy in France, and Malines in Belgium were assemblage points from which detainees were moved eastward. Theresienstadt located in the Czech Protectorate was called a ghetto but was also used as a transit facility for the shipment of Jews to death camps. The numerous slave labor camps and their even more numerous satellites dotted the Nazi occupied landscape like hundreds of pustules. Mauthausen in Austria was one of the worst of these, Neuengamme and Stutthof in northern Germany were other examples. Ravensbrueck, also in Northern Germany, imprisoned Christian women; most came from France and Poland and only during the last few months were Jewish women pushed into its overcrowded barracks. Ordinary concentration camps, if one may use that term, were detention compounds in which prisoners languished for indeterminate periods of time. From there they might be transferred to work sites or to death factories. Dachau, Bergen–Belsen and Buchenwald, all in Germany, fit into this category. Often the functions of camps changed and overlapped. The Auschwitz network, for example, was utilized as a slave labor facility, its death chambers had the largest capacity and sometimes prisoners were transferred to other facilities. Because all camps had high death rates it could be said that all were accessories to the annihilation process. (*The Macmillan Atlas of the Holocaust* by Martin Gilbert contains excellent maps on the geography of the Holocaust).

GAS CHAMBERS

The first gas chambers installed by Wirth were placed in the Belzec camp which was located on the railway line between Lublin and Lvov. Considerable effort was made to conceal the true purpose of the structure in order to deceive the victims. Signs, such as THIS WAY TO THE DISINFECTION ROOM, and arrows pointing TO THE SHOWER BATH were designed to prevent panic. The diesel engine that fed the gas into a sealed chamber was activated as soon as the prisoners were locked in. Roughly thirty minutes later, the "special treatment" had been administered. Thus, mass murder had been made easier for the killers, as direct contact with the victims was at a minimum.

The men of the special *Totenkopfverbaende,* the SS Deathhead Formations whose ranks constituted the concentration camps' guard units, found it reassuring to regard themselves as faithful civil servants. Himmler visited often to tell them so; they were merely following orders and doing a very difficult but necessary job of destroying a dangerous pestilence. The guards at Chelmno, where many sick Jews were gassed, actually received bonus pay as if they were really killing people with infectious diseases. Although every concentration camp survivor witnessed and/or suffered many incidents of sadistic treatment by guards, the SS's official position discouraged private acts of degenerate behavior and a Nazi Commission of Special Inquiry investigated some of the most flagrant cases. Two hundred complaints, (of course none were heard from the victims), resulted in convictions for corruption and unauthorized murder. Most infamous among the condemned was Karl Koch, commandant of Buchenwald and Lublin. He was given the death sentence for pursuing private wealth and for indulging his sadistic cravings. In the world of Nazism, only the state had the right to loot, torture, maim, and kill. It is safe to assume that an unknown number of guards who were never indicted would have been judged criminally insane or guilty of heinous crimes in any court of law.

THE MANY FORMS OF DECEPTION

The question "Why did nearly all the condemned Jews go so quietly to their deaths?" is raised in every Holocaust history class. Although a precise analysis of this question is not feasible, a response should be attempted.

First, it is necessary to understand the prevailing conservative, paternalistic society of Eastern Jewry during the first half of the twentieth century. This is a difficult leap into a past wherein the word of the father was unquestioned law. And fathers were unwilling to urge their children to endanger themselves, their family and the community by disobedience to the Germans. The desire to keep the family together was compelling beyond logic; there was the hope that the ordeals to be endured could be eased by a comforting word, a gesture of love. Permitting one's children to escape the ghetto and face cold, hunger and an unknown fate without their support terrified most parents. Even so, some children, even babies, were left in the care of Gentiles by desperate mothers and fathers. Most, however, clung to one another until the end. As we will note in the following chapter, when no illusions of survival were left, the young people in several ghettos defied their elders and resisted the Nazis.

Nothing in the history of the last thousand years had prepared Jews to fight for their lives with weapons. As strangers, more or less tolerated by reluctant host countries, they had relied on petitions, on the goodwill of a few friendly officials or kings and on bribery as a means of survival. The past had taught them to absorb the blows of their enemies because striking back, even in self-defense, resulted in catastrophic retaliation against the entire community. The nightmare of Russian pogroms had not faded from the collective memory. Jewish boys were taught to bring honor to their families by virtue of scholarship, not through physical strength and skill. And always, after each assault, the remnant had rebuilt Jewish life. This had been their formula for survival in the Diaspora.

Those of us who study the Holocaust from a distance of more than a half century, find the deliberate murder of people who broke no laws and posed no danger to the Germans very difficult to comprehend. We know the facts, have met survivors, read the admissions of the perpetrators, and still cannot grasp the death factories. How much more difficult it must have been for the Jews who had lined up in front of the false showers to understand their fate. Human intelligence has limits of comprehension and the human spirit has limits of endurance. Self-deception or denial of reality relieves the mind of its suffering when all else fails. It was easier to deny the truth about the strange, acrid smell in the air and the meaning of the ashes coming from the chimney than to face reality. Some of the victims, so completely and suddenly deprived of every aspect of their former lives, had turned into automatons. They were robots, empty shells, going here, standing there, their reasoning ability had already ceased to function. The tattered ones who had come from starvation-plagued ghettos or other concentration camps resembled the walking dead. Unable to absorb the past, they could not comprehend the present and surely it was a blessing that they could not see their future.

The commanders of various death camps devised their own methods of keeping their installations running smoothly. Deception and trickery reinforced the prisoners' hope for life. In Auschwitz-Birkenau, the arriving trains were met by music from an orchestra; in Treblinka, flowers bloomed at the railway depot. Here the SS guards grouped them according to their skills, carpenters here, tailors there, to create the impression that after resettlement they would work in their trades. In the entry of the "showers," prisoners were told to tie their shoes together to prevent later mix-ups and to remember the number of the peg on which they hung their clothing. The women were reassured that their hair would grow back; the shaving of heads was a sanitary measure, lice cause typhus. And mothers were urged to hold their babies close so none would get lost in the confusion.

The Jews complied. What could they have done, these rows of naked men and women, facing the SS with their loaded guns, their dogs, and whips? Had the Germans not proven time and again that disobedience by one would cause the death of many? Who would dare to lift a hand, or try to run away when the retaliation would be so swift and so terrible? And finally, who among them had the energy of mind and body to resist? Many who knew that death was a certainty had but one wish: Let it be over with; let it end.

SONDERKOMMANDOS

All the death camps were located on or near railroad lines. The first arrivals came from Poland and Slovakia, then from Germany, the Low Countries, France, Greece, the Balkans, the Soviet Union, and, finally, Italy and Hungary. The SS was in charge, their numbers augmented by auxiliary troops made up of volunteers from the local population. Jewish prisoners, organized into *Sonderkommandos,* were employed for some of the most repugnant work. When the rail cars were unlocked, a putrid stench escaped from the interior. Depending on the length of the journey, the severity of the crowding, the degree of cold or heat endured, and the number of days spent without food and water, prisoners were in a state of partial or complete shock. They had no idea where they were; often the windowless cars had not allowed them to see the terrain through which they had passed. Rumors, fear, and often darkness had added to the trauma of the journey.

Those who were able jumped from the train, the others were pushed or beaten into an orderly procession, destined either for work or the gas chambers. Every car had a number of dead propped up among the living. Members of the *Sonderkommandos* hauled them away and then hosed down the filthy wagons. They worked hard and fast, screaming at the prisoners, sometimes hitting them in order to impress the SS with their usefulness. Some dared to whisper a word of advice to a new arrival: "Don't carry the baby," "Stand up straight," "Say you know how to sew." They labored because they knew how easily they could be replaced and forced to join the line to the deadly showers. Death camps, as opposed to the slave-labor camps, required only small work forces. That meant that nearly all, and in many instances every single person coming off a train was immediately dispatched to die. Women and children had virtually no chance of surviving death camp selections.

In some death camps, *Sonderkommandos* were replaced frequently; in others they lived for several months. The Nazis made use of these prisoners before and after the gassing. With German orderliness, barbers shaved the hair of the women, others cleaned and sorted the belongings of the dead, piling up eyeglasses, tons of hair, baby shoes, and crutches. The most fortunate inmates worked in the offices, preparing reams of paperwork and keeping accounts for Himmler's comptrollers in Berlin. The most harrowing duty entailed the handling of corpses. First, the dead had to be removed from the gas chambers, which then had to be cleaned of human waste. Disposal of the corpses, however, could not take place until a final act of robbery and desecration was committed. Members of the *Sonderkommando* were required to pry open the jaws of the dead and remove any gold from their teeth; others searched for jewels that might have been hidden in any bodily orifices. Depending on the facilities of the camp, the corpses were turned into ashes in the ovens of the crematoria or buried in mass graves or soaked with gasoline and burned in pits.

Most of the camps built cremation facilities as a solution to the problem of disposing of so many hundreds of thousands of bodies. This method was also useful in destroying the evidence of the crimes, an issue that became more important after the initial German victories in the Soviet Union turned into military reversals. During the last few months of the war, a frantic attempt was made to incinerate bodies of victims that earlier had been thrown into mass graves. But time ran out. It took six hours to burn 100 paraffin-soaked bodies. There was never enough gasoline to speed the process. Advancing Russian troops encountered evidence of heaps of partially burnt corpses as they fought their way toward Germany.

AUSCHWITZ'S ORGANIZATION

Some 160 miles southwest of Warsaw, in a swampy marsh near the German border of upper Silesia, the Nazis established the largest and most complex of their many concentration camps. The demented world of Auschwitz gave full expression to the worst betrayal of humanity found in the annals of history. Because of its size and the completeness of its facilities, this camp merits a closer look. Its name is rightfully placed at the center of the genocide of European Jewry.

The concentration camp was established in 1940 as a place of incarceration for a large variety of people declared dangerous by the Nazis. The wrought-iron legend over its main gate, *Arbeit macht frei* (Work gives freedom) encapsulated the irony of a place where only death brought freedom. The barbed wire fences were electrified; sentries with machine guns looked down upon the hapless masses day and night. From time to time shots were fired by members of the SS simply to raise the level of anxiety by killing a few prisoners. Two hundred dogs trained in tracking and killing were kenneled just behind the SS barracks. Auschwitz was the only camp where prisoners who survived their immediate destruction were branded with a number that was tattooed on the inside of their left forearm. Even before the addition of the slave labor and death camp facilities, the entire installation was designed to speed the "natural" reduction of prisoners. Hunger, cold, disease, terror tactics, and executions were the norm in this upside down world.

The Nazis adopted the techniques first established in the older camps such as Dachau, Buchenwald, and Sachsenhausen. To keep SS personnel at a minimum, they used inmates to supervise other inmates. As the camp expanded, a hierarchy of prisoner functions developed. Positions such as Camp Elders, Block Elders, and Room Orderlies which allowed the Nazis to run their prisons with relatively few guards. The term Elders, however, belies the type of inmates who held these posts. The SS preferred non-Jewish convicted criminals, mostly from Germany and some from the conquered countries for these appointments, but there were also a number of Jewish Kapos (from the Italian word meaning head) in the camps. Since it was their function to maintain rigid discipline, the most vicious among them were apt to be chosen.

A Kapo, that is, a prisoner in charge of other prisoners, held the power of life and death over his charges even though the SS could execute him as indifferently as any other inmate. If he struck an inmate and marked his face by the blow, that man would not survive the next selection for the gas chambers. The Kapo's authority to make work assignments was equivalent to deciding if an already weak or ill man would or would not live another day. On the other hand, a choice job in the kitchen or in any enclosed structure extended some inmates' chance of survival. Obviously, many prisoners lived in constant fear and secret rage. Mastering these emotions, however, was vital in a place where an average prisoner remained alive for three months.

Although Jews made up the majority of men and women who died in Auschwitz, many Gentiles, particularly Poles who had somehow run afoul of the Nazis, were among the imprisoned. Also, there were Germans convicted of crimes ranging from robbery to antisocial behavior (such as unwillingness to work), Gypsies, whose fate was not decided for years, pacifists such as Seventh Day Adventists, and homosexuals. After June 1941, Soviet prisoners of war were kept there, and hundreds of thousands were deliberately starved to death in complete disregard of the international conventions regarding the treatment of POWs. They were also the first victims of the Zyklon-B gas experiments. Jews began to arrive en masse after the Wannsee Conference, first from nearby Poland and Silesia, later from the entire European continent. The great majority were immediately conveyed to the gassing facilities at Birkenau.

Auschwitz grew constantly between 1941 and 1944 until the map was dotted with names like Auschwitz I (the main camp); Auschwitz II (the Birkenau killing factory); Auschwitz III (Monowitz, the slave labor camp for Buna, the IG Farben oil and rubber plants). Many other factories, including Siemens-Schuckert and Krupp, clustered nearby. Few Jewish arrivals, about 10 percent of the men, considerably fewer women, and none of the children and older generation, were permitted to live and work. The imprisoned non-Jews fared better and comprised the majority of the slave workers until 1944 when the Hungarian Jews filled their thinning ranks. The pull between the Germans who wanted to use Jewish labor in war related industries and the push from the Nazi fanatics who were bent on total annihilation, was never quite resolved. The number of survivors, estimated at a maximum of a half million, compared to the 6 million who died, justified the Nazis' claim of victory in their war against the Jewish people.

CHEAPER THAN SLAVES

The industrial complex at Auschwitz encompassed several square miles. The IG Farben cartel, Germany's largest industrial enterprise, had established an extensive compound, which included the Buna Werke for the manufacture of synthetic rubber, and a coal-based oil refinery. To save the workmen some strength, they were no longer marched the several miles from the main camp, but were housed and fed in barracks near the factories. In fact, they were leased chattel, easily replaced when worn out, for whom the SS received payment. Only toward the end of the war, when the need for workers became acute and the SS Economic and Administrative Department under Oswald Pohl was given authority over the inmates, did conditions improve slightly.

The workday usually started at three or four in the morning and lasted until late evening. In addition to laboring in the factories, quarries, and various road construction projects surrounding the camp, a number of Jews were used to process the by-products of death. Aside from their earlier mentioned labor, the *Sonderkommandos* were assigned to the huge storage structures called "Canada" (a place of riches). Here, they counted, cleaned, sorted, and readied for shipment to Germany the enormous quantities of goods left behind by the murdered Jews. Depending on their former status, the dead were now robbed of everything from hair ribbons to diamonds sewn into hems. Inmate accountants recorded every item, for as the Germans so often said; *"Ordnung muss sein"* (There must be order). Members of the SS took personal advantage of the pool of talent at their disposal. Jewish tailors fashioned suits, coats, and uniforms for the SS and their families; former cobblers made them shoes and fine boots; jewelers created lovely pieces from the abundant gold and precious stones. For most of the period of Auschwitz's existence, Rudolf Hoess was its commander. Whenever he wanted to impress visiting dignitaries, or amuse himself and his staff, he could count on the availability of talented musicians and actors to brighten their dreary life in the Polish wasteland.

HUNGER

The inmates of Auschwitz had less value than slaves. They cost nothing because the *Judenraete* had paid the price of their transportation to the camp. They were doomed at any rate and could be replaced at will. Inmates were deliberately given starvation rations. Hunger, the sort one cannot even imagine, gnawed at the men and women relentlessly. While there was no general formula for survival in Auschwitz, and while every individual had to find his and her own strength to get through another day, the one common memory of survivors is hunger. Enduring terror, dehumanization, deprivation of the simplest human sanitary needs, and the fear for missing loved ones, each prisoner dealt with such suffering in ways unique to his and her personality. But hunger was the universal dimension, the single most remembered agony.

A thin soup with a few grams of black bread made of some substitute for grain was the main meal at midday. Mornings and evenings, a liquid called coffee and another piece of bread were doled out. Naturally, a forbidden trade developed. Prisoners who had the energy and will bought and sold any item that could eventually be turned into food. That required access to "Canada," where everything could be obtained, or to the machine shops or any place at all where theft might go

Jewish women selected for slave labor in Auschwitz-Birkenau.   (Courtesy United States Holocaust Memorial Museum.)

unnoticed. A homemade tin cup for a cigarette, a cigarette for a vest, a vest for a piece of chocolate, a piece of chocolate for an apple. . . .

These were the "organizers"; they risked punishment, even death, with their trades and smuggling. They became experts, bartering item for item, but at the end of the chain was something edible. The "organizers" were akin to the *Prominenten,* the men and their female counterparts who by virtue of their luck and pluck maintained the outward aspects of their humanity. Often they bore low numbers on their arms, indicative of their early arrival and amazingly long survival in the camp. The men shaved, using the precious hot liquid at breakfast and dull knives; the women exchanged a meal for a comb or a toothbrush. They washed their clothes and, without a place to hang them to dry, put them on wet, even in winter. Sooner or later, the SS noticed them and considered them reliable. Sometimes they were rewarded with positions of some authority, or were permitted to work indoors, or given a Red Cross package. Such gifts were life-giving. Unlike the Kapos, the *Prominenten* were generally respected and often helpful to others. They set an example of how to remain civilized in a savage and brutal environment.

Not only the death camps in Poland, but all concentration camps were intended to reduce the number of inmates by "natural" attrition. There was, of course, nothing natural about 500-calorie-a-day diets, lack of proper clothing, long hours of exhausting labor, beatings, or overcrowded barracks where two or three slept in the space for one. There was nothing natural about the institutionalized dehumanization designed to break the spirit. The SS knew that the will to live was essential to survival and used their dehumanization techniques to speed up the genocide process. Don't let a prisoner wash, don't let him go to the latrine, curse him, never let him look at you, make him watch the hangings and shootings of his fellow prisoners, and soon his broken spirit will pull his body into the grave. In the language of the *Lager* (shortened from *Konzentrationslager*), the prisoners who had reached the end of their strength were called "Musselmen." It was easy to recognize their empty stare, their uncoordinated movements. They cowered, unseeing, unspeaking and from a distance they resembled Muslims kneeling at prayer. They no longer washed nor picked the lice from their bodies. Waiting for death without impatience, without any visible emotion, they were sure to disappear at the next selection.

THE HUNGARIAN TRAGEDY

Hungary had been a more or less reluctant ally of the Nazi regime in order to fulfill its own goals of aggrandizement. With Hitler's approval, Hungary had expanded its territory at the expense of Slovakia, Romania, and Yugoslavia. Although Hungarian troops were active on the Russian front, Germany found this ally lacking in commitment to the war. The Hungarian government under the Regent Nicholas Horthy had also resisted Nazi pressure to deliver its approximately 800,000 Jews into German captivity. Thus, this ancient and renowned Jewish community believed it had weathered the Holocaust. It was hoped that since the Germans were losing the war, the Nazi nightmare would soon be over.

The situation, however, changed rapidly and tragically in 1944. Internal turmoil instigated by the extreme political right weakened the Horthy government. The dilemma worsened when Hitler suspected that Horthy planned to negotiate a separate peace with the advancing Soviet Union. By kidnapping Horthy's son, the regent was forced to cede power to the pro-Nazi Arrow Cross Fascists who took their orders from Berlin. For all intents and purposes, Hungary became an occupied nation and the Jews lost their protection.

Beginning in March of 1944, just eleven months before Budapest was captured by the Russian army, the Jews faced the terror of Eichmann. His experienced and well-oiled organization set up ghettos, appointed *Judenraete,* and confiscated "abandoned" properties and set in motion the machinery for transport of the Jews. Eichmann had long hoped to get his hands on this, the largest remnant of European Jewry and with the eager aid of the Hungarian fascist Arrow Cross police, the roundups and deportation began almost at once. The first thousands of victims came from the provinces at the periphery of the nation, and the intent was to deport the Jews of Budapest as soon as these regions were *Judenrein.*

Without a shred of doubt, the Germans had lost the war. But the killing of Jews continued without letup. This belated onslaught did not go unnoticed by the international community. The American and British governments and the Pope at long last raised their voices in protest. There was also the promise by the Allies that the Nazis' crimes against civilians would not go unpunished. But despite these efforts, the process of annihilation did not cease. Hungarian Jews were sent to Auschwitz until Himmler ordered the closing of the camp because Soviet armies were nearly at the gates. The confusion of the final battles between the Allies and Germany made it impossible to get the trains the SS so urgently demanded for the Budapest Jews. Eichmann then organized treks to march them north across Austria. This took place in the winter of 1944–1945, and the loss of life was enormous. Mauthausen concentration camp was made an interim destination, but by the end of the war Hungarian survivors were found in many German camps. Even when the Russians were in the suburbs of the capital, Eichmann's compulsion to destroy Jews never abated. Gas chambers, starvation, freezing, and illness killed thousands of Hungarian Jews every day. Their death toll, so close to the fall of the Third Reich, was a staggering 500,000. Only in the besieged city of Budapest did some 160,000 Jews survive.

SURVIVING A CONCENTRATION CAMP

Not the prisoners, nor the psychiatrists, and certainly not the historians can unravel the mystery of who would live and who would die in Auschwitz and its counterparts. The obstacles that had to be overcome were vast and varied. The initial decision, made at the railroad siding upon arrival, was a matter of chance. Were any workers needed from this shipment? Did the woman carry a child? Was she pregnant? Did Dr. Mengele or his fellow doctors not like a face, a body? Did the commander need a violinist for the camp orchestra? Or an electrician? Did the prisoner look older or younger than approximately forty years? For such reasons the arm or the riding crop pointed to the right or the fatal left. There simply was no rational explanation why some lived beyond their first day.

But what of the inmates who survived the first and many other selections? Their memories and memoirs fill us with awe. Terrorized, emaciated, exhausted drudges, they endured. The SS expected most of their slave workers to die within three months of so-called natural causes or they were killed. And yet some of the prisoners, men and women who never cooperated with the murderers, who never did anything to betray their decency, survived; some for the astounding period of five years.

Why? How? Victor Frankl, himself a prisoner and a psychiatrist, believed that survival was connected to the successful search for a meaning to one's suffering. Physical strength, status of health, erstwhile occupation, all that meant nothing. If a prisoner could find a rationale for his agony, he might hold out against all odds. If he could discover a reason to endure his suffering, then his mind and body might resist the welcome relief of death. It did not matter what inspired his resistance as long as it filled him with a passion to live. Perhaps he or she wanted to see the day of Germany's defeat, or take revenge against a tormentor, or bear witness to what happened here, or search for members of his family who might have escaped, or, because just one more time, he wanted to eat enough to feel satisfied. The voices of many survivors point toward the need to live to fulfill some obligation: "I had to take care of my sister"; "I knew God had a purpose for me"; "If we all died, who would believe this ever happened?"

Recent studies indicated that women imprisoned in concentration camps had a better survival rate than men. Reared in the tradition of nurturers, women created artificial families in their barracks. Small groups, perhaps four or five girls who may have come from the same town or spoke the same dialect or arrived on the train together, bonded with one another. They shared what little they had, tried to protect each other, and they talked, always, they talked. Often, an older woman would take on the role of mother; she comforted her girls, advised them, assured them that their menstrual periods would return once they ate properly, and yes, they would have husbands and children someday. Because they were always hungry, food was a prime topic of conversation. How carefully they described each detail of the traditional Passover meals they had prepared in the past. Sometimes, they sang together, even laughed. The Orthodox remembered the dates of Jewish holidays and tried to recall the appropriate prayers. And, of course, they often wept, but not alone. Custom and social conventions expected men to suffer in silence, crying and complaining were unmanly. Thus, most of the men suffered isolation within the camp in addition to the sense of abandonment by the world outside the barbed wire while many women found comfort in sharing their tears and their humanity in the most inhuman places on earth.

Communal grave at the Bergen-Belsen concentration camp.   (Courtesy Corbis.)

THE DOCTORS

In Auschwitz medical doctors did not practice the art of healing. There was no treatment for the sick or injured, not even an aspirin for pain and fever. The only surgery performed was related to experiments so diabolical that they dishonored the name of science. In all the slave labor and concentration camps, doctors routinely condemned the men and women to death because they judged who was fit or unfit to work; in the death camps, they were participants in the murder of millions.

The plunge from healer to killer originated in Nazi ideology gone berserk. The doctrine of the Aryan super-German was given official credibility by calling it racial science. Biologists and physicians established criteria for the pure Nordic type: skin tones, bone structure, eye color, height, weight, and so on. A distortion of Darwin's theories led to the "purification" of Germany by eliminating its supposedly mentally and physically flawed population. In the Thousand Year Reich, only those declared fit according to government standards had the right to live. Nazi doctors determined who could live and who must die. They called this program euthanasia, but it was murder. In Hitler and Himmler's world, the annihilation of a people declared dangerous—the Jews—was the next logical step. Medical personnel accepted their genocidal assignments and became docile instruments and partners in mass murder.

Doctors functioned in three areas related to the Holocaust. They dictated life or death for prisoners at the railroad sites and at the *Appells* (roll calls, or inspections); they conducted medical experiments that were certain to kill their subjects; and they injected fatal phenol into the hearts of inmates in their hospitals.

The infamous Dr. Mengele enjoyed his role at the railroad siding. Dubbed "the angel of death" at Auschwitz, he was a handsome man, immaculate in his SS uniform as he pointed with his riding crop to the right or to the left; one line for the gas chambers, the other to labor barracks. Surviving the initial selection, however, guaranteed nothing; selections for death occurred continuously. Every morning, the prisoners stood at attention to be counted and recounted during the dreaded *Appell*. Black clad SS doctors moved up and down the rows of men or women to supply fodder for the gas chambers. The weak, the ill, the bruised, the men or women who simply did not please the SS men, were ordered to join the lines leading to the deadly showers.

The medical experiments conducted at Auschwitz and several other camps were cruel beyond belief. Ostensibly to advance medical research, these scientists with credentials from German universities used human beings in ways that ordinary language cannot portray, nor a rational mind comprehend. They tested various types of male and female sterilization techniques and competed to see how many hundreds of sterilization procedures a single doctor could perform in a day. They sought the limits of human endurance to heat and cold and deprivation of oxygen by using prisoners in deadly experiments. Infections were artificially introduced to discover when the disease would kill the subject. New mothers had their breasts bound to observe how soon they would die of deadly fever. Doctors supervised forms of torture to learn what breaks a man and finally destroy him.

Dr. Mengele's experiments with twins were expected to yield information that would increase the number of multiple births for Aryan women. Few adults or children survived his vivisections of their bodies. He was also fascinated with dwarfs and hunchbacks and kept them in the hospital facilities until his experiments killed them. The Nazi racial and eugenic medical establishment in Berlin approved and welcomed the findings of camp doctors. After all, no other place on earth afforded such unlimited access to people whose screams they did not hear.

Camp hospital facilities doubled as medical killing centers. Some Jewish and non-German doctors were permitted to assist the Nazis in the camps. Their efforts to do some healing, to help some patients should be noted, but overall they could not be effective. When it was doubtful that a prisoner could return to work, when the hospital wards were too crowded, the phenol injections were ordered. Patients had no idea what it meant when a doctor or an orderly, needle in hand, told them to cross their arms over their eyes. Only when inmates were sure that their illness or exhaustion made them certain targets for the next selection did they venture into the hospital. There was always a chance they could survive if unnoticed, if allowed a few days' rest and slightly better food. It was a risk taken only as a last resort.

CAMPS IN CENTRAL EUROPE

The death camps were located in Poland but the concentration camp system spread across Central Europe from the borders of France and Holland into Austria and Czechoslovakia. Some of the sites confined permanent prisoners, others were used as stopovers for the eastward journey. Moving inmates from one camp to another was a common practice; some survivors could recall more than a dozen in their personal history. The map of Germany was dotted with *Lagers,* some huge, others holding a few hundred slave laborers for a nearby factory. The prison population always included Jews, but they were not necessarily in the majority. Only after the advance of the Soviet armies impelled the Nazis to march the inmates westward were the German camps deluged with the pathetic, dying remnant from Poland.

During the early years of the Third Reich, Dachau, Buchenwald, and Sachsenhausen were the destinations of political dissenters, trade union leaders, and members of religious organizations who opposed the Nazis. Most were held without trials and served sentences of indeterminate length. When the harshness of German rule over their foreign conquests created opposition, the Gestapo seized hundreds of thousands of accused resistance fighters. It was never clear why the Nazis shot some suspects immediately while others were shipped to death camps and still others to concentration camps. The arrests of underground resisters required expansion of the number and size of camps. When the Nazis began to force foreign workers and prisoners of war into the German defense industry, many slave labor camps, often indistinguishable from concentration camps, were constructed. In addition, there was an increase of German citizens who ran afoul of the secret police for such crimes as grumbling against the war and the nebulous offense of defeatism. Although only estimates are available, the total of prisoners numbered not in the hundreds of thousands, but in the millions. Nor will it ever be known how many died due to starvation, disease, despair, beatings, or shootings.

THERESIENSTADT AND RAVENSBRUECK

Every concentration camp had unique features due to its geography, its administration, its inmates, and/or its work requirements. Two of the *Lagers* were extraordinary and merit particular attention. Theresienstadt (Terezin), located in the Bohemian section of Czechoslovakia, was established by Heydrich in 1941. It was organized to resemble a ghetto, with a council of elders and a chairman running the internal affairs of the Jewish community. Originally a military fortress, the site had stables, workshops, and a street of ramshackle houses. Theresienstadt was reputed to be the most humane camp in the constellation of German camps. Well connected elderly German Jews, decorated Jewish war veterans, prominent scholars, and Jews married to Aryans paid with their life's savings for the opportunity to go there. The Germans had promised that some privileged few could live out their pleasant retirement years in lovely Bohemia. Once the Jews arrived and realized they had been deceived, they were unable to escape their prison/ghetto. The inmates who were permitted to remain had a fair chance of survival, but their numbers were small. It has been suggested that the Nazis considered some of these "residents" to be worth more alive than dead as possible pawns in exchange for German prisoners or for purposes of blackmail.

Theresienstadt had two faces. One looked like an impoverished but viable Jewish community of old people who sustained themselves by their own work in several cottage industries and through gifts from the Red Cross. Families lived together; the food was poor, but lectures and music nourished the soul. These inmates were not as cut off from the rest of the outside world as were other camp prisoners. The SS dealt with the council rather than with individuals. Almost the entire group of Danish Jews who had not taken part in the great escape from Denmark (see Chapter 10) survived here due to the scrupulous vigilance of the Danish government. When the Nazis were pressured by the International Red Cross to permit an inspection of the camp, they grudgingly gave permission. The inspectors were treated to an elaborate charade. After an intensive cleanup, flowers appeared on the sidewalks, well-dressed people sipped tea in the afternoon, and children played around the well-stocked pushcarts of street vendors. The sham lasted one day. The Red Cross representatives saw nothing of the suffering of the hidden camp and wrote a favorable report on their findings.

Theresienstadt, however, was also a stopover for thousands of Jews on their way to Auschwitz and other camps. While waiting for transport east, they lived in overcrowded misery for weeks or months. There was no fuel to heat their stone-walled rooms, too little food, and the ever-present fear of where the next train would take them. The former Chief Rabbi of Germany, Leo Baeck, was among the prominent Jews imprisoned in Theresienstadt. He knew what "resettlement to the East" actually meant and resolved not to reveal the truth. One can only guess what that decision must have cost him. Many Jews from Prague, Berlin, and Vienna were routed through Theresienstadt to Auschwitz as well as the dreaded stone quarries at Mauthausen in Austria. Much of the work of organizing the transfers was handled by the Jewish council, which hoped to save a remnant by cooperating with the Nazis.

Ravensbrueck, established in 1939, was a camp for women only. Before the influx of Jewish women at the approach of the Soviet armies, the majority of inmates were not Jewish. Like so many other concentration camps, it was located in a swampy, unhealthy area. The internal camp management was largely in the hands of German women who were convicted criminals. But its population was international. Prisoners included female Russian soldiers, nurses, Red Cross workers from everywhere in Europe, and resistance fighters, especially from France and Poland. The latter were subjected to medical experiments involving the transplanting of human bones. Their suffering resonated in the bodies of all inmates who tried to alleviate their pain by words and deeds of solidarity. The main industry employing the prisoners was somewhat strange in a country under bombardment on three fronts and from the air: the remodeling of the furs expropriated from Nazi victims. If nothing else, the wives of Nazi leaders would wear lovely fur coats.

Inmates in their barracks at the Buchenwald concentration camp. (Courtesy Corbis.)

It is probable that 50,000 women perished in the camp. The number would have been higher but for a last minute rescue of 14,000 women in April of 1945. Himmler finally agreed to the entreaties of the Swedish diplomat Count Folke Bernadotte to permit their release. Himmler was then entertaining the illusion that the Allies would allow him to represent Germany in peace negotiations, thus his gesture of goodwill. At this late moment of the war and of the Holocaust a single meal could make the difference between life and death.

THE DEATH MARCHES

The encirclement of Germany was almost complete in the late winter of 1944 and early spring of 1945. Soviet armies rolled across the Polish plains and the Western Allies moved up from Italy and crossed into Germany from France. The deadly showers were closed during November 1944 as frantic efforts were exerted to cover up Nazi crimes. Huge shipments of goods taken from the dead were hurriedly sent to Germany, gas chambers and crematoria were blown up, and bodies were disinterred from mass graves and burned. Mountains of accumulated paperwork were thrown into the flames, but time was running out. Some of the inmates were able to hide vital Nazi records before the evacuations virtually emptied the death camps.

During the final months of the Thousand Year Reich, the remaining prisoners, many of whom were recent arrivals from Hungary, presented a problem for the SS. The nation was engulfed in last ditch fighting; it was a time of complete confusion, yet most of the concentration camp guards obeyed their final orders to march their prisoners westward. The roads were choked with fleeing Germans, there was no food or shelter, and the SS had no instructions as to how they were expected to reach their first stopover at the Silesian camp of Gross Rosen. A final tragedy was the inevitable result. The roads on which starved, freezing, barely alive survivors were hurried along were littered with the dead and dying. Many were left where they fell; others were shot by the SS. Just a few hours from liberation, from food and medical care, from life itself, they were claimed by the Shoah.

CHAPTER 10

Resistance and Rescue

For decades after the liberation of the Jewish remnant, the image of the Jew during the Nazi *Endloesung* was woefully one-sided. The unfortunate depiction of victims waiting for death like lambs going to their slaughter ignored the fact that some Jews resisted the Nazis, that they fought back and did so under extremely difficult conditions. In the more recent past, books, movies and television programs have dealt with the topic of opposition more frequently but not necessarily with accuracy. It is fair to state that yes, Jews offered opposition, but it is also correct to say that their participation in the military defeat of the Germans in World War II was not significant. Nonetheless, their choice—and it was a choice—to take a stand had great psychological significance. Their heroism lives as a definitive symbol of courage against overwhelming odds.

In the context of Jewish opposition to the Nazis, the term resistance requires some definition. Does the word refer only to organized combat, such as military action, or does it include individual assaults against the Germans? Is the use of weapons required or is nonviolent opposition rightfully classified as resistance? Is it appropriate, as has been suggested, that survival itself was a form of resistance because the Nazis sought the death of EVERY Jew? Surely, the Jewish men and women who fought as members of partisan organizations in occupied lands were resisters. How should one characterize the workers in ghettos and in slave labor camps who sabotaged the economic enterprises of the Nazis by producing flawed goods? What of the Jewish writers who risked their lives to publish forbidden newspapers and teachers who defied the Gestapo when they secretly instructed their students? The illegal smuggling of food delayed the total collapse of ghetto life and was frequently carried out by children. Did they not offer resistance? The historian Emanuel Ringelblum and others collected and preserved information on the fate of ghetto Jews in defiance of orders. Art and music, as well as poetry, expressed opposition to the Nazis in the ghettos and camps. Clearly, resistance had many forms, and it is necessary to establish its definition as used in this text.

Without intending to diminish the heroism of the many individuals who defied the Nazis in various ways, in this context resistance designates systematic or organized guerilla type clashes between Jews and Germans. Many silent acts of heroic opposition will never come to light nor can their effectiveness be measured. The dimensions and results of industrial sabotage are equally difficult to gauge. German industrialists complained frequently about the low productivity of their forced laborers, but it is not possible to know if the cause was physical and emotional exhaustion or subversive action or all three. It is credible however, to assess the impact of organized Jewish resistance both as members of insurgent units as well as that of ghetto and concentration camp fighters.

The Germans did not consider the Jews who had escaped them to be dangerous to them. Some believed their own propaganda which had marked Jews as cowards while others realized that the practical difficulties facing Jewish resisters, especially in the Polish countryside, were nearly insurmountable. They would be faced with such obstacles as these: The number of Jews with military training was small; procurement of weapons was almost impossible; animosity between Jews and Poles created great danger for Jews trying to find food, medicine, clothing and secure hiding places. No wonder the Nazi felt secure that they had nothing to fear from them.

The actual number of Jews engaged in organized anti-German actions is not clear because many thousands fought as Yugoslavs, Frenchmen, Russians, and alongside other guerilla forces rather than as independent Jewish battalions. Many of the Polish underground units, however, refused to allow Jews to join them and therefore separate Jewish companies were formed.

SHEEP OR WOLVES?

Some historical events speak so clearly that they need no interpretation; others evolve into controversial expositions. The problem of Jewish militancy belongs to the latter category. Some scholars, notably Raul Hilberg and Hannah Arendt, stated that the Jews were passive and consequently they and the activities of the *Judenraete* rendered valuable aid to the Nazis. The death toll, in their view, would have been smaller without the cooperation of the victims. Opposing this concept are, among others, Yehuda Bauer and Schmuel Krakowski. Their research led them to the conclusion that Jews tried to fight Germans whenever and wherever they could, at some cost to the Nazi war effort.

It is a fact that 6 million were killed. It is also true that relatively few Jews resisted as they moved toward the deadly ditches or the gassing chambers. The hundreds of thousands who constituted the armies of slave workers followed Nazi instructions because they hoped that work would give them life. Nearly all of the Jewish elders, before and after ghettoization, urged compliance with Nazi orders out of fear of retaliation. A case from the history of the Vilna ghetto made the point.

A group of young Jews had escaped and joined the partisans in the forest. The Germans ordered the execution of the families they left behind. The head of the *Judenrat,* Jacob Gens, called the escapees traitors who endangered all the inhabitants of the ghetto.

Compliance, however, does not represent the complete picture. A body of evidence exists which recognizes the fact that Jews fought against the Nazis. In some cases Jewish resistance predated the native anti-Nazi underground movements in the conquered nations. As will be noted below, Jews carried out revolts in several Polish ghettos and death camps. They also organized into resistance groups in the forests of Poland and western Russia. When Jewish men and women were accepted into anti-Nazi guerilla organizations, they fought side by side with their Christian counterparts. If rejected, they formed their own partisan groups although they usually had little or no military training, owned few weapons, were constantly on the move for fear of denunciation by Nazi collaborators and had to spend much of their strength in the daily struggle for food. The Germans, on the other hand, had ample manpower, all the arms, food and communications equipment they needed. Only in their zeal to kill the enemy did the guerillas exceed the Nazis; most of the Jewish fighters were the sole survivors of their families. Hatred and the hope to avenge the death of their loved ones gave them daring and resilience beyond all expectations.

What were the chances for Jews to survive in Nazi-occupied Europe by evading capture, by disobeying the demand that they present themselves at train stations or in town squares? The likelihood that they might live through the occupation years was slight, yet survival was more likely for them than for their comrades who followed the Germans' orders. Much depended on the attitude of the Gentile world around them. Would they protect a fleeing Jew or denounce him? Was the geography favorable? Forest and mountains offered the best opportunities. Could he or she pass as a Gentile by virtue of an "Aryan" appearance? Did he/she speak the vernacular language without an accent? What about false identification papers? Money? So many variables, so many dangers.

How many Jews might have saved themselves by flight from the conquered territories? In Eastern Europe their number might have been considerable if they had been warned by their rabbis and elders of the danger facing them. We know this because in eastern Europe the majority of survivors were families who escaped toward the Russian hinterlands. Some traveled as far as Siberia. Conditions were harsh, but they lived to rebuild their lives. But most community leaders did not know what lay ahead, did not urge their people to disappear, to run for their lives.

THE WARSAW GHETTO REVOLT

For the past several decades Jews throughout the world commemorate the anniversary of the Holocaust during the middle of April. They gather for religious and secular observance of Yom Hashoah, the day of remembrance. The date was selected because it marks the start of the Warsaw ghetto uprising. Although this was not the only revolt of Jews against the Nazis, it amazed the world and influenced others to defy the Nazis. Not until 1944 when Christian Poles rose up and were defeated by the Germans, did citizens of any other city take up arms against the Nazis. Even the brutally treated Russian prisoners of war did not do battle against their tormentors until the end of the war.

A brick wall with an 11 mile circumference had been erected and enclosed the Warsaw ghetto since the summer of 1940. It was 10 feet high and the cost of construction had to be paid by the *Judenrat*. Enclosing an area of 3.5 sqare miles, it confined as many as 360,000 Jews. When its 22 gates were sealed that November, a drastic increase in the death toll by starvation resulted. Eventually the daily losses reached 300 to 400 people and the total death rate due to famine was 80,000. But these numbers were deemed insufficient after the Nazis had decided that total destruction was the meaning of the Final Solution. On July 22, 1942, deportations to the death camp Treblinka began. Within two months the ghetto population was reduced by a staggering 300,000. The *Judenrat* was compelled to deliver 6,000 victims daily to the *Umschlagplatz* where the trains were loaded. It was no longer possible to hide the truth that deportation was equivalent death. At this point, with just 120,000 Jews remaining, the Jews rejected the authority of the Council of Elders; their acquiescence to German demands in the hope of saving lives had proven to be a total failure. A new breed of leaders emerged; they were younger, committed to resist, to kill Germans, and, if necessary, to die fighting.

Several political organizations had continued to function in the ghetto and from the ranks of these groups came the ghetto fighters. Most had been affiliated with the Socialists and the Zionists. Now they set aside their theoretical differences to forge a united front. Six days after the deportations to Treblinka began, they joined to become the ZOB (*Zydowska Organizacja Bojowa* or Jewish Combat Organization), headed by Mordekhai Anielewicz. Their combined strength approximated 700 to 1,000 men and women willing to take up arms. At this point, most of the remaining ghetto population gave them support and cooperation. These young people had no illusions. They knew what choice awaited them, not between life and death but between death in combat or death in Treblinka. They transformed their grief for the loved ones they had lost into a resolve for revenge and their hatred into the courage of the already condemned.

Anielewicz combined the attributes of the idealist with the activism of the realist. He came from a working class family and as a youth had been attracted to Zionism. In the ghetto he published an underground newspaper, *Against the Stream,* wherein he called for Jewish resistance. Other young men and women were drawn to him and to his determination to make a stand. During the final months of the ghetto's life, he was its military leader and the virtual chief of its public administration.

The first order of business was the procurement of arms. In this effort the ZOB was never very successful. Contact with the Polish Home Army, the major underground militia of the Polish people, resulted in a few guns and some explosives. At first the Poles were not convinced that the Jews would actually fight and were reluctant to give up any of their own few and precious weapons. On January 18, 1943, however, it became clear that the ghetto was ready to resist the Nazis. On that day, as a large group of deportees was escorted out of the ghetto, Mordekhai Anielewicz with a small number of his men attacked the Nazi escort. In military parlance this was merely a skirmish, but it was the first time that the German sustained losses at the hands of Jews. While the astounded SS troopers were responding to the assault in the street, a second cadre of the ZOB attacked Nazis inside a building. On that day the myth of Jewish cowardice was dispelled.

The Polish partisans were impressed and increased their contribution of weapons to the ZOB. By April, when earlier skirmishes had come to resemble battles, the ghetto arsenal included many revolvers, grenades, homemade bombs, and one machine gun. Although pitifully inadequate, by means of resourceful deployment, the small army snatched from the Germans their ability to do whatever they pleased within the ghetto.

It would have been foolhardy for Mordekhai's few hundred, ill-equipped fighters to meet the Germans in any sort of battle formation where the enemy's superior weapon would quickly annihilate them. Clearly, the Jews had to attack from entrenched positions, retreat, regroup, and fight from another bunker. By repeating this formula they gave the impression of much greater fire power than they actually had. With great ingenuity, the people in the ghetto built bunkers, connected houses and constructed escape routes. Tunnels were dug which led from one cellar to another to another, routes were created up to rooftops and attics and down to cellars and to sewage pipes. At various points they cached food, water, and ammunition and some of these shelters were equipped with electricity and radios. The ghetto became a maze of hide-out and combat positions, designed to maximize the fire power of a small army that must be able to move from one position to another without exposing its fighters.

While this feverish activity was taking place, the Nazis were unable to bring their quota of victims to the *Umschlagplatz* and the trains. The Jews, no longer deceived by the resettlement fiction, were hiding. Threats of dire consequences had lost their power and now the SS tried persuasion. They posted notices that there would be no further expulsions from the city, it was safe to come into the streets, that German employers needed workers in their factories. Amnesty would be given to all who willingly came forward. Most tempting was the promise that bread and jam would be distributed at the *Umschlagplatz*. But the duplicating machines of the ZOB were busy as well. They distributed leaflets which countered the German lies with the truth: Death awaits you if you go on the train; stand firm, do not leave your hiding places, evade the Germans by any means you can.

The German realized that the destruction of the Jews of Warsaw would require more than orders from the now impotent *Judenrat*. On the first day of Passover, April 19, 1943, they were ready to attack with military force. A new commander, Major-General Juergen Stroop of the *Waffen SS,* had been assigned to the task of clearing out the ghetto. He had under his command a force estimated at between 2,000 and 5,000 which was composed of SS troops, Polish and Baltic auxiliaries, and policemen. They expected to finish their job in three days. Before dawn they surrounded the ghetto to prevent escapes. Then they moved through the gates with their arsenal of hand-held weapons, their armored vehicles and, emphasizing their determination to make this a short campaign, they brought in tanks.

The ghetto fighters responded from their hiding places. The Germans were met with a barrage of bullets, with grenades, and homemade Molotov cocktails. By shooting from attic bunkers that faced each other, they caught Stroop's men in their cross-fire. Because the ZOB troops rushed from place to place, the Germans thought their number greater than it was. Again and again the Nazi were forced to withdraw to reorganize their attack. On the third day they changed their tactics and called in aerial support. Thus began the firebombing of the ghetto. To find the secret bunkers the Germans used listening devices which could detect life beneath the rubble. But the ghetto continued its effective resistance. Finally, Stroop was convinced that there was only one way to end this embarrassment to his honor, that his best option was to raze the entire ghetto, burn it to the ground.

At least 50,000 Jews were still in hiding, Jews that Himmler wanted in Treblinka. They refused to follow German orders even when SS guns attacked their hiding places. Only flame throwers or gas bombardments caused some of the trapped Jews to run into the open. They were killed on the spot or transported to death or concentration camps. German incendiary weapons created a veritable holocaust, a sea of flames. Stroop, with the approval of his superiors, torched the ghetto, house by house, block by block. Six hundred and thirty-one bunkers were destroyed. When the beautiful main synagogue would not go up in flames, it was dynamited.

Day by day the number of defensive positions shrank. On May 7, eighteen days after the start of the insurrection, the Nazis found the Anielewicz headquarters on Mila Street. All means of resistance had been exhausted and just one option was left: How shall we die? The remnant of the Warsaw ghetto fighters used their final bullets to commit suicide or kill each other. That was preferable to falling into the enemy's hands. Among the dead was Mordekhai Anielewicz. He was twenty-four years old. Seventy-five of the surviving fighters had been able to escape through the sewers that ran beneath the ghetto wall. They continued their resistance with Polish partisans in the forest. Only a handful lived to see the end of the war. The ghetto lay in rubble. Nearly all its inhabitants were dead. On May 10, Stroop informed his superiors that the battle was over. He could claim victory.

RESULTS AND SIGNIFICANCE

But was this a German victory? The ZOB had never claimed that defeat of the Germans was an achievable goal, never had that been considered a realistic prospect. Yes, the Germans had won, they had destroyed the ghetto. But the ZOB fighters, had accomplished the goal they had set for themselves: to prove that not all Jews were passive victims, that they could and did give battle against overwhelming odds in defense of their freedom and their honor. Furthermore, their revolt gave other oppressed subjects of the Nazis the incentive to resist. If a few hundred Jews could hold off the mighty Germans for nearly a month, then the power of the Germans was not unassailable. Prisoners in other ghettos, concentration and death camps, partisans in the forests, and underground fighters throughout the Axis world saw events in Warsaw as a model they could emulate. When the final moments of the ghetto were near, Anielewicz sent a stirring message of defiance in the face of death to the world outside the walls. It reached the Polish government in exile in London and was read over the radio. Young Jews in several Polish ghettos paid homage to their dead comrades by their refusal to obey SS orders.

The estimates of German casualties in Warsaw range widely. Stroop admitted to only sixteen dead and eighty-five wounded; the Polish Home Army's assessment was 500 Germans killed. No matter what the true number of casualties, the symbolic importance of the ghetto revolt was never in question. The Warsaw uprising was fought by Jews only. Appeals by the ZOB for assistance from the Polish partisan army were refused. While the ghetto fought without hope of victory, the Poles decided to delay their armed struggle until there was a chance for victory. In the fall of 1944, as the Red Army advanced into Poland, and with Soviet encouragement, the Polish underground thought their time had come. It was a tragic irony of fate that the Home Army was left to fight and die alone, without Russian assistance. The Germans crushed the Warsaw uprising of Gentile Poles, and some 200,000 members of Polish partisan battalions died. Only after the Nazis had smashed the Polish insurgents did the Red Army march toward Warsaw. The establishment of a pro-Soviet regime in Poland was facilitated by the losses sustained by the resistance army.

OTHER CAMP REVOLTS: AN OVERVIEW

Conditions in the ghettos made armed resistance extremely difficult, but organizing a revolt in the camps seemed totally impossible. Only in the death camps and only near the end of the war did prisoners in Treblinka, Sobibor, and Auschwitz-Birkenau attempt to resist their killers. The plotters hoped that an uprising would result in a breakout, and some of the prisoners might escape. Even that limited goal was far-fetched. An abbreviated account of their overwhelming obstacles included the following:

1. The isolation of prisoners in death camps was nearly total. Not only was there no contact with the outside world, but within the camps various work battalions were prevented from communicating with one another. Organizing and planning any coordinated resistance required ingenious and dangerous circumvention of Nazi surveillance.

2. The prisoners lived under inhumane and debilitating conditions. Everything they had valued in their former lives was gone and the temptation to let go, to end their suffering, was inescapable. Suicides were common.

3. Newly arriving prisoners required some time to orient themselves to the camp before it was possible to organize a circle of co-conspirators. However, the

longer an inmate was in the camp, the greater was his/her loss of physical and mental stamina.

4. The opportunity to buy weapons was almost nil. Slave laborers who worked with the property of murdered Jews managed to hoard some valuables, but to exchange jewels for arms was a deadly business. Some members of the Ukrainian and other auxiliary troops were willing to take the risk for the right payment, but such arrangements were infrequent. Most of the arms used by the camp rebels were stolen from German armories or were put together from parts filched from workshops. The number of weapons accumulated was pitifully small; clubs and shovels had to do for most of the resisters.

5. If the miracle of a breakout was accomplished, the escapees faced a second hurdle of awesome proportions. The chances of survival on the other side of the barbed wire were precarious at best. They were dressed in prison stripes, and they had no money and probably no friends in the surrounding area. Helping an escapee was a crime the Nazis punished with execution. The SS camp guards reacted with fierceness to any act of Jewish resistance and their use of tracking dogs reduced the chances of evasion to nearly zero.

Revolts in three of the death camps confirmed the desperation underlying this unequal struggle. As symbolic actions, these efforts merit respect; as battles to save Jewish lives they failed. The resistance group at Treblinka revolted in August 1943, two months before the official closing of the camp. There were 700 Jews working in the facility, mainly sorting the goods of dead victims or disposing of corpses. Upon a given signal, a group of conspirators rushed to recover their few hidden guns and grenades. With these they forced open a door into the SS arsenal. Two hundred men helped themselves to firearms; the others used whatever was at hand that could serve as a weapon. The crematoria were set on fire as well as several other buildings. The Germans responded with rage and called in additional troops. Most of the rebels were killed within the compound. Between 150 and 200 men made their escape, but only 12 survived the intensive German manhunt. At the end of the rout, the gas chambers were still functional, and their operation was resumed.

The Sobibor uprising took place in October of 1943. This death factory, located near the Bug River, was enclosed by three circles of barbed wire, a minefield, and a ditch. An adjoining dense forest improved chances for a successful escape. The leader of the resistance was a Jewish Soviet prisoner of war whose military background contributed to the partial success of the breakout. In Sobibor's workshops, the SS had employed Jews to make items for their personal use. On October 14, the tailors and shoemakers arranged staggered appointments for fittings for their "clients." As individual SS men stepped into the workrooms, they were attacked and killed by prisoners who had been waiting in hiding. By the time the general attack began in the evening, nineteen officers, including the camp commander, were dead. The resulting confusion enabled some 400 of the 600 prisoners to escape. Of these, many died when they stepped on mines, some were killed in the manhunt organized by the Germans, others joined partisan groups in the woods. Only forty of the men survived to see the end of the war. But they had the satisfaction of knowing that as a result of their attack, the gas chambers at Sobibor were permanently closed down. Himmler ordered the camp to be leveled two days after the uprising.

At Auschwitz-Birkenau, an international resistance movement had been secretly organized. Although the members of the *Sonderkommando* who worked with the corpses in the death factories were kept apart from other inmates, a tenuous line of communication was established between them and the other inmates. Plans to stage a revolt involving both groups were developed but never completed. The men of the *Sonderkommando* knew their days were numbered when Eichmann's trains with Hungarian victims arrived less frequently. Unable to convince the underground leadership in the main camp to coordinate an uprising, the men working at the crematoria revolted on October 7, 1944.

These men had no weapons but they had a small store of explosives. Women prisoners who worked in a German factory had smuggled the chemicals to them over a period of months. How they managed to hide forbidden materials beneath the rags they wore to cover their emaciated bodies was in itself a story of heroism. The rebel Jews killed several SS guards and blew up one of the four crematoria. About 600 of them were able to break out through the barriers, but their freedom was short-lived. Several hundred SS troops went into immediate pursuit, and it is believed that all the prisoners were killed. An investigation by the Gestapo revealed the involvement of Rosa Robota as the leader of the dynamite smugglers. Rosa was tortured but never betrayed the names of her friends. Nonetheless, she and three other girls were publicly hanged. These events took place when the war was drawing to its inevitable conclusion. One might have expected the SS to be too preoccupied with the cover up of their crimes rather than the fate of a few hundred Jews. On January 18, 1945 those inmates able to walk were marched westward, guarded by men still loyal to Himmler and Hitler.

WITH THE PARTISANS

The degree of harshness of Nazi rule differed widely from conquest to conquest. Nazi racial theories played a major role in their posture toward the defeated peoples, but military necessities and the need for food and oil also compromised the realization of Himmler's Aryan fantasy. The treatment of Frenchmen, Danes, or Norwegians, for example, was quite dissimilar to the conduct of the conquerors toward the eastern Slavs. The great majority of all the subjugated people responded to the German presence with emotions ranging from dislike to hatred, and every nationality had its anti-Nazi heroes as well as its eager collaborators.

Between 1942 and 1943 secret anti-Nazi organizations began to develop in German-occupied nations. Romanticized in many movies and novels, freedom fighters performed daring exploits despite hated Gestapo agents and their use of terror and torture. Actually, groups rather than individuals carried out the most successful missions. With the exception of Yugoslavian and some Russian underground organizations, they were unable to engage the German army in battles and had to resort to hit-run–hide guerrilla tactics. They became adept in sabotage, derailing of trains and rescuing imprisoned comrades. Included in their groups were experts who printed counterfeit identity papers, committed theft and robbery to finance their operations, and killed selected enemies. In the Western-occupied nations, they often attempted, and sometimes succeeded, in saving Jews from arrest and shipment to the death camps. Whether urban cells or forest guerrillas, the objectives were the same: Hasten the day of liberation by fighting the invader. In contrast with the uprisings in the ghettos and death camps, these resisters had reasonable expectations of surviving the war.

Many underground organizations were formed from the remnants of outlawed political parties. Long-standing affiliations and old friendships promoted unity and trust among the members. Outlawed and unable to promote their political agenda, Communists, Socialists, and Zionists organized to battle the Germans as underground fighters. But old animosities did not always disappear; rivalries and antipathies plagued the factions throughout their existence and often hampered their best efforts.

By 1943, when Polish underground units became effective, the destruction of the Jews was almost completed. The leaders of some of the ghettos facing total liquidation finally urged their young people to escape into the countryside to join, or create, partisan units. The obligation to God to preserve a remnant that might someday rebuild Jewish life finally won out over every other consideration, even as it tore families apart. Escape from the ghetto was harrowing because the most fit had to abandon their helpless relatives. Nevertheless, the number of Eastern Jews who fled was believed to reach tens of thousands. Their survival rate, however, was very poor. Many Polish, Ukrainian, and Baltic antiSemites denounced them to the Germans or killed them for whatever possessions they still had. Some died during the winters, freezing and starving to death. Their best hope lay in acceptance by one of the partisan organization that were hidden in the dense forests of the Baltic States, eastern Poland, or the western Soviet Union. Generally only Jews who had weapons were admitted to join the Polish Home Army. That meant that only a few qualified no matter how eager they were to fight the Germans. In brigades commanded by Russians and/or Polish Communists, their chances of acceptance were better. Considering the intensity of hatred that Jews harbored for Nazis, the policy of refusing any of them an opportunity for revenge was self-defeating.

A number of family camps, a mixture of old and young, able-bodied and dependent Jews, were established in the woods. These groups were particularly vulnerable. Unless the local farmers gave or sold them food, they starved. When, in desperation, they tried to steal from the fields, they were hunted like animals. Family camps greatly burdened the partisans who protected them. Supplying them with even the most basic staples, potatoes, beets, and bread was the most pressing problem, but the inability to pick up and move to another location at a moment's notice restricted the vital mobility of guerrillas. The fact that several such groups maintained themselves in hiding throughout the war was a tribute to the endurance of its members as well as to the humanity of the Jewish and non-Jewish resistance fighters who provided for their needs.

Brigades that included complements of Jews were most numerous in eastern Poland and western Russia. In these regions some units were organized and commanded by Soviet soldiers who had been parachuted in for this purpose. These officers (some were Jewish) enrolled all who were willing and able to fight and several of them accepted the obligation to safeguard family camps. In the forests near Vilna, a Lithuanian Jewish brigade operated; in White Russia and the vicinity of Minsk, Jewish guerrillas formed effective combat battalions. If the estimate of 20,000 Jews survivors in the Eastern wilderness is correct, much of the credit must go to the Soviets.

In the Western-occupied nations, Jews had no difficulty in joining the resistance movements. In France and the Low Countries, they played prominent roles as part of the native underground fighters. French Jewry, 1 percent of the population, was represented by 15 to 20 percent in their resistance activity. There was also a Jewish Maquis organization, founded and led by Robert Ganmzon. He was reputed to have killed more than a thousand Nazis and committed many hundreds of acts of sabotage. Other distinctly Jewish battalions smuggled Jewish children into neutral safe havens. In the Balkans and in Greece, young Jewish men and women were active in their national liberation movements. Some 2,000 Jews fought with Tito's army. In Italy, a Jewish unit was formed which later merged with other freedom fighters. It operated in Piedmont and in the Italian Alps. In Slovakia, Jews were among the original organizers of that resistance.

Clearly, history and the many medals for courage awarded to Jewish fighters, often posthumously, contradict the allegation that during the Holocaust all Jews were passive. Where circumstances permitted, they fought with distinction. The military history of Israel could not have been written by a people unwilling or unable to defend itself. In fact, the surviving partisans who made their way to Israel invigorated the Jewish homeland's defense units when the infant nation was attacked by its neighbors in 1948.

RESCUE: TOO LITTLE, TOO LATE

Very little was done by the world to rescue Jews during the Holocaust. It would be convenient to simply condemn the Allies and neutrals for their lack of compassionate action and claim that antiSemitism was at the root of this evil. Such a wide brush stroke, however, discounts the unsung heroes and martyrs who aided Jews at their own peril. It is equally important to give credit to the efforts of a number of organizations and the courageous stand taken by the leaders of several governments who resisted German demands that they deliver their Jews into Nazi hands.

What causes individuals to act with compassionate courage? Psychologists have been unable to provide definitive answers to this ancient puzzle. Questions regarding genetic predisposition, the influence of religion, of family environment, or social pressure all deserve consideration but conclusions are lacking. The men and women whose names appear on the list of the Righteous at Yad Vashem came from all social classes, rich, poor and middle class; their education ranged from exceptional to very limited. It appears that age and sex played no part in their altruistic decisions, men and women and teenagers all are represented. As noted above, their nationalities encompassed a wide variety and the circumstances which led them to help a hunted fellow human being do not provide any clues.

Until we understand the enigma of benevolence, we must be content to examine the facts, the responses of governments, organizations, and individuals to the plight of the Jews. Specifically, we ask: What was known, what was believed, what was done, what might have been done? Our answers, however, must not be distorted by the improved vision of hindsight. And that means placing events into the context of a period of Western history that was fraught with emotional, political and economic shocks which influenced decisions at every level.

When the concentration camps were liberated and the Jewish survivors counted, their number approached 40,000. The great majority were in miserable physical and emotional condition. There is no dearth of rationalization, breast-beating, or excuses to account for the failure of powerful nations and institutions that allowed the Nazis to kill 6 million. In fact, several successful rescue efforts, such as in Denmark, in Bulgaria, and belatedly in Hungary, demonstrated that much more might have been done. As the leader of the free world during the war, the burden of inactivity falls heavily upon the United States. Great Britain, because of its policy of restricting immigration to Palestine, must also share the guilt. No doubt, the failure of the refugee commissions of the League of Nations, the International Red Cross, and the international conferences in Evian and Bermuda, as well as the lack of activism by the great churches, contributed to the genocide. Would the losses have been smaller if American Jewry had adopted a less diffident attitude toward Roosevelt? And how destructive was the prevailing attitude that held only the perpetrators accountable but not the mute bystanders?

ORDINARY PEOPLE

Who were the people that accepted the dangerous moral challenge to try and save Jewish lives? As a rule, individuals demonstrated greater courage than institutions. Thus, nuns in convents saved Jewish children, while the papacy was silent; consuls representing governments as diverse as Japan and Switzerland defied their official instructions and provided visas for doomed Jews in contravention of their national policies. In the occupied nations, and, yes, in Germany too, gallant men and women from every walk of life ignored the Nazis' dire warnings not to aid the persecuted. They took great risks, and some paid the ultimate price to help people they often did not know. After the war, when Madame Trocmé of Le Chambom in France asked why she and her husband, Pastor André Trocmé, endangered their own families and friends in their successful rescue of hundreds of Jews, she replied: "They came to my door, hunted, fleeing and I said 'come in, come in'. What else could I do?"

In Jerusalem, the Israeli government's Authority of Heroes and Martyrs at Yad Vashem designates rescuers of Jews as Righteous Among the Nations. The title is bestowed on men and women who saved a Jewish life and derived no personal gain from their selflessness. In 2002 the list contains nearly 20,000 names who came from 41 nations and the search for others continues. It should be noted that the largest number thus distinguished were from Poland, followed by the Netherlands, France, the Ukraine and Belgium. When a name is proposed to the Yad Vashem Authority, a board of inquiry examines the validity of the recommendation before the designation of Righteous Among the Nations is awarded. The recipients are officially thanked by the Israeli government and aside from a visit to see the installation of their names, they receive no monetary compensation.

While most political leaders, whether from Vichy France, the United States, or England theorized about the difficulties of saving Jewish lives, individuals, alone or in groups, risked their lives to keep them safe. They represent the gamut of society; among them were dock workers, shopkeepers, farmers, and schoolteachers. They hid Jews in attics, shared their food rations, and carried out pails of waste. Often they were forced to deceive their own families because a slip of the tongue by a child might find its way to the Gestapo. Collaborators with the Nazis were a great danger to them whether a "guest" stayed a night, for several weeks, or months, and even years.

Fleeing Jews passed along the names and addresses of safe houses, which in turn increased the danger to the hosts. Whenever possible, the fugitives were spirited across borders into neutral territory. Spain, Switzerland, England, and Palestine were the sometimes legal, often illegal destinations of these border crossings. As noted earlier, the search for Jews continued even when invasion threatened the German heartland. That meant that in Germany, Austria, Poland, and Czechoslovakia some Jews were hidden and supported for as long as six years. The memoirs of survivors emphasize the physical and emotional strain experienced by both Jews and Gentiles who shared lives of unrelenting anxiety.

QUESTIONS OF OPPORTUNITIES

The feasibility of saving Jews greatly depended on the type of control the Germans established in a region. Where Nazi authority reached into every sphere of human activity, such as in Germany and Poland, rescue attempts were most perilous. Where puppet governments had been installed, as in Vichy France and Norway, the possibility for covert defiance of the regime was greater. The level of assimilation of the Jewish population also had an impact. For example, many of Italy's long-integrated Jews could disappear from German eyes by claiming to be Catholic and/or moving to a new neighborhood; on the other hand, a Latvian Orthodox Jew whose mastery of the native language was poor could not vanish among the local factory or farm workers. Physical appearance also mattered, and blond blue-eyed Jews had a distinct advantage.

Every nation can point to examples of righteous people among its citizens. The entrepreneur celebrated in the book and movie *Schindler's List* was Sudeten German. Notable among the champions of Christian ethics in action were the villagers of Le Chambon sur Lignon in Vichy France. Under the leadership of their Huguenot pastor, they created a safety zone for Jews. Hundreds of members of the pastor's congregation conspired to protect thousands of Jewish children and adults. Some of them they handed over to the French underground to be escorted to nearby Switzerland, others remained in the village and surrounding farms until liberation. *The Diary of Anne Frank* is so well known that the compassion, generosity, and courage of some Dutch people needs no further amplification. From the Pyrenees to the Urals, in an era when might made right, perhaps five percent of the population stayed faithful to their concepts of decency, humanity, and courage.

Within Germany and in the occupied nations, no information of the genocide was permitted to reach the public. Stories about mass murders and death camps were whispered in some circles but lacked verification. The United States and Great Britain were fighting on three continents and the fate of European Jewry was not central to their efforts. None of the Allied Nations wanted to be accused of fighting the war for the sake of the Jews. Then, in August 1942, indisputable evidence reached the desk of Gerhart Riegner, an observer for the World Jewish Congress in Switzerland. A German industrialist contacted Riegner when he learned of the Wannsee Conference's decision. He had hoped Riegner's contacts in America would find a way to stop the killings. Riegner was stunned but sought confirmation. He did not have to wait long before other sources corroborated the information. In keeping with previous arrangements, he passed this information through U.S. State Department channels to be forwarded to Rabbi Stephen S. Wise, the major spokesman for American Jewry. The State Department sought its own verification before contacting Rabbi Wise. The officials turned to the Vatican to confirm or deny Riegner's information because the Pope maintained international contacts. But the papacy would not or could not confirm the ongoing massacres. Unable to understand the lack of any American reaction, Riegner alerted the British. Now the U.S. government had no choice but to notify Rabbi Wise. Eleven weeks had passed since the receipt of the first cable.

Though the alarm had been sounded, it did not cause a furious uproar in the Gentile world. With some notable exceptions, the Jews were alone in their distress. The general public and the Roosevelt administration expressed concern, but that was all. On December 17, 1942, the United States joined the other Allies in a general condemnation of German atrocities, but no other action was taken. Some of the rationale for the apathetic response will be discussed later, for now it should be noted that the world outside of Hitler's European fortress was apprised of the fate of the Jews while the majority of them were still alive.

The fact of the ongoing atrocities was no longer in doubt. The Polish government in exile supplied much of the documentation, escaped prisoners told their horror stories, even photographs, taken secretly and at great risk, were now available. But the focus of the world was elsewhere. Except in the Jewish press, newspaper reports on events such as the destruction of the Warsaw ghetto were consigned to the inside pages. The war against the Nazis made headlines while the war against the Jewish people was shunted aside.

THE PROBLEM WITH NUMBERS

The statistics representing the national percentages of Jews murdered during the Holocaust do not reflect several factors related to the difficulties or possibilities of rescue. As mentioned, the specific framework of Nazi rule, the degree of Jewish assimilation into the native mainstream, the number of Jews in danger, all affected the opportunities for sheltering Jews. Other variables must also be considered. Certainly, the length of German domination had a direct bearing. For example, in Germany or Austria, a Gentile might have to look after a hidden Jew for seven years while in Hungary, the Nazis were in direct control for only one year. Topography, too, mattered. In the flat and almost woodless terrain of Holland, concealment was very difficult, while the mountains and forests of western Russia could swallow up thousands of refugees. The type and amount of aid dropped by Allied planes or smuggled across borders to support underground fighters varied considerably from place to place. Difficult to appraise but surely significant was the quality of political and religious leadership. Thus, the Metropolitan of the Holy Synod of Bulgaria set an example that strengthened the resolve in that country to withstand German pressure to transfer Jews into Nazi hands. By contrast, Premier Laval of Vichy France tried to ingratiate himself with the SS by eagerly enacting anti-Jewish legislation.

The lack or prevalence of antiSemitic tradition related directly to Christians' willingness or reluctance to aid Jews. Some righteous Poles were hesitant to disclose their altruism even after the war ended because they feared that their neighbors would frown at their actions. The Jews of Budapest were saved largely as a result of the work of American Jews and the U.S. government. The rescue of Danish Jewry was an entirely Christian effort by the native population. Within each of the conquered countries the Germans had no choice but to allow some local autonomy. They simply did not have sufficient manpower to manage every phase of administration. Puppet regimes received anti-Jewish directives, and local police or militia were commonly used to round up Jews for deportation. The native authorities could obey Nazi instructions without protest or they could try to protect the Jewish population. Until the moment the trains to the death camps were sealed, some choices were still possible in the occupied areas: Obey and ingratiate yourself; disobey and risk retaliation. The numbers cited below make for interesting contrast and comparison.

Approximate Percentages of Surviving Jews:

Austria	33%
Baltic States (Lithuania, Latvia, Estonia)	10%
Belgium	55%
Czechoslovakia	17%
Denmark	99%
Greater Bulgaria	80%
France	70%
Greece	20%
Germany	20%
Holland	25%
Hungary	50%
Italy	85%
Poland	15%
Rumania	50%
USSR (occupied territories)	29%
Yugoslavia	27%

DELAY AND OBSTRUCTION IN THE UNITED STATES

Nearly 60 years have passed since the death of Franklin Delano Roosevelt but his name and his policies continue to arouse both admiration and scorn. His first inauguration and that of Adolf Hitler took place within a few weeks of each other. Interesting, too, is the fact that both were called upon to solve such serious problems as severe unemployment, disillusionment with government, pressures from the radical right and left to use drastic measures to alleviate problems and disappointment which had resulted in World War I. On both sides of the Atlantic the general misery encouraged a search for scapegoats. Jews and Communists were often held conveniently responsible for all social and political ills. In Germany, however, the remedy was infinitely worse than the problems.

Some observers, including historians, pronounced harsh judgment upon FDR for his lack of action on behalf of European Jewry. The occasionally voiced accusation that he was antiSemitic has not been substantiated. In fact, nearly all American Jews admired him, voted for him and were grateful to him. Religious discrimination was not discernible in his personal relationships or in his political appointments. His directives opened many more civil service jobs to the merit system, and many bright young Jewish college graduates found employment in government agencies. It must be remembered that in the United States during the 1930s, few hospitals, law firms, banks, universities or large industrial and manufacturing companies hired Jews regardless of their qualifications. When Roosevelt broadened the civil service system and nominated Jews to his cabinet and to the Supreme Court, he never again needed to be concerned about the Jewish vote. It was his for the asking. A much larger constituency, however, opposed these and other New Deal efforts.

When the news of the ongoing genocide reached the United States, Jewish leaders believed that the President would share their deep distress and provide a haven for the persecuted. Perhaps Roosevelt did care, but not to the extent of jeopardizing the delicate balance of party politics. Congress had severely restricted immigration to this country between 1924 and 1929. The quota system was particularly inequitable toward immigrants from Eastern and Southern Europe. The legislature showed no inclination to lift these limitations in the 1930s when the number of jobless at home was high and anti-Jewish feeling was substantial. The incident involving the ship *St. Louis* was a tragic case in point. Nine hundred German Jews had boarded the ship, confident that their visas to enter Cuba were valid. Upon reaching Havana, the Cuban government refused to accept their documents and did not permit the passengers to land. Urgent appeals to the American government requesting that the passengers be permitted to disembark in Miami were rejected. Florida, so clearly visible from the deck of the ship, remained a forbidden fantasy even though the American Jewish community was willing to defray all costs. The ship was forced to return to Hamburg and many of the men, women, and children became victims of the Nazis.

After 1942, the Germans no longer permitted Jews to leave; however, there were still possibilities for rescue. One can speculate that if the United States had provided energetic leadership, several of the neutral nations would have done more to provide havens for victims of the Holocaust. Perhaps if Great Britain had been willing to ignore the illegal immigration to Palestine, other non-European nations might have offered visas to the fleeing Jews. Opportunities to save hundreds of children were frittered away by long bureaucratic delays in the United States State Department. Temporary reception centers could have been set up in neutral areas. American bombing missions could easily have inflicted damage on the perimeters of the death camps and the rail lines leading there. Several State Department officials, such as Breckenridge Long who controlled the immigration desk, were actively involved in preventing "these people" from entering the United States. Members of Congress counted the votes from the folks back home and decided that no action was their best action.

It must be remembered that during the early 1940s, the United States was going through a national trauma. Most of the fleet had been sunk at Pearl Harbor, the war in the Pacific was going badly, England was hanging by a thread, and Hitler was at the gates of Moscow. This country exerted its supreme and total effort toward winning the war. To the cries for help for Europe's Jews, the administration responded again and again with assurances that winning the war was the first priority; the sooner Germany was defeated, the sooner Hitler's victims would be freed. How few Jews would remain alive to benefit from future assistance was as yet unimagined.

AMERICAN JEWRY

American Jews were not passive in the face of the genocide. They organized rallies, circulated petitions, lobbied members of Congress, and collected money. Even though their voices were joined by some prominent Christians, they never became a resounding chorus. Today, after Martin Luther King, Jr., and others have instructed protesters in the art of civil disobedience, the activities of the Jews seem modest. They feared that too much pressure would backfire, first by increasing American antiSemitism and second, by enraging the Nazis, causing them to commit greater atrocities. The ideological split between Zionists and anti-Zionists further weakened the advocacy for immediate rescue attempts. It seemed to many American Jews that vigorous support for the establishment of a Jewish homeland might be viewed as unpatriotic, likely to create the impression that their allegiance was divided. The Jewish conservative establishment was dismayed when the radical Committee for a Jewish Army ran an advertisement: "For Sale, 70,000 Jews; guaranteed to be human beings; at $50.00 a piece," in response to a Romanian initiative to "sell" its Jews. This, as well as many other suggestions, was refused by the State Department.

At the eleventh hour, the administration was finally energized. Secretary of the Treasury Henry Morgenthau provided the impetus. He had become aware of the inertia, even obstructionism, in the State Department. At his behest, a brief was prepared that exposed the tactics of the immigration officials who prevented the entry of Jews, even within the established limits of the law. Morgenthau handed the President this exposé, provocatively entitled "On the Acquiescence of the Government of the Murder of the Jews." Roosevelt was shocked. He immediately initiated the War Refugee Board. Its purpose was rescue; its partner was the World Jewish Congress.

THE WAR REFUGEE BOARD

In January 1944, the greatest number of Jews in immediate danger of annihilation were the 144,000 assembled in Budapest. Eichmann was there, loading trains to Auschwitz. The resettlement myth was no longer believed, and there was no doubt regarding the actual fate of the deported Jews. The Nazis were not without opposition in the destruction of this last of the major Jewish population centers. Efforts to save Jews had been mounted by the Hungarian Zionist Youth, by the International Red Cross, by the papal nuncio who issued false baptismal papers, and by the Swiss consular staff. The Swiss embassy, flying its neutral flag, had become a haven for hundreds of Jews whom Eichmann could not claim. Nonetheless, the death trains were filled every day with terrified victims. This was the state of affairs when the American War Refugee Board went into action.

When the Board asked a young Swedish diplomat, Raoul Wallenberg, to undertake the mission to save Jews in Hungary, they made a brilliant choice. Wallenberg was daring, ingenious, and his pockets were filled with American money. His arrival in Budapest marked the beginning of a new intensity in rescue activities. Officially a member of the Swedish legation, he issued passports and safe conduct passes, and bought houses in the name of the Swedish government. The protection of the neutral flag afforded safety to thousands. He organized a squad of 400 operatives, young Jews who imitated his bluff and bravado as they pulled prisoners out of transports, claiming they were under Swedish protection. The thousands thus saved required housing, food, medicine and confidence; all of which the remarkable Wallenberg provided. His greatest exploit was executed as the Soviet Army approached the city. The SS commander of Budapest had been ordered to murder all the remaining 70,000 Jews before pulling out of the city. Wallenberg, with a combination of threats and persuasion, convinced the German general not to undertake such a horrendous massacre. It is tragic that the righteous Swede disappeared on the very day the Russians entered Budapest. Nothing was ever admitted, but it is probable that he was arrested by the Soviets who mistakenly believed him to be an American anti-Communist agent. Despite intensive inquiries, the exact nature of his fate remains unknown.

SURVIVAL IN BULGARIA

Not every country within the German sphere became a partner in genocide. There was Finland, an uneasy ally of Germany in the war against the USSR, which simply said "no" to Himmler and kept its Jewish community of 2,000 intact. Franco of Spain, the Fascist dictator who had accepted German aid to attain power, remained neutral during the war. He turned a deaf ear to the complaints of the SS that he was obstructing Hitler's intent to blot out Jewish existence. Franco's policies were responsible for saving 40,000 Jews; most were refugees who made their way to the Spanish coast and overseas. Franco reversed history when he declared that Sephardic Jews, whose ancestors had been expelled by Ferdinand and Isabella in 1492, were de facto Spanish citizens, thus entitled to asylum in Spanish embassies. In Italy, even when Mussolini was in power, Jews who had fled from Greece, France, and Yugoslavia found protection. Only after Germany occupied Italy did the trains begin to roll toward Auschwitz. The majority of Italian Jews lived through that traumatic final year of the war because the Italian people and their institutions were supportive.

Bulgaria was home to about 50,000 Jews, 0.8 percent of its population. Most belonged to the middle class and lived in the capital, Sofia. The majority of Bulgarians were Eastern Orthodox Christians who traditionally accepted their Jewish fellow citizens with tolerance. Until 1941 the government, headed by Czar Boris III, had remained neutral in the war but this policy changed when Germany permitted Bulgaria to annex long desired Greek and Yugoslav border territories. The Czar joined the Axis powers and to appease their new partners, a reluctant parliament passed a version of Hitler's Nuremberg laws. Bulgarian Jews were now subjected to discrimination and economic exploitation. Much of their property was seized, and they were ordered to wear a yellow star. Many of the younger men were forced to work in road building gangs. But the German authorities demanded complete compliance with their racial principles, they wanted the Jews delivered into their hands. The Bulgarian government agreed to give the SS free reign to deport the Jews living in their recently acquired regions of Thrace and Macedonia. And so, in 1943 SS roundups began. More than 11,000 were shipped to Auschwitz and of these nearly 95 percent were killed.

Next the Nazis began their preparations for an *Aktion* against the Bulgarian Jews. The date was set, in fact, arrests were in progress when the Bulgarian government called for a postponement. Behind the scenes the leaders of the Jewish community and their Christian friends had worked a miracle. The rumors that "resettlement" meant death had been confirmed and the majority of Bulgarians did not want their government to be an accessory to mass murder. A public protest and the intervention of the head of the church, the Metropolitan Stephen, won a stay of execution for tens of thousands of Jews. An anti-Nazi resistance movement had been organized whose members equated saving Jews to opposing the Germans.

In 1943 the Czar went to see Hitler and returned in the Fuehrer's private plane. Within a few days he died, perhaps a victim of poison. If he was killed, the plot misfired because succeeding governments continued to oppose deportation of Bulgarian Jews. Their rescue was due to the combined efforts of the leaders of the Jewish community, the resistance of the parliament to German demands and to the opposition of the Holy Synod. The fact that German victory in the war was no longer a certainty may well have entered into the resolve of the Bulgarians.

THE DANES MOBILIZE FOR RESCUE

No Holocaust history is complete without some detailed reference to Denmark. The number of Jewish survivors in that small occupied nation was a remarkable 99 percent. How and why was such an extraordinary rescue achieved? Events resemble a play in three acts: the first sets the scene, the second reveals the plot against the Jews, the third unveils the rescue operation.

The 6.5 million Danes were swept into the German hegemony in a bloodless invasion during the spring of 1940. Danes were considered to be Aryans, and cooperation was deemed to be cheaper than force, therefore the Germans opted for a lenient occupation policy. King Christian X, the parliament (which included several Jewish members), the cabinet, and even Denmark's small army were left in place. Danish autonomy was, however, restricted in regard to its economic output and its foreign policy. As long as Danish food poured into the Reich, the German military presence under General Hermann von Hannecken and the diplomatic representative, Dr. Werner Best, were fairly unobtrusive.

Dr. Best, however, was an ambitious Nazi. What better way to ingratiate himself with his masters in Berlin than to institute anti-Jewish measures in Denmark? When Best approached Prime Minister Scavenius, he was told the Danish cabinet would resign rather than pass such legislation. The king replied in the same manner, stating that there was no Jewish problem and all his subjects were equal.

That nearly 8,000 Danish Jews walked freely and unmarked on the streets of Copenhagen stuck like a bone in Werner Best's throat. Other problems were developing as well. The Danes had organized an effective anti-German underground, which sabotaged goods going to Germany. German occupation soldiers complained that the Danes treated them with disdain and thus the hope of continued cooperation eroded. Best's situation became worrisome when Hitler berated him and warned him to do better. Empowered to teach the Danes the meaning of obedience, Best changed his approach. The executive and legislative branches of the Danish government were dissolved, the king became a virtual prisoner in his palace, and the army was forced to disband. This, predictably, increased the numbers and activities of the anti-German partisans. Werner Best ordered the seizure of the records of the Jewish community which enabled him to identify nearly all the Jews in the kingdom. He inquired whether or not the Danish civil service would participate in any anti-Jewish action and the answer was a clear "no." Nonetheless, he decided that the time had come to execute a lightning strike against the Jews; surely that would restore him to Hitler's good graces.

THE PLOT

Best decided to arrest all Danish Jews on October 13, 1943, the eve of the Jewish New Year when most of them would be conveniently assembled in synagogues for religious services. In order to transport the intended prisoners as quickly as possible, he imported SS, German police, and railroad cars. Ships were readied in the harbor to ferry the sealed trains across the sea to Germany. General von Hannecken was opposed to the entire enterprise and had to be persuaded to allow fifty of his men to be available in case of disturbances. The plan required the expertise of a maritime specialist. Best called in a German who was a longtime resident of Denmark, Georg F. Duckwitz. When apprised of the scheme, Duckwitz was appalled. At this juncture, Duckwitz decided that he must follow the dictates of his conscience. He called on an old friend, a Dane, and revealed to him the fate awaiting the Jews of Denmark in just a few days.

A chain reaction was set into motion. The Danish underground was notified and its members decided to do everything in their power to protect the Jews. But where could thousands of men, women, and children be hidden? Certainly not in Denmark. Duckwitz went to Sweden to ask if that governments would receive the Danish Jews if the landed on their shores. That assurance was given without reservations. Now the details of the rescue had to be organized. First, however, the Jewish leadership had to be convinced that the threat was real. On the eve of the Jewish New Year service, the rabbi stood before his stunned congregation to tell them what the Germans had planned. No, you cannot return to your homes, you must disappear. Not next week, not tomorrow, but at once. At first there was disbelief, but the rabbi persisted until the congregation accepted the fact that here they were, dressed for the holy day and yet in mortal danger. Because it had yet not been possible to obtain transport to Sweden, it was necessary to find temporary hiding places for thousands of men, women, and children. And at this point it seemed that the entire population of Denmark participated in an enormous conspiracy to save their Jews and defy the Nazis.

As word of the immediate danger spread throughout Copenhagen and to other Jewish communities, the intended victims simply vanished. When the SS entered the main synagogue on Rosh Hashanah, it was empty. Hotels, hospitals, private homes in remote villages, Christian friends, churches, funeral parlors, taxis, ambulances, and even the police became partners in a single objective: Hide the Jews; do not, by a word or a glance allow the Germans to find a single one. Some of the Danes went through the telephone books, search for Jewish names and called the numbers to sound the alarm. Amazingly, the secret was kept, and the promise that the Jews of Denmark would not be abandoned was fulfilled.

THE ESCAPE

A few dozen Jews were caught in the German net. They were people who refused to believe that they were in danger or did not hear of the planned arrests. Several Polish refugees committed suicide; they could not imagine that Gentiles would risk their lives to save them. The captured Danish Jews were deported to the Theresienstadt concentration camp where nearly all survived due to the continued vigilance and food packages of the Danish Red Cross. The hidden Jews, meanwhile, had to be whisked out of the country as quickly as possible. Members of the underground found fishermen who were willing to transport Jews to the Swedish shores. Throughout October there were daily departures. Danish doctors and nurses stood by every night to give injections to keep children asleep during the crossing. German ships patrolled these waters constantly and a crying child could endanger everyone on board.

The Germans suspected that certain villages along the coast were used as departure points and tried to barricade the roads. In the skirmishes between the underground fighters and the SS, several Danes were killed. But, unlike the unfulfilled and wasted lives of so many millions, their deaths enabled others to live. The sea did not part on this exodus; instead, Danish fishermen carried the Jews across the waters of the Kattegat to safety.

Until the end of the war, for nearly two years, the hospitality and generosity of the Swedish people and their government sustained the Danish Jews. When they returned home, they found their gardens had been tended by neighbors, their pets had been cared for, and their Torahs had been hidden in churches.

ACCOUNTING FOR THE DANISH ACHIEVEMENT

It is very tempting to use the Danish experience as an example of the possibilities of rescue that other peoples did not attempt. No doubt, a greater humanitarian commitment could have saved lives, but it is a fallacy to believe the success of the Danes could easily have been duplicated elsewhere. Every European nation had distinct and unique problems during the Nazi era. Prevailing attitudes toward Jews differed widely, native and occupation administrations varied considerably and diverse geographic factors affected the possibility of keeping Jews safe.

The Danes saw an opportunity and went into action; that fact is forever to their credit. Their achievement was predicated on some, perhaps all, of the following prerequisites:

1. The Danes had a well-established humanitarian attitude toward their fellow men. AntiSemitism had been outlawed since 1814!
2. The political leadership set the tone for ethical behavior.
3. The Christian religious leadership was not intimidated and from their pulpits urged their parishioners to aid their imperiled countrymen.
4. When the Germans executed Danish saboteurs, they believed the population would be cowed; instead the opposite effect resulted.
5. The willingness and proximity of neutral Sweden provided a necessary haven for the potential victims.
6. The underground movement was well organized and eager to prove its effectiveness.
7. The Jews were well integrated into Danish society; their numbers were small and the rate of intermarriage with Christians was high.

SOME CONCLUDING THOUGHTS

The Holocaust is largely a history of human failure. We cherish the exploits of a Wallenberg or the victory of the Danes because they lit a candle in the darkness of savagery and irrationality. Hitler and Himmler represent the triumph of absolute evil. They were criminals who were totally indifferent to the human suffering they inflicted. German Nazis and their foreign collaborators camouflaged their criminality with patriotic slogans. The Holocaust repudiated the concept that the teachings of Christ were practiced in the daily lives by most of those who professed to be believers. The onlookers who averted their eyes in order to keep their consciences untroubled were guilty of responding with silence to the question, "Am I my brother's keeper?"

When, in 1948, the United Nations voted the state of Israel into legitimate existence, it discharged an act of international contrition. Perhaps a sense of guilt also motivated the unprecedented support by American Jews for that small, beleaguered nation. Israel is of extraordinary significance to the Jews of the world. It ended a sometimes hidden, sometimes overt sense of rootlessness and alienation experienced even by the many Jews who were well integrated into their native countries. Israeli success in its struggle to survive against great odds is a legacy for all Jews. The image of the powerless, submissive Jew has faded throughout the world, and the tragic lesson of the Holocaust can be summed up in two words: Never again.

Epilogue

Among the questions raised at the conclusion of a course in Holocaust history, two recur most frequently: What happened to the liberated remnant of European Jewry? And how did the Allies deal with the men responsible for the genocide? Students hope to complete this distressing chapter of man's inhumanity with an uplifting account of compensation and retribution. The facts, however, do not grant us the satisfaction of a fitting closure. The victims did not triumph and most of the persecutors were never punished. One can merely say that neither the tormented nor their tormentors ever received a full measure of justice.

POSTWAR GERMANY

In order to understand the plight of the liberated Jews, several issues must be considered. When Germany surrendered in May of 1945, much of the nation lay in rubble. A half million German civilians had perished during Allied intensive bombing raids, and many cities were unable to provide even the most basic services required to sustain life. At this point, Germany was a nation virtually without able-bodied men. The male population between 16 and 70 years of age had been drafted into one or another of the various military and paramilitary forces. As a result, women, children, and old men were left to struggle in a world that lacked electric power, health facilities, government services, food, fuel, water supply, schools, and public transport. In most cities industry was disrupted, paid employment was scarce, and many homes and apartment houses were uninhabitable. To add to the chaos, some 10 million Germans were fleeing westward from regions east of the

Oder-Neisse line. The Soviet Union had handed this territory to Poland to compensate for Russian annexation of lands in eastern Poland. The newly installed Polish occupation authorities ordered that this region be made *Deutschrein*, free of German inhabitants and, depending on the location, gave them a day, perhaps a week to leave. In addition to these massive shifts in population, German soldiers who had evaded capture by the Allies were trying to make their way home. To add to the waves of trekkers crisscrossing the nation, the approximate 7 million forced and volunteer laborers from all parts of the continent were choking the roads. Some of these foreign nationals were eager to get home, but large numbers refused to return to states that were now ruled by Soviet-sponsored Communist regimes.

ZONES OF OCCUPATION

A year before the collapse of the Reich, the Allied leaders had agreed that when Germany was defeated, the country would be divided into temporary zones of military occupation. The conquest of the Axis powers was completed in the spring of 1945, and by summer the German territory had been divided by the victors. The area west of the Elbe River was shared by American, British, and French occupation forces; the eastern region, except for Berlin, was held by the Soviets. The German capital was partitioned into four districts, which mimicked the division of the Reich itself. An agency, named the Allied Control Commission, was set up in order to formulate and enact a joint occupation policy. It was presumed that the suffering now experienced by the German people would discredit Nazism and militarism. When the Allied military authorities deemed that reeducation had progressed satisfactorily, democratic elections would gradually empower the Germans to govern themselves.

The occupation zones had been envisioned as a temporary measure while the occupation powers planned for the future of Germany. But that prospect depended on continued cooperation between the Soviets and the Western Allies. It soon became clear that Stalin had his own agenda. He succeeded in his quest to dominate Eastern and Balkan Europe. Where Soviet soldiers had marched to liberate the people from Nazi oppression, a different dictator now dominated their lives. Soviet-trained politicians were placed in positions of control, and satellite nations dotted the map. Stalin acted the obstructionist at the Allied Control Council meetings again and again until, in 1948, the Soviets walked out. The military zones now hardened into the formation of two German states, East and West. The three western zones combined in 1949 to form the Federal Republic of Germany, with its capital in Bonn; in the East, the DDR, or German Democratic Republic, became a Communist state, a Soviet satellite governed from East Berlin. Thus, the Cold War had its genesis in Germany and Germany continued to play a major role in the struggle between the Communist and non-Communist world.

The end of the war had exposed the magnitude of the problems facing the victors. It was impossible for the Control Council to meet even the must urgent needs of the millions of people under its authority. Immediate essentials required immediate actions and it became necessary for each of the commanders of the military zones of occupation to act on instructions from his own government. The men on the scene, not distant ministries, made the assessments and sought the solutions to alleviate the suffering of the civilian population. Soldiers who were poorly or not at all trained in the work of restoring a devastated country generally worked with diligence and often with great ingenuity to restore conditions to some level of civilized life.

JEWS AND OTHER DISPLACED PERSONS

The suffering of the defeated Germans and the displaced persons was not comparable to the anguish of the liberated concentration camp survivors. These tens of thousands of men and women and a few hundred children were physically and emotionally on the brink of death. When a stunned General Dwight D. Eisenhower, chief of the European Theater of Operations, saw his first concentration camp, he cabled newspapers in the United States and elsewhere to send reporters to the scene. He feared that without pictures and descriptions the world simply would not believe the truth about Nazi atrocities. Indeed, it became clear that earlier accounts of the genocide, which had often been characterized as exaggerations, could not approach the sights and smells of the dead and half-dead inmates.

At the destinations of the death marches, whether at Neuengamme, Ravensbrueck, Sachsenhausen, Bergen-Belsen, Flossenbuerg, Dachau, Mauthausen, or Buchenwald, the prisoners had been dumped behind the barbed wire fences. The SS guards disappeared, leaving the prisoners in worse conditions than they had ever experienced. The camps were overcrowded and lacked any sanitation facilities; there was no food or water, and no one to care for the sick or bury the dead. The liberators were not prepared for the enormity of the task they faced. Their initial hope was to save many of the starving Jews by providing them with nourishing food; this turned into a medical disaster. The months or years during which their bodies had been famished had robbed their intestinal systems of normal digestive abilities. There simply was no medical knowledge on how to deal with such emaciation, and thousands died because they ravenously filled their stomachs. The resulting diarrhea sapped their strength at the moment of their possible rebirth.

How many Jews survived the Holocaust? The answer is subject to definition as well as discernment. Who should be counted as a survivor? Only those who had been in concentration camps? What of the hidden Jews, the partisan fighters, those who fled to Russia before the German armies, and the Jews who passed as Gentiles? What of the half Jews, the offspring of mixed marriages? Clearly, the numbers are subject to interpretation. In the chaos of the weeks, months, and even years following the end of the war, no agency was in a position to keep accurate records. The victors were faced with pleas for food, clothing, housing, and medical aid for some 7 million homeless non-Germans as well as for the millions of despairing Germans whose cities had been bombed. As far as we know, Soviet authorities did not differentiate between Jewish and non-Jewish survivors.

Experts at the U.S. Holocaust Memorial Museum in Washington indicate that in 1945 the number of Jews in DP camps was 69,098. A year later it had risen to 173,592, and in 1947 reached 182,000. The continuing increase was probably the result of the longing of most of the survivors to live among their fellow Jews. They streamed into the DP camps after they gave up their initial search for members of their families. Only about 20–30 percent of Jewish Displaced Persons lived in German towns and cities. Of the total number of survivors, more than three-fourths were Polish nationals, the rest mainly Hungarian and Czech.

It is estimated that approximately 50,000 were liberated from the concentration camps. Because thousands died within days after liberation, even this number cannot be cited with accuracy. What can be said without fear of contradiction concerns the condition of the survivors. Many were near death, often numbed by emotional and physical exhaustion. They greeted their liberators with disbelief, with tears of joy, and with stunned silence. But after the momentary euphoria of liberation, the survivors had to face the reality of their position. And that reality was bleak.

JEWISH SURVIVORS' SPECIAL PROBLEMS

They found themselves on German soil, often among hated Germans and Nazi collaborators who were confined in the same facilities. The military authorities had designated all the homeless as DPs, displaced persons, including former prisoners of war, slave laborers, concentration camp survivors, and even criminals. The shortage of housing in Germany was acute, and several concentration camps were used as holding facilities. Jewish survivors constituted about one-fourth of the total number of DPs. For weeks, in some cases months, they were identified and billeted according to their national origin; that meant German Jews were housed with Nazis, Polish Jews with antiSemites, etc. Obviously, this arrangement caused great tensions.

The Jews were liberated, but were they free? The guards outside the barbed wire were no longer the blackshirted SS, but they were soldiers nonetheless who had orders to prevent the inmates from roaming the countryside. For medical aid they had to rely on German doctors whom they had learned to fear. Because so many of the homeless and stateless people wanted to be in the American zone of occupation, U.S. camps were particularly overcrowded. The original number of Jewish survivors in the American zone, estimated at 30,000, grew by a third when 10,000 Polish Jews made their way west. These were survivors who had retraced their steps back to their hometowns as soon as they could in order to search for members of their families. Some had hoped to reestablish themselves on familiar soil. What they found instead was devastating beyond all expectations. Most, often all of their family members were dead and the Poles living in their houses were generally hostile to them. Clearly, Jewish life could not be renewed on Polish soil and so they tramped westward toward the DP camps. A further, even larger increase resulted from the arrival of tens of thousands of Polish Jews who had fled to the Soviet Union during the war. They did not want to live under a Communist regime, many were Zionists hoping to get to Palestine. Among this last group were many of the partisan fighters.

The new arrivals presented new and different problems to the U.S. camp administrators, who, as a rule, were ill prepared to meet the challenge. Many survivors had difficulties in facing and adjusting to the realities of their losses; to their half-free, half-dependent existence; to communal kitchens; and to the continued lack of privacy. The military occupation officials were overwhelmed by the physical and emotional troubles of their charges. In their later recollections, survivors gratefully commended the heroic efforts of individuals who tried to help them. Some Jewish and non-Jewish soldiers and especially the army chaplains worked indefatigably to meet the needs of the Nazis' victims. They had little or no training in assisting victims of such extensive abuse, but met the psychological and physical needs of their charges with kindness, and a willingness to listen. They made use of every facility of the armed forces to improve conditions within the DP camps. In tandem with American Jewish organizations, these men played an important role in changing U.S. policies. President Truman was made aware of the urgency of the needs of Nazi survivors and he appointed Earl G. Harrison to conduct an official investigation. The report, completed in August 1945, was sharply critical. As a result, many of the worst problems were alleviated.

Among the many issues facing the liberated remnant, two questions arose invariably: Am I the sole survivor of my family? and Where can I go to start rebuilding my life? Jewish organizations assembled and distributed lists of names which facilitated the search for relatives. Reunions were rare indeed and were celebrated with joy and envy. The realization of the many, however, that their parents, children, wives, or husbands were dead, caused psychological disorders from which many survivors never recovered completely.

The aim of Allied DP policy was repatriation. Most of the Christian workers, those who had volunteered as well as most of those who had been forced into labor service by the Germans, went home. Willingly or reluctantly, they were pushed out of the military zones. But what was to be done about the Eastern Jews? It was no secret that survivors who had returned to Poland had encountered rabid antiSemitism and that some of the returnees were murdered when they tried to reclaim their possessions. Clearly, repatriation was not an option for this group. To remain in Germany was equally out of the question. Survivors' hopes revolved around two destinations: The majority wanted to emigrate to Palestine, and most of the others hoped to put down new roots in the United States. The years of suffering had greatly encouraged the growth of Zionism. Clearly, the Jews needed a national home of their own. But the path to either haven, Palestine or the United States, was blocked by many obstacles.

As a result of the revelations of the Harrison report, the Jews gained separate housing, either within existing camps or at other sites. As soon as they were settled, they requested permission to govern themselves. The American and British occupation forces gladly granted them autonomy. The survivors held elections, organized associations according to religious or political preferences, negotiated with the Allied authorities, established recreational and educational facilities, and conducted religious services; in other words, they tried to create the best possible conditions within the restrictions imposed upon them. The desire to establish families and give newborn babies the names of murdered relatives resulted in many marriages. Every birth was an occasion for joy as a symbol of Jewish survival. Meanwhile, they prepared for their future by learning trades and studying English and Hebrew. Jewish organizations from the United States and Palestine and the United Nations' Relief and Rehabilitation Administration (UNRRA) provided financial and emotional support. American Jews engaged in intense lobbying to ease U.S. and British immigration restrictions. The search for a home, for a place to resume a normal life, remained the most urgent all-consuming quest.

SEEKING REFUGE: THE UNITED STATES

The international press had feasted on the pictures and stories of the Nazi camps for months. Nonetheless, the expectation that sympathy for the survivors would be quickly translated into offers of asylum remained unrealized. They were, of course, dirt poor. Many had aged before their time. They had no political or economic power. Politicians in the United States as well as in Great Britain were preoccupied with adjusting from war to the peacetime needs and saw no necessity to relax their immigration restrictions. American quotas remained in force and the British government, long uncomfortable in its role as the mandatory authority over Palestine, feared Arab reaction if a flood of Jewish settlers were to enter the region.

Since 1929 the immigration policy of the United States was based on the national origins law, the Johnson-Reed Act. The law established a quota system that favored Northern and Western Europeans and severely limited immigration from Eastern and Southern Europe. This bias was rationalized by the theory that the preferred groups would assimilate more easily to American life than, for example, Poles, Italians, Greeks, or Russians. Most of the DPs, both Jewish and non-Jewish, were born in nations whose American quota was very small. As the months of waiting turned into years and the camps still teemed with the homeless, their earlier hopes often turned into despair. Congress, under the pressure of public opinion, was finally moved to change the immigration policy. The remedy, called the Displaced Persons Act of 1948, only opened the door a crack. The law did not set aside the quota system. Instead, it permitted DPs to "borrow" against future quotas of up to 205,000 persons in two years. Few of the survivors were able to obtain visas under restrictions that still discriminated against Jews and Catholics. Finally, in 1950, that is five years after liberation, an amendment provided some additional relief: 415,000 DPs would be permitted to enter within a four-year period. Thus it was possible for 80,000 survivors who chose to make this their homeland to become a grateful and valuable component of our citizenry.

PALESTINE

The record of British reaction to the longing of the survivors to settle in Palestine is a sorry tale. The government had to choose between incurring the wrath of the oil-rich Arabs who wanted to maintain numerical superiority in the holy land and the struggling half-million Palestinian Jews who were eager to welcome the European remnant of their people. The Arabs won. In 1939, the British government had issued its so-called White Paper, which stipulated that during the following five years Jewish immigration to Palestine could not exceed 75,000. Thus, the earlier Balfour Declaration of 1917, which had supported Zionist aspirations for a Jewish homeland, was scrapped in order to appease the Arabs.

The restrictions imposed in 1939 were precisely, even cruelly, enforced. Throughout the war the British fleet turned back the ships, usually barely or not at all seaworthy, which tried to carry fleeing Jews to Palestine. Certificates of entry were actually held below the promised 75,000 until the drowning of refugees in the Mediterranean aroused a storm of criticism. The cabinet then permitted the quota to be filled. But what of the bulk of the survivors still lingering in Germany? The Labor party government led by Ernest Bevin decided to permit the paltry number of 1,500 individuals to enter Palestine each month. About 12,000 Jews who were caught trying to evade the restrictions were seized by the British en route and kept in detention camps on the island of Cyprus. Despite the worldwide recognition of the plight of concentration camp survivors, this policy remained in force until the establishment of the Jewish state in May 1948.

But even the determined hostility of the British government could not stop a continuous, though small, stream of survivors from reaching the destination of their hopes and dreams. They came via several illegal escape routes. These schemes were conceived, funded, organized and run by Jews. Among the most active members of this group were veterans of the Jewish Brigade, soldiers who fought as an independent unit in the British army. They were combat experienced and at the end of the war many of them decided to use their training to aid the Holocaust survivors. The appearance of Jewish soldiers, young, strong, in uniforms with a star on their shoulders, created a sensation in the DP camps. Their optimism was infectious, and their escape plans seemed workable. With the help of money from American contributors, members of the Brigade leased ships and secretly escorted survivors across borders to reach Mediterranean harbors. Most of their vessels were intercepted by the English fleet, and the Jews were interned on Cyprus until the creation of the State of Israel finally allowed them to reach their destination. Those ships which eluded British patrols were anchored off shore and their passengers were transferred onto small fishing boats. When they reached land, they were taken in hand by the Jewish underground army, the Haganah. At this point, English authorities could do nothing because the refugees disappeared into the mainstream of life with the aid of a welcoming and supportive Jewish population.

THE ISRAELI INGATHERING

In 1947, the British decided to liquidate their Palestine mandate. No doubt, the bad press over such incidents as the ship *Exodus* had sullied their reputation and tried their patience. The *Exodus* hoped to take about 5,000 Jews to Palestine when the British forced it to return to the hated soil of Germany. The outcry over this and other incidents reverberated across the Western world. The Bevin government had quite enough. It deposited the question the future of the Holy Land into the lap of the United Nations. In November 1947, that body voted in favor of Arab and Jewish partition. The British withdrew in May of 1948 and tiny, beleaguered, newly born Israel opened its doors to all Jews. Despite the enormous difficulties that beset the new nation, Israel managed to integrate the survivors of Hitler's war against the Jewish people into its precarious existence. It should be noted that in the Arab-Israeli wars that followed the partition, Holocaust survivors contributed significantly to Israeli victories.

JUSTICE FOR THE MURDERERS?

Among the many problems facing the victorious Allies in their aim to decentralize, democratize, and demilitarize their respective zones of occupation, two have direct impact on Holocaust history: First was the demand for punishment of the Nazis who had turned so much of Europe into a cemetery, and second the need to root out Nazi ideology and its supporters. Both efforts were undertaken to ready the German people for eventual democracy.

The Allies, after many discussions and delays, agreed to create an international tribunal that would try the most infamous Nazis. The court was constituted to collect evidence, present the charges in public hearings and permit the defendants legal council and arguments. In those cases where a guilty verdict was reached, the court could and did mete out the punishment. Many other trials followed Nuremberg; some continue to the present day. Such cases may concern Nazis who had not been arrested until after the Nuremberg sessions ended or the accused would be brought to justice in the nations in which their crimes were committed.

To rid Germany of the advocates of Nazism was a complicated and perplexing task for the occupying Allies. The effort, however, was essential in laying the groundwork for a democratic future. The dual processes of reeducation and denazification were required to reshape German political life. An immediate inducement to renounce Nazism was all around the German people: Millions were dead and millions missing; the disgrace of their mass murders was broadcast to a shuddering world; their own cities lay in desolation. To reenforce such graphic lessons, the Allied occupation forces instituted changes in the school curricula. The objectives of denazification were to punish those Nazis criminals and purge ex-Nazis from positions they still held in the many administrative jobs and in industry. But it was not easy to replace old Nazi party members with "good Germans." As might be

The crematoria at Buchenwald. The remains in the oven are of women. (Courtesy AP/Wide World Photos.)

expected, there were no "true" Nazis in the defeated Reich, only people who had "pretended" to follow the Fuehrer for one reason or another. And, of course, every German now had a favorite Jew whom he/she tried to help.

THE NUREMBERG TRIALS: 1945–1946

The Bavarian city of Nuremberg had been a favorite showpiece of Nazi pomp and ceremony. From here the anti-Jewish racial laws of 1935 had been issued. To conduct the trial of twenty-two leaders of the Third Reich against this background seemed eminently appropriate.

That such a prosecution took place at all was a victory for humanity. It implied acceptance of the concept that international law may supersede national law when heinous criminal acts are committed regardless of national boundaries. The topic of punishment for the Nazis was first raised at the 1943 Teheran Conference of Allied chiefs of state. There, Stalin had suggested the liquidation of the entire German General Staff. In the United States, Secretary of the Treasury Henry Morgenthau had urged that Germany should be reduced to an agricultural country. At the Potsdam meeting in 1945, the various draconian proposals were rejected in favor of convening an international extraordinary court of justice. Specifically, high-ranking Nazis were to be tried on charges of crimes against peace, against humanity, and against defenseless minorities. The original objections of some jurists and some members of the public concerning the lack of legal precedents were muted as the full testimony of Nazi terror was unveiled.

The presiding justice of the Tribunal was British, Lord Chief Justice Geoffrey Lawrence. The United States was represented by Attorney General Frances Biddle; France sent an expert on international law, Henri Donnedieu de Vabres; and the Soviet judge was Major General I.T. Nikitchenko. Each of the four participating Allies also sent several prosecutors to Nuremberg. The U.S. team was led by Robert Jackson, an Associate Justice of the Supreme Court. The accused were permitted German defense attorneys and procedures were fixed according to legal principles. The defendants, used to Nazi justice, were surprised that the trial was not a sham but was conducted with careful attention to their rights.

Since Hitler, Himmler, and Goebbels had committed suicide, Hermann Goering emerged as the highest ranking of the Nazis. Among the indicted were men who held high positions in the military, the foreign office, and the economic and propaganda ministries. Holocaust survivors noted with satisfaction that Hans Frank, Governor-General of much of occupied Poland, stood in the dock, as well as Ernst Kaltenbrunner, who had succeeded Reinhard Heydrich as head of the security and other police organizations. Julius Streicher, publisher of antiSemitic hate material and Alfred Rosenberg, whose Nordic superiority theory had dovetailed with *Mein Kampf*, were also among the defendants. The tribunal condemned several organizations, such as the *Fuehrerkorps*, composed of the upper echelons of the Nazi party, the Gestapo, the SS, and the SD. Officials of these organizations could expect to be arrested. Even simple membership was equated with commission of a criminal act. It should be noted that, in the long run, prosecution of all members of these associations was not feasible.

THE VERDICTS

The amount of evidence collected for the Nuremberg tribunal filled forty-two volumes. Bushels of documents, many signed by the defendants, attested to their guilt. Their letters, directives, orders, and speeches, and the testimony of witnesses whose recollections reduced listeners to tears, all combined to condemn all but three of the twenty-two defendants. Sentenced to death by hanging were Hermann Goering, *Reichsmarshall* and head of the air force; General Wilhelm Keitel, Chief of the High Command of the armed forces; Joachim von Ribbentrop, Foreign Minister; Ernst Kaltenbrunner, successor to Heydrich as head of the SD and RSHA; Alfred Rosenberg, promoter of Aryan superiority and minister for Eastern-occupied areas; Hans Frank, Governor-general in occupied Poland; Wilhelm Frick, Minister of the

Interior and NSDAP leader; Julius Streicher, publisher of a violently antiSemitic newspaper; Fritz Sauckel, Minister of Labor; General Alfred Jodl, Chief of Armed Forces Operational Staff; Artur Seyss-Inquart, whose last appointment was as Reich Commissioner for the occupied Netherlands. Prison sentences were pronounced on Rudolf Hess, Hitler's early deputy; Walther Funk, president of the national banking system; Admiral Karl Doenitz, the naval chief; Admiral Erich Raeder, earlier chief of the German navy; Baldur von Schirach, leader of the Hitler Youth organizations; Albert Speer, Minister of Armaments; and Constantin von Neurath, who had administered occupied Bohemia and Moravia. The minister of economics and chief of the banking system, Hjalmar Schacht, who left government office in 1939, was acquitted, as were Franz von Papen, ranking official in the foreign service, and Hans Frizsche, who had headed the radio division in the propaganda ministry. Martin Bormann, who had not been found, was sentenced to death *in absentia*.

In a last-minute act of defiance, Goering escaped the hangman by means of a long-hidden cyanide capsule.

FURTHER TRIALS

The Nuremberg tribunal was a showcase event that set up the parameters for many other trials. Some were conducted during the Allied military occupation but as soon as the Germans organized their own courts, they brought Nazis to trial. The penalties they handed down were generally more severe than those of the international court. As the nations that had suffered under German domination reestablished their judiciaries, they brought the men who had committed crimes as conquerors as well as many collaborators before their own courts. For example, the infamous commandant of the Auschwitz camps, Rudolf Hoess, was sentenced to death by a Polish court, and Hitler's puppet in Norway, Vidkun Quisling, was tried and shot in Oslo. The most notorious Nazi to be brought to justice long after Nuremberg was Adolf Eichmann. He had been one of the major criminals to carry out the Final Solution and had escaped to South America in 1945. After years of pursuit he was located by Israeli agents who smuggled him out of Argentina. At the conclusion of his spectacular trial, an Israeli court condemned him to death in 1960.

Even now the search for former Nazis who are accused of crimes continues. They are tried by courts in many countries including France, Canada, the United States, and even Australia.

DENAZIFICATION: THE CONCEPT

The Allied Control Commission's directive concerning denazification charged the occupation forces with dual duties: Remove Nazis from positions of responsibility and punish individuals who had violated principles of justice and humanity. The commanders of all four zones were expected to establish procedures that would speedily replace Nazis in prominent positions with men and women whose pasts were politically unblemished. The methods followed by the three Western powers did not differ in the essentials. This cannot be said, however, of the Soviet zone. There, the military commanders were ordered to lay the foundation for a Communist government in East Germany. Anyone, except the most notorious Nazis, was accepted to serve in positions of authority as long as they swore to uphold and promote communism. The need for civil servants to help in the reorganization of the Soviet Zone was pressing. Obviously, many former Nazis swore loyalty to the new master and escaped punishment.

THE WESTERN MILITARY ZONES

It was relatively simple to outlaw the NSDAP and its accessory organizations and to arrest their leaders. Men who had volunteered for the SS, Gestapo, SD, or held high office in the Third Reich were identified, removed from their positions, and charged with crimes if the evidence warranted. But to fill positions that required public confidence with men and women who had not been Nazis was extremely difficult. Precisely what was the definition of a Nazi? Many organizations had been incorporated into the party without consent of its members. Employment in numerous occupations had required party membership. Advancement in business, industry, and the civil service usually had required the telltale swastika pin in one's lapel. Hitler Youth enrollment had been virtually coerced; artists, writers, and musicians had found it nearly impossible to obtain work without party affiliation; and the list goes on and on. If denazification were enforced in the broadest definition, then who would be left to restore civic and economic life in Germany? Obviously a distinction needed to be made between nominal and active Nazis.

In October of 1946, the Allied Control Council tried to solve the dilemma by establishing categories of Nazis that ranged from major offender, offender, lesser offender, and follower, to the exonerated. Adults in the Western zones were ordered to register and complete a lengthy questionnaire, the *Fragebogen*. The responses to 131 questions, as well as other documents, were used as criteria for positions of public trust and/or possible trial. German courts, conducted by known anti-Nazis, aided in the processing of millions of people. It was fortunate that Hitler ruled Germany for only twelve years, and some retired jurists were available to participate in the cleansing action. According to a 1950 report by the U.S. High Commissioner for Germany, General Lucius D. Clay, in the American zone 27 percent of the adult population, more then 13 million people, were registered as a prelude to further investigation. That number was reduced by amnesties for the very young, the very poor, for returning prisoners of war, and several other categories. But nearly a million ex-Nazis were tried, often accused by people from their own communities. Sentences were imposed, which ranged from execution to the payment of fines.

RESULTS

The effort to denazify was unprecedented in its aim and scope. No doubt, many inequities in the application of the law took place. It is not possible to know just how many Nazi criminals escaped their punishment. Even the German Federal Republic, which pursued the guilty with great diligence, could not prevent the infiltration of prominent ex-Nazis into the ranks of its government. As was noted earlier, the files on the prosecution of leading Nazis are still open, but of course, old age and death are fast overtaking justice.

The attempt was a noble effort. It would be absurd to claim that the punishments meted out compensated for, or even fit the crime of genocide. Perhaps we can take some solace from the fact that it appears that the German people have turned their backs on totalitarianism. Germany, made *Judenrein* in 1945, today has a vibrant Jewish presence. Hebrew prayers rise from synagogues and Jewish day schools echo with young voices. And some people say that history is a rational study. . . .

A Postscript: Germany and the Jews Today

This history text began with a letter to students and it seems appropriate to close it with a PS. Despite the initial caution that study of the Shoah leaves one with more questions than answers, the "yes, buts". . . and "what ifs". . . surge around the lecture room until the last day of classes. Unfortunately, most of the issues raised remain unresolved, but there is a response I believe to be appropriate.

A theme which sooner or later enters into the debate concerns man's apparent inability to learn from the lessons of the past. The fact that civilized society was, and is, appalled by the atrocities committed by the Nazis, that Hitler's very name has become a synonym for absolute evil, has not stopped further killing of the innocents. Since 1945 massacres have taken the lives of hundreds of thousands of guiltless men, women, and children. Whether called ethnic cleansing, or a search for political unity, or the observance of an alleged religious obligation, the results are equally devastating. Man's inhumanity to man appears to be a seamless cycle in which we run without ever moving, much like the gerbil on his treadmill.

But that is not entirely true. The contemporary picture of the human condition may indeed be bleak, nonetheless it is possible to shine a beam of light onto the canvas. And that beam originates in the most unlikely place, in Germany.

The government of the present day German republic is democratic and we may infer that its leaders carry out the wishes of the majority of its citizens. When autonomy was returned to the German people by the occupying Allied powers, the political leadership and their parties had a choice: Blame the Nazi crimes on "a few madmen" or accept culpability for the savagery of the dictatorship. Put in a different context the question was: Shall we whitewash our past or shall we accept the guilt? The notion that "all but a few of us were also victims of the Nazis" had obvious appeal, but in its official voice the Germans refused to take that road. The members of the government decided to use unvarnished history, indeed, the truth, as a lesson for the future.

What evidence can be presented to confirm such an assessment? Actually, a great deal. Most convincing is the revival of Jewish life in Germany. At this time about 120,000 Jews live in Germany; most are immigrants from parts of the former Soviet Union. This group constitutes the fastest-growing minority population in Europe. They have recreated a vibrant Jewish life in places that Hitler had pronounced to be *Judenrein*. Synagogues have been rebuilt at government expense, Jewish day schools receive government support, or the children may attend public schools. A new generation of Jews calls Germany its homeland. If they are unhappy there, they need not stay, Israel would gladly bid them welcome.

German children learn early and often about their country's Nazi past. The lessons are presented with an honesty that must make their grandparents cringe. Academic studies of the Holocaust are re-enforced with field trips to the sites of mass murder. One cannot visit Dachau or Auschwitz without meeting classes of German children and their teachers. The success of these educational programs can be measured by the fact that several top universities now offer doctoral degrees in Judaic Studies.

Even the vaunted army has not been spared its share of disgrace. For decades after the end of the war, most Germans believed that their military forces had played no part in the murder of civilians. But that illusion was shattered by an exhibit of photographs called *Crimes of the Wehrmacht*. Graphic pictures proved that the regular army had participated in the round-ups and in the shooting of civilians. The success of the exposition amazed its curators as nearly a million Germans filed through the gallery and viewed the pictures in shocked silence.

German municipalities have erected and maintain many Holocaust memorials. Every city has a plaque or a museum or a sculpture to recall its own lost Jews. Large communities may have dozens of reminders; in Berlin huge tablets stand in the streets with the inscription: LEST WE FORGET, followed by the names of concentration camps. Many synagogues which had been destroyed during *Kristallnacht* have been repaired and serve as educational centers and/or houses of worship. The magnificent dome of Berlin's once grand *Neue* Synagoge has been restored and since 1995 the facility is used as a research center. The site of the Wannsee Conference has been turned into an archive of shame. More recently, a remarkable museum has opened in the center of the German capital. This rather strange looking building, with its slanting walls and uneven floors expresses in steel and cement the sense of loss caused by the Nazi tragedy and seeks to balance that grief with the remembrance of German Jewish achievements in the more distant past. The focus is educational, Germans are reminded that the Holocaust is not the only connecting link between German Jews and Christians.

A national memorial center is slated for completion in 2004. It will stand near Berlin's *Brandenburger Thor*, probably the most recognizable location in the country. At ground level it will resemble a cemetery with a field of vertical slabs, but below it

Berlin street scene. The words above the names of the concentration camp warn: PLACES OF HORROR WHICH WE MUST NEVER FORGET. (Photo by Leonard Botwinick.)

will be housed the most complete research facility of the history of the Holocaust. Scholars and students from around the world will have access to its files.

The German legislature has enacted persuasive evidence that it is the will of the people to reverse their xenophobic past. It is illegal to deny the Holocaust; to publish antiSemitic books or articles, or to exhibit Nazi paraphernalia in public. Anti-Jewish remarks by politicians are punished by expulsion from the party. Laws have been passed which resulted in restitution payments to Holocaust survivors and the state of Israel. Ninety billion Marks have already been disbursed and reparations continue to aid the Israeli economy and many aging survivors.

The governments of Germany and Israel have entered into a special relationship of support and friendship. Aside from the United States, the next largest contingent of visitors to the Jewish State are from Germany and treaties of cooperation and trade have been concluded. As early as 1951 the President of Germany, Richard von Weizaecker, set the tone when he said:

> The Federal Government and with it the majority of The German people are aware of the immeasurable suffering that was brought upon Jews in Germany and in the occupied territories. . . . Unspeakable crimes have been committed in the name of the German people calling for moral and material indemnity.

In the same year Chancellor Konrad Adenauer stated that Germany could not become a respected member in the family of nations until it had recognized and proven its will to make amends.

For a fitting voice to conclude this postscript we turn once more to Richard von Weizaecker. On the occasion of the first visit to Germany by a President of Israel, Chaim Herzog in 1987, he made these comments:

> The fact that you are the first president of the State of Israel to visit our country makes this a most outstanding event in the history of our two peoples. . . . Official intergovernmental contacts are normal and rest on firm foundations. Practical cooperation is broad ranging and is borne by a spirit of mutual trust. But besides the intergovernmental relations there are human beings with feelings. We cannot simply put them on the same level. No Israeli can meet a German without recalling the suffering of the Jews under National Socialism. . . . There can be no forgetting the Holocaust. . . . We must be honest with one another and that means first of all being honest in our recollection of the past. Only in this way can a credible and lasting relationship grow between the generations who at that time had not been born and who, today and tomorrow, will have to live and get along with one another in this one world.

And so, dear student, I hope to leave you with a modicum of hope that it is possible to get off the treadmill, to break the cycle of hatred and learn to live together on this, our one small world.

Glossary and Abbreviations

Abwehr: German military counterintelligence.

Allied Control Commission: Organization of senior administrators of the military zones of postwar Germany.

Appell: Roll call, often lasting hours, used in concentration camps.

Aktion: Nazi operation involving the deportation and/or killing of Jews.

Anschluss: German annexation of Austria, March 1938.

Aryanization: Nazis force Jewish businessmen to sell to Aryans at bargain prices

Bermuda Conference: Anglo–USA conference, which failed to solve the refugee problem, April 1943.

Boycott: Nazi order to the German public to stop all economic dealings with Jews, April 1933.

Bund: Anti–Zionist Jewish socialist party, originated in Poland.

CV: Centralverein deutscher Staatsbuerger juedisches Glaubens, Union of Jewish citizens of Germany.

Denazification: Removal of Nazis from important positions by the Allies at the end of the war.

Der Stuermer: The Attacker, Julius Streicher's violently anti–Jewish weekly newspaper.

Displaced Persons (DPs): Europeans made homeless by the Nazis or as a result of World War II.

Displaced Persons Camp: Facilities, often former concentration camps, used to house displaced persons in the military zones.

Einsatzgruppen: Mobile killing units of SS and SD members used mainly in Poland and Russia.

Endloesung: See Final Solution.

Evian Conference: International conference held in 1938, which failed to alleviate the refugee problem.

Final Solution: Nazi plan to solve Jewish problem by annihilation.

Fuehrerprinzip: Leadership principle; Nazi concept that all power belongs in the hands of the totalitarian leader.

Gauleiter: Nazi administrative leader in a *Gau,* or district.

General Government: Western Polish territory conquered by Germany and administered by Hans Frank.

Genocide: The partial or total destruction of a racial, religious, or national group.

Gestapo: Geheime Staatspolizei, Nazis' secret state police.

Gleichschaltung: Consolidation of all political activities and nonpolitical organizations under Nazi dictatorship.

Judenrat: Jewish council of elders, used by Germans in ghetto administration.

Judenrein: Cleansed of Jews; Nazi policy of removal of Jews.

Kapo: Prisoner in a concentration camp who was in charge of other inmates.

Kristallnacht: Night of broken glass, pogrom carried out between November 9–10, 1938, in Greater Germany.

Lager: Camp, as in concentration or death camp.

Lebensborn: Kidnapping by SS of "desirable" foreign children.

Lebensraum: Room to live, euphemism for German policy of expansion.

Madagascar Plan: Briefly considered notion by Germany to ship 4 million Jews to the island of Madagascar.

Maquis: French anti–Nazi guerrilla fighting organization during World War II.

Mischlinge: Nazi classification for people of Jewish–Christian parentage.

Mein Kampf: My Struggle, book by Adolf Hitler, which outlined his program.

Munich Agreement: Appeasement policy of England and France, which permitted Hitler to take part of Czechoslovakia.

Musselman: Term denoting a concentration camp prisoner who had given up the struggle to stay alive.

NSDAP: Nationalsozialistische Deutsche Arbeiterpartei, National Socialist German Workers' Party, the Nazi party.

Nuremberg Laws: German legislation, which deprived Jews of citizenship rights, passed in 1938.

Nuremberg Trials: An International Military Tribunal tried 22 Nazi leaders, 19 were found guilty of war crimes.

Pogrom: Organized violence directed against Jews.

Protocols of the Elders of Zion: AntiSemitic forgery claiming an international plot by Jews to attain world domination.

Putsch: Attempted coup d'état.

Righteous of the Nations or Righteous Gentiles: Non-Jews who saved Jewish lives during the Holocaust.

RSHA: Reichssicherheitshauptamt, Central German security department under the Nazis.

SA: Sturmabteilung, the Brownshirts; Nazi political storm troopers.

SS: *Schutzstaffel,* the Blackshirts; elite of Nazi storm troopers.

Shtetl: Eastern European town or village with large Jewish population.

Third Reich: Germany under the Nazis.

Umschlagplatz: Assembly place for deportees, usually at rail junctions.

Wannsee Conference: 1942 meeting of Nazi leaders, which confirmed the implementation of the Final Solution.

War Refugee Board: U.S. government special agency to rescue and aid victims of Nazi persecution.

Wehrmacht: German armed forces.

World Jewish Congress: A voluntary association of major Jewish organizations.

Yad Vashem: Israeli authority of commemoration and research on the Holocaust.

ZOB: *Zydowska Organizacja Bojowa,* Jewish fighting organization in Poland, active in Warsaw ghetto uprising.

Time Line

1920	Hitler announced NSPAP program in Munich
1921	SA organized
1923	Failure of the Hitler/Ludendorff Beer Hall Putsch
1924	Nazi Party won 6.4 percent of votes in Reichstag elections
1925	*Mein Kampf* published
1928	Nazi Party won 2.5 percent of votes in Reichstag elections
1929	Joseph Goebbels made chief of propaganda for NSDAP
1930	Nazi Party won 18 percent of votes in Reichstag elections
1931	Hitler lost presidential election to Paul von Hindenburg
1932	Hitler granted German citizenship
1933	Hitler appointed Chancellor by Hindenburg
	The Reichstag fire and subsequent emergency powers given to Hitler
	Dachau concentration camp opened; SS organized
	Adoption of Enabling Act gave Hitler totalitarian power
	Boycott of Jewish businesses and professionals
	Gleichschaltung consolidated political, social, and economic institutions under Nazi control
	Gestapo organized
	Jews ousted from government position
	Books deemed undesirable or dangerous burnt

	Concordat between papacy and Germany signed
1934	Germany and Poland signed ten-year nonaggression pact
	Heinrich Himmler appointed acting chief of the Gestapo
	Blood purge (Night of the Long Knives) carried out
	Death of Hindenburg; Hitler assumed title of Fuehrer
	Plebiscite concerning Hitler's new role; nearly 90 percent voted yes
1935	Military conscription enacted; Jews barred from military
	Nuremberg Laws deprived Jews of rights of citizenship
	Definition of who is a Jew or *Mischling*
1936	Rome/Berlin Axis formed
	Jewish doctors forbidden to practice
	Sachsenhausen concentration camp opened
1937	Buchenwald concentration camp opened
	Hitler nullified Treaty of Versailles
1938	Austrian *Anschluss* accomplished
	Jews must register ownership of all property
	Munich Appeasement by France and Great Britain
	Deportation of Polish Jews from Germany
	Hershel Grynzpan killed vom Rath in Paris followed by Crystal Night pogrom; Jews forced to pay 1 billion marks
	Aryanization of Jewish businesses
	Jewish children expelled from German schools
1939	Molotov/Ribbentrop nonagression pact signed
	German invasion of Poland; the start of the Second World War; Poland defeated
	Establishment of Polish ghettos begun; Polish Jews must wear identifying stars
	Jews expelled from Vienna
1940	Germans conquered Norway, Denmark, the Netherlands, Belgium, and France
	The Battle of Britain began
	Japan joined Axis powers
	Italy invaded Greece and required Germans to come to their aid; the Warsaw ghetto was sealed off
1941	The war spreads to the Balkans
	Deputy Fuehrer Rudolf Hess landed in Scotland; Martin Borman named his successor
	Germany attacked the USSR

Himmler opened Maidanek, Sobibor, and Auschwitz camps

German Jews sent to Eastern concentration and death camps

Pearl Harbor attacked by Japan; Germany declared war on United States

1942 Wannsee Conference confirmed "Final Solution to the Jewish question"

First use of gas in Auschwitz, Belzec, and Sobibor

French, Belgian, Dutch, Croatian, Greek, Norwegian, and remaining German Jews sent to Polish death camps

Battle of Stalingrad ended German advance into USSR

Jewish resistance organizations formed

1943 Warsaw Ghetto revolt

Italy surrendered to Allies

Revolt of Auschwitz prisoners

Rescue of Danish Jews

1944 D-Day landings of Allied armies established a second front in Europe

Attempt to assassinate Hitler failed

Nazis began deportation of Hungarian Jews

Death marches of remaining concentration camp survivors

Allies defeated German troops in Eastern and Western offensives

1945 Russian and Western Allies' armies joined near Berlin

Hitler, Goebbels, Himmler commit suicide

Concentration camp inmates freed by Allied soldiers

V-E Day proclaimed on May 8

V-J Day marked end of war in Pacific theater on August 14

DP camps established in Germany

1946 International War Crimes Tribunal met in Nuremberg

Bibliography and Selected Readings

The amount of material on the Holocaust is massive and the following books represent a small selection. The rationale for including a book while excluding hundreds of other excellent works was based on these factors: (1) Most students read English only, thus the research published in other languages is not useful; (2) most books on Holocaust history contain further bibliographies; a long list here is likely to be redundant; (3) the books catalogued below are based on recommendations by students and the author of this text; (4) the works listed should be easily available in university and public libraries.

ANTHOLOGIES AND ESSAY COLLECTIONS

Bettelheim, Bruno, *Surviving and Other Essays*. New York: Vintage Books, 1980.

Chartok, Roselle, and Jack Spencer, eds., *The Holocaust Years: Society on Trial*. New York: Bantam Books, 1978.

Friedlander, Albert H., ed., *Out of the Whirlwind*. New York: Schocken Books, 1976.

Furet, François, *Unanswered Questions: Nazi Germany and the Genocide of the Jews*. New York: Schocken Books, 1989.

Laska, Vera, *Women in the Resistance and in the Holocaust, The Voices of Eyewitnesses*. Westport, CT: Greenwood Press, 1983.

Niewyk, Donald, ed., *Problems in European Civilization: The Holocaust*. Lexington MA: D.C. Heath and Company, 1992.

Ritter, Carol, and Sondra Myers, *The Courage to Care, Rescuers of Jews during the Holocaust*. New York: New York University, 1986.

Roth, John K., and Michael Berenbaum, eds., *Holocaust: Religious and Philosophical Implications*. New York: Paragon House, 1989.

ANTI-SEMITISM IN HISTORY

Abel, Ernest L., *The Roots of Anti–Semitism*. Cranbury NJ: Associated University Presses, 1975.

Hay, Malcolm, *Thy Brother's Blood: The Roots of Christian Anti–Semitism*. New York: Hart, 1965.

Katz, Jacob, *From Prejudice to Destruction, Anti–Semitism, 1700–1933*. Cambridge MA: Harvard University Press, 1980.

Rose, Paul Laurence, *German Question/Jewish Question: Revolutionary Antisemitism from Kant to Wagner*. Princeton: Princeton University Press, 1990.

Smith, Helmut Walser, *The Butchers Tale Murder and Anti–Semitism in a German Town*. New York and London: W.W.Norton & Company, 2002.

DOCUMENT COLLECTIONS

Arad, Yitzhak, Yisrael Gutman, Abraham Margialot, eds., *Documents on the Holocaust*. Jerusalem: Yad Vashem, 1981.

Botwinick, Rita Steinhardt, ed., *A Holocaust Reader From Idealogy to Annihilation*. Upper Saddle River, NJ: Prentice Hall, 1997.

Hitler, Adolf, *Mein Kampf*. Trans. by Ralph Manheim. Boston: Houghton Miflin, 1943.

Mosse, George L., ed., *Nazi Culture*. New York: Schocken Books, 1981.

Noakes, J. and G. Pridham, eds., *Nazism: A History in Documents and Eyewitness Accounts*. Vols. 1–2. New York: Schocken Books, 1990.

Remack, Joachim, *The Nazi Years: A Documentary History*. Prospect Heights, IL: Wavelength Press, Inc., 1990.

Snyder, Louis, ed., *Hitler's Third Reich: A Documentary History*. Chicago: Nelson Hall, 1981.

GENERAL HOLOCAUST HISTORIES

Bauer, Yehuda, *A History of the Holocaust*. New York: Franklin Watts, 1982.

Dawidovicz, Lucy S., *The War against the Jews 1933–1945*. Philadelphia: Jewish Publication Society, 1975.

Friedlaender, Saul, *Nazi Germany and the Jews*. Vol. 1. New York, N.Y.: Harper Perennial, 1997.

Hilberg, Raul, *The Destruction of the European Jews*. Vols. 1–3. New York and London: Holmes & Meier, 1985.

Kaplan, Marion A., *Jewish Life in Nazi Germany*. New York: Oxford University Press. 1998.

Poliakov, Leon, *Harvest of Hate: The Nazi Program for the Destruction of the Jews of Europe*. New York: Holocaust Library, 1979.

Yahil, Leni, *The Holocaust*. Trans. by Ina Friedman and Haya Galai. New York and Oxford: Oxford University Press, 1990.

MODERN GERMAN HISTORIES

Carr, William, *A History of Germany, 1815–1900*. London: Edward Arnold, 1991.

Elon, Amos, *The Pity of it All, A History of Jews in Germany 1743–1933*. New York, N.Y.: Metropolitan Books, 2002.

Eyck, Eric, *A History of the Weimar Republic*. Vols 1 and 2. Trans. by H.P. Hanson and R. G. L. Waite. New York: Antheneum, 1970.

Halperin, S. William, *Germany Tried Democracy*. New York: Thomas Y. Cromwell Co., 1946.

Herf, Jeffrey, *Divided Memory: The Nazi Past in Two Germanys*. Cambridge and London: Harvard University Press, 1997.

Shirer, William, *The Rise and Fall of the Third Reich*. New York: Simon and Schuster, 1960.

Spielvogel, Jackson J., *Hitler and Nazi Germany*. Englewood Cliffs, NJ: Prentice Hall, 1992.

Valentin, Veit, *The German People*. New York: Alfred A. Knopf, 1946.

MONOGRAPHIC WORKS

Ainsztein, Ruben, *The Warsaw Ghetto Revolt*. New York: Holocaust Library, 1979.

Arad, Yitzhak, *Belzec, Sobibor, Treblinka. The Operation Reinhard Death Camps*. Bloomington IN: Indiana University Press, 1987.

Barnett, Victoria, . *For the Soul of the People Protestant, Protest Against Hitler*. York: Oxford University Press,1992.

Breitman, Richard, *The Architect of Genocide. Himmler and the Final Solution*. New York: Alfred A. Knopf, 1991.

Donat, Alexander, *The Holocaust Kingdom*. New York: Holocaust Library, 1978.

Gilbert, Martin, *Auschwitz and the Allies*. New York: Henry Holt and Company, 1981.

Gutman, Ysrael, *The Jews of Warsaw*. Bloomington IN: Indiana University Press, 1982.

Hoehne, Heinz, *The Order of the Death's Head*. Trans. by Martin Secker & Warburg Limited. Hamburg: Verlag der Spiegel, 1966.

Lifton, Robert, Jay, *The Nazi Doctors, Medical Killings and the Psychology of Genocide*. Scranton PA: Harper Collins Publishers, 1986.

Lipshitz, C. U., *Franco, Spain, the Jews and the Holocaust*. New York: KTAV Publishing House, Inc., 1984.

Marrus, Michael, and Robert O. Paxton, "The Nazis and the Jews in Western Occupied Europe 1940–1944." *Journal of Modern History*, 54, New York: Basic Books, 1981.

Mueller, Ingo, *The Courts of the Third Reich*. Trans. by Deborah Lucas Schneider. Cambridge: Harvard University Press, 1993.

Novitch, Miriam, *Sobibor, Martyrdom and Revolt*. New York: Waldon Press, 1980.

Oliner, Samuel P., and Pearl M. Oliner, *The Altruistic Personality*. New York: The Free Press, 1988.

Steiner, Jean-François, *Treblinka*. New York: The New American Library, 1979.

Thalmann, Rita, and Emanuel Feinermann. *Crystal Night, 9–10 November, 1938*. Trans. by Gilles Cremonesi. New York: Holocaust Library, 1974.

Thomas, Gordon, and Max Morgan Wilts, *Voyage of the Damned*. New York: Stein and Day, 1974.

Tusa, Ann, and John Tusa, *The Nuremberg Trial*. New York: Antheneum, 1986.

Waite, Robert L., *The Psychopathic God: Adolf Hitler*. New York: Basic Books, 1977.

Wyman, David S., *The Abandonment of the Jews: America and the Holocaust, 1941–1945*. New York: Random House, 1984.

Zuccotti, Susan, *The Italians and the* Holocaust. New York: Basic Books, 1987.

OTHER RELATED BOOKS

Allport, Gordon W., *The Nature of Prejudice*. Reading, MA: Addison Publication Co., 1986.

Aly, Goetz, *Final Solution: Nazi Population Policy and the Murder of European Jews*. Trans. from German by Allison Brown. London: Arnold, 1999.

Arendt, Hannah, *The Origins of Totalitarianism*. New York: Harcourt Brace, 1958.

Engelmann, Bert, *In Hitler's Germany: Daily Life in the Third Reich*. Trans. by Krishna Winston. New York: Pantheon Books, 1986.

Howe, Irving, *World of Our Fathers*. New York: Harcourt Brace Janovich, 1976.

Patai, Raphael, *The Vanished World of Jewry*. New York: Macmillan Publishing Co. Inc., 1980.

Sachar, Abram Leon, *A History of the Jews*. New York: Alfred A. Knopf, 1958.

PERSONAL AND BIOGRAPHICAL WORKS

Astor, Gerald, *The Last Nazi: The Life and Times of Dr. Joseph Mengele*. New York: Donald I. Fine, Inc., 1985.

Borowski, Tadeus, *This Way for the Gas, Ladies and Gentlemen*. Trans. by Barbara Vedder. New York: Penguin Books, 1959.

Botwinick, Rita, *Winzig, Germany 1933–1946. The History of a Town Under the Third Reich*. Westport CT: Praeger, 1992.

Crome, Len, *Unbroken: Resistance and Survival in the Concentration Camps*. London: Lawrence and Wishart, 1988.

Des Pres, Terrence, *The Survivor: An Anatomy of Life in Death Camps*. New York: Oxford University Press, 1976.

Friedlaender, Saul, *When Memory Comes*. New York: Farrar and Straus, 1979.

Gross, Leonard, *The Last Jews of Berlin*. New York: Simon and Schuster, 1982.

Heck, Alphons, *A Child of Hitler*. Fredrick CO: Renaissance House, 1985.

Kershaw, Ian, *Profiles in Power—Hitler*. London: Longman Group, 1991.

Korczak, Janus, *Ghetto Diary*. New York: Holocaust Library, 1978.

Levi, Primo, *Survival in Auschwitz: The Nazi Assault on Humanity*. Trans. by Stuart Woolf. New York: Collier, 1966.

Mayer, Bernard, *Entombed My True Story: How Forty-Five Jews Lived Underground and Survived the Holocaust*. Ojus, FL: Aleric Press, 1994.

Meed, Vladka, *On Both Sides of the Wall*. New York: Summit Books, 1986.

Rubinstein, Erna F., *The Survivor in Us All: Four Young Sisters in the Holocaust*. Hamden CT: The Shoe String Press, 1983.

Salvaged Pages: Young Writers' Diaries of the Holocaust. Collected and edited by Alexandra Zapruder. New Haven: Yale University Press, 2002.

Wiesel, Eli, *Night*. Trans. by S. Rodway. New York: Bantam Books, 1960.

REFERENCE BOOKS

Encyclopedia Judaica. Jerusalem: Keter Publishing, 1973.

Gilbert, Martin, *Atlas of the Holocaust*. New York: Da Capo Press, Inc., 1982.

Marrus, Michael R., *The Holocaust in History*. Hanover, NH and London: University Press of New England, 1987.

Snyder, Louis L., ed., *Encyclopedia of the Third Reich*. New York: Paragon House, 1989.

RIGHTEOUS CHRISTIANS

Anger, Per, *With Raoul Wallenberg in Budapest*. Trans. by David Mel Paul and Margarita Paul. New York: Holocaust Library, 1981.

Flenders, Harold, *Rescue in Denmark*. New York: Holocaust Library, 1963.

Hallie, Phillip, *Lest Innocent Blood Be Shed: The Story of Le Chambon and How Goodness Happened There*. New York: Harper Torchbooks, 1979.

Tec, Nechama, *When Light Pierced the Darkness: Christian Rescue of Jews in Poland*. New York: Oxford University Press, 1986.

SELECTED WEBSITES

BBC's History Section on the Holocaust
    HTTP://WWW.ST.-EDMUNDS.CAM.AC.UK

German Website on the Shoah
    HTTP://WWW.ST-EDMUNDS.CAM.AC.UK

The Imperial War Museum Holocaust Exhibition
    HTTP://WWW.1WM.ORG/LAMBETH/HOLOC-EX1.HTM

Jewish Museum in Berlin
    HTTP://WWW.JMBERLIN.DE

PBS Holocaust Website
    HTTP://WWW.PBS.ORG/HOLOCAUST

Simon Wiesenthal Museum of Tolerance
    HTTP://MOTLC.WIESENTHAL.COM

The Women of the Holocaust
    HTTP://WWW.INTERLOG.COM/~MIGHTY

United States Holocaust Museum
    HTTP://WWW.USAMM.ORG

Index